Themis
Bar Review

Multistate Bar Exam
Lecture Handouts

MBE Introduction and Workshops

Civil Procedure

Constitutional Law

Contracts & Sales

Criminal Law

Criminal Procedure

Evidence

Real Property

Torts

All other trademarks are the property of their respective companies.

The material herein is intended to be used in conjunction with the myThemis Portal™ in order to provide basic review of legal subjects and is in no way meant to be a source of or replacement for professional legal advice.

ISBN 978-1-943808-82-3
1-943808-82-1

MBE Workshop

MBE WORKSHOP: INTRODUCTION
PROFESSOR LISA MCELROY
DREXEL UNIVERSITY SCHOOL OF LAW

The seven subjects on the MBE:

1. _____

2. _____

3. _____

4. _____

5. _____

6. _____

7. _____

Number of questions on the MBE: _____

Organization of the MBE:

_____

_____

_____

Scoring: _____

TOP FIVE THINGS TO KNOW FOR THE MBE

1. In each subject area, one topic is tested more than any other. Know this topic cold. Don't sweat the small stuff.

_____

_____

_____

2. For every single MBE question, ask yourself: What is the cause of action?

_____

_____

_____

3. Remember that it doesn't matter where you get the points. Rack up points in your stronger subjects.

_____

_____

_____

4. Short, easy questions are worth just as much as long, difficult questions.

_____

_____

_____

5. You only need to get a D- on this exam. In most jurisdictions, if you get about 65% of the questions correct (130/200), you are in the passing range.

_____

_____

_____

MBE WORKSHOP: CIVIL PROCEDURE
PROFESSOR LISA MCELROY
DREXEL UNIVERSITY SCHOOL OF LAW

CHAPTER 1:   **CIVIL PROCEDURE**

> **Editor's Note 1:** The below outline is taken from the National Conference of Bar Examiners' website.

NOTE: Examinees are to assume the application of (1) the Federal Rules of Civil Procedure as currently in effect and (2) the sections of Title 28 to the U.S. Code pertaining to trial and appellate jurisdiction, venue, and transfer. Approximately two-thirds of the Civil Procedure questions on the MBE will be based on categories I, III, and V, and approximately one-third will be based on the remaining categories II, IV, VI, and VII.

I. Jurisdiction and venue

    A. Federal subject matter jurisdiction (federal question, diversity, supplemental, and removal)

    B. Personal jurisdiction

    C. Service of process and notice

    D. Venue, forum non conveniens, and transfer

II. Law applied by federal courts

    A. State law in federal court

    B. Federal common law

III. Pretrial procedures

    A. Preliminary injunctions and temporary restraining orders

    B. Pleadings and amended and supplemental pleadings

    C. Rule 11

    D. Joinder of parties and claims (including class actions)

    E. Discovery (including e-discovery), disclosure, and sanctions

    F. Adjudication without a trial

    G. Pretrial conference and order

IV. Jury trials

    A. Right to jury trial

    B. Selection and composition of juries

    C. Requests for and objections to jury instructions

V. Motions

    A. Pretrial motions, including motions addressed to face of pleadings, motions to dismiss, and summary judgment motions

    B. Motions for judgments as a matter of law (directed verdicts and judgments notwithstanding the verdict)

    C. Posttrial motions, including motions for relief from judgment and for new trial

VI. Verdicts and judgments

    A. Defaults and involuntary dismissals

    B. Jury verdicts—types and challenges

    C. Judicial findings and conclusions

    D. Effect; claim and issue preclusion

VII. Appealability and review

    A. Availability of interlocutory review

    B. Final judgment rule

    C. Scope of review for judge and jury

TOP FIVE THINGS TO KNOW FOR CIVIL PROCEDURE

1. Think about how to make the case go away.

_____

_____

_____

2. If the fact pattern includes dates, make a timeline. Many rules revolve around the number of days allowed to do something.

_____

_____

_____

3. Be open-minded about jurisdiction.

_____

_____

_____

4. Carefully note the cause of action.

_____

_____

_____

5. Recognize that this is a new subject on the MBE; you are just as prepared as everyone else!

_____

_____

_____

Tip #1: Think about how to make the case go away.

A bank properly filed an action in federal district court to collect on an overdue promissory note. The defendant, who was the alleged maker of the note, asserted in his answer that the signature on the note was a forgery. The answer was prepared, submitted, and signed by his attorney. The bank timely filed a summary judgment motion. As part of the motion, the bank, in addition to attaching the note, attached an affidavit by a bank officer in which the officer swore that she had witnessed the signing of the note and that the signer had been the defendant. The defendant replied to the motion by noting the statement in his answer that he had not signed the note. Determining that there were other issues in dispute, the court refused to grant a partial summary judgment with respect to the issue of forgery.

Was the court's denial of a partial summary judgment with respect to the issue of forgery correct?

A. Yes, because the affidavit by the bank officer was self-serving.

B. Yes, because a partial summary judgment is not permitted under the federal rules.

C. No, because the bank eliminated the possibility that the signature on the note was a forgery.

D. No, because the defendant failed to carry his burden to show that there was a genuine dispute as to the authenticity of the signature.

Answer choice D is correct. With respect to a summary judgment motion, the movant must show that there is no genuine dispute as to any material fact and that the movant is entitled to judgment as a matter of law. Here, with regard to the issue of forgery, the bank presented an affidavit that the defendant was the person who signed the note. This evidence, if uncontradicted, is sufficient to entitle the bank to judgment as a matter of law that the signature on the note is not a forgery. Consequently, the burden shifts to the defendant to present evidence that would dispute this fact. A party opposing a motion for summary judgment may not rely merely on allegations or denials in her own pleading, but she must set out specific facts showing a genuine dispute for trial. In this case, while the defendant did point out to the court a statement contained in his answer, merely alluding to a statement made in a pleading does not constitute evidence. Because the defendant did not offer evidence that would dispute the bank officer's affidavit, the bank was entitled to a partial summary judgment with respect to the issue of forgery. Answer choice A is incorrect because, although the bank officer, as an agent of the bank, was likely biased in favor of the bank and thus the statement might be characterized as self- serving, the fact that evidence is self-serving does not prevent its introduction into evidence. Evidence presented by a party is typically self-serving, in that it supports the party's position. Answer choice B is incorrect because a partial summary judgment is permitted under the federal rules. Answer choice C is incorrect because the bank as movant is not, at least initially, required to eliminate the possibility that the signature on the note was a forgery. Instead, the bank meets its burden of production by making a prima facie showing that the signature on the note is genuine. If the defendant then introduces evidence that the note is a forgery, the bank would have to present evidence that there is no genuine dispute as to the issue of forgery. In this case, however, the defendant failed to present such evidence.

Question notes:

_____

_____

Tip #2: If the fact pattern includes dates, make a timeline. Many rules revolve around the number of days allowed to do something.

Family members of a deceased individual properly filed an action for money damages in federal court against a funeral home for negligent infliction of emotional distress based on the alleged mishandling of the remains of the deceased. The funeral home timely and properly served an answer to the complaint. Thirty days later, including eight weekend days, the family members served a demand for a jury trial on the funeral home. The demand was served on a holiday. On the following day, a non-holiday weekday, the family members filed the jury trial demand with the court.

Was the family member's demand for a jury trial timely?

A. No, because the demand for a jury trial was not served on the funeral home within 14 days of service of the answer.

B. No, because the demand for a jury trial was not filed with the court within 21 days of service of the answer.

C. Yes, because the last day for making the demand was a holiday.

D. Yes, because weekend days are not counted in determining whether the demand was timely.

Question notes:

_____

_____

_____

_____

Tip #2 Answer Explanation

Answer choice A is correct. A demand for a jury trial must be served within 14 days after service of the last pleading directed to the issue that is sought to be tried by a jury. Here, the complaint sought damages, which is an action at law for which a jury trial may be had. However, the demand was not made within 14 days of service of the funeral home's answer, which is the only responsive pleading the funeral home may make that is directed to the plaintiff's complaint. Therefore, the demand for a jury trial was not timely. Answer choice B is incorrect. While a defendant has 21 days to respond to a complaint, a demand for a jury trial must be served on the other parties within 14 days after service of the last pleading directed to the issue for which the jury trial is sought. Answer choice C is incorrect. In computing whether a party has complied with the rules for undertaking an action within the specified time period, when the last day of the period would otherwise fall on a holiday, the action may be undertaken on the next non-holiday weekday. However, in this case, because the time period is 14, not 21 days, the time period for making a jury trial demand expired prior to the family members' service of the jury trial demand. Answer choice D is incorrect. Weekend days are counted in determining whether a party has taken action, such as making a demand for a jury trial, within the permissible time period.

Question notes:

_____

_____

_____

_____

Tip #3: Be open-minded about jurisdiction.

A plaintiff sued a defendant in federal district court following a car accident between the parties that occurred in the state where the federal district court is located. The plaintiff asserted a negligence claim under state law, and in good faith alleged damages of $100,000. At the time of the car accident, both parties were domiciled in the forum state. Following the accident, but before filing the complaint, the plaintiff accepted a full-time job in another state and moved to that state with the intent of living there permanently. After a bench trial, the judge ruled for the plaintiff and awarded $70,000 in damages. The defendant appealed the decision, asserting for the first time that the trial court lacked subject-matter jurisdiction.

Is the defendant likely to succeed in his appeal?

A.   No, because the defendant waived the issue by failing to raise it in the lower court.

B.   No, because the requirements for diversity jurisdiction were satisfied.

C.   Yes, because the plaintiff recovered less than $75,000 in damages.

D.   Yes, because the parties were not citizens of different states when the claim arose.

Question notes:

_____
_____
_____
_____
_____

Tip #3 Answer Explanation

Answer choice B is correct. U.S. district courts have diversity jurisdiction when both (i) no plaintiff is a citizen of the same state as any defendant and (ii) the amount in controversy in the action exceeds $75,000. To be a citizen of a state, a person must be a citizen of the United States and a domiciliary of the state. Domicile is determined at the time the action is commenced. In this case, the requirements for diversity jurisdiction were satisfied because the parties were citizens of different states at the time the action was commenced, and the amount in controversy was more than $75,000. Answer choice A is incorrect because an objection to subject-matter jurisdiction can be raised at any stage of a proceeding, including on appeal. Answer choice C is incorrect because the amount in controversy is determined at the time the action is commenced in federal court. If the plaintiff eventually recovers an amount that is less than the statutory jurisdictional amount, that fact will not render the verdict subject to challenge on appeal for lack of jurisdiction. In this case, the plaintiff asserted over $75,000 in damages, and thus satisfied the amount-in-controversy requirement. Answer choice D is incorrect because diversity must exist at the time of filing of the lawsuit, not when the claim arose. A party may establish or defeat diversity by changing state citizenship after the accrual of a cause of action but before the commencement of a lawsuit. In this case, although the parties were citizens of the same state when the accident occurred, the plaintiff was a citizen of a different state than the defendant when the lawsuit was commenced, and thus the requirements for diversity jurisdiction were satisfied.

Question notes:

_____

_____

_____

_____

Tip #4: Carefully note the cause of action.

An employer properly filed a complaint in federal district court seeking an injunction to enforce a covenant not to compete against a former employee. The former employee properly filed an answer that contained a counterclaim for damages stemming from alleged unpaid wages. The employer timely filed a demand for a jury trial with regard to the counterclaim. The former employee timely filed a motion challenging this demand.

How should the court rule on the former employee's motion?

A. Deny the motion, because the employer is seeking an injunction.

B. Deny the motion, because the former employee is seeking damages.

C. Grant the motion, because the employer is not seeking damages.

D. Grant the motion, because only a defendant may demand a jury trial.

Answer choice B is correct. Any party may make a jury trial demand with regard to an action at law, which includes any claim for damages. The right to trial by jury is evaluated for each claim. Because the former employee is seeking damages in the counterclaim, the employer is entitled to a jury trial on this issue. Consequently, the court should deny the former employee's motion that challenged the employer's demand for a jury trial on the counterclaim. Answer choice A is incorrect. While the employer is seeking an injunction (equitable relief) and thus the parties are not entitled to a jury trial with respect to the employer's complaint, either party may assert its right to a jury trial with respect to the former employee's counterclaim that seeks relief in the form of damages. Answer choice C is incorrect. Even though the employer is not seeking damages, the employer may assert its right to a jury trial with respect to the former employee's counterclaim that seeks relief in the form of damages. Answer choice D is incorrect because either party may make a jury trial demand.

Question notes:

_____

_____

_____

_____

_____

_____

MBE WORKSHOP: CONSTITUTIONAL LAW
PROFESSOR LISA MCELROY
DREXEL UNIVERSITY SCHOOL OF LAW

CHAPTER 1: CONSTITUTIONAL LAW

> **Editor's Note 1:** The below outline is taken from the National Conference of Bar Examiners' website.

NOTE: The terms "Constitution," "constitutional," and "unconstitutional" refer to the federal Constitution unless indicated otherwise. Approximately half of the Constitutional Law questions on the MBE will be based on category IV, and approximately half will be based on the remaining categories—I, II, and III.

I. THE NATURE OF JUDICIAL REVIEW
Organization and relationship of state and federal courts in a federal system
A. **Jurisdiction**
 1. Constitutional basis
 2. Congressional power to define and limit
 3. The Eleventh Amendment and state sovereign immunity
B. **Judicial review in operation**
 1. The "case or controversy" requirement, including the prohibition on advisory opinions, standing, ripeness, and mootness
 2. The "adequate and independent state ground"
 3. Political questions and justiciability

II. THE SEPARATION OF POWERS
A. **The powers of Congress**
 1. Commerce, taxing, and spending powers
 2. War, defense, and foreign affairs powers
 3. Power to enforce the 13th, 14th, and 15th Amendments
 4. Other powers
B. **The powers of the president**
 1. As chief executive, including the "take care" clause

 2. As commander in chief
 3. Treaty and foreign affairs powers
 4. Appointment and removal of officials
C. **Federal interbranch relationships**
 1. Congressional limits on the executive
 2. The presentment requirement and the president's power to veto or to withhold action
 3. Non-delegation doctrine
 4. Executive, legislative, and judicial immunities

III. THE RELATION OF NATION AND STATES IN A FEDERAL SYSTEM
A. **Intergovernmental immunities**
 1. Federal immunity from state law
 2. State immunity from federal law, including the 10th Amendment
B. **Federalism-based limits on state authority**
 1. Negative implications of the commerce clause
 2. Supremacy clause and preemption
 3. Full faith and credit
 4. Authorization of otherwise invalid state action

IV. INDIVIDUAL RIGHTS
A. **State action**
B. **Due process**
 1. Substantive due process
 a. Fundamental rights

b. Other rights and interests
2. Procedural due process, including personal jurisdiction
C. **Equal protection**
   1. Fundamental rights
   2. Classifications subject to heightened scrutiny
   3. Rational basis review
D. **Takings**
E. **Other protections, including the privileges and immunities clauses, the contracts clause, unconstitutional conditions, bills of attainder, and ex post facto laws**
F. **First Amendment freedoms**
   1. Freedom of religion and separation of church and state
      a. Free exercise
      b. Establishment

2. Freedom of expression
   a. Content-based regulation of protected expression
   b. Content-neutral regulation of protected expression
   c. Regulation of unprotected expression
   d. Regulation of commercial speech
   e. Regulation of, or impositions upon, public school students, public employment, licenses, or benefits based upon exercise of expressive or associational rights
   f. Regulation of expressive conduct
   g. Prior restraint, vagueness, and overbreadth
3. Freedom of the press
4. Freedom of association

TOP FIVE THINGS TO KNOW FOR CONSTITUTIONAL LAW

1. Think in terms of black and white; there is no gray on the MBE.

_____
_____
_____

2. Focus on questions asking about individual rights.

_____
_____
_____

3. Remember that the test covers the U.S. Constitution, not federal statutes.

_____
_____
_____

4. Know the hierarchy of laws (checks and balances).

_____
_____
_____

5. Always ask "Where am I?"

_____
_____
_____

CHAPTER 2: CONSTITUTIONAL LAW -- PRACTICE QUESTIONS

Tip #1: Think in terms of black and white; there is no gray on the MBE.

A state enacted a law that prohibited the sale of violent video games to minors and imposed a fine for each violation. The legislative history demonstrated a concern that there was a correlation between playing such games and subsequent violent behavior. A maker of video games brought suit contending that this law violated its First Amendment right of free speech.

Is this law unconstitutional?

A. Yes, because the costs of such a restriction on speech outweigh its benefits.

B. Yes, because the state law is a content-based restriction.

C. No, because video games do not qualify for First Amendment protection.

D. No, because states have the power to protect children from harm.

Answer choice B is correct. The state law prohibited a particular type of speech (i.e., violent video games), and thus contained a content-based restriction subject to strict scrutiny. Such regulations must be necessary to achieve a compelling government interest and narrowly tailored to meet that interest. A mere correlation between violent video games and violent behavior does not constitute a compelling interest to regulate such games. Accordingly, the law is unconstitutional. Answer choice A is incorrect because a balancing test is not the correct test to determine the constitutionality of contest-based regulations. Rather, content-based regulations are subject to the strict scrutiny test. Answer choice C is incorrect because video games communicate ideas, and are thus a form of speech protected by the First Amendment. Answer choice D is incorrect because, although a state possesses the power to protect children from harm, a state may not shield children from speech absent a recognized limitation on the speech, such as obscenity.

Question notes:

_____

_____

_____

_____

_____

_____

_____

_____

_____

Tip #2: Focus on learning the rules of law related to individual rights.

A city ordinance provided that only applicants under the age of 50 would be considered for the city's fire department, even though the employees of the fire department may serve until they reach the age of 55. A 50-year-old man applied for a position in the fire department, and his application was rejected solely because he did not meet the age restrictions in the ordinance. The applicant sued the city, alleging that the ordinance violated the Equal Protection Clause of the Fourteenth Amendment.

What statement most accurately describes the burden of proof?

A. The city must show that the ordinance is the least restrictive means to achieve a compelling government interest.

B. The city must show that the law is substantially related to a legitimate government interest.

C. The applicant must show that the ordinance is not substantially related to an important government interest.

D. The applicant must show that the ordinance is not rationally related to a legitimate government interest.

Question notes:

_____
_____
_____
_____
_____
_____
_____
_____
_____
_____
_____

[Answer explanation on next page.]

Tip #2 Answer Explanation

Answer choice D is correct. When reviewing government action under equal protection theories, a court applies one of three levels of review, depending on the classification of persons or the type of right concerned. The rational basis standard is used in all cases in which one of the higher standards (intermediate or strict scrutiny) is not applicable, including laws drawing distinctions based on age. A law passes the rational basis standard of review if it is rationally related to a legitimate government interest. Laws are presumed valid under this standard, so the burden is on the challenger to overcome this presumption. Answer choice A is incorrect because it describes the strict scrutiny standard, which applies only if the case involves a fundamental right or suspect classification, such as race, ethnicity, national origin, or alienage. Answer choice B is incorrect because it describes the intermediate scrutiny test, which applies in the case of a classification based on gender or status as a non-marital child.

Answer choice C is incorrect because, although the burden of proof does fall on the applicant, the required proof is not the intermediate scrutiny standard; rather it is the rational basis standard.

Question notes:

_____
_____
_____
_____
_____
_____
_____
_____
_____
_____

Tip #3: Remember that the test covers the U.S. Constitution, not federal statutes.

An engineer worked for a private company that had a mandatory retirement policy. All employees were required to retire at age 65. The engineer, who had children later in life, wanted to continue working until age 67, as he had two college tuitions to pay. On his 65th birthday, however, the head of human resources for the company sent him a termination notice.

If the engineer brings an equal protection claim against the private company, he will most likely:

A. Win, because federal statutes prohibit discriminating against workers on the basis of age.

B. Win, because the agency will not be able to show that its policy is necessary to further a compelling state interest.

C. Lose, because there is no state action.

D. Lose, because the engineer's reason for wanting to continue working is not compelling or necessary.

Answer choice C is correct. Constitutional equal protection claims apply only to governmental entities, not to private companies. Because the engineer's claim is an equal protection one, he will not prevail against his employer. Answer choice A is incorrect because, while there are federal statutes that prohibit age discrimination, the engineer has not raised a statutory claim. Furthermore, the Constitutional Law questions on the MBE do not test the application of federal statutes, merely constitutional provisions. Answer choice D is incorrect because, under an equal protection claim based on age discrimination, the engineer would have to prove that the employer's policy is not rationally related to a legitimate government interest. However, that standard does not apply in the absence of state action.

Question notes:

_____
_____
_____
_____
_____
_____
_____

Tip #4: Know the hierarchy of laws (checks and balances).

On behalf of the United States, the President of the United States entered into a valid federal treaty with a foreign island nation. Under the ratified treaty, a U.S. territory that bordered that foreign island nation could freely trade with the island nation certain agricultural products, including bananas. Shortly thereafter, a nearby U.S. state passed a law allowing for a free transfer of goods between the state, the territory, and the island nation. Several years later, Congress passed a statute requiring a mark of origin on all agricultural products from all foreign countries. Last year, the President of the United States entered an executive agreement with the leader of a second foreign country, promising that the United States, including its territories, would buy all of the bananas that the United States requires from this foreign country, and would only buy bananas from other foreign countries if the United States' demand exceeded the country's supply. In exchange, the foreign country would first buy its wheat supply from the United States. Citizens of the U.S. territory want to continue to freely buy bananas from the island nation.

Which of the laws is likely to govern whether the U.S. territory can buy bananas from the island nation?

A. The executive agreement

B. The federal statute passed by Congress

C. The federal treaty

D. The state law

Question notes:

_____
_____
_____
_____
_____
_____
_____
_____

[Answer explanation on next page.]

Tip #4: Answer Explanation

Answer choice C is correct. Federal statutes and treaties take precedence over executive agreements. Here, the federal treaty and the executive agreement directly conflict with one another, so the federal treaty would govern whether the territory can buy bananas from the island nation. Answer choice A is incorrect because, even though the President does have the power to enter into executive agreements with foreign nations, including reciprocal trade agreements, the executive agreement is subject to federal treaties and statutes. Answer choice B is incorrect because, although a federal statute would take precedence over an executive agreement, the two here do not really conflict. The federal statute does not govern whether the territory can buy bananas from the island nation; it only requires that a mark of origin be included on those bananas. Answer choice D is incorrect because federal actions, whether statutes, treaties, or executive agreements, take precedence over state laws.

Question notes:

_____

_____

_____

_____

_____

_____

_____

_____

Tip #5: Always ask, "Where am I?"

For years, a federal agency regularly contracted with a construction company to perform renovations on federal government buildings within a state. The agency properly chose to contract with the company following a federally mandated competitive bidding process. Although representatives from the agency and the company would meet to discuss and negotiate contracts for the upcoming year every January, each individual renovation project was covered by a separate contract. The company made a political contribution to an interest group whose interests were adverse to the current administration. As a result, the agency decided to prohibit the company from participating in the bidding process and therefore terminated the possibility of contracting with the company at all. After the most recent competitive bidding process, the agency gave all of the upcoming renovation projects for the year to the company's competitor. The company brings a proper suit to enjoin the agency from contracting with the competitor.

Did the agency's decision to stop contracting with the company violate the Contracts Clause?

A.   Yes, because the government cannot cancel a contract based on a party's political affiliations.

B.   Yes, because it constituted impairment by the government of a public contract without a compelling government interest.

C.   No, because the interference was reasonably necessary to serve an important government interest.

D.   No, because there was no state legislation that impaired the contract.

Answer choice D is correct. Article I states that no state legislation may retroactively impair the obligation of contracts. The article does not apply to federal action or to court decisions. In this case, there was no state action at all, let alone state action that retroactively impaired an existing contract. Answer choice A is incorrect because there was no contract that the government cancelled. The government simply chose to award contracts to another party. There is no fundamental right to a government contract. Answer choice B is incorrect because it is not an impairment of a contract, as there was no existing contract cancelled. In addition, the Article I prohibition on impairment of contracts applies to state legislation, not to the federal government; and it misstates the standard of proof in the event that the impairment of a contract by state action was at issue--the standard, if applicable, is that the interference was reasonably necessary to serve an important government interest. Answer choice C is incorrect because, while it does state the correct standard of review, it is an irrelevant answer because the Article I prohibition applies to state legislation, not the federal government.

Question notes:

_____

_____

_____

MBE WORKSHOP: CONTRACTS
PROFESSOR LISA MCELROY
DREXEL UNIVERSITY SCHOOL OF LAW

CHAPTER 1:   CONTRACTS

Editor's Note 1: The below outline is taken from the National Conference of Bar Examiners' website.

NOTE: Examinees are to assume that Article 2 and Revised Article 1 of the Uniform Commercial Code have been adopted and are applicable when appropriate. Approximately half of the Contracts questions on the MBE will be based on categories I and IV, and approximately half will be based on the remaining categories—II, III, V, and VI. Approximately one-fourth of the Contracts questions on the MBE will be based on provisions of the Uniform Commercial Code, Article 2 and Revised Article 1.

I. **Formation of contracts (with part IV, 50% of the exam)**
   A. Mutual assent
      1. Offer and acceptance
      2. Indefiniteness or absence of terms
      3. Implied-in-fact contract
      4. "Pre-contract" obligations based on reliance
   B. Consideration
      1. Bargain and exchange and substitutes for bargain: "moral obligation," reliance, and statutory substitutes
      2. Modification of contracts: preexisting duties
      3. Compromise and settlement of claims

II. **Defenses to enforceability**
   A. Incapacity to contract
   B. Duress
   C. Undue influence
   D. Mistake, misunderstanding
   E. Fraud, misrepresentation, and nondisclosure
   F. Illegality, unconscionability, and public policy

   G. Statute of frauds
III. **Parol evidence and interpretation**
IV. **Performance, breach, and discharge**
   A. Conditions
      1. Express
      2. Constructive
      3. Obligations of good faith and fair dealing in performance and enforcement of contracts
      4. Suspension or excuse of conditions by waiver, election, or estoppel
      5. Prospective inability to perform: effect on other party
   B. Impracticability and frustration of purpose
   C. Discharge of contractual duties
   D. Express and implied warranties in sale-of-goods contracts
   E. Substantial and partial breach and anticipatory repudiation
V. **Remedies**
   A. Measure of damages for breach; protecting the expectation interest

B. Consequential damages: causation, certainty, and foreseeability
C. Liquidated damages and penalties
D. Avoidable consequences and mitigation of damages
E. Rescission and reformation
F. Specific performance; injunction against breach; declaratory judgment
G. Restitutionary and reliance recoveries
H. Remedial rights of breaching parties

VI. Third-party rights
A. Third-party beneficiaries
1. Intended beneficiaries
2. Incidental beneficiaries
3. Impairment or extinguishment of third- party rights
4. Enforcement by the promisee
B. Assignment of rights and delegation of duties

TOP FIVE THINGS TO KNOW FOR CONTRACTS

1. Focus on contract formation.

_____

_____

_____

2. Where there's a UCC rule, learn the distinction between common law and UCC.

_____

_____

_____

3. Ask yourself whether there's an enforceable agreement and, if not, explore other theories of recovery.

_____

_____

_____

4. Dates can be very important – where many dates appear in a fact pattern, draw a timeline.

_____

_____

_____

5. If a fact pattern mentions a conversation or a telephone call, take note.

_____

_____

_____

CHAPTER 2: CONTRACTS - PRACTICE QUESTIONS

Tip #1: Focus on contract formation.

A homeowner entered into a contract with a landscaper. The contract specified that the homeowner would pay the landscaper $10,000 upon completion of a list of projects. The landscaper performed the work while the homeowner was away on vacation. When the landscaper sought payment, the homeowner refused, noting that a tree had not been trimmed as required by the contract. The landscaper responded that, since he would now have to forego other work in order to trim the tree, he would do it but only if the homeowner agreed to pay him a total of $10,500 for his services. The homeowner, desperate to have the work completed, agreed. Once the work was completed, however, the homeowner gave the landscaper a check for $10,000, and refused to pay more. The landscaper sued for breach of contract.

Is the landscaper likely to succeed in his claim?

A.   No, because an enforceable contract cannot be renegotiated.

B.   No, because there was no consideration for the promise to pay $10,500 and no unanticipated circumstances arose.

C.   Yes, because there was a valid modification of the contract.

D.   Yes, because the landscaper suffered a detriment by foregoing other work.

Answer choice B is correct. At common law, a promise to perform a preexisting legal duty does not qualify as consideration because the promisee is already bound to perform. In this case, the landscaper had a preexisting legal duty to trim the tree, and thus there was no consideration to support the homeowner's promise to pay an additional $500. Answer choice A is incorrect because an enforceable contract may be renegotiated. Even when there is a preexisting legal duty, there will be consideration if the promisee gives something in addition to what is already owed or varies the preexisting duty. Answer choice C is incorrect because modification of a services contract must be supported by consideration. Or some circumstances that were not anticipated when the contract was made must have arisen, and modification is fair and equitable in light of those circumstances. Answer choice D is incorrect because the fact that the landscaper had to forego other work would not serve as consideration in this case because the landscaper was under a preexisting legal duty.

Question notes:

_____
_____
_____
_____
_____
_____
_____
_____

Tip #2: Where there's a UCC rule, learn the difference between the common law and the UCC.

Completing an online form, a customer ordered a handmade colored glass ornament to hang in the window of her home. In a box labeled "Comments," the customer wrote, "red, please." Via email, the online retailer sent a notice acknowledging the order, but reserving the right to send an ornament in any color. The retailer shipped the customer a green ornament.

Which of the following arguments would not support the customer's position that she does not have to pay for the ornament?

A. The retailer shipped nonconforming goods.

B. The customer did not separately agree to receive an ornament in any color.

C. Because customer was not a merchant, the retailer's additional term in acknowledgment is not part of contract.

D. The retailer's acceptance did not mirror the customer's offer.

Question notes:

_____
_____
_____
_____
_____
_____
_____
_____

[Answer explanation on next page]

Tip #2 Answer Explanation

Answer choice D is correct. The mirror image rule, which states that acceptance must mirror the terms of the offer, does not apply to a sale of goods, such as a glass ornament. Answer choices A, B, and C are incorrect because they all support the customer's position that she does not have to pay for the ornament. Answer choice A is incorrect because the failure of the retailer to ship conforming goods (i.e., a red ornament) would constitute a breach of the retailer's contract obligations. Answer choice B is incorrect. Because the customer is not a merchant, any additional terms in the acceptance are treated as a proposal. This proposal must be separately accepted by the customer in order to become part of the contract. Answer choice C is incorrect because, if the acknowledgement is an acceptance, since the customer is not a merchant, a different term (i.e., an ornament of any color) is not part of the contract.

Question notes:

_____

_____

_____

_____

_____

_____

_____

Tip #3: Ask yourself if there's an enforceable agreement, and, if not, explore other theories of recovery.

A local philanthropist, during a lecture to a class of high school students, promised to pay the college tuition of any student who received a perfect score on a college admissions test. Immediately after the lecture, a student told the philanthropist that he accepted the philanthropist's promise. The student thereafter signed up for a preparatory class for the test, hired a private tutor at significant expense, and quit all of his extracurricular activities. Shortly before the student took the test, the philanthropist's assistant contacted the student and told the student that the philanthropist withdrew his promise to pay for college. The student took the test and received a perfect score. The student sued the philanthropist based on the promise.

Is the student likely to receive relief in his suit against the philanthropist?

A. No, because the philanthropist revoked his offer before the student received a perfect score.

B. No, because there was no consideration for the philanthropist's promise.

C. Yes, because the student detrimentally relied on the philanthropist's promise.

D. Yes, because the student accepted the philanthropist's offer prior to revocation.

Answer choice C is correct. The doctrine of promissory estoppel (detrimental reliance) can be used under certain circumstances to enforce a promise that is not supported by consideration. A promise is binding if the promisor should reasonably expect it to induce action or forbearance, it does induce such action or forbearance, and injustice can be avoided only by enforcement of the promise. In this case, the student enrolled in a test preparation course, hired a private tutor, and quit his extracurricular activities in reliance on the promise. Moreover, the philanthropist should have reasonably expected such actions. Accordingly, the student will likely receive some relief, although he may receive reliance damages (e.g., money expended to pass the test) rather than expectation damages (i.e., payment of the student's college tuition). Answer choice A is incorrect because, although an offer can generally be revoked at any time before acceptance, an offeror's power to revoke an offer is limited when an offeree has detrimentally relied on the promise. Answer choice B is incorrect because the doctrine of promissory estoppel would likely apply to allow the student some relief despite the absence consideration. Answer choice D is incorrect because the offer could be accepted only by performance, that is, by achieving a perfect test score.

Question notes:

_____

_____

_____

_____

_____

_____

_____

_____

_____

_____

Tip #4: Where dates appear in a fact pattern, draw a timeline.

A homeowner met with a contractor regarding remodeling the homeowner's kitchen. At the conclusion of their meeting, the contractor told the homeowner that he would charge her $9,000-$10,000 for the work, but that he would get back to her with a definite price once he returned to his office. When he arrived at his office, the contractor had a voicemail from the homeowner, saying that she would pay him
$9,000 for the work they discussed. The contractor promptly returned her phone call, and left her a voicemail saying that he would do the work for $9,500, which the homeowner received. The next day, the contractor, having a change of heart, tried unsuccessful to reach the homeowner by phone. He left her a voicemail that he would do the work for $9,000 after all, and that he would start the following day unless he heard otherwise from her. The next day, the contractor showed up at homeowner's house, ready to begin.

What best describes the relationship between the parties?

A. A contract was formed when the contractor left the final voicemail.

B. A contract was formed when the homeowner received the final voicemail.

C. A contract was formed when the contractor showed up to begin work on the kitchen.

D. There is no contract between the parties.

Question notes:

_____
_____
_____
_____
_____
_____
_____
_____

[Answer explanation on next page]

Tip #4 Answer Explanation

Answer choice D is correct. An offer is terminated by rejection. A modification of the terms of the offer acts as a rejection of the original offer and as a new counteroffer. In this case, the contractor's first voicemail served as a rejection of the homeowner's original offer of $9,000 and a counteroffer of $9,500. The original offer was terminated; the contractor could not later accept the homeowner's offer. Accordingly, no contract was formed. Answer choices A, B, and C are incorrect because the contractor rejected the homeowner's offer and thus there was no contract.

Question notes:

_____

_____

_____

_____

_____

_____

_____

Tip #5: If a fact pattern mentions a telephone call or a conversation, take note.

An adult daughter called a local restaurant to place a large delivery order. The restaurant generally requires a credit card for all delivery orders, but the daughter's father, who is a regular at the restaurant and happened to be there when the daughter placed the order, told the clerk that, in the event the daughter failed to pay for the food, he would do so. The restaurant delivered the order to the daughter, who, having decided to order something else instead, refused to accept or pay for the food.

Can the restaurant collect from the father?

A. No, because the father's promise was made orally.

B. No, because a third party will not be held liable for the contract obligations of another.

C. Yes, because the father promised to pay.

D. Yes, because a parent is liable to pay for necessities provided to a child.

Answer choice A is correct. The Statute of Frauds applies to suretyship agreements (i.e., one person's promise to pay the debts of another). Here, the daughter ordered food and was obligated to pay for the food. However, the father also promised to pay for the food if the daughter did not. This promise created a suretyship agreement. Since this agreement was not in writing, the restaurant cannot enforce it. Note that some oral suretyship contracts can be enforced (indemnity contracts and contracts wherein the surety's main reason for paying the debt is the surety's own economic advantage), but those circumstances are not present here. Answer choice B is incorrect because third parties may be liable for the debts of another if they agree to be sureties. In such cases the surety agreement must generally be in writing. Answer choice C is incorrect because, although the father did promise to pay for the food if his daughter failed to do so, the Statute of Frauds applies to a suretyship agreement. Since the agreement was not in writing the father's promise is unenforceable. Answer choice D is incorrect because, although a parent is liable for necessities, such as food, provided by a third party to a minor child, a parent is not liable for necessities provided to an adult daughter or son.

Question notes:

_____

_____

_____

_____

_____

_____

_____

_____

MBE WORKSHOP: CRIMINAL LAW
PROFESSOR LISA MCELROY DREXEL
UNIVERSITY SCHOOL OF LAW

CHAPTER 1:   CRIMINAL LAW

> **Editor's Note 1:** While the below outline is taken from the National Conference of Bar Examiners' website, the notes and comments in italics are notes from Themis staff attorneys.

NOTE: Approximately half of the Criminal Law and Procedure questions on the MBE will be based on Criminal Law.

> **Editor's Note 2:** While you should assume that applicable law is common law unless told otherwise, the MBE does also test the Model Penal Code.

I. **HOMICIDE** *(note that this includes common-law murder, felony murder, and statutory murders)*
   A. Intended killings
      1. Premeditation, deliberation
      2. Provocation
   B. Unintended killings
      1. Intent to injure
      2. Reckless and negligent killings
      3. Felony murder
      4. Misdemeanor manslaughter

II. **OTHER CRIMES**
   A. Theft
      1. Larceny
      2. Embezzlement
      3. False pretenses
   B. Receiving stolen goods
   C. Robbery
   D. Burglary
   E. Assault and battery
   F. Rape; statutory rape

   G. Kidnapping
   H. Arson
   I. Possession offenses

III. **INCHOATE CRIMES; PARTIES**
   A. Inchoate offenses
      1. Attempts
      2. Conspiracy
      3. Solicitation
   B. Parties to crime

IV **.GENERAL PRINCIPLES**
   A. Acts and omissions
   B. State of mind
      1. Required mental state
      2. Strict liability
      3. Mistake of fact or law
   C. Responsibility
      1. Mental disorder
      2. Intoxication
   D. Causation
   E. Justification and excuse
   F. Jurisdiction

TOP FIVE THINGS TO KNOW FOR CRIMINAL LAW

1. Focus on murder/manslaughter and then on crimes against property.

_____

_____

_____

2. Know the elements cold! Most questions revolve around the elements of the cause of action.

_____

_____

_____

3. Remember that the best defense is that the prosecution cannot sustain its burden; don't go with an affirmative defense unless it's the only option.

_____

_____

_____

4. Use the answer choices to help you figure out which crimes are in play.

_____

_____

_____

5. Rack up the points here; they'll offset the more difficult Contracts & Property questions.

_____

_____

_____

CHAPTER 2: CRIMINAL LAW -- PRACTICE QUESTIONS

Tip #1: Focus on murder/manslaughter.

Immediately after she arrived home from work, a woman found her husband engaged in sex with a female who worked in the husband's office. Enraged, the woman retrieved a handgun from her dresser drawer. She fired the gun, intending to shoot her husband's co-worker. Her shot missed the co-worker, and instead killed her husband. The woman was charged with common law murder of her husband.

Based on the foregoing facts, should she be convicted?

A.   Yes, because the woman acted with reckless indifference with regards to her husband's life.

B.   Yes, because of the doctrine of transferred intent.

C.   No, because the act was provoked.

D.   No, because the woman's extreme temporary distress completely excuses her actions.

Answer choice C is correct. Voluntary manslaughter is murder committed in "the heat of passion," that is, in response to adequate provocation. The woman's enraged mental state mitigates the crime from murder to voluntary manslaughter. Answer choice A is incorrect because, while firing a handgun in a bedroom in the direction of the victim could arguably constitute the intent necessary for murder, the provocation would reduce the crime to voluntary manslaughter. Answer choice B is incorrect because, while the doctrine of transferred intent could supply the necessary intent for the killing of the husband to constitute murder, the adequate provocation would reduce the crime to voluntary manslaughter.
Answer choice D is incorrect because a defendant's action in the "heat of passion" does not serve as a complete defense to any crime related to the killing. The woman could be convicted of voluntary manslaughter.

Question notes:

_____

_____

_____

_____

_____

_____

_____

_____

_____

Tip #2: Know the elements cold!

A woman who had been drinking heavily took her neighbor's truck without the neighbor's permission. The woman intended to drive the truck up to a local bar and then return the truck later that evening. On the way to the bar, the woman crashed the truck and totaled it. The woman is subsequently arrested and charged with larceny in a jurisdiction that follows the common law.

Should the woman be convicted?

A.   Yes, because of her intent to take the car.

B.   Yes, because the car was destroyed and could no longer be used by the neighbor.

C.   No, because she lacked the specific intent required for larceny.

D.   No, if she establishes she was intoxicated at the time she took the car.

Question notes:

_____

_____

_____

_____

_____

_____

_____

_____

[Answer explanation on next page]

Tip #2 Answer Explanation

Answer choice C is correct. Common law larceny requires the intent to permanently deprive the person who owns the property of the property that is taken. The intent to permanently deprive must be present at the time of the taking. Here, the woman took the truck with the intent to return it later that evening. Accordingly, the specific intent required for larceny is not present. Answer choice A is incorrect. If the defendant intends only to borrow the property with the ability to return it at the time of the borrowing, the taking does not constitute a larceny because the defendant lacked the intent to permanently deprive the owner of the property. Answer choice B is incorrect because the fact that the car was destroyed is irrelevant. What controls is the woman's intent at the time she took the car. Here, it was to borrow the car, with the ability to return it. Answer choice D is incorrect. While voluntary intoxication may prevent the formation of the required intent in specific intent crimes, there is no need to prove intoxication here because the woman never had the specific intent to permanently deprive the neighbor of the truck in the first place. Therefore, even if she does not raise intoxication as a defense, she would still not be convicted.

Question notes:

_____

_____

_____

_____

_____

_____

_____

Tip #3: Remember that the best defense is that the prosecution cannot sustain its burden; don't go with an affirmative defense unless it's the only option.

While shopping in a department store, a man saw an expensive wallet on display, and slipped it into his girlfriend's purse without her knowledge as a practical joke to embarrass her. He intended for her to find it as she reached into her purse to pay for other items at the cashier's station and turn it over to the cashier. The couple shopped for the next hour, and the man forgot about the wallet. Before they could pay for their purchases, the couple got into an argument, abandoned their intended purchases, and headed toward an exit. When they attempted to leave the store, they were detained by a store security officer who found the wallet in the purse. Both parties were charged with larceny.

Of the following, which would provide the man with his best defense to larceny?

A. The woman, and not the man, carried the wallet away from the display.

B. There was not a trespassory taking of the wallet since the man was on the store premises as a customer.

C. The man did not understand the nature of his actions.

D. The man lacked the necessary intent to steal the wallet.

Answer choice D is correct. Larceny requires the intent to permanently deprive another person with superior rights to the property of that property. In this case, the man did not intend to permanently deprive the department store of the wallet. Rather, he intended for the girlfriend to return the wallet when she found it at the cashier's station. Therefore, the man did not possess the specific intent required for the crime of larceny. Answer choice A is incorrect because larceny can occur if property is taken and carried away by an agent, even if the agent is unaware that she is doing so. Answer choice B is incorrect because a trespassory taking requires only that the taking occur without the owner's permission, and not that the defendant be a trespasser when the taking occurs. Answer choice C is incorrect because, even if the man could satisfy the test for insanity, he would never have to do so if the prosecution could not prove that he had the requisite intent.

Question notes:

_____

_____

_____

_____

_____

_____

_____

_____

Tip #4: Use the answer choices to help you figure out which crimes are in play.

A runner was in the midst of his morning run when the defendant jumped out from behind a bush and tripped the runner, intending to steal the runner's wallet. The runner was not carrying a wallet, however. Frustrated, the defendant tore off the runner's hat. The runner tried to grab the hat back from the defendant, but the defendant pulled it away and ran off. The struggle caused the defendant to lose his balance, and he dropped the hat a few feet from the runner. The runner then picked up his hat and completed his run.

What is the most serious crime, listed in order of increasing seriousness, for which the defendant may be convicted?

A. Attempted larceny.
B. Larceny.
C. Battery.
D. Robbery.

Answer choice D is correct. Robbery is larceny by force or intimidation, taking the property from the person or in the presence of the victim. The force need not be great, but must be more than the amount necessary to effectuate taking and carrying away the property. The elements of larceny were met as soon as the defendant carried away the hat. Moreover, the force element was satisfied when the defendant tripped and then struggled with the defendant. Answer choices B and C are incorrect because battery and larceny are less serious than robbery. Although the elements of each of these crimes are satisfied, they would merge into the crime of robbery. Answer choice A is incorrect because larceny merely requires a taking and carrying away of the personal property of another with the intent to steal. These elements were satisfied as soon as the defendant took away the hat, so the defendant actually completed the crime of larceny.

Question notes:

_____

_____

_____

_____

_____

_____

_____

MBE WORKSHOP: CRIMINAL PROCEDURE
PROFESSOR LISA MCELROY
DREXEL UNIVERSITY SCHOOL OF LAW

CHAPTER 1:   CRIMINAL PROCEDURE

> **Editor's Note 1:** The below outline is taken from the National Conference of Bar Examiners' website

NOTE: Approximately half of the Criminal Law and Procedure questions on the MBE will be based on Criminal Procedure.

CONSTITUTIONAL PROTECTION OF ACCUSED PERSONS

A. Arrest, search and seizure

B. Confessions and privilege against Self-incrimination

C. Lineups and other forms of identification

D. Right to Counsel

E. Fair trial and guilty pleas

F. Double jeopardy

G. Cruel and unusual punishment

H. Burdens of proof and persuasion

TOP FIVE THINGS TO KNOW FOR CRIMINAL PROCEDURE

1. Focus your studies on the Fourth Amendment and exceptions to the warrant requirement.

_____
_____
_____

2. Remember that the state almost always wins!

_____
_____
_____

3. Be sure you understand the probable cause and reasonable suspicion standards and when they apply.

_____
_____
_____

4. Remember that defendant rights are usually very limited.

_____
_____
_____

5. New cases (from the last 6-8 months) do not matter.

_____
_____
_____

CHAPTER 2: CRIMINAL PROCEDURE - PRACTICE QUESTIONS

Tip #1: Focus on the Fourth Amendment and exceptions to the warrant requirement.

A police officer, acting on an anonymous tip that a farmer was illegally growing opium poppies in his fields, entered the farm without permission of the farmer by climbing over a locked gate and despite the presence of several "No trespassing" signs. Searching the property, the officer found the poppies growing in a field that was surrounded by woods and consequently not visible from any other privately owned or public property. In addition, the farmer had deployed camouflage netting to forestall detection of the poppies from the air. Based on her observations, the police officer arrested the farmer and seized the poppies. Prior to the farmer's trial for illegally growing opium poppies, the farmer filed a motion to suppress the poppies on the basis that they were seized in violation of his constitutional rights.

Should the poppies be suppressed?

A. No, because the Fourth Amendment protection against unreasonable searches and seizures does not extend to open fields.

B. No, because the police office had probable cause to search the farmer's property without a warrant.

C. Yes, because the police officer gained knowledge of the poppies by trespassing on the farmer's property.

D. Yes, because the farmer made reasonable efforts to exclude the public from his lands.

Answer choice A is correct. By its terms, the Fourth Amendment is limited to "persons, houses, papers and effects;" it does not extend to open fields. Whether a location is an open field does not turn on whether the owner of the field has taken measures to keep it private, but on whether such expectations of privacy are objectively reasonable. For activities conducted outdoors, a person generally has no reasonable expectation of privacy. For this reason, answer choice D is incorrect. Answer choice B is incorrect because an anonymous tip, without more, is not sufficient to constitute probable cause to conduct a search. Answer choice C is incorrect because, although the police officer may be liable in tort to the farmer or even subject to criminal action for trespassing, the officer's trespass does not prevent her search from being constitutional. The law of trespass proscribes intrusions upon land that the Fourth Amendment does not.

Question notes:

_____

_____

_____

_____

_____

_____

Tip #2: Remember that the state almost always wins!

Police officers, responding to a complaint about noise, discovered a party going on at a residence. Approaching the front door of the residence, the officers witnessed an altercation, which took place inside the residence. One of the guests, despite being restrained by other guests, nevertheless managed to punch another guest in the nose, giving that guest a bloody nose. After announcing their presence, the officers entered the residence without a warrant for the purpose of arresting the guest who committed the assault and did so. That guest was subsequently charged with assault. At trial, the guest sought to suppress evidence of the assault and dismiss the charge.

Should the court suppress this evidence?

A.   Yes, because the officers arrested the party guest at a residence without a warrant.

B.   Yes, because the officers entered the residence for the purpose of arresting the party guest rather   than to prevent further violence or to render aid to the injured guest.

C.   No, because exigent circumstances justified the arrest of the party guest.

D.   No, because the police announced their presence.

Question notes:

_____

_____

_____

_____

_____

_____

_____

_____

_____

[Answer explanation on next page]

Tip #2 Answer Explanation

Answer choice C is correct. While generally a police officer cannot effect an arrest within a residence without a warrant, a police officer may do so where exigent circumstances exist. Here the officers witnessed an altercation within the residence that had the potential for continuing and a victim that could require assistance. The fact that the officers entered for the subjective purpose of arresting the perpetrator of the assault does not negate the objective justification for the officer's entry into the residence (i.e., the prevention of violence and the rendering of aid to the victim of violence). For this reason, answer choices A and B are incorrect. Answer choice D is incorrect because the announcement by police of their presence before entering a home does not justify a warrantless entry.

Question notes:

_____

_____

_____

_____

_____

_____

_____

Tip #3: Be sure you understand the probable cause and reasonable suspicion standards and when they apply.

An employee of a storage company informed police that the owner of the company was involved in a conspiracy to steal goods and then sell them. According to the employee, the owner permitted the storage of the stolen goods in his warehouse, typically only overnight, before the goods were transported elsewhere for resale. Acting on reliable information from the employee that the warehouse was due to receive a shipment of stolen goods that evening, a police officer immediately sought and obtained a warrant from a neutral and detached magistrate to search the warehouse upon the arrival of the stolen goods. The warrant failed to specify the condition that had to occur before the search was authorized by the warrant. Properly executing the warrant, the police seized the stolen goods. The warehouse owner was charged with conspiracy to commit larceny and possession of stolen goods. The owner sought to suppress the evidence of the stolen goods on the grounds that the seizure was unconstitutional.

Should the court suppress this evidence?

A. Yes, because an anticipatory warrant is per se unconstitutional.

B. Yes because the failure to state the triggering condition in the warrant caused the warrant to fail for lack of particularity.

C. No, because the warrant satisfied the probable cause requirement of the Fourth Amendment.

D. No, because warrant is not needed to search business premises such as a warehouse.

Answer choice C is correct. An anticipatory warrant is not unconstitutional simply because the items to be seized are not located on the premises to be searched at the time that the warrant is issued. The probable cause requirement is satisfied where, at the time that the warrant is issued, there is probable cause to believe that the triggering condition will occur and, if that condition does occur, there is a fair probability that contraband or evidence of a crime will be found in a particular place. For this reason, answer choice A is incorrect. Answer choice B is incorrect because a warrant need not state any condition that is precedent to its validity. Answer choice D is incorrect because the warrant requirement generally does apply to the search of a business, particularly where the search is made in regard to criminal activity rather than for administrative purposes.

Question notes:

_____

_____

_____

_____

_____

_____

Tip #4: Remember that defendant rights are usually very limited.

Federal agents were investigating a drug trafficking ring. The agents received reliable information that the drug ring used a drug dealer's basement as the primary storage site for their drugs. Relying on this information, the agents obtained a warrant to search the drug dealer's basement for drugs and related paraphernalia. After failing to find any evidence in the basement, the agents searched the drug dealer's bedroom and seized a notebook they found on the dresser. The notebook contained a ledger, with the names of the drug dealer's suppliers and clients, as well as statements of their accounts. One of the drug dealer's suppliers named in the ledger was later arrested, charged, and tried jointly with the drug dealer. The drug dealer's supplier seeks to suppress evidence of the ledger at trial, arguing that the seizure of the ledger was illegal.

Should the judge grant the supplier's motion?

A. No, because the supplier lacks standing to challenge the seizure of the ledger.

B. No, because the ledger was seized legally.

C. Yes, because the ledger was not specifically named in the warrant.

D. Yes, because the agents exceeded the scope of the warrant when they searched the drug dealer's bedroom.

Question notes:

_____

_____

_____

_____

_____

[Answer explanation on next page]

Tip #4 Answer Explanation

Answer choice A is correct. Fourth Amendment rights are personal and may not be asserted vicariously. The defendant must be the alleged victim of the unreasonable search or seizure in order to assert a claim. A defendant cannot raise the constitutional rights of a co-defendant. In this case, the supplier was not the victim of an illegal search, and his rights were not violated. Thus, he cannot challenge the seizure. Answer choice B is incorrect because the seizure of the ledger was in fact illegal. A search warrant confers authority to search only the places and persons named in the warrant. In this case, the warrant allowed the agents to search only the drug dealer's basement, and the agents exceeded the scope of the warrant when they searched the bedroom. Answer choice C is incorrect because, even if the seizure of the ledger was illegal, the supplier lacked standing to challenge its illegal seizure. Thus, the fact that the ledger was not named specifically in the warrant would not bar its admission. Answer choice D is incorrect because, although the seizure did in fact exceed the scope of the warrant, and was thus illegal, the defendant lacks standing to challenge the seizure.

Question notes:

_____

_____

_____

_____

_____

_____

_____

Tip #5: New cases (from the last 6-8 months) do not matter.

A highway was known as a drug corridor used to transport drugs between two cities. The drug unit of a state police force launched an initiative to combat drug trafficking along this section of highway. They formulated a plan to conduct checkpoint stops to check for drugs along certain sections of the highway. Under the plan, the police would stop every hundredth car that passed the checkpoint, and a trained canine would sniff for the presence of drugs. The defendant was stopped at a checkpoint, and the canine detected the presence of cocaine in the trunk of his car. The police then searched the trunk, where they found large amounts of cocaine. The entire stop lasted less than three minutes. The defendant was charged and tried for drug trafficking crimes. At his trial, he moved to suppress evidence of the drugs found during the search.

Are the drugs likely to be suppressed?

A. No, because the canine sniff provided probable cause to search the trunk.

B. No, because the checkpoint stop was based on neutral, articulable standards.

C. Yes, because the checkpoint stop constituted an unreasonable seizure.

D. Yes, because a canine sniff of a car may not be performed without probable cause.

Answer choice C is correct. Police may stop an automobile at a checkpoint without reasonable, individualized suspicion of a violation of the law if the stop is based on neutral, articulable standards and its purpose is closely related to an issue affecting automobiles. A roadblock to perform sobriety checks has been upheld, while a similar roadblock to perform drug checks has not. In this case, the checkpoint stops would constitute an unreasonable seizure because their purpose was to only to perform drug checks rather than to prevent an issue affecting automobiles (for example, driving safely). Answer choice A is incorrect because although the sniff provided probable cause for the search of the trunk, the evidence seized would not be admissible because the stop itself violated the Fourth Amendment.

Answer choice B is incorrect because, even if the standards are neutral and articulable, the purpose of the stop must be permissible. Checkpoint stops to perform drug tests are not permissible. Answer choice D is incorrect because the use of a trained dog to sniff for the presence of drugs does not violate the reasonable expectation of privacy present during a valid stop. Thus, a canine search may be performed without probable cause, provided the stop itself meets other constitutional requirements.

Question notes:

_____

_____

_____

_____

MBE WORKSHOP: EVIDENCE
PROFESSOR LISA MCELROY
DREXEL UNIVERSITY SCHOOL OF LAW

CHAPTER 1:   EVIDENCE

> **Editor's Note 1:**   The below outline is taken from the National Conference of Bar Examiners' website.

NOTE: All Evidence questions should be answered according to the Federal Rules of Evidence, as currently in effect. Approximately one-quarter of the Evidence questions on the MBE will be based on category I, one-third on category II, one-quarter on category V, and the remainder on categories III and IV..

I. PRESENTATION OF EVIDENCE
  A. Introduction of evidence
    1. Requirement of personal knowledge
    2. Refreshing recollection
    3. Objections and offers of proof
    4. Lay opinions
    5. Competency of witnesses
    6. Judicial notice
    7. Roles of judge and jury
    8. Limited admissibility
  B. Presumptions
  C. Mode and order
    1. Control by court
    2. Scope of examination
    3. Form of questions
    4. Exclusion of witnesses
  D. Impeachment, contradiction, and rehabilitation
    1. Inconsistent statements and conduct
    2. Bias and interest
    3. Conviction of crime
    4. Specific instances of conduct
    5. Character for truthfulness
    6. Ability to observe, remember, or relate accurately
    7. Impeachment of hearsay declarants
    8. Rehabilitation of impeached witnesses
    9. Contradiction
  E. Proceedings to which evidence rules apply

II. RELEVANCY AND REASONS FOR EXCLUDING RELEVANT EVIDENCE
  A. Probative value
    1. Relevancy
    2. Exclusion for unfair prejudice, confusion, or waste of time
  B. Authentication and identification
  C. Character and related concepts
    1. Admissibility of character
    2. Methods of proving character
    3. Habit and routine practice
    4. Other crimes, acts, transactions, and events
    5. Prior sexual misconduct of a defendant
  D. Expert testimony
    1. Qualifications of witnesses
    2. Bases of testimony
    3. Ultimate issue rule
    4. Reliability and relevancy
    5. Proper subject matter for

expert testimony
- E. Real, demonstrative, and experimental evidence

III. PRIVILEGES AND OTHER POLICY EXCLUSIONS
- A. Spousal immunity and marital communications
- B. Attorney-client and work product
- C. Physician/psychotherapist-patient
- D. Other privileges
- E. Insurance coverage
- F. Remedial measures
- G. Compromise, payment of medical expenses, and plea negotiations
- H. Past sexual conduct of a victim

IV. WRITINGS, RECORDINGS, AND PHOTOGRAPHS
- A. Requirement of original
- B. Summaries
- C. Completeness rule

V. HEARSAY AND CIRCUMSTANCES OF

ITS ADMISSIBILITY
- A. Definition of hearsay
  1. What is hearsay
  2. Prior statements by witness
  3. Statements attributable to party- opponent
  4. Multiple hearsay
- B. Present sense impressions and excited utterances
- C. Statements of mental, emotional, or physical condition
- D. Statements for purposes of medical diagnosis and treatment
- E. Past recollection recorded
- F. Business records
- G. Public records and reports
- H. Learned treatises
- I. Former testimony; depositions
- J. Statements against interest
- K. Other exceptions to the hearsay rule
- L. Right to confront witnesses

TOP FIVE THINGS TO KNOW FOR EVIDENCE

1. Focus on hearsay and the hearsay exceptions.

_____

_____

_____

2. Always ask yourself: For what purpose is the party trying to introduce this evidence?

_____

_____

_____

3. Know when and how you can introduce evidence of character (defendant and third-party witness).

_____

_____

_____

4. Evidence questions are short but tricky. Take your time.

_____

_____

_____

5. Almost all Evidence questions are based on the FRE; the ones that aren't are mostly on privileges.

_____

_____

_____

CHAPTER 2: EVIDENCE - PRACTICE QUESTIONS

Tip #1: Focus on hearsay and the hearsay exceptions.

The owner of a restaurant sued a real estate developer from whom the owner had purchased land. The owner alleged that the developer had lied to the owner during the contract negotiations for the purchase of the land. According to the owner, the developer had told the owner that he was in the final negotiations to develop the surrounding area for a large retail complex. The developer denied that he had made these statements. At trial, the owner sought to introduce an affidavit from the attorney who had negotiated the land sale contract on his behalf. In the affidavit, the attorney swore that the developer did make the assertion at issue to the owner in the attorney's presence. The attorney had moved to a foreign country and refused to appear to testify. The owner did not submit the land sale contract negotiated by the attorney into evidence. The developer objected to the introduction of the affidavit.

Is the affidavit admissible?

A. No because the best evidence rule requires that the owner submit the original contract.

B. No, because the affidavit is hearsay not within any exception.

C. Yes, because the attorney is unavailable to testify.

D. Yes, because an affidavit meets the former testimony exception to the hearsay rule.

Answer choice B is correct. The affidavit is an out-of-court statement offered for the truth of the matter asserted, or hearsay. Because it does not fall within any hearsay exception, it is inadmissible. Answer choice A is incorrect because the best evidence rule does not apply in these circumstances. The best evidence rule requires that a party produce the original document when the contents of a writing are at issue. In this case, the contract itself is not at issue, and thus need not be produced. Answer choice C is incorrect because the affidavit does not fit within any of the hearsay exceptions that apply when a declarant is unavailable. Answer choice D is incorrect because the affidavit does not meet the former testimony hearsay exception. The former testimony of an unavailable witness given under oath in a hearing or deposition is admissible if the party against whom it is being offered had a similar motive and opportunity to develop the testimony. An affidavit does not qualify as former testimony because it is not given during a hearing or deposition and there is no opportunity for the other party to cross- examine the individual providing the affidavit.

Question notes:

_____
_____
_____
_____
_____
_____
_____

Tip #2: Always ask yourself: For what purpose is the party trying to introduce this evidence?

During a defendant's civil trial for assault, a witness for the plaintiff testified that, shortly after the assault took place, the defendant had admitted to her that he did assault the plaintiff. On cross-examination, the defendant's counsel asked the witness whether she had testified in the defendant's prior criminal prosecution for assault that she had never spoken to the defendant before. The plaintiff objected to the defendant's question.

May the court allow the question over the plaintiff's objection?

A.   Yes, but only to prove that the defendant did not commit the assault.

B.   Yes, but only to impeach the credibility of the witness.

C.   Yes, both to prove that the defendant did not commit the assault and to impeach the credibility of the witness.

D.   No, because the defendant did not first allow the witness the opportunity to explain or deny the statement.

Question notes:

_____
_____
_____
_____
_____
_____
_____
_____
_____
_____
_____

[Answer explanation on next page]

CHAPTER 3: EVIDENCE - PRACTICE QUESTIONS

Tip #2 Answer Explanation

Answer choice C is correct. A witness's prior inconsistent statement is always admissible to impeach the witness. Such a statement is also admissible substantively as non-hearsay if the statement was made under oath, as this one was at the prior criminal proceeding. Answer choices A and B are incorrect because they each only recognize one of the two admissible uses for the evidence here. Answer choice D is incorrect because, while the witness must be given the chance to explain or deny the inconsistent statement, the opportunity to explain or deny need not take place before the statement is admitted into evidence.

Question notes:

_____
_____
_____
_____
_____
_____
_____
_____
_____

Tip #3: Know when and how you can introduce evidence of character (defendant and third-party witness).

A high school teacher played on a hockey team in a local recreational league. During a league game, the teacher was involved in a fight with another hockey player. That player sued the teacher in a battery action to recover for injuries inflicted during the fight. The teacher contended that he had acted in self- defense. The teacher called his principal to testify that the teacher had a reputation within the school community for peacefulness. The plaintiff, who had not introduced evidence of the teacher's character for violence, objected to this testimony.

Should the court admit this testimony?

A. Yes, because the defendant is entitled to introduce evidence of a pertinent good character trait.
B. Yes, because character evidence may be introduced through reputation testimony.
C. No, because the plaintiff had not introduced evidence of the teacher's character for violence.
D. No, because such evidence is not admissible in a civil action.

Answer choice D is correct. Evidence of a defendant's character is inadmissible in a civil case to prove that the defendant acted in conformity with that character trait unless the defendant's character is an essential element of a claim or defense. Since the defendant's character for peacefulness is not an element of either battery or self-defense, the principal's testimony is not admissible. Answer choice A is incorrect because, although a defendant is permitted to introduce evidence of a pertinent good character trait in a criminal case, such evidence is not admissible in a civil case. Answer choice B is incorrect because, although reputation testimony is an acceptable form of presenting character evidence when such evidence is permitted, character evidence is generally not admissible in a civil action. Answer choice C is incorrect because it is not relevant that the plaintiff has not introduced such evidence. Such evidence is not permitted in a civil case, whether introduced by the plaintiff or the defendant.

Question notes:

_____

_____

_____

_____

_____

_____

_____

_____

_____

_____

Tip #4: Evidence questions are short but tricky. Take your time.

A defendant was charged with theft of a valuable watch belonging to an elderly resident at the retirement facility where he worked. The defendant argued that he was not a dishonest person. At trial, he sought to introduce the testimony of a resident of the facility that the defendant had found and returned her diamond wedding ring.

Is the woman's testimony likely to be admitted?

A.   No, because a defendant may not introduce evidence of his good character.

B.   No, because the defendant may not introduce specific instances of conduct to prove character.

C.   Yes, because a criminal defendant may introduce evidence of his own good character.

D.   Yes, because the defendant's character for honesty is relevant to the crime for which he is charged.

Question notes:

_____
_____
_____
_____
_____
_____
_____
_____
_____
_____

[Answer explanation on next page]

Tip #4 Answer Explanation

Answer choice B is correct. A defendant may introduce evidence of his good character as inconsistent with the type of crime charged. Proof of good character offered by the defendant must be in the form of reputation testimony or opinion testimony. Specific instances of a person's conduct are not admissible. Answer choice A is incorrect because a criminal defendant may generally introduce evidence of his good character; however, it must take the form of reputation or opinion testimony.
Answer choice C is incorrect because, although a criminal defendant may introduce such evidence, it must be in the form of reputation or opinion evidence. Answer choice D is incorrect because, although the defendant's trait for honesty is relevant to the crime of theft for which he is charged, proof of good character offered by the defendant must be in the form of reputation testimony or opinion testimony.

Question notes:

_____
_____
_____
_____
_____
_____
_____
_____
_____
_____

Tip #5: Almost all Evidence questions are based on the FRE; the ones that aren't are mostly on privileges.

A lawyer represented a sole proprietor in a federal income tax refund case in U.S. district court in which the sole proprietor was claiming certain additional business expense deductions based on sales expenses that had inadvertently been left off of his tax return for the year.

In this case, which of the following is most likely protected from admission into evidence under the attorney-client privilege?

A.   An employment contract between the sole proprietor and a salesperson drafted by the lawyer.

B.   Sales records created by the sole proprietor and provided to the lawyer to enable the lawyer to prepare for the litigation.

C.   A letter sent to the lawyer by the sole proprietor detailing business expenses.

D.   The sole proprietor's tax return for the tax year in question, which was prepared by the lawyer.

Answer choice C is correct. The letter is a communication by a client to his attorney about a matter under litigation. (Note that, while the letter itself is protected by the attorney-client privilege, the information contained in the letter, i.e., the sole proprietor's business expenses, is not protected by this privilege.) Answer choice A is incorrect because, even though the contract was prepared by the lawyer at the client's request, the contract was between the client and a third party and was intended to be shared with the third party. Consequently, the contract does not constitute a confidential communication. Answer choice B is incorrect because, even though the records were provided by the client to the lawyer and pertained to the legal matter at hand, the records were not prepared in order to obtain legal advice. Answer choice D is incorrect because the tax return is a document that the client filed with government and therefore it was not intended to be kept in confidence.

Question notes:

_____
_____
_____
_____
_____
_____
_____
_____
_____

MBE WORKSHOP: REAL PROPERTY
PROFESSOR LISA MCELROY
DREXEL UNIVERSITY SCHOOL OF LAW

CHAPTER 1:   REAL PROPERTY

Editor's Note 1: The below outline is taken from the National Conference of Bar Examiners' website.

NOTE: Approximately one-fifth of the Real Property questions on the MBE will be based on each of the categories I through V.

I. OWNERSHIP OF REAL PROPERTY
A. PRESENT ESTATES AND FUTURE INTERESTS
1. Present estates
    a. Fees simple
    b. Defeasible fees
    c. Life estates
2. Future interests
    a. Reversions
    b. Remainders, vested and contingent
    c. Executory interests
    d. Possibilities of reverter, powers of termination
    e. Rules affecting these interests (including survivorship, class gifts,   waste, and cy pres)
B. COTENANCY
1. Types: tenancy in common and joint tenancy
2. Rights and obligations of cotenants
    a. Partition
    b. Severance
    c. Relations among cotenants
C. LANDLORD-TENANT LAW
1. Types of tenancies
2. Possession and rent
3. Transfers by landlord or tenant

4. Termination (including surrender, mitigation of damages, anticipatory breach,   and security deposits)
5. Habitability and suitability
D. SPECIAL PROBLEMS
1. Rule against perpetuities: common law rule and statutory reforms
2. Alienability, descendibility, and devisability of present and future interests
3. Fair housing/discrimination
4. Conflicts of law related to disputes involving real property

II. RIGHTS IN REAL PROPERTY
A. RESTRICTIVE COVENANTS
1. Nature and type
2. Creation
3. Scope
4. Transfer
5. Termination
6. Property owners' associations and common interest ownership communities
B. EASEMENTS, PROFITS, AND LICENSES
1. Nature and type
2. Methods of creation
    a. Express
    b. Implied

            c. Prescription
        3. Scope and apportionment
        4. Transfer
        5. Termination
    C. FIXTURES
    D. ZONING (FUNDAMENTALS OTHER THAN REGULATORY TAKING)
        1. Zoning laws
        2. Protection of pre-existing property rights
        3. Rezoning and other zoning changes

III. **REAL ESTATE CONTRACTS**
    A. REAL ESTATE BROKERAGE
    B. CREATION AND CONSTRUCTION
        1. Statute of frauds and exceptions
        2. Essential terms
        3. Time for performance
        4. Remedies for breach
    C. MARKETABILITY OF TITLE
    D. EQUITABLE CONVERSION (INCLUDING RISK OF LOSS)
    E. OPTIONS AND RIGHTS OF FIRST REFUSAL
    F. FITNESS AND SUITABILITY
    G. MERGER

IV. **MORTGAGES/SECURITY DEVICES**
    A. TYPES OF SECURITY DEVICES
        1. Mortgages (including deeds of trust)
            a. In general
            b. Purchase-money mortgages
            c. Future-advance mortgages
        2. Installment land contracts
        3. Absolute deeds as security
    B. SECURITY RELATIONSHIPS
        1. Necessity and nature of obligation
        2. Mortgage theories: title, lien, and intermediate
        3. Rights and duties prior to foreclosure
        4. Right to redeem and clogging the equity of redemption
    C. TRANSFERS
        1. By mortgagor

            a. Assumption and transfer subject to
            b. Rights and obligations
            c. Application of subrogation and suretyship principles
            d. Restrictions on transfer (including due-on-sale clauses)
        2. By mortgagee
    D. DISCHARGE OF THE MORTGAGE
        1. Payment (including prepayment)
        2. Deed in lieu of foreclosure
    E. FORECLOSURE
        1. Types
        2. Acceleration
        3. Parties to the proceeding
        4. Deficiency and surplus
        5. Redemption after foreclosure

V. **TITLES**
    A. ADVERSE POSSESSION
    B. TRANSFER BY DEED
        1. Requirements for deed
        2. Types of deeds (including covenants for title)
        3. Drafting, review, and negotiation of closing documents
        4. Persons authorized to execute documents
    C. TRANSFER BY OPERATION OF LAW AND BY WILL
        1. In general
        2. Ademption
        3. Exoneration
        4. Lapse
    D. TITLE ASSURANCE SYSTEMS
        1. Recording acts
            a. Types
            b. Indexes
            c. Chain of title
            d. Hidden risks (e.g., undelivered or forged deed)
        2. Title insurance
    E. SPECIAL PROBLEMS (INCLUDING ESTOPPEL BY DEED AND JUDGMENT AND TAX LIENS)

TOP FIVE THINGS TO KNOW FOR PROPERTY

1. Focus on easements and other rights to enter onto another's land.

_____

_____

_____

2. Don't stress about RAP.

_____

_____

_____

3. Diagram! Draw pictures!

_____

_____

_____

4. Property questions are long. Keep track of people and dates.

_____

_____

_____

5. A little work goes a long way in Property.

_____

_____

_____

CHAPTER 2: REAL PROPERTY - PRACTICE QUESTIONS

Tip #1: Focus on easements and other rights to enter onto another's land.

A brother and sister own parcels of adjacent property. Their father had owned the land in its entirety, and when the siblings graduated from college, he split his estate in two and gave each sibling a parcel. The brother's property was landlocked, so his sister granted him an easement over her property in order to access the sole public road. The easement was not recorded. Five years later, the brother, having never set foot on his parcel, sold it to his sister. The sister eventually resold this parcel to a stranger, after telling the stranger about the easement she had granted her brother. Shortly thereafter, she sold her own parcel to a colleague. The stranger seeks access over the colleague's parcel in order to reach the public road, but the colleague refuses.

Does the stranger have a right to an easement across the colleague's parcel?

A. No, because the brother's easement was not recorded.

B. No, because the brother's easement was extinguished upon the sister's acquisition of her brother's parcel.

C. Yes, because the stranger requires an easement by necessity.

D. Yes, because the colleague had notice of the brother's easement.

Answer choice C is correct. An easement by necessity arises when property is virtually useless without the benefit of the easement across neighboring property, such as when it is landlocked. In order for an easement by necessity to exist, there must be a necessity, the dominant and servient estates must have once been owned by the same person, and the necessity must have arisen at the time that the property was severed and the two estates were created. Here, these requirements are met: the stranger cannot access his land without the easement, both the stranger's and colleague's parcels were under the common ownership, and the necessity arose at the time that the sister sold the parcel to the stranger.

Answer choice A is incorrect because an easement by necessity need not be recorded. In fact, it need not even be written. An easement by necessity is binding on the servient estate as long as the necessity exists. Answer choice B is incorrect because, while merger of the dominant and servient estates did terminate the easement granted by the sister to her brother, the stranger enjoys an easement by necessity upon the separation of the parcels again. Answer choice D is incorrect. Although the stranger's notice of the brother's easement might have prevented the enforcement of that easement against the colleague if the easement had not been terminated through merger, the stranger's easement is based on necessity; it is not necessary that the colleague have notice of the easement.

Question notes:

_____

_____

_____

_____

_____

_____

Tip #2: Don't stress about RAP.

A philanthropist conveyed a residence that he owned to a local charity for use as a homeless shelter. The deed stated that the parcel was transferred "in fee simple so long as the residence is used as a homeless shelter." After using the residence as a homeless shelter for twenty-two years, the charity recently closed the shelter and put the building up for sale. The philanthropist sought to prevent the sale of the residence. The jurisdiction has retained the common-law Rule Against Perpetuities and imposes a 20-year period for adverse possession.

May the philanthropist stop the sale of the residence?

A.   Yes, because the doctrine of cy pres does not apply.

B.   Yes, because the philanthropist is the owner of the residence.

C.   No, because the charity owns the residence by adverse possession.

D.   No, because the philanthropist's reversionary interest violates the Rule Against Perpetuities.

Answer choice B is correct. The deed, through the use of the phrase "so long as," created a fee simple determinable interest in the residence held by the charity and the possibility of reverter in the philanthropist as grantor. Upon the termination of the condition that the residence be used as a homeless shelter, the ownership of the residence automatically reverted to the philanthropist. As the rightful owner of the residence, the philanthropist can prevent its sale by the charity. Answer choice A is incorrect because the doctrine of cy pres is irrelevant to the philanthropist's ability to stop the sale. The doctrine, which permits a court to redirect a trust established for one charitable purpose to another, does not apply to this situation because there is no charitable trust. This fact is irrelevant to whether the philanthropist can prevent the sale of the residence by the charity, however. Answer choice C is incorrect because the charity's possession of the residence did not become adverse until the charity ceased to use the residence as a homeless shelter. Since this cessation occurred recently, the length of the charity's subsequent possession of the residence has not met the 20-year requirement for adverse possession. Answer choice D is incorrect because the Rule Against Perpetuities does not apply to a reversionary interest, such as a possibility of reverter.

Question notes:

_____

_____

_____

_____

_____

_____

_____

_____

Tip #3: Diagram! Draw pictures!

A widow transferred land that she held in fee simple to her only heir, her nephew, for his life, to her nephew's wife for the wife's life if she survived him, and then to any of the nephew's children who reached the age of 21. The widow later died intestate. Shortly after the widow's death, her nephew and his wife had their first and only child, a daughter. Five years ago, immediately prior to dying, the nephew's wife transferred her interest in the land to her daughter. One year ago, when the daughter was 18 years old and possessed legal capacity to transfer real property, she sold any interest she then owned in the land to a speculator. Recently, the nephew died and left everything to his daughter by his will. The jurisdiction recognizes the majority rule regarding inter vivos transfers of contingent remainders and executory interests.

Which of the following would be the daughter's best argument that she is entitled to current possession of the land?

A. The daughter was transferee of her mother's interest in the land.

B. The daughter took the nephew's interest in the land upon his death.

C. The daughter's contingent remainder in the land was not transferable inter vivos.

D. The daughter was the only child of the nephew and his wife.

Question notes:

_____
_____
_____
_____
_____
_____
_____
_____

[Answer explanation on next page]

Tip #3 Answer Explanation

Answer choice B is correct. At the time of the widow's death, the nephew held a life estate, his wife a contingent life estate, any children of the nephew a contingent remainder, and the widow's estate a reversionary interest. Because the widow died intestate, the reversionary interest passed to the widow's only heir, the nephew. Upon the nephew's death, his life estate terminated and the reversionary interest was transformed in the current possessory interest in the land (i.e., a fee simple subject to an executory interest). This fee simple estate passed by the terms of the father's will to the daughter. However, at the time of the daughter's sale of any interests in the land to the speculator, the daughter had only a contingent remainder, which, upon her father's death, became a springing executory interest. This interest is not a current possessory interest. It will become one, if at all, only when the daughter reaches age 21. Accordingly, the speculator does not have a current possessory interest. Answer choice A is incorrect because the nephew's wife held only a contingent life estate in the land. This interest, which was transferred by the nephew's wife to her daughter inter vivos, terminated upon the death of the nephew's wife, since she did not survive her husband. Answer choice C is incorrect because, in most states, a contingent remainder may be transferred inter vivos. Answer choice D is incorrect because the daughter's status as a child of the nephew and his wife is relevant only with respect to her rights to the contingent remainder/springing executory interest, which is not a current possessory interest.

Question notes:

_____

_____

_____

_____

_____

_____

_____

_____

Tip #4: Property questions are long. Keep track of people and dates.

On April 15, a librarian purchased a vacation home from a seller for $200,000 cash. She placed the deed in a safety deposit box but did not immediately record it. On April 20, the seller sold the vacation home to an engineer, who had no knowledge of the prior sale, for $250,000 cash. On April 22, the librarian recorded her deed. The engineer, who had placed the deed in a drawer and forgotten about it, did not record the deed until June 1. The recording statute in the jurisdiction states: "No conveyance or mortgage of real property shall be good against subsequent purchasers for value and without notice unless the same be recorded according to law."

In a subsequent action, who will prevail?

A. The librarian, because she was first to record the deed.

B. The librarian, because the engineer had constructive notice of her deed when he recorded his deed on June 1.

C. The engineer, because the librarian did not record her deed until after the engineer purchased the vacation home.

D. The engineer, because the paid value of his purchase was greater than that for the librarian.

Answer choice C is correct. All states have enacted recording acts, which establish priorities among conflicting claims to land and promote certainty of title. These recording acts may be notice, race, or race-notice statutes. The statute in this case is a notice statute. In a notice jurisdiction, a purchaser need only purchase without notice of the prior interest to prevail. If a subsequent purchaser purchases a property which a prior grantee failed to record, and the subsequent purchaser had no notice of the prior interest, the subsequent purchaser prevails over the prior interest regardless of who recorded the deed first. Because the engineer did not have actual, inquiry, or constructive notice of the librarian's interest when he purchased the property, his claim will prevail over the librarian's, even though he recorded his deed later in time. Answer choice A is incorrect because in a notice jurisdiction, it is irrelevant who recorded the deed first, as long as the subsequent purchaser had no notice of the prior interest at the time of the sale (e.g., as long as the prior interest was not recorded before the sale).
Answer choice B is incorrect because it is not relevant whether the engineer had constructive notice of the librarian's deed at the time of recording. Because the engineer did not have notice when he purchased the property, he would prevail. Answer choice D is incorrect because it is not relevant that the engineer "paid value" in an amount greater than the librarian.

Question notes:

_____
_____
_____
_____
_____
_____
_____
_____

MBE WORKSHOP: TORTS
PROFESSOR LISA MCELROY
DREXEL UNIVERSITY SCHOOL OF LAW

CHAPTER 1:   TORTS

> **Editor's Note 1:**   The below outline is taken from the National Conference of Bar Examiners' website.

NOTE: The Torts questions should be answered according to principles of general applicability. Examinees are to assume that there is no applicable statute unless otherwise specified; however, survival actions and claims for wrongful death should be assumed to be available where applicable. Examinees should assume that joint and several liability, with pure comparative negligence, is the relevant rule unless otherwise indicated. Approximately half of the Torts questions on the MBE will be based on category II, and approximately half will be based on the remaining categories—I, III, and IV.

I. INTENTIONAL TORTS
A. Harms to the person, such as assault, battery, false imprisonment, and infliction of mental distress; and harms to property interests, such as trespass to land and chattels, and conversion
B. Defenses to claims for physical harms
   1. Consent
   2. Privileges and immunities: protection of self and others; protection of property interests; parental discipline; protection of public interests; necessity; incomplete privilege

II. NEGLIGENCE
A. The duty question, including failure to act, unforeseeable plaintiffs, and obligations to control the conduct of third parties
B. The standard of care
   1. The reasonably prudent person: including children, physically and mentally impaired individuals, professional people, and other special classes
   2. Rules of conduct derived from statutes and custom
C. Problems relating to proof of fault, including res ipsa loquitur
D. Problems relating to causation
   1. But for and substantial causes
   2. Harms traceable to multiple causes
   3. Questions of apportionment of responsibility among multiple tortfeasors, joint and several liability
E. Limitations on liability and special rules of liability
   1. Remote or unforeseeable causes, legal or proximate cause, and superseding causes
   2. Claims against owners and occupiers of land
   3. Claims for mental distress not arising from physical harm; other intangible injuries
   4. Claims for pure economic loss
F. Liability for acts of others
   1. Employees and other agents
   2. Independent contractors and nondelegable duties
G. Defenses
   1. Contributory fault, including common law contributory negligence and last clear chance, and the various forms of comparative

negligence
2. Assumption of risk

III. STRICT LIABILITY AND PRODUCTS
LIABILITY: common law strict liability, including claims arising from abnormally dangerous activities, and defenses to such claims; claims against manufacturers and other defendants arising out of the manufacture and distribution of products, and defenses to such claims

IV. OTHER TORTS
A. Claims based on nuisance, and defenses
B. Claims based on defamation and invasion of privacy, defenses, and constitutional limitations
C. Claims based on misrepresentations, and defenses
D. Claims based on intentional interference with business relations, and defenses

TOP FIVE THINGS TO KNOW FOR TORTS

1. Focus on negligence. About ½ of the questions will touch on this topic.

_____
_____
_____

2. Do the math!

_____
_____
_____

3. A correct answer to a negligence question will almost always include the word "reasonable" or "foreseeable" – often both!

_____
_____
_____

4. Know the elements cold! Most questions revolve around the elements of the cause of action.

_____
_____
_____

5. Use the answer choices to help you figure out which torts are in play.

_____
_____
_____

CHAPTER 2: TORTS - PRACTICE QUESTIONS

Tip #1: Focus on negligence. About one half of the questions will touch on this topic.

The plaintiff and his friend were walking on a city sidewalk. The friend jokingly pushed the plaintiff after the plaintiff started making fun of the friend's taste in music. This caused the plaintiff to trip over his own feet and stumble into the bike lane of the street. The defendant driver, who was involved in a heated argument on his cell phone, had veered into the bike lane and did not see the plaintiff. He hit the plaintiff, causing the plaintiff numerous injuries. The plaintiff has sued the driver. The evidence at trial shows that the plaintiff's injuries were caused by the negligence of both the friend and the defendant. The state has adopted a system of pure several liability.

Is the plaintiff likely to prevail in a negligence claim against the defendant?

A. No, because the plaintiff's injuries were caused by multiple tortfeasors.

B. No, because the state does not recognize joint and several liability.

C. Yes, because the defendant and the friend were independent tortfeasors.

D. Yes, because the defendant's conduct was the actual cause of the plaintiff's injury.

Answer choice D is correct. In order to prove negligence, the plaintiff must establish that the defendant's actions were both the actual cause and the proximate cause of the plaintiff's injury. Generally, the plaintiff must show that his injury would not have occurred but for the defendant's conduct. When multiple defendants have contributed to the plaintiff's injury, the plaintiff may establish causation by showing that the defendant's conduct was a substantial factor in causing the plaintiff's injury. In this case, the defendant and the friend were both the actual causes of the plaintiff's injury, and the plaintiff could recover against either or both of them. Answer choice A is incorrect because a plaintiff may recover against a single tortfeasor when his injuries were caused by multiple tortfeasors so long as the plaintiff can show that the defendant's conduct was the "but for" cause or a substantial factor in causing the injuries. Answer choice B is incorrect because, under joint and several liability, when two or more persons are responsible for a plaintiff's harm, the plaintiff may sue any one of them and obtain a full judgment. Under a system of pure several liability, a tortfeasor is generally only liable for his comparative share of the plaintiff's damages. In this case, the plaintiff could likely collect only a share of the full damages from the defendant. This does not, however, prevent the plaintiff from successfully pursuing a negligence action against the defendant alone. Answer choice C is incorrect because when more than one individual is the cause of a plaintiff's harm, the plaintiff may choose to sue only one defendant regardless of whether the defendants acted in concert with one another or were independent tortfeasors.

> **Editor's Note 1:** The Professor misspoke when discussing pure several liability. Under pure several liability, a tortfeasor is generally only liable for his comparative share of the plaintiff's damages. Note that this distinction does not impact the correct answer choice.

Question notes:

_____

_____

_____

_____

_____

Tip #2: Do the math!

A skier took his skis to a ski shop to have the bindings tuned ahead of an upcoming ski vacation. Unbeknownst to the skier, the shop tuned only his right ski. On the first day of his vacation, the skier fell and broke his left leg after being hit by a snowboarder. It was later determined that the left binding was rusted, and that his injuries would have been less severe if the binding had been intact. The skier has sued the ski shop and the snowboarder. The jury has awarded damages of $100,000, and determined that the skier was 20% at fault, the ski shop was 20% at fault, and the snowboarder was 60% at fault.
The jurisdiction recognizes pure comparative negligence and joint and several liability.

How much can the skier collect from the ski shop?

A. $20,000.00
B. $80,000.00
C. $100,000.00
D.   The skier cannot collect anything from the ski shop.

Question notes:

_____

_____

_____

_____

_____

_____

_____

_____

_____

_____

[Answer explanation on next page]

CHAPTER 3: TORTS - PRACTICE QUESTIONS

Tip #2 Answer Explanation

Answer choice B is correct. Under the doctrine of joint and several liability, each of two or more defendants who is found liable for a single and indivisible harm to the plaintiff is subject to liability to the plaintiff for the entire harm. Thus, a plaintiff can collect the full damages to which he is entitled from any of the defendants. Under a system of pure comparative negligence, a plaintiff's damages are reduced by the proportion that his fault bears to the total harm. In this case, the plaintiff would be entitled to $80,000 in damages because his total damages would be reduced by 20%, or the proportion of his fault. He could collect this entire amount from the ski shop. Answer choice A is incorrect because it ignores the effect of joint and several liability. The skier is entitled to $80,000 in total damages, and he could collect this entire amount from the ski shop. Answer choice C is incorrect because the skier cannot collect the $20,000 in damages attributable to his own negligence. Answer choice D is incorrect because it ignores the effect of the comparative negligence doctrine. At common law, the theory of contributory negligence barred a plaintiff from recovery when his own negligence contributed to his injury. Under the theory of comparative negligence, however, a plaintiff's own negligence is not a complete bar to recovery.

Question notes:

_____

_____

_____

_____

_____

_____

Tip #3: A correct answer to a negligence question will almost always include the word "reasonable" or "foreseeable" – often both!

A woman told her friend that she believed she had a peanut allergy, although it had not been diagnosed. In an attempt to prove her long-held theory that peanut allergies do not really exist, the friend decided to surreptitiously give the woman some peanuts. The friend invited the woman over for lunch, assuring her that the lunch was peanut-free. In fact, the friend had substituted peanuts for pine nuts in the pesto on their sandwiches. After they finished eating, the friend began to feel guilty and admitted to her plan. When the woman saw hives forming on her arm, she decided to go to the doctor. The doctor told the woman that the hives were likely due to anxiety, but that he would provide an ointment. Due to a mix- up, the doctor ordered the nurse to provide the woman with an antibiotic to which the woman was allergic. The woman suffered a severe reaction to the antibiotic. The woman has sued her friend and her doctor for negligence. The friend has filed a motion to dismiss the claims against her.

Is the friend likely to succeed in having the claims against her dismissed?

A.   No, because the doctor's error and the resulting harm were foreseeable.

B.   No, because the friend's actions were the direct cause of the woman's injuries.

C.   Yes, because the doctor's error was the direct cause of the woman's injuries.

D.   Yes, because the doctor's error was a superseding cause of the woman's injuries.

Answer choice A is correct. To succeed on a negligence claim, the plaintiff must prove proximate causation. Proximate cause exists when the defendant's actions are a direct cause of the plaintiff's injuries. Or, if an intervening force occurs between the defendant's act and the plaintiff's injury, the defendant still may be liable if the intervening force was foreseeable. Medical malpractice is a foreseeable intervening force. In this case, the doctor's error was foreseeable after the friend intentionally gave the woman a food to which she may have been allergic. Accordingly, the friend was the proximate cause of the woman's injuries. Answer choice B is incorrect because the doctor's negligence in providing the woman with the wrong medication was the direct cause of the woman's injuries. Answer choice C is incorrect because, although the doctor's error was the direct cause of the woman's injuries, the doctor's actions were a foreseeable intervening force. Accordingly, the friend is unlikely to succeed in having the claims dismissed. Answer choice D is incorrect because the doctor's actions were not a superseding cause of the woman's injuries. When an intervening cause is unforeseeable, it may become a superseding cause and cut off the defendant's liability. Medical malpractice is foreseeable, however. Thus, the doctor's actions were not a superseding cause.

Question notes:

_____

_____

_____

_____

_____

_____

Tip #4: Know the elements cold! Most questions revolve around the elements of the cause of action.

Two high school students, dressed as robbers for Halloween, were playing tag and chasing each other in the street outside of their dormitory. One of the students hid behind a shrub and waited to surprise the other. Before the other student appeared, an elderly woman passed the shrub. The student, hearing footsteps and thinking it was the other student, jumped in front of her and shouted, "Got you!" Before the student could touch her, the elderly woman shrieked and jumped backward. She dropped a bag of groceries but was otherwise unharmed.

The woman sued the student for assault. Will the woman prevail in her suit against the student?

A.   Yes, because the woman was placed in reasonable apprehension of imminent battery.

B.   Yes, because the student's words, coupled with the act of jumping from the shrub, constituted an overt act.

C.   No, because the woman sustained no damages for which she could collect.

D.   No, because the student did not have the necessary intent to commit a tort.

Question notes:

_____
_____
_____
_____
_____
_____
_____
_____
_____
_____
_____

[Answer explanation on next page]

CHAPTER 4: TORTS - PRACTICE QUESTIONS

Tip # 4 Answer Explanation

Answer choice D is correct. An assault occurs when the defendant's intentional overt act causes the plaintiff to experience reasonable apprehension of an imminent battery. The act must be volitional and performed with intent to place someone in apprehension of imminent harm or offensive contact. The doctrine of transferred intent applies to the tort of assault. Here, although the student startled the woman, who was reasonably frightened by the student's actions, the student lacked tortious intent.

Had the student intended to assault or commit battery against another person, the doctrine of transferred intent would have applied, but the facts do not suggest that the student had any intent to commit any sort of tort, and was merely playing a game of tag with a friend. Answer choice A is incorrect because, although the woman was placed in reasonable apprehension, this element alone does not suffice to prove an assault. Answer choice B is incorrect because, while an overt act is one of the elements of the tort of assault, it requires an intent to place someone in imminent apprehension of a battery, which is not present here. Answer choice C is incorrect because no proof of harm is required; the plaintiff may recover nominal damages even though no actual damage occurred.

Question notes:

_____
_____
_____
_____
_____
_____
_____

Tip #5: Use the answer choices to help you figure out which torts are in play.

Two high school students, dressed as robbers for Halloween, were playing tag and chasing each other in the street outside of their dormitory. They decided it would be fun to scare passersby. They hid behind a shrub and peeked out, waiting for someone to pass. When an elderly woman passed the shrub, one student jumped in front of her and shouted, "Hands up!" Before the student could touch her, the elderly woman shrieked and jumped backward. She dropped a bag of groceries but was otherwise unharmed.

Under what tort theory is the woman most likely to prevail?

A. Negligent infliction of emotional distress.
B. Intentional infliction of emotional distress.
C. Battery.
D. Assault.

Answer choice D is correct. An assault occurs when the defendant's intentional overt act causes the plaintiff to experience reasonable apprehension of an imminent battery. The act must be volitional and performed with intent to place someone in apprehension of imminent harm or offensive contact. Here, although the student (dressed like a robber and shouting something that sounded like a robbery) startled the woman, who was reasonably frightened by the student's actions. Answer choice A is incorrect because the facts say that the woman was unharmed. Negligent infliction of emotional distress requires physical harm. Answer choice B is incorrect because, while scaring someone is offensive, it probably does not rise to the level of extreme and outrageous, particularly on Halloween. Answer choice C is incorrect because the facts indicate that the student did not touch the woman. Battery requires an offensive touching.

Question notes:

_____
_____
_____
_____
_____
_____
_____
_____
_____
_____

CIVIL PROCEDURE
PROFESSOR JOHN C. JEFFRIES, JR.
UNIVERSITY OF VIRGINIA SCHOOL OF LAW

INTRODUCTION

A. In General

- Added to MBE for February 2015
- Similar to state civil procedure in most states

  o State rules often patterned on Federal Rules of Civil Procedure

B. MBE

- Includes 25 scored questions on Federal Civil Procedure
- Important topics:

  o Pleadings
  o Discovery
  o Motions

    ▪ Motion to Dismiss
    ▪ Motion for Summary Judgment
    ▪ Motion for Judgment as a Matter of Law

- MOST important topic:

  o **Jurisdiction**

CHAPTER 1:   INTRODUCTION TO JURISDICTION AND SUBJECT MATTER JURISDICTION

A. Introduction to Jurisdiction

1. **Subject Matter Jurisdiction**

   Power of the court to decide _____

2. **Personal Jurisdiction**

   Power of the court to decide the rights and liabilities of _____

3. **Venue**

   Determining the appropriateness of deciding the case in a particular court which has subject matter jurisdiction and personal jurisdiction over the defendant (i.e., which district(s))

B. Subject Matter Jurisdiction (SMJ)

1. In General

- Issue: Does this court have the power to decide this kind of case?
- Federal courts are courts of _____ subject matter jurisdiction.

    - *Compare with state courts* - courts of _____ subject matter jurisdiction.

        > **Exam Tip 1:** For the MBE, unless you are provided with a state statute that explicitly limits state court jurisdiction (e.g., only small claims or probate), assume state courts have subject matter jurisdiction over any kind of case.

2. Pleading SMJ

Basis for SMJ must be _____ in every case.

- If challenged, must prove there is a basis for SMJ.

3. Waiver

- _____ of SMJ
- Lack of SMJ cannot be waived by failing to object or by affirmative consent.

4. Objection to SMJ

- Lack of SMJ can be raised by _____ at _____, including by the plaintiff.
- Can be brought for the first time on appeal

C. Federal Question Jurisdiction ("Arising Under")

1. Basis

Exists for a claim that arises under _____

2. Well-Pleaded Complaint

- **Plaintiff's claim** must be based on federal law - look to the face of the complaint.

    - Presence of a federal defense does not matter.

- *Louisville & Nashville R.R. v. Mottley*

    - Accident on railroad, Mottleys received lifetime passes on the railroad in settlement of their claim.
    - Congress subsequently passed a statute which prohibited lifetime passes, according to the railroad; railroad stopped honoring the passes.
    - Mottleys brought suit, claiming that the federal statute does not bar lifetime passes, but if it did, then it is unconstitutional.

- Issue: Is there federal question jurisdiction?
- Answer: _____ - Mottleys' claim was for specific performance of a contract.
  - Claim arises under state law (contracts)
  - Federal law is only raised by the defendant's argument that it is barred by the federal statute from continuing to honor its contract.

D. Diversity Jurisdiction

1. Basis

- Cases between citizens of _____, or citizens of a state and a foreign country, if the amount in controversy **EXCEEDS** $_____, exclusive of interest and costs.
- *Exceptions*: _____ and _____ actions cannot be brought in federal court under diversity jurisdiction.

2. Complete Diversity

a. General rule

- The diversity statute requires ***complete diversity***.
- Every citizenship represented on the plaintiff's side of the case must be different than every citizenship on the defendant's side.
- Does NOT mean every plaintiff must be diverse from every other plaintiff or that the defendant must be diverse from every other defendant.
  - Diversity must only be complete as ***between plaintiffs and defendants***.

  Example 1: *Pennsylvania Plaintiff 1 and Pennsylvania Plaintiff 2 sue a New York Defendant. Complete diversity exists.*

  Example 2: *Pennsylvania Plaintiff and New York Plaintiff sue a New York Defendant. There is _____ diversity.*

b. Minimal diversity (exception to complete diversity requirement)

- Provided by a few statutes
- Exists when any plaintiff is diverse from any defendant
- Minimal diversity is permitted in the following circumstances: federal interpleader act, class actions with claims more than $_____, and interstate mass torts (e.g., airline crash).

  Editor's Note 1: With regard to a federal statutory interpleader action, diversity exists if any two adverse claimants are diverse from each other.

  c. **Time for determination of diversity**

    ▪ Must exist when the complaint is _____

    ▪ Does NOT matter that diversity did not exist when the cause of action _____

    ▪ Does NOT matter that diversity no longer existed when the case came to trial

 3. **Citizenship of the Parties**

  a. **Individuals**

    ▪ Citizen of the state or country of _____

    ▪ Domicile is permanent residence.

      • Residence + an intention to remain indefinitely

      • Can only have _____ domicile at a time

  b. **Aliens**

  Diversity jurisdiction exists for controversies between a citizen of a state and a citizen of a foreign country.

  c. **Representative parties**

    ▪ Generally, the citizenship of the _____ controls.

      Example 3: *In a suit by Trustee on behalf of a trust, the Trustee's citizenship will control.*

    ▪ *Exception*: For the legal representative of a decedent's estate (e.g., executor or personal representative), the citizenship of the _____ controls.

    ▪ *Exception*: For the legal representative of an infant or an incompetent person (e.g., guardian), the citizenship of the _____ or the incompetent person controls.

  d. **Class actions**

    ▪ Citizenship of the _____ counts

    ▪ Class members not named may join without regard to citizenship.

  e. **Corporations**

    ▪ Citizen of (1) the state, states, or countries in which it is _____ *and* (2) the state or country of its _____ (i.e., the "nerve center," where its executive offices are located).

      Exam Tip 2: When dealing with a corporation, be sure to consider every state where the corporation has citizenship.

    f. **Partnerships and unincorporated associations**

    ▪ Citizen of *every* state of which its _____ are citizens

    ▪ Applies to unions, trade associations, partnerships, and limited partnerships

4. **Devices to Create or Destroy Diversity**

    ○ Actions that create or defeat diversity are permitted so long as they are not "shams" or fraudulent.

    ○ *Moving* – permitted, even if it was done with the purpose of affecting diversity, so long as the change in domicile is genuine, not a sham.

    ○ *Assignment of a claim* - permitted so long as the assignment is complete and real and not collusive.

    ▪ *Partial assignment of a claim for debt collection* - does NOT affect citizenship if the assignor retains an interest in the claim.

    • Assignor's citizenship will count for purposes of diversity.

5. **Amount in Controversy (AIC)**

    a. **Rule**

    ▪ Must EXCEED $_____, exclusive of interest and costs

    ▪ ONLY relevant in a diversity case

    ▪ General rule: Any *good faith allegation* will suffice.

    • Case will only be dismissed for failure to meet the AIC when it appears to a _____ that recovery in excess of $75,000 cannot be had.

    b. **Aggregation**

    ▪ Adding up smaller claims to exceed $75,000

    ▪ *One plaintiff vs. one defendant:* plaintiff can aggregate all his claims against the defendant to meet the AIC requirement.

    ▪ *One plaintiff vs. multiple defendants:*

    • If the defendants are **jointly liable**, plaintiff can aggregate all of his claims against the defendants (treated as one defendant).

    • Otherwise, plaintiff _____ add up all his claims against multiple defendants; claim against EACH defendant must meet AIC requirement.

    ▪ *Multiple plaintiffs:*

    • *General rule* - Each plaintiff's claims must meet the AIC requirement.

    • **Supplemental jurisdiction:**

- o If one plaintiff has a claim exceeding $75,000, the claims of additional plaintiffs can be heard regardless of the amount if all of the claims: (1) arise out of the same _____ and (2) complete diversity is maintained.

- o If a plaintiff has a claim based solely on diversity jurisdiction against one defendant exceeding $75,000, the plaintiff can join claims against other defendants only if (i) complete diversity is maintained and (ii) the claims against each defendant exceed $75,000.

> **Editor's Note 2:** The lecturer misstated the rule regarding joinder of claims against other defendants in a diversity case. The correct rule, as included above, is the following: when a plaintiff has a claim based solely on diversity jurisdiction, the plaintiff can join claims against other defendants only if (i) complete diversity between the plaintiff and the defendants is maintained, and (ii) the claims against *each defendant* exceed the jurisdictional amount in controversy of $75,000.

c. **Counterclaims**

> **Exam Tip 3:** Most frequently asked question regarding procedure on the bar exam.

- ▪ Does a counterclaim in a diversity action have to meet the jurisdictional minimum of $75,000+?

- ▪ _____ - if the counterclaim is *compulsory*.
- ▪ _____ - if the counterclaim is *permissive*.

CHAPTER 2: SUBJECT MATTER JURISDICTION: SUPPLEMENTAL AND REMOVAL JURISDICTION

A. **Supplemental Jurisdiction**

1. **In General**

- o Allows a federal court with subject matter jurisdiction over a case to hear additional claims over which the court would not independently have jurisdiction if ALL the claims constitute the same _____.

- o Claims constitute the "same case or controversy" if they arise out of a *common nucleus of operative fact*.

   - ▪ Means all the claims arise out of the same

   _____

- o 28 USC § 1367

2. **Federal Question**

- o Issue: whether a federal court can hear related state-law claims.

Example 4:   *Federal and state law claims against Defendant A. If the two claims share a common nucleus of operative fact, the federal court **may** hear the pendent state law claim under supplemental jurisdiction.*

Example 5:   *Federal claim against Defendant A and a related state-law claim, arising out of the same transaction or occurrence, against Defendant B. The federal court **may** hear both the federal claim against A and the pendent state-law claim against B. Called "pendent party" jurisdiction.*

3. **Diversity Jurisdiction**

   a. **Counterclaims**

   - A federal court sitting in diversity has supplemental jurisdiction over a _____.

      - Compulsory counterclaim - one that **arises out of the same transaction or occurrence** as the main claim.
      - A compulsory counterclaim can be heard in a diversity action regardless of the amount.

   - A _____ (one that does NOT arise out of the same transaction or occurrence) can only be heard if it independently satisfies diversity jurisdiction (i.e., complete diversity and $75,000+).

   b. **Cross-Claims**

   - Supplemental jurisdiction applies.
   - Claim by a plaintiff against another plaintiff, or by a defendant against a co-defendant
   - Cross-claim and main claim must share a common nucleus of operative fact.
   - Does NOT matter that the co-plaintiffs or co-defendants are not _____ or that the cross-claim is worth less than $75,000+.

   c. **Multiple Plaintiffs/Permissive Joinder/Class Action**

   - If the claim of one diverse plaintiff against Defendant A satisfies the jurisdictional amount, other diverse plaintiffs who have related claims against Defendant A sharing a common nucleus of operative fact (same transaction or occurrence) can also be heard even if their claims do NOT satisfy the jurisdictional minimum.

   Example 6:   *Class action is brought with 5 representative parties who are all diverse from the defendant. One of the representative parties has a claim for more than $75,000. The claims of other class members can be heard even if they do not meet the jurisdictional amount ($75,000+).*

   Note 1: Remember that there is also a statute that allows federal subject matter jurisdiction over class actions wherein the total amount in controversy exceeds $5 million, so long as there is minimal diversity between one plaintiff and one defendant.

  d. Supplemental Jurisdiction NOT Permitted

- Means these additional claims/parties can be brought into a diversity action only if the additional claims maintain complete diversity and exceed $75,000
- Includes the following claims:
    - Claims by plaintiffs against _____ under Rule 14
    - Claims by plaintiffs against _____ joined as necessary parties under Rules 19 and 20
    - Claims by _____ under Rule 24
    - Claims by plaintiffs joined **involuntarily** under Rule 19

4. Summary

- Supplemental jurisdiction works for federal question cases across the board.
- Works in **diversity** cases for: (1) _____ counterclaims; (2) _____ ; and (3) for voluntary joinder of plaintiffs (whether in or out of a class action) when there is complete diversity with all named plaintiffs, when one of them has a claim exceeding $75,000, and all claims arise out of the same transaction or occurrence.
- Supplemental jurisdiction establishes the court's power to hear additional claims; whether the court exercises that power is up to its _____, based on the practicalities of the case.

B. Removal Jurisdiction

1. Terminology

- Removal moves case from _____ to _____ court.
- Transfer moves case from one _____ court to another _____ court.
- No procedure for removal of a case from federal court to state court.
    - Federal court can abstain from hearing the case (very narrow circumstances).

2. General Rule

- Removal is proper only if the case **could have been brought originally** in _____.
- Only _____ may remove.
    - ALL defendants must consent to removal.

- o Case had to have come within original jurisdiction of the federal court
- o Hypothetical to determine whether removal is proper:
  - If the plaintiff had sued in federal court in the first place, would the federal court have had subject matter jurisdiction?

3. **Federal Question**

- o Well-pleaded complaint rule
- o FQ jurisdiction exists only when the federal question appears on the face of the well-pleaded complaint.
- o Removal - if the well-pleaded complaint discloses that the plaintiff's claim is based on federal law, then the defendant may remove to federal court.
  - If the plaintiff's claim is based on state law, defendant _____ remove even though the defendant has a *federal defense*.

4. **Diversity**

- o Removal based on diversity jurisdiction is proper only if:
  - There is complete diversity;
  - The amount in controversy exceeds $75,000; and
  - The action is brought in a state of which no _____ is a citizen.
- o ***One-year limit on removal*** - must remove within one-year of the commencement of the action in state court, unless the plaintiff has acted in _____ to try to make the case non-removeable.

5. **Removal Procedures**

- o A *notice of removal* is filed in the _____ court, copy to the _____ court.
- o When the removal notice is filed, the case is removed automatically; the state court's jurisdiction ceases.

6. **Improper Removal**

- o Plaintiff can file a petition for _____.
  - Federal court holds hearing to determine whether removal is proper.
    - If proper, remand is denied - case stays in federal court.
    - If improper, remand is granted - case goes back to state court.

CHAPTER 3:   PERSONAL JURISDICTION; IN PERSONAM JURISDICTION

A. Personal Jurisdiction (PJ)

1. **In General**

   o Concerns the power of the court to adjudicate the rights and liabilities of this defendant

   o Questions of PJ always concern the _____.

   o Personal jurisdiction is generally the same in federal and state court.

      ▪ Federal courts generally rely on the long-arm statutes of the states

      _____.

      ▪ Long-arm statute - chief means of asserting PJ over out-of-state defendants.

   o **Overview:** *Every* personal jurisdiction issue involves two questions (**both** must be addressed):

      ▪ Has the particular basis for exercising personal jurisdiction over an out-of-state defendant been _____ by statute or by rule of court?

      ▪ Is the particular basis for exercising personal jurisdiction permitted by the _____?

2. **Types of Personal Jurisdiction**

   o _____: against the person

   o _____: against the thing

   o _____: "sort of" against the thing

3. **Constitutional Aspect**

   o Due process requires _____ between the defendant and the forum state, such that it is consistent with traditional notions of *fair play and substantial justice* to sue the defendant here.

      ▪ Basically, is it _____ to sue the defendant here?

   o In assessing minimum contacts, courts look for a _____ by the *defendant* of the protections of the forum's law.

      ▪ Contacts between the forum and the _____ do NOT suffice.

4. **Waiver**

   o Unlike subject matter jurisdiction, lack of personal jurisdiction _____ be waived.

   o Voluntarily litigating on the merits waives any objection to lack of PJ (i.e., a general appearance).

- o A defendant waives any objection to personal jurisdiction by

  _____ on

  the merits *before* raising that objection.

  - ▪ Includes almost anything other than challenging jurisdiction

- o **Federal Rules:** A defect in personal jurisdiction must be raised at the

  _____ or it is waived.

  - ▪ "First opportunity" - a pre-answer motion to _____

    if the defendant chooses to file one, OR if the defendant chooses not to file a pre-

    answer motion, must be raised in the _____.

5. **Federal Exceptions**

- o Generally, federal courts follow the personal jurisdiction law (i.e., long-arm statutes) of the states in which they sit.

- o Federal courts can assert broader personal jurisdiction in the following cases:

  - ▪ Federal Interpleader Act ("statutory interpleader") - authorizes *nationwide service of process*

  - ▪ The *Bulge Provision* of the Federal Rules - allows service anywhere within

    _____ miles of the federal courthouse, even if in another state, in *two situations*:

    - • For *impleading third-party defendants* under Rule 14; and

    - • For joining _____

      under Rule 19.

  - ▪ Unusual provision – narrow authorization of nationwide service of process when the defendant is not subject to personal jurisdiction in ANY state court

    - • Suit may be brought in federal court so long as there are minimum contacts w/ the United States

B. **In Personam Jurisdiction**

1. **In General**

- o Federal courts follow the personal jurisdiction law of the states in which they sit.
- o There is some variation state to state, but not much.
- o *General in personam jurisdiction* - the defendant can be sued on any claim whatsoever, even if it is unrelated to the defendant's contacts with the forum state.
- o *Specific in personam jurisdiction* - the _____ statute; only applies when the dispute *arises out of that contact* with the forum.

2. Bases for General In Personam Jurisdiction

a. _____

- Service of process on the defendant while she is physically present in the state
- *Exceptions*: the defendant was in the state only to answer a summons or was brought there by force or fraud.

b. _____

c. _____

- Express or implied
- Can be given by contract or by appointing an in-state agent for receiving service of process

d. **For a corporation**

- General in personam jurisdiction applies only to corporations that are "at home" in the state.
- "At home":
  - The state of _____
  - The _____
- Simply "doing business" (e.g., having a branch office, or an interactive website) in the state is not enough when the claim is wholly unrelated to that in-state activity.

CHAPTER 4:   SPECIFIC IN PERSONAM JURISDICTION, IN REM, AND SERVICE OF PROCESS

A. Specific In Personam Jurisdiction

1. In General

- Every state has a long-arm statute.
- Gives courts in personam jurisdiction over out-of-state defendants but ONLY for the particular transactions in the state - *jurisdiction is specific to the in-state activity*.

2. Common Bases for Specific In Personam Jurisdiction

- Any act or omission in the state causing injury to a person or property here or elsewhere
- Any act or omission _____ the state causing injury to a person or property here, provided that the defendant conducted activities here or introduced goods into the flow of commerce
- Any claim arising out of a contract to perform _____ in the state or to pay someone in the state to perform services elsewhere, or out of the actual performance

o Any claim arising out of a contract to _____ to or from the state, or arising out of the shipment of such goods

o Any claim regarding local property

o Any action against a director or officer of a domestic corporation

o Any contract of insurance where the plaintiff is a resident of the state where the claim arose

> **Exam Tip 4:** Almost everything is covered by a state's long-arm statute, so long as the *claim arises out of the transaction* involving that state.

B. In Rem and Quasi In Rem Jurisdiction

- **In rem:** suit against any kind of property, real or personal, so long as the property is located in _____ (i.e., the state has physical power over the property).

- **Quasi-in-rem jurisdiction:** Tries to use in-state property as a basis for forcing an out-of-state defendant to litigate an unrelated claim.

  o Seize the in-state property

  o Supreme Court - quasi in rem is subject to the same _____ test as in personam jurisdiction.

  o Much less important source of jurisdiction today

C. Notice and Service of Process

1. In General

  o Service of a _____ on the defendant while the defendant is in the jurisdiction.

  o Establishes _____ of the defendant in the jurisdiction and gives the defendant notice of the action

  o _____ is the type of service of process used to assert in personam jurisdiction.

  ▪ Should also be used in in rem and quasi-in-rem actions when the identity of an interested party is _____.

  o Federal Rules have their own rules for service and also authorize service in accordance with state law *where the federal court sits*.

  o Federal Rules for service of process on an individual:

  ▪ _____;

  ▪ Leaving the summons at the defendant's _____ or usual place of abode with a *person of suitable age and discretion*;

  ▪ Delivery of the summons to an _____; and

  ▪ For *persons in foreign countries*, service can be made by _____, return receipt requested.

> **Note 2:** Service by mail is generally **NOT** accepted for service of process UNLESS state law so provides.

2. **Special Rules for Service of Process**

   a. **Infant**

      Service on the infant AND on the _____ or guardian

   b. **Adjudicated incompetent**

      Service must be made on the incompetent AND her guardian

   c. **Partnership**

      Service on a _____, an attorney in fact, or an authorized agent

   d. **Corporation**

      Service on an _____, _____, managing agent, or an agent appointed for receiving service of process (corporations doing business in the state must have one)

   e. **Non-resident motorists**

      ▪ Claims arising out of in-state accidents
      ▪ Generally, service can be made on a state official who forwards a copy to the out-of-state defendant.

3. **Service of Process for In Rem and Quasi-in-rem Actions**

   o You must make a _____ to locate all claimants to the property (res) and serve them personally.
   o If the claimants cannot be located, then notice by publication is permitted.
   o CANNOT rely on notice by publication if you actually know or can readily find out the names and addresses of the other claimants – must serve personally.

D. **Summary**

   • There are several bases for general in personam jurisdiction.
   • State long-arm statutes allow very broad reach against out-of-state defendants so long as the claim arises out of the specific contact with the state.
   • In every case, there must be a rule or statute authorizing personal jurisdiction and the assertion of PJ must be based on minimum contacts between the defendant and the forum state such that it is fundamentally fair to sue the defendant in the state.
   • PJ of federal court is usually the same as that of the state in which it sits.

○ But, federal courts have nationwide in personam jurisdiction in statutory interpleader cases and expanded PJ under the "Bulge provision."

CHAPTER 5:   VENUE AND CHOICE OF LAW

A. Venue

1. **In General**

   ○ Matter of administrative convenience
   ○ Asks where among the courts in this judicial system is the appropriate place to hear the case
     ▪ Federal system – whether this district is a proper court to hear this action
   ○ Defendant's obligation to object if venue is improper.
     ▪ Failure to make a timely objection results in waiver.
   ○ Under federal law, a claim of improper venue must be made at the _____ or it is waived.
     ▪ Either a pre-answer motion to _____ if the defendant chooses to file one, or the _____, if no pre-answer motion is made
   ○ Venue rules for state and federal courts are *completely different*.
   ○ Federal venue concerns which **district** should hear a case.

2. **General Rule**

   ○ Federal venue is proper in a district:
     ▪ Where *any defendant resides*, if ALL defendants reside in the _____; or
     ▪ Where the _____– i.e., where a *"substantial part of the events or omissions"* on which the claim is based occurred or where a *"substantial part of the property"* that is the subject of the action is located.
   ○ If neither of the above (rare), *any* district where

   _____

   has venue.
   ○ For federal venue, the _____ residence does NOT count.

3. **Residence**

   ○ Where does the defendant reside?
     ▪ For *individuals* - residence means _____.
     ▪ For *business entities* - a business entity resides in every district in which

     _____ exists.

4. **Special Provisions**

   o For a case begun in state court and ***removed*** to federal court, venue is automatically proper in the federal district where the _____ court sits, even if that district would not have been proper originally.

5. **Transfer**

   o General rule - transfer is only to a district with proper venue.

      ▪ Exception: Transfer to a district without proper venue may occur when ALL parties agree.

   o A case brought in a district *with proper venue* may be transferred for convenience to another district with proper venue.

   o A case brought in a district *without proper venue* may be transferred to a district with proper venue or dismissed by the court.

   o ***Choice of law:***

      ▪ If suit was brought in a district *with proper venue* and the case is transferred to another district, the law of the _____ forum controls.

      ▪ If suit was brought in a district *without proper venue* and transferred to another district, the law of the _____ court controls.

B. **Choice of Law – The Erie Doctrine**

   1. **General Rule**

      o *Erie* says that in a diversity case, a federal court applies state _____ law.

   2. **State Substantive Law**

      State substantive law includes:

         ▪ The substantive rules on what must be proved to win a case and what defenses may be asserted (i.e., who wins and who loses);

         ▪ _____ on state causes of action;

         ▪ The _____ on state claims or defenses; and

         ▪ State rules on _____.

      Example 7: *A federal court in New York with diversity jurisdiction over a state tort claim will apply state law on (i) the existence and definition of that tort, (ii) the limitations period within which that cause of action may be brought, (iii) the burden of proof for any elements of the tort claim or any defenses, and (iv) in a situation in which there is a question as to which state's law governs, the federal court will apply New York law on choice of law.*

3. **Federal Procedures**

   o *Hanna v. Plumer* - anything covered by the _____ is procedure.

   o FRCP **always** apply in federal court, even if the substance of the claim is governed by state law (i.e., a diversity action).

   > **Editor's Note 3:** Professor Jeffries misspoke with regard to the court. The FRCP always apply in **federal** court.

4. **No Federal Statute or Rule on Point**

   o Looks procedural, but not covered by Federal Rules

   o When there is no federal rule or statute on point, then the court must determine whether the matter is substantive (follow state law) or procedural (apply federal law) by consulting the **twin aims of Erie**:

   - To avoid _____ (i.e., situations where there is a different result in state and federal courts); and

   - To avoid _____ administration of justice.

   o **Two common applications of Erie:**

   - If the choice of the procedure would be *outcome determinative* (change the result), the federal court should usually apply _____ law to prevent forum shopping.

   - The role of the jury in federal court is **entirely controlled** by _____ law.

5. **Federal Common Law**

   o Judge-made federal law

   o Overrides _____ state or local law/rule

   o Federal courts make federal common law only when they encounter **important** _____ that are not covered by a statute.

   o **Examples -** Federal common law applies to:

   - Boundary disputes between _____; and

   - _____ preclusion.

6. **Determining Applicable State Law**

   o Follow precedent from the _____.

   o If there is no precedent, _____ how the highest state court would rule.

   o Give respectful attention to the decisions of _____ (not binding).

CHAPTER 6: PLEADINGS AND DEFENSE MOTIONS

A. Commencement of Proceedings

- Federal civil action is begun by filing a _____ with the court clerk.

- For diversity actions, however, _____ law controls when an action is begun.

B. Types of Pleadings

1. _____

   o Used to state a claim for relief

   o The plaintiff or the defendant may file a claim against a co-party, called a

   _____.

   o A defendant files a _____
   to implead a third-party defendant.

2. _____

   o Filed by the opposing party in response to the complaint

   o It may contain responses to the allegations of the complaint,

   _____, and

   counterclaims.

3. _____

   o Used by the plaintiff to answer a counterclaim

C. Claim for Relief

- Recovery is not limited by the claim for relief as stated in the complaint, except for default judgments.

- Special rule for tort and punitive damages – if suing for punitive damages in excess of $10,000, must state "suing for tort or punitive damages in excess of $10,000."

D. Notice Pleading

- Historically, pleading was difficult because each kind of claim had its own special rules of pleading. The pleading had to match the proof.

  o Litigation was often resolved on the pleadings, rather than the merits.

- One of the chief aims of the Federal Rules - reform pleading.

  o Standardize pleading across all civil actions

  o Simplify pleading

  o Shift emphasis from pleading to the merits of the case

- _____ pleading under the Federal Rules

- o A pleading need not detail the facts of the plaintiff's case or spell out the legal theory
- o Only must give _____ of the pleader's claim
- o **Rule:** All that is required is a _____ statement of the claim.

E. Special Pleading

1. Definition

- o Alleged with particularity/specificity
- o No particular form of words

2. Types of Claims Requiring Special Pleading

a. _____ or mistake

b. _____

- ▪ Damages that do not ordinarily follow from the wrong complained of

  Example 8: *You are hit by an automobile and you claim medical expenses, personal injury, and pain and suffering—all these may be alleged generally. But let's say you allege in your complaint that you lost a major business deal because the accident prevented you from making an appointment and the opportunity slipped away. That is not the type of damages that ordinarily result from the accident, so those damages must be stated with particularity.*

F. Recent Decisions

- • Supreme Court "cut-back" on notice pleading.
- • Required that the allegations in the complaint state a _____ case for recovery.
- • Important and controversial cases:
  - o *Bell Atlantic v. Twombly* (2007)
    - ▪ Antitrust case - plaintiffs alleged that defendants had made an illegal agreement in restraint of trade.
    - ▪ Plaintiffs had NO evidence that the defendants had actually made such an agreement; only had evidence of the opportunity to make such an agreement.
    - ▪ Plaintiffs' claim would have been sufficient under notice pleading, thereby opening the door for discovery.
    - ▪ *Holding:* Complaint should be dismissed because the allegations were ***not sufficiently plausible***.
      - • Trial court should determine whether a complaint was sufficiently convincing to allow discovery to go forward; if not, dismiss the case.

- *Ashcroft v. Iqbal* (2009)
  - Constitutional tort action against Attorney General of the United States
  - Allegations were exceedingly thin, but would have been sufficient under notice pleading to obtain discovery
  - *Holding:* Complaint should have been dismissed because the allegations **did not make a plausible case** for overcoming the defendant's defense of qualified immunity.
- The two cases do NOT abandon notice pleading, but they do curtail it.
  - Empower district judges to dismiss, before discovery, complaints that they think are *obviously unfounded*.

> **Exam Tip 5:** These two cases could be raised by an essay question on the MEE (issue spotting).

CHAPTER 7: PLEADINGS AND DEFENSE MOTIONS (CONT'D.)

A. Defense Motions Against the Complaint

1. Motion to Dismiss

- May be used to raise:

  - Lack of _____ jurisdiction
  - Lack of _____ jurisdiction
    (including defects in service of process)
  - Improper _____
  - Failure to state a claim upon which relief can be granted
  - Failure to join a _____ party
  - Forum non conveniens

- Claim of no personal jurisdiction or a claim of improper venue must be made at the _____ (either a pre-answer motion to dismiss or the answer).

- Lack of subject matter jurisdiction _____ be waived.

  - **Can be raised by any party at any time**, including for the first time on appeal or by the court itself.

- Most claims are waived if NOT timely raised.

2. Motion for Judgment on the Pleadings

- Applies when the pleadings agree on all the facts and only the law is in dispute
- Unusual
- If there is any factual dispute, you have a case for

  _____.

3. **Motion for a More Definite Statement**

   o Asks that a pleading be made more specific

   o Judges usually disfavor this motion.

4. **Motion to Strike**

   o Can be used to delete from a pleading _____ or prejudicial matters that are **NOT relevant** to the case at hand

   o Also used by the plaintiff to strike a legally invalid defense

B. **Answer**

   1. **In General**

      o Used to respond to any form of a complaint.

      o The answer may contain _____, _____, and counterclaims.

   2. **Responses**

      o The failure to respond is an _____.

      o Unless cured by amendment, the admission is binding in the action.

      o Usual practice - include a "boilerplate" denial of everything not specifically admitted.

   3. **Affirmative Defenses**

      o Defenses which require _____.

      o Common affirmative defenses include assumption of _____, contributory negligence, _____, fraud, release, Statute of _____, and statute of _____.

      o Basically, any defense that has a name is an affirmative defense and must be raised in the answer.

   4. **Timing**

      Must ordinarily be served within _____ **days** of service of the pleading to which it responds.

C. **Reply**

   • Plaintiff's answer to a counterclaim

   • Rules governing answers apply to a reply.

D. **Amendments to Pleadings**

   1. **As of Right**

      o May be amended **once** at any time within _____ days of service of the pleading or within _____ days of the defendant's response, if there is one.

2. **By Leave of Court**

   o After the party has amended once, leave to amend must be sought from the court.

   o Amendment by leave of court should be _____.

     ▪ Judge must have a reason for denying leave to amend.

     ▪ E.g., too late and would be prejudicial to the other side, or the pleader has had a prior opportunity to amend but has not corrected the problem

3. **Statute of Limitations and the Doctrine of Relation Back**

   o In some circumstances, an amendment is deemed to _____ to the date the original pleading was filed.

   o If the *statute of limitations has NOT yet run (still open)*, this doctrine does not matter.

   o If the *statute of limitations has run*, then relation back determines whether the amended pleading is allowed (relates back) or time-barred (does not relate back).

   o ***An amendment relates back*** to the date of the original IF it concerns the same _____ as the original pleading.

   o The key here is _____ - cannot have the effect of "surprising" the other party.

4. **Amendment to Add or Change a Party**

   o An amendment to ***add or change a party against whom a claim is asserted*** must:

     ▪ Concern the *same conduct, transaction, or occurrence* as the original pleading; and

     ▪ The party to be added must have _____ or had _____ that the action should have been brought against that party but for the mistake.

     Example 9: Suit is filed against a corporate subsidiary, and the complaint is later amended to name the parent company. Meanwhile, the statute of limitations runs. Is the amended pleading timely as against the parent company? _____. The amended pleading concerned the same transaction as the original pleading and the suit filed against the subsidiary gave the parent notice of the issue.

     Example 10: Suppose a plaintiff slips and falls on a sidewalk in a shopping area and sues a store. After the statute of limitations has run, it becomes clear that the plaintiff has sued the wrong store. If the plaintiff tries to amend the complaint to sue the correct store (change the defendant), the amendment is time-barred because the original complaint did not give the correct store notice of the claim.

E. **Certification of Pleadings**

- **Verification**: Most pleadings are NOT verified (not sworn to), nor do they have to be.
- **Certification:** Pleadings and all other documents—including **motions** of all kinds and **discovery** requests—must be

  _____.

  o The signature certifies that:

  - There is an appropriate _____
    basis for filing;
  - Attorney certifies that to the best of her knowledge after

    _____ there

    is **NO improper purpose** (e.g., harass or needlessly increase costs);
  - The legal contentions are warranted by existing law or by a

    _____ argument for a

    change in the law; and
  - The factual allegations have _____
    or are likely to have such support after discovery.

    - Denials must have such support or must be reasonably based on lack of information or belief.

  o Violation of certification requirement: can be raised by court or opposing party.

  - Move to dismiss or seek sanctions (Rule 11)
  - The attorney can be made to bear the cost of baseless or improper filing.

    - Opposing party's attorney's fees

CHAPTER 8: MULTI-PARTY LITIGATION

A. **Two Minor Topics**

1. **Real Party in Interest**

   o The right plaintiff
   o An action should NOT be dismissed for having the wrong plaintiff until a reasonable time has been allowed for the *substitution* of the correct plaintiff (the real party in interest).

2. **Capacity to Sue**

   o *Minors* and *incompetents* may sue or be sued only through a _____.
   o Partnerships can sue or be sued as an entity if federal jurisdiction is based on federal question.

   - If jurisdiction is based on *diversity*, then each and every partner's citizenship counts; every partner must be listed as a party to the litigation (complete diversity applies).

B. Permissive Joinder of Parties

- Joinder by _____
- Any number of **plaintiffs** may join if they assert claims arising out of the

  _____ AND there is a

  _____ of law or fact.
- Any number of **defendants** may be joined in the same action if the claims against them arise out of the same transaction or occurrence and there is a common question of law or fact.
- **Diversity cases** - NO party can be joined, either as a plaintiff or a defendant, whose presence would defeat _____.

  o   If complete diversity is maintained, and if one plaintiff has a claim that exceeds $75,000, other plaintiffs with smaller claims can come in under

  _____.

C. Compulsory Joinder of Parties

- Joinder by _____
- **Necessary party** – a person whose participation in the lawsuit is necessary for a

  _____.

  o   Absent that party, complete relief cannot be accorded to the existing parties;
  o   Necessary party has an interest in the litigation which will be impeded if the litigation goes forward without that party; OR
  o   There is a substantial risk of double liability.
- MUST be joined if feasible

  o   Feasible if (1) it will not deprive the court of SMJ (will not destroy complete diversity) and (2) the court can assert _____ over the necessary party.
  o   "Bulge provision" - in addition to all other grounds for serving an out-of-state defendant, a necessary party may be served anywhere within _____ miles of the federal courthouse.
- If a necessary party CANNOT be joined, the court decides whether to continue without the necessary party (typically the case) or dismiss the suit (rare).

  o   When the suit is dismissed, party is described as being _____.

D. Intervention

- Outsider who *volunteers* to enter a lawsuit
- Chiefly concerned with _____
- **Intervention as of right** - may be had when the outsider claims an interest in the subject matter of the lawsuit that, as a practical matter, may be _____ by the disposition of the pending action.

- *Permissive intervention* - may be allowed whenever there is a **common** _____ between the intervenor's claim and the main claim.

  o Must ask the court's permission - matter of court's sound discretion

- Both types must be timely - "reasonable promptness"
- NO _____ _____ for either kind of intervention.

  o Diversity case – intervenor must satisfy _____ and have a claim that exceeds $75,000.

E. Interpleader

1. In General

  o Used to resolve the problem of competing claims to the *same property*

  o Designed to avoid inconsistent obligations or multiple claims

  o Property at issue - _____

  - May be real or personal, tangible or intangible

  o Person holding the property - _____

  o Persons claiming the property - _____

  - Stakeholder may also be a claimant.

  o Stakeholder can invoke interpleader either as a plaintiff OR a defendant.

  - Stakeholder-plaintiff sues all the claimants as defendants.

  - Stakeholder-defendant is one who has been sued by a claimant; all the other claimants are joined as plaintiffs.

2. Rule Interpleader

  o Authorized by Rule 22

  o Remedy available in a lawsuit otherwise within the court's _____

3. Statutory Interpleader

  o Federal Interpleader Act

  o Has special provisions:

  - Special jurisdictional amount: Need only exceed $_____

  - _____ service of process

  - Venue is proper in any district where _____.

  - SMJ based on _____ diversity.

    - Any two claimants are from different states

CHAPTER 9: **MULTI-CLAIM LITIGATION, IMPLEADER, AND CLASS ACTIONS**

A. **Joinder of Claims**

- As between the *same plaintiff and the same defendant*, ALL claims may be joined.

  o Need not be related

- Diversity case - plaintiff can add up ("aggregate") all claims against the same defendant to exceed the jurisdictional minimum ($75,000+).

- Federal question case – if diversity is lacking for additional state-law claims, additional state-law claims can be joined only if they are covered by supplemental jurisdiction (i.e., arise from the same transaction or occurrence as the original claim).

B. **Counterclaims**

1. **Definition**

   o Claim by the defendant against the plaintiff

   o Pleaded in the defendant's answer

2. **Compulsory Counterclaims**

   o Lost if not pleaded - must be raised now

   o A counterclaim is compulsory if it arises out of the

   _____

   as the claim to which it responds.

   o _____ jurisdiction covers compulsory counterclaims.

     ▪ If there is SMJ over the main claim, there is SMJ over a compulsory counterclaim.

     ▪ Diversity case – amount of compulsory counterclaim does not matter.

   o ***Statute of Limitations*** - filing of the original complaint _____

   the SOL for the original claim AND any compulsory counterclaim(s).

3. **Permissive Counterclaims**

   o May be pleaded now OR raised later

   o Counterclaims that do NOT arise out of the same transaction or occurrence – unrelated.

   o Requires an independent jurisdictional base - must be a

   _____ claim or there must be

   _____ of citizenship with $75,000+ in issue.

   o SOL - A permissive counterclaim must be timely as of the date it is filed or it's time-barred.

C. **Cross-claims**

- Claims asserted against a _____

  o Plaintiff v. co-plaintiff, defendant v. co-defendant

- MUST arise out of the _____
  as the original claim
- Never _____

D. Impleader (Third-Party Practice)

1. In General

Device by which the defendant brings into the suit someone who is or may be liable to the
_____ for all or part of the
_____ claim against him

2. Vocabulary

- o Impleaded party - _____
- o Original defendant - _____
  as against the third-party defendant

> ***Example 11:*** *Contribution among joint tortfeasors. Two tortfeasors injure a plaintiff. The plaintiff sues one but not the other. That defendant has a right to seek contribution from the other tortfeasor if he is found liable to the plaintiff. The sued defendant can implead the other tortfeasor, not because the other tortfeasor may be liable to the plaintiff, but, given the right of contribution, because the other tortfeasor is or may be liable to the defendant for all or part of the defendant's liability to the plaintiff.*

> ***Example 12:*** *Contract of indemnification. A general contractor makes contracts with subcontractors. Each contract requires the subcontractor to indemnify the general contractor for any defect in that subcontractor's work. If the owner sues the general contractor, the general contractor can implead the subcontractor, who may be liable to the general contractor (the defendant) for all or part of the owner's claim against him.*

3. Subject Matter Jurisdiction

- o Diversity cases - impleader comes within the court's
  _____ jurisdiction.

  - ▪ Citizenship of the third-party defendant does NOT matter
  - ▪ Amount of claim against third-party defendant does NOT matter
  - ▪ Extends to claims by the defendant against a third-party defendant

- o Supplemental jurisdiction does NOT extend to claims by the original
  _____ against the impleaded third-party
  defendant.

  - ▪ Plaintiff cannot make a claim against the third-party defendant UNLESS complete diversity is met (or there is federal question jurisdiction for the claim).

4. **Personal Jurisdiction**

   o   In addition to all other methods for asserting personal jurisdiction, impleader allows the assertion of PJ by service of process anywhere within 100 miles of the courthouse.

E. **Class Actions**

   1. **Prerequisites**

      Prerequisites for a class action are:

      o   **Numerousness** - too many parties to be joined conventionally

      o   _____ of law or fact

      o   _____ of claims by the class representatives

      o   _____
          by the representatives' lawyer(s)

   2. **Dismissal or Compromise (Settlement)**

      Requires _____

   3. **Diversity Jurisdiction**

      _____ representatives must be completely diverse from the defendants AND at least _____ has a claim worth $75,000+

   4. **Class Action Fairness Act of 2005**

      o   Allows very large class actions, involving _____ or more members with more than $_____ at stake

      o   _____ diversity

CHAPTER 10:   SCOPE OF DISCOVERY

A. **Mandatory Disclosures**

   1. **In General**

      o   Designed to streamline discovery
      o   Means disclosure without having to wait for a discovery request

   2. **Three Stages**

      a. **Initial disclosures**

         ▪   _____ of persons with potentially discoverable information
         ▪   Copies or descriptions of relevant _____ or things
         ▪   Computation of _____ claimed

- Applicable insurance agreement(s)

 b. **Disclosure of expert witnesses**

- Names of expert witnesses who will be called at trial
- Qualifications, publications, opinions, information on which they will base their opinions, other cases in which they have testified, and compensation

 c. **Pretrial Disclosures**

- _____ days before trial
- List of witnesses and exhibits
- Any objections must be made within 14 days after disclosure or they are waived unless excused by the court for good cause.

B. Scope of Discovery

1. In General

- General rule is _____.
- You can discover anything that might be admissible at trial *OR* that might lead to something that might be admissible at trial.
- **Key point** - the scope of discovery _____ limited to admissible evidence.

  - E.g., hearsay is NOT a valid objection to discovery - might lead to other evidence that is admissible.

2. Proportionality

- Discovery is limited to matters _____ to the needs of the case.
- Courts are to consider the importance of the issues, the amount at stake, the parties' resources and access to information, the value of discovery in the case, and, most importantly, whether the _____ of discovery outweighs its likely benefit.

3. Exceptions to Discovery

 a. **Evidentiary privilege**

  Anything covered by an evidentiary privilege, e.g., attorney-client privilege, is NOT discoverable.

 b. **Work product rule**

  Exam Tip 6: High priority topic for the bar exam.

- Basic idea: preparation for litigation by one party cannot be discovered by the other.
- The attorney work product rule protects:

- _____ and things (not information),

Example 13: A lawyer has made notes after interviewing witnesses to a car accident. The lawyer's notes are protected by the work product rule and cannot be discovered by the other side. The other side, however, can ask for the names and addresses of the witnesses. The other side may then interview those witnesses and discover the same information and introduce it at trial. Only the lawyer's notes recording the testimony of the witnesses is protected by work product.

- Prepared in _____,
    - Documents prepared before the cause of action arose are NOT protected by the work product rule.
- By or for _____ or her
    _____.

- Creates a _____ immunity from discovery:
    - Can be overcome if the party seeking discovery shows:
        - _____ for the document or thing; and
        - That the information cannot be obtained elsewhere.

Example 14: A lawyer interviews a witness and has notes of the witness's statements. The notes are work product and are protected against discovery. But, if the witness dies after the interview, suddenly becomes senile, or refuses to talk about the matter, the other side may be able to access the lawyer's notes because it needs the information and cannot get it elsewhere.

- Notwithstanding the above, you can always get a **copy of your own statements** whether you are a party or a mere witness, but you can NEVER discover the _____ of the lawyer.

4. **Experts**
    - Distinction between experts who will be called to testify at trial and those who will not
        - If expert is going to be called, the other side, in fairness, has to prepare for cross-examination.
        - Other side can always discover the _____ of the testifying expert.
            - Draft reports are generally NOT discoverable.
        - Communications between the lawyer and the expert are generally NOT discoverable.

- Can discover the amount of compensation, and the facts, data, and assumptions provided to the expert by the lawyer
  - o If expert is NOT going to be called as a witness, no discovery absent exceptional circumstances.

5. Protective Orders

- o Court orders to compel or restrain discovery
- o For _____ shown, court can basically do anything it wants, in its discretion, that justice may require.

CHAPTER 11: DISCOVERY DEVICES

A. Six Discovery Devices

1. Oral Deposition

- o Questions are asked and answered orally and under _____.
- o Limited to _____ depositions, unless the court allows more
- o Each is limited to one day of 7 hours, unless the court allows more.
- o Any kind of notice suffices for the deposition of a _____; but a deposition of a nonparty witness requires a _____.
- o A *subpoena duces tecum* requires the deponent to bring specified documents or things.
- o Deposing an organization – serve notice or subpoena on organization; organization then selects person who will be deposed
- o Can be taken at any time after the party has made mandatory disclosures
- o May be taken before any notary public who is not otherwise disqualified

2. Written Deposition

- o Questions asked in writing are delivered to an officer who asks orally the questions and the witness answers orally under oath.
- o Rarely used

3. Interrogatories

- o Questions asked in _____ to be answered under oath in writing
- o May only be used against a _____
- o Limited to _____ interrogatories, unless the court allows more
- o Responses required within _____ days

4. Discovery and Inspection of Documents and Land

- o Called a *request to produce and permit inspection*
- o Applies only to documents, things, and land under the control of a _____

- o The thing to be produced and inspected must be described with

  _____.

- o Response is due within 30 days.

5. Physical and Mental Examinations

- o Available only against a _____

- o Only permitted when the party's physical or mental condition is in

  _____

- o Only for _____ shown

6. Request for Admission

- o Used to streamline the lawsuit

- o Failure to respond within 30 days is an _____.

- o *Certification:* Responses to requests for admissions (and all other documents) must be signed by the attorney of record.

  - ▪ The signature certifies that there is a _____

    and ***good faith*** for denying the request.

- o Admissions have no _____ effect.

  - ▪ Only binding in the current lawsuit
  - ▪ Cannot be used against the party in any future proceeding

B. Use of Depositions

- • Discoverability does not equal _____.

- • Deposition of ***an adverse party*** is admissible as an _____

  against interest.

- • Deposition of a witness can be used to _____.

- • Deposition of a witness who does NOT testify can be used if the witness is dead or beyond the court's subpoena power or otherwise unavailable.

  - o Can also be used if the witness is more than _____ miles from the place of trial.

C. Enforcement Sanctions

- • The court can ***immediately impose sanctions*** in three instances of complete default:

  1) Failure to attend one's own _____;

  2) Failure to respond to _____; and

  3) Failure to respond to a request for documents or things.

- • In all other cases, the party seeking discovery must go to court and obtain an order compelling discovery; the court should first issue an **order to compel** based on the party's request before imposing sanctions.

D. **Electronically Stored Information**

- Should be preserved
- If lost through the _____ of a party, the court may order measures to cure the prejudice to the other party.
- If the material was destroyed with the _____ to prejudice the other party, the court may instruct the jury that it must presume the information was unfavorable, or even order the end of the litigation.

CHAPTER 12: PRE-TRIAL AND TRIAL PROCEDURE

A. **Pre-Trial Conference**

- Must be attended by the attorneys who will conduct the trial
- Must file a _____ detailing:
  - Claims and defenses, itemization of damages, requests for stipulations and admissions, list of all witnesses and exhibits, etc.
- Failure to comply usually means that the attorney pays the costs and the other side's attorney's fees.

B. **Termination Without Trial**

1. **Devices**

    - Judgment on the _____;
        - Rarely used
        - Appropriate only when the pleadings agree on all of the facts

    - _____ judgment;
    - _____ dismissal (dismissal *without* prejudice);
    - _____ dismissal (dismissal *with* prejudice); and
    - _____ judgment.

2. **Voluntary Dismissal**

    - "Without prejudice" - plaintiff whose claim has been dismissed can bring that claim again in a new lawsuit.
    - Plaintiff has a *right* to a voluntary dismissal *once* at any time prior to the defendant serving an _____ or a motion for _____.
        - The defendant's motion to dismiss (e.g., for lack of jurisdiction or improper venue) before filing an answer does NOT cut off the right to a voluntary dismissal.

- o After a defendant has filed an answer or motion for summary judgment, or if the plaintiff has already voluntarily dismissed once, plaintiff may seek a dismissal without prejudice on _____.

3. **Involuntary Dismissal**

- o Involuntary dismissal for *lack of jurisdiction*, *improper* _____, or *failure to join a necessary party* is _____ prejudice.
- o All other cases - involuntary dismissal is _____ prejudice.
  - ▪ Dismissal with prejudice is **an adjudication on the merits**.
  - ▪ Given full _____ effect (preclusive)
- o May be imposed for plaintiff's failure to prosecute or for failure to comply with the FRCP or any court order
- o Standard for appellate review: abuse of discretion

4. **Summary Judgment (SJ)**

- o Distinguish from a motion to dismiss for failure to state a claim upon which relief can be granted (12(b)(6)):
  - ▪ Only tests the _____ of the plaintiff's claim
- o Summary judgment can be used to test both the facts AND the law.
- o "Partial summary judgment" - SJ be granted only for certain parties, certain claims/defenses, or certain issues.
- o *Standard*: there is **no genuine dispute as to any material fact** and the moving party is entitled to judgment _____.
  - ▪ "No genuine dispute" - no reasonable juror could find the other way.
- o May be sought by either side
- o Must be supported or opposed by particular *materials in the record*, such as:
  - ▪ _____
  - ▪ _____
  - ▪ Affidavits
  - ▪ Stipulations
- o Materials in the record must generally be _____ statements.
  - ▪ Pleadings are generally NOT sworn statements.
  - ▪ Mere assertion or denial of a fact in a pleading does NOT create a genuine dispute.
- o Sworn statement - made on _____.

> *Example 15:* *Ethel sues Fred for injuries in an automobile accident and then moves for summary judgment. Ethel supports her motion with her affidavit, describing the accident. Fred cannot oppose summary judgment simply by relying on the denials in his answer nor by saying that he will call witnesses who will testify in a certain way. Fred must file a sworn statement based on personal knowledge that raises a genuine dispute as to a material fact. For example, Fred could file an affidavit asserting that he was in Philadelphia at the time of the accident.*

C. Trial by Jury

1. Right to Jury Trial

- o 7th Amendment right to trial by jury depends on the division between law (juries) and equity (no juries) as of 1791.
- o Equity issues, such as _____ and _____, do NOT require trial by jury.
- o _____ - classic remedy at law; triggers right to jury trial.
- o Legal and equity issues overlap in one lawsuit - try the _____ issues first.

> *Example 16:* *The plaintiff sues the defendant for an injunction (equity); the defendant counterclaims for money damages (law). The defendant wants a jury trial. The court must try the counterclaim first so that it will be heard by a jury.*

2. Demand for Trial by Jury

Must be made not later than _____ days after service of the answer

3. Jury Selection

- o Minimum of _____; maximum of _____
- o All must participate in verdict unless dismissed for good cause.
- o Each litigant gets _____ peremptory challenges (no need to explain or have a good reason).
    - ▪ Cannot be used for _____ or gender reasons

4. Bench Trial

Judge is required to make _____ and state conclusions of law.

5. Jury Instructions

- o Parties may request specific instructions.

o   Judge must inform the parties of his actions on those requests and the court's proposed instructions before final argument.

o   Court must provide an opportunity to object to proposed instructions - objections must be on the record.

o   Any objection to the instructions must be made BEFORE the

_____.

D. **Motion for Judgment as a Matter of Law (formerly Directed Verdict)**

-   Essentially a motion for summary judgment AFTER the trial has begun.

-   *Standard*: viewing the evidence in the light *most favorable to the opposing party*, the evidence cannot support a _____

   and the moving party is therefore *entitled to judgment as a matter of law*.

-   Credibility of a witness - if the case turns on this issue, then there is a dispute as to an issue of material fact and the motion for JMOL will be denied; the issue is for the jury.

-   Typically made by the _____

   at the close of the plaintiff's case and by either or both sides at the close of ALL evidence.

E. **Renewed Motion for Judgment as a Matter of Law (formerly J.N.O.V.)**

-   A motion for JMOL made at the close of all the evidence and denied by the court may be *renewed* after the verdict.

-   Standard is the same: the ***evidence cannot support the jury's verdict*** and the ***moving party is therefore entitled to judgment as a matter of law***.

-   Prior motion is required: It is a *condition precedent* to a post-verdict motion that the motion for JMOL had been made at the close of all evidence.

   o   If you fail to ask originally, you cannot renew.

-   Usually made with a motion for a new trial

CHAPTER 13:   APPEALS

A. **Motions to Terminate Without Trial**

-   A motion to dismiss for failure to state a claim, motion for judgment on the pleadings, motion for summary judgment, or motion for judgment as a matter of law made before the jury retires are _____ if the moving party proceeds with trial once the motions are denied.

-   Preliminary motions are *no longer relevant* once there has been a full trial.

-   Appellate review is based on the judgment rendered after full trial, not the earlier motion.

B. **New Trial**

-   Usually made with a renewed motion for judgment as a matter of law, but very different.

-   Grounds for new trial include:

- Errors during trial that rendered the judgment _____;
- _____ evidence;
- **Prejudicial misconduct** by a lawyer, party, or juror; and
  - For jurors, includes the failure to answer voir dire honestly if an honest response would have been a valid basis for challenging the juror's service
- Excessive verdict and the winning party refused to accept a reduction (remittitur).
- The court must _____ the reason(s) for granting a new trial in its order.
  - Reason for granting a new trial is **_purely a question of law_** – appellate court reviews the question(s) of law _____.
  - Most grounds for new trial are within the _____ of the trial court - reviewed on appeal only for _____.

C. Appeals

1. Final Judgment Rule

- Ordinarily, appeals lie only from final judgments.
  - Resolves ALL the _____ of ALL the _____ on the _____
- **_Partial final judgment:_** the court may, by express designation, enter a final judgment on some claims.
  - Such a judgment is _immediately appealable_.
- A judgment becomes final when entered by the clerk on the court's docket.
- Notice of appeal must be filed in the trial court within _____ days of entry of judgment.
  - A timely post-judgment motion (e.g., renewed motion for JMOL or a new trial motion) _____ the 30-day limit.

2. Interlocutory Orders

a. Interlocutory Orders Immediately Appealable as of Right

- _____ (granting or modifying)
- Any order that changes or affects _____

b. **Discretionary Interlocutory Appeal**

   ▪ Any interlocutory order is appealable on

   _____.

      • BOTH the trial and appellate courts must agree to allow the appeal.

   ▪ The trial court can issue a certificate for interlocutory appeal stating:

      • That it involves a _____;
      AND

      • That the immediate appeal may _____
      termination of the litigation.

   ▪ The appellate court must then agree to accept the appeal.

3. **Collateral-Order Doctrine**

   ○ Authorizes immediate appeal of orders *separable from* and *collateral to* the main suit and *too important to deny immediate review*

   ○ Most likely case: The denial of a motion to dismiss for *forum non conveniens* is almost always a collateral order and immediately appealable.

4. **Mandamus**

   Provides for immediate appellate review of an order that is an _____ of authority

5. **Class Actions**

   Appellate courts have discretion to hear interlocutory appeals from orders _____ or refusing to certify a class action.

6. **Standards of Review**

   a. **Questions of Law**

      Appellate review is _____.

   b. **Findings of Fact**

      Appellate review is more limited:

      ▪ **Jury verdicts** must be affirmed if supported by

      _____.

      ▪ **Judge's findings of fact** must be affirmed unless

      _____.

      ▪ **Judge's conclusions of law** are reviewed _____.

c. **Matters of Discretion**

- Standard of appellate review is

_____.

- Any reasonable decision will be upheld.

D. **Full Faith and Credit**

- Courts in the United States, both state and federal, must give full faith and credit to judgments rendered by courts of other states, provided that the rendering court had

_____.

CHAPTER 14: THE EFFECT OF FORMER ADJUDICATION

A. **Introduction**

- Preclusion consists of *two* doctrines:

    o _____ preclusion (res judicata)
    o _____ preclusion (collateral estoppel)

- Ask two questions:

    (1) Is the _____ in the second suit precluded by the prior adjudication?

    (2) If not, is the _____ in the second suit precluded by the prior adjudication?

    Exam Tip 7: Always ask these questions separately and in order.

B. **Claim Preclusion**

1. **Rule**

    o A final judgment on the merits of a claim bars re-litigation of that claim by the same parties or those in privity with the parties.
    o Prevents re-litigation of every claim that was raised OR should have been raised in the first suit.

2. **Three Requirements**

    o There must have been a final judgment _____ in the first suit;
    o The second suit must be between the _____ or their successors in interest; and
    o The second suit must involve the ***same claim or cause of action***.

3. **Final Judgment on the Merits**

    o Includes a _____ judgment, _____ judgment, and dismissal with prejudice o   NOT necessary that there had been a trial

4. **Re-litigation between the Same Parties or Their Successors in Interest**

o   _____ parties must have been parties to the first action or successors in interest to the original parties.

o   Same parties - must be same plaintiff and same defendant

> *Example 17:* *Father is criminally prosecuted by the government for failing to provide child support and is acquitted. Mother then brings a civil action for child support against the father. Is the second suit barred by claim preclusion?*
>
> *Answer: _____. The first action was a government prosecution brought by the government, and the second was a civil action brought by the mother. Different plaintiffs, different parties, different claims.*
>
> *Example 18:* *A person injured by a defective vehicle sues the dealer and the dealer wins. Subsequently, the injured person sues the vehicle manufacturer for the same defect. Is the second suit barred by claim preclusion?*
>
> *Answer: _____. The first suit was against the dealer, and the second was against the manufacturer. No re-litigation between the same parties.*

o   The only "exception" is when re-litigation involves successors in interest - stands in the shoes of his or her predecessor.

o   Examples of successors in interest include:

▪   The *assignor* and *assignee* of a claim;

▪   A *decedent* and the *executor* of the estate; and

▪   The *executor* of an estate and *persons who claim* under the will.

o   Class action - each member is bound by the judgment, considered to have had their opportunity in court even if not a named representative.

5. **Re-litigation of the Same Claim or Cause of Action**

o   ALL legal theories to recover for harm arising out of a single transaction or occurrence are

_____.

o   Unless state law provides otherwise, if both contract and tort claims seek redress for the same harm, they are the SAME claim.

o   Installment sales - creditor must sue for all that is due at the time of the suit. All debt owed at the time of the action is one claim even if it was due in 3 or 4 separate payments. Creditor cannot sue for payments that are not "due and owing." Future debts or obligations are another claim.

> *Example 19:* *A tenant is in default on the rent for three months (January, February, and March). On April 1st, the landlord brings suit but unwisely sues*

only for the January rent and wins. He subsequently brings a second suit to collect the February and March rent. Can he collect?

Answer: _____. *All the rent that was due when suit was brought in April is one claim, even though it involved three payments.*

Example 20: *Landlord sues the tenant for all the rent due and owing and gets a default judgment (final judgment on the merits). The next month, the same dispute arises and the landlord sues again, seeking to invoke claim preclusion against the tenant. Is the tenant precluded from defending the second suit on the ground that the lease was invalid or the rent had been paid?*

Answer: _____. *The defenses for the next month were not and could not have been litigated in the earlier suit. The next month is a new claim.*

- Look out for installment sales contracts that provide if a purchaser misses a payment, the entire outstanding balance becomes due and owing (acceleration of obligation).

C. Issue Preclusion

1. Three Requirements

- The same _____ must arise in two suits;
- That issue must have been ***actually and necessarily decided*** in the first suit; and
- The party _____ must have been a party to the first suit.

2. Same Issue of Fact

It doesn't matter if the two suits involve entirely different claims, so long as they have a factual issue in common.

Example 21: *Assume that the person injured by a defective motor vehicle sues the dealer and loses. The jury found that the vehicle was not defective. Then the injured person sues the manufacturer for the same defect. Is there claim preclusion?*

Answer: _____. *The second suit involved a different defendant and therefore a different claim.*

Is there issue preclusion?

Answer: _____. *The same issue arose in both suits and it was actually and necessarily decided in the first suit. Finally, the party to be precluded, the injured person, was a party to the first suit.*

3. Actually and Necessarily Decided

- Only applies to issues actually litigated; not to those that MIGHT have been litigated

- o ***Default judgment*** - results in full _____ preclusive effect, but no _____ preclusive effect.

4. **Party to be Precluded Must Have Been a Party to the First Suit**

   - o The party *against whom preclusion is invoked* must have been a party to the first suit or a successor in interest.
   - o The party invoking preclusion _____ have been a party to the prior action, nor in any way involved in the action.
   - o NO requirement for mutuality of estoppel

     - ▪ Rule at least applies to the *defensive use* of issue preclusion.
     - ▪ Whether a succession of plaintiffs could invoke issue preclusion *offensively* is not clear.

       Example 22: *Fred and Ethel # 1. Fred and Ethel are involved in an auto accident with Mort and Myrtle. Fred sues Mort, the driver of the other car, and loses. The jury found that Mort's car was not operated negligently. Fred then sues Myrtle, the passenger in Mort's car, claiming that she caused the car to be operated negligently. Can Myrtle preclude re-litigation of the negligence issue in the second suit?*

       Answer: *No claim preclusion because the first suit was against a different defendant and thus raises a different claim. But there is issue preclusion. Fred was a party to the first suit. The issue of negligent operation of the vehicle was fully litigated and actually decided against him. Fred is precluded from re-litigating the issue of negligence.*

       Example 23: *Fred and Ethel # 2. Fred and Ethel are involved in an auto accident with Mort and Myrtle. Fred sues Mort, the driver of the other car, and loses. The jury found that Mort's vehicle was not operated negligently. Ethel, the passenger in Fred's car, then sues Mort, claiming that he operated his vehicle negligently. Can Mort, who has already litigated and won this issue, preclude Ethel from re-litigating it in the second suit?*

       Answer: _____. *No claim preclusion because a suit by a different plaintiff is a different claim. There is no issue preclusion because Ethel (the party to be precluded) was not a party to the first suit. She has not had her day in court. Issue preclusion cannot be invoked against her.*

D. **Summary**

   - • Remember that claim preclusion and issue preclusion are separate doctrines and must be addressed separately and in order.

     - o *Ask first* whether claim preclusion bars the second suit. If so, that ends the matter.
     - o *If not*, ask whether issue preclusion bars the second suit.

E. Conclusion

- Remember to concentrate your attention on the areas most often tested:

    o   Jurisdiction (subject matter, personal, and venue) - MOST important;

    o   Pleadings, especially amendments;

    o   Discovery, especially the work-product rule;

    o   Motions practice, especially summary judgment and the two stages of motion for judgment as a matter of law; and

    o   The effect of former adjudication, namely claim and issue preclusion.

[END OF HANDOUT]

Constitutional Law

CONSTITUTIONAL LAW
PROFESSOR JOHN C. JEFFRIES, JR.
UNIVERSITY OF VIRGINIA SCHOOL OF LAW

CHAPTER 1:   THE JUDICIAL POWER

A. **Source, Scope, and Limitations**

- **Source**: Article III

- **Scope**: The jurisdiction of federal courts is limited to cases or controversies.

- **Limitations**: The Eleventh Amendment and State Sovereign Immunity

  o   Article III lists the kinds of cases that come within the judicial power of the United States—the most important are diversity jurisdiction and federal question jurisdiction (cases arising under the laws of the United States).

  o   A **major exception** to the judicial power is created by the _____ Amendment and by the preexisting concept of state sovereign immunity.

     ▪   Rule: You cannot sue a state for _____ damages in either state or federal court unless the state _____ or the U.S. Congress expressly says so to enforce _____ rights.

     > **Editor's Note 1:**   The rule is that you cannot sue a state for money damages in either the state's *own court* or federal court unless the state consents or Congress expressly says so. You may sue a state for money damages in a sister state's court. *Nevada v. Hall*, 440 U.S. 410 (1979).

        - Note that the Eleventh Amendment protects states and state agencies, not _____ governments (no immunity for cities, counties, or towns).

        - Note also that a state's sovereign immunity applies in both _____ and _____ court, unless the state consents, or Congress _____ to enforce Fourteenth Amendment rights.

           o   When enforcing individual rights, Congress can _____ Eleventh Amendment immunity. It can force states to pay money damages for violating individual rights, but it must say so **expressly**.

           o   Any lack of clarity will preclude damages.

     ▪   Whom can you sue then? Answer: a _____

        - Can always get injunctive relief simply by enjoining the appropriate state officer (e.g., sue the state attorney general)

        - Can also get money damages, but only from the officer _____

- Damages from the state treasury are **barred** (unless state consents or Congress expressly says so to enforce individual rights).

B. Jurisdiction of the Supreme Court

1. Original Jurisdiction

A case may be filed first in the Supreme Court (controversies between states, mostly).

2. Appellate Jurisdiction

Mostly, the jurisdiction of the Supreme Court is appellate.

a. Certiorari

- Almost all cases come to the Supreme Court by way of writ of certiorari.
- Key factor is that certiorari is _____ with the court.
- The Supreme Court is the _____ federal court that exercises discretionary jurisdiction.

b. Limitations on the Supreme Court's appellate jurisdiction

- Congress can make exceptions to the Court's appellate jurisdiction. In other words, Congress can effectively control the Supreme Court's docket (its appellate jurisdiction) by legislating exceptions to its appellate jurisdiction.

c. Adequate and Independent State Grounds (AISG)

- Arises *only* in the U.S. Supreme Court, and it arises only when the Supreme Court reviews a _____ judgment.

   Exam Tip 1: Frequently tested topic

- Rule: The Supreme Court can review a state court judgment *only* if it turned on _____ grounds. The court has no jurisdiction if the judgment below rested on an adequate and independent _____ ground.

  - **Adequate:** the state ground must control the decision no matter how a federal issue is decided. When does this happen? When the federal claimant (the party claiming a federal right) wins anyway under state law.

    Example 1: A criminal defendant objects to the legality of a search and asks for the evidence to be suppressed under both the 4th Amendment and under the analogous search and seizure provision of the state's constitution. Suppose the state court says it is unsure about the 4th Amendment, but under the state law, the search was illegal and the evidence must be suppressed. This kind of case cannot be reviewed by the U.S. Supreme Court—the federal claimant wins anyway under state law. Therefore, there is no live federal issue.

    Note 1: *Remember this key point*: The U.S. Constitution is a floor, not a ceiling, for individual rights. A state court construing a state constitution can always give you more. A state can never give you less than the federal constitution requires.

- **Independent:** The state law does not _____ on an interpretation of federal law. No AISG if state law adopts or follows federal law.
- When a state court decision is unclear as to whether it rests on federal grounds or state grounds, the Supreme Court _____ the federal issue. If the Supreme Court agrees with the state court's decision of federal law, it affirms the decision. If the Supreme Court disagrees with the state court's understanding of the federal issue, it remands the case to state court, so that the state court can reconsider state law.

Example 2: Michigan v. Long: Defendant moved to suppress evidence under both the 4th Amendment and the analogous search and seizure provision of the Michigan Constitution. The highest court in the state ruled that the search was illegal but it did not make clear whether it was illegal as a matter of state law or federal law, or both. The Supreme Court took the case, reviewed the federal issue, found that the search was valid, that the evidence could lawfully be used under the 4th Amendment, and remanded the case to the Michigan Supreme Court to reconsider whether the search was lawful under the state constitution.

CHAPTER 2: THE JUDICIAL POWER (CONT'D): CONCEPTS OF JUSTICIABILITY

A. Standing to Sue

Standing requires _____, _____, and _____.

1. **Injury**

   - Almost anything can be injury, especially if Congress says so (either past or future).
   - Must be concrete (not abstract), but need not be economic

     - If your freedom of movement or enjoyment of public space is impaired, that constitutes injury.

   - Mere ideological objection is not injury.
   - An organization has standing if its _____ have standing.

2. **Causation**

   A defendant's act must have caused or will cause the injury.

3. **Redressability**

   - A court can remedy or redress the injury.
   - If the injury is in the past, the redress is _____.
   - If future injury is threatened, the redress is an _____.

o   Past injury does not give automatic standing to seek an injunction for future injury. You must show that it will happen again.

4.   **Standing Examples and Commonly Tested Standing Issues**

> *Example 3:*   *Corporation A applies for a business license, but is turned down. Corporation B applies for the same license and gets it. Corporation A sues to enjoin the government from licensing Corporation B. Does Corporation A have standing? _____. The relief sought would not redress the wrong to Corporation A. The wrong to Corporation A was a wrongful denial of a license. Corporation A should sue for its own license.*

o   Federal taxpayers **always** have standing to challenge their own tax liability. However, taxpayers do not have standing to challenge government expenditures.

■   *Narrow exception* under the Establishment Clause: An establishment of religion challenge to _____ congressional appropriations can be challenged by _____. (Note also that state courts often allow municipal taxpayers to challenge a municipality's expenditures.)

o   Legislative standing: Legislators _____ have standing to challenge laws that they voted against.

o   "Third-party standing" refers to the question of whether you can raise the rights of someone else.

■   Generally, the answer is _____.

■   **Exception**: Parties to an _____ or _____ can raise the rights of other parties to that exchange or transaction.

> *Example 4:*   *Doctors who were not compensated for providing abortion services can raise the rights of women who wanted to have abortions provided. The doctor has injury because he wasn't paid but he wants to raise the rights of his patient to have an abortion, not his own. The doctor and the patient are involved in an exchange or transaction.*

> *Example 5:*   *A seller of beer in a saloon can raise the rights of 18-year-old boys to buy beer at the same age as 18-year-old girls. The saloon keeper is injured because she is not making money. She wants to raise the rights of the underage boys because that is gender discrimination. She can raise the claims of those customers or would-be customers because they are parties to an exchange or transaction.*

B.   **Timeliness (Ripeness and Mootness)**

•   Ripeness concerns prematurity of a case. You must show _____ or an _____ threat of harm.

- Mootness cases are overripe and are dismissed whenever they become moot. Cases can become moot during trial or on appeal.

  o **Exception**: Controversies capable of _____, yet evading _____, are not moot, even though they look like it.

    ▪ Such controversies always have an *internal time limit* (e.g., pregnancies and abortion).

C. Advisory Opinions

- Federal courts cannot issue advisory opinions.
- Cannot rule on the constitutionality of _____ legislation

> **Exam Tip 2:** Commonly tested
>
> ***Example 6:*** *If disputes about federal grants and aid projects were to be litigated, the judgment of the federal court would take effect only if the federal agency, or the executive officer, agreed with it. This is an unconstitutional advisory opinion. Federal courts decide cases; they do not make recommendations to executive officers.*

D. Political Questions

- A non-justiciable question—courts will not decide because there are no manageable standards for judicial decision-making
- Examples of non-justiciable political questions include:

  o _____ Clause (protecting the republican form of government);
  o Foreign affairs, such as opening or breaking off diplomatic relations with another country;

  > ***Example 7:*** *Congress enacted a law stating that American citizens born in Jerusalem could list Israel as their place of birth on their passports, which the executive branch challenged. The Court held that a dispute over the regulation of passports is not a non-justiciable political question.*

  o _____ procedures; and
  o Political gerrymandering (drawing districts to establish a political advantage of one party over another).

    ▪ The court has found no judicially manageable standards for determining what is and what is not acceptable in the area of drawing districts.

CHAPTER 3: THE LEGISLATIVE POWER

A. Introduction

- In theory, the federal government is a government of limited powers. In fact, the federal government can do almost anything it likes, so long as it does not violate individual rights.

> **Exam Tip 3:** On the Multistate, you'll be given a federal statute, and you'll have to give the strongest argument in favor of congressional power for passing that legislation. Three wrong answers:
>
> - Promoting the _____ is not a power of Congress.
>
> - The federal government does not have a general _____ _____ .
>
> - _____ is not a free-standing power of Congress. It works only as an add-on to some other legislative power.

- There are many powers of Congress, but the three big ones for the bar exam are: **taxing**, **spending**, and **commerce**.

> **Exam Tip 4:** The general rule for the bar exam:
>
> - Pick the _____ power when the law involves a tax.
>
> - Pick the _____ power whenever federal money is spent or disbursed.
>
> - When in doubt, pick the _____ power.

> **Example 8:** There is a federal law that states that every state that receives federal highway funds has to limit its speed limit to 65 mph. What is the strongest argument Congress has to accomplish this? Answer: The _____ clause. What if the law simply caps the highway speeds at 65 mph without saying anything about federal highway funds? Answer: Regulation of _____ .

B. The Powers

1. The Commerce Power

- Almost anything can be regulated as interstate commerce.
- Congress can regulate:
    - The _____ of interstate commerce (highways, seaways, airways, etc.);
    - The _____ of interstate commerce (cars, trucks, ships, railroads, etc.); and
    - *Intrastate* [and interstate] activity (economic or commercial) that has a _____ _____ on *interstate* commerce.
        - Substantial effect is judged in the _____ . The question is always whether the aggregate activity of everyone doing the same thing has a substantial effect on interstate commerce, and the answer is almost always *yes*.
        - Not within the Commerce Clause: For non-economic, non-commercial activity, Congress can regulate intrastate actions only by *actually* demonstrating a

substantial effect on interstate commerce (substantial effect is presumed for economic or commercial activity). Thus, Congress cannot regulate purely intrastate, non-commercial, non-economic activity for which a substantial effect on interstate commerce has not been shown.

Example 9: *Wickard v. Filburn (wheat growing case where growing crops for sale was judged in the aggregate and a substantial effect was demonstrated)*

Example 10: *Gonzales v. Raich (where the cultivation and medical use of marijuana was judged in the aggregate and a substantial effect was demonstrated)*

Example 11: *United States v. Lopez (illegal to have a firearm within 1000 feet of a school—could not be proved that it was an economic or commercial activity, and it couldn't be demonstrated that there was a substantial effect on interstate commerce)*

Example 12: *United States v. Morrison (federal remedy for gender-motivated violence—could not be shown that, in the aggregate, the activity had a substantial effect on interstate commerce)*

Example 13: *2012 Affordable Health Care case (individual mandate required individuals to buy health insurance or to pay a penalty for not doing so – Court said that forcing individuals who are not engaged in commercial or economic activities to buy health insurance they do not want cannot be sustained as a regulation of interstate commerce.)*

2. **The Taxing and Spending Power**

   Think of these as separate powers even though they are lumped together in one clause.

   a. **Taxing**

      ▪ The Taxing Clause is the right answer whenever Congress imposes a _____, even when the tax is actually used to prohibit the good or activity in question.
      ▪ The tax must be _____ to raising revenue.

   b. **Spending**

      ▪ The Spending Power includes spending for the _____.
      ▪ Congress can use the Spending Power to accomplish things it could not do by direct regulation under the Commerce Clause.

      Example 14: *South Dakota v. Dole. Congress imposed a 21-year-old minimum drinking age throughout the United States. However, the 21st Amendment repealed Prohibition and gave states the power to control the regulation and consumption of alcohol. Thus, in order to pass the 21 year-old drinking age law,*

Congress passed a "bribe." If states wanted to receive federal highway funds, they had to raise their drinking age to a minimum of 21.

3. **Anti-Commandeering**

    o   Congress cannot force states to adopt or enforce _____ programs. It cannot commandeer state and local officers to carry out federal programs.

    > ***Example 15:*** *The Brady Gun-Control Act required background checks for people wanting to purchase firearms, and it required that state and local law enforcement carry out those background checks. The Supreme Court said this was unconstitutional.*

    o   What can Congress do to enforce regulatory programs?

    ▪   It can bribe states through use of the _____ power.

    ▪   It can adopt its own regulatory program and enforce it with federal officers.

4. **The War and Defense Powers**

    o   Congress has the power to _____ and the power to maintain the Army and Navy.

    o   Congress has the power to provide for military discipline of United States armed forces members.

    o   Congress can provide for military trial of enemy combatants and enemy civilians.

    o   Congress _____ provide for military trial of U.S. civilians.

CHAPTER 4:   THE LEGISLATIVE POWER (CONT'D): THE POWER TO ENFORCE THE CIVIL WAR AMENDMENTS

A. **Thirteenth Amendment**

    •   Congress has broad power to legislate against _____ discrimination, whether _____ or _____.

    •   Includes purely private racial discrimination

B. **Fourteenth Amendment**

    •   Congress has the power to _____ violations of _____ rights by the government, but only as those rights have been defined by the courts.

        o   Does not enable Congress to redefine constitutional rights by legislation

    •   To be properly remedial, the legislation must have "congruence" and "proportionality." That is, there must be a _____ between the remedial law enacted by Congress and the constitutional right as declared by the Supreme Court.

    •   Congress does not have the power to overrule the Court's decisions and define new rights.

Example 16: *The Religious Freedom Restoration Act (RFRA)*

Overview: Neutral, generally applicable laws regulating conduct can validly be applied despite religious objections. Everyone can be made to obey the law whether they believe in it or not.

Background: Religious individuals often claimed a right of accommodation to religious belief. They were demanding special treatment, or a special exemption from a law applicable to everyone else, despite the lack of a compelling interest. The Supreme Court stated that there is no constitutional right to accommodation of religious belief.

Congress disagreed with the Supreme Court and passed RFRA, which declared that religious believers have the right not to obey otherwise valid laws, unless the government can show a compelling interest in enforcing the law against them.

The Supreme Court struck down RFRA, as it went beyond federal legislative power, because it was not really remedial. It was not narrowly aimed at the kinds of things the Supreme Court had declared unconstitutional – laws aimed at religion. In RFRA, Congress passed a law that declared illegal any state or local laws that had an incidental burden on religion.

Congress could have made it a crime for the government to discriminate against religious belief. Congress could say that any government or any official who discriminated against religious belief had to pay money damages. Congress could give the Department of Justice special enforcement powers to look into religious discrimination and make sure it is rooted out. All of these actions would have been reasonable remedies against a recognized constitutional violation of discrimination against religious belief.

Congress basically said even wholly non-discriminatory laws were invalid if someone had a religious objection to the law. The Supreme Court stated that RFRA was an attempt to overrule the Court and that is a power Congress does not have. RFRA was found unconstitutional as beyond federal legislative power.

Note: RFRA was only unconstitutional as it applied to states and localities. RFRA is valid as it applies to federal laws, as Congress's powers over the Army and the Navy, the District of Columbia, the post office, etc., include the power to accommodate religious beliefs.

C. Fifteenth Amendment

Congress has the power to ensure no racial discrimination in voting.

CHAPTER 5:   THE EXECUTIVE POWER AND INTERBRANCH RELATIONS

A. The Powers of the President—Domestic

- Has the power to _____ the law, not to make it or break it
- The power to enforce is greatest when authorized by _____. Generally, the President's powers are subject to control by statute.
- Few powers that are *exclusively executive* and, therefore, **not subject** to statutory control:

  o **Pardon Power**: The President can pardon or commute punishment for all _____ offenses. (Governors have a similar power for state crimes.) This power _____ be limited by Congress.

  o **Veto Power**: The President has 10 days to veto legislation. He can veto for any reason or no reason, but cannot veto specific items in the legislation and accept others. Overriding a veto requires a _____ majority vote of each house.

  o **Appointment and Removal of Executive Officers**: Only the President (or his appointees) can _____ or _____ executive officers. Some senior officers (cabinet officers, ambassadors, federal judges) require the advice and consent of the Senate. The Senate has a power of rejection. The Senate's approval power does not translate into a power of appointment.

    ▪ Who are executive officers? Anyone who _____ on behalf of the U.S.

    ▪ Just as Congress cannot hire or fire an executive officer, it cannot give executive power to anyone it can hire or fire.

    > **Exam Tip 5:** In the question, it tells you that a certain officer is appointed by the Speaker of the House of Representatives (under legislative control). Be alert to the fact that the officer cannot be given executive power to act on behalf of the United States.

B. The Powers of the President—Foreign Affairs

- Commander in Chief: The President has control over military decisions, although Congress has exclusive power to _____.
- Treaties and Executive Agreements

  o Treaties are negotiated by the President, but require approval by a _____ vote of the Senate. Once a treaty is ratified (approved), it has the same authority as a statute.

  o Executive agreements are presidential negotiations not submitted for approval by the Senate. They can be authorized, precluded, or overridden by statute, but they take precedence over conflicting state laws. They do not have the binding status of a treaty.

C. Interbranch Relations

1. Congressional Limits on the Executive

a. Impeachment

- Applies to executive officers
- An accusation of high crimes or misdemeanors requiring a majority vote of the House of Representatives.
- Trial in the Senate
- Conviction requires a two-thirds vote of the Senate.
- The remedy is _____ from office. No other penalty applies.

b. Impoundment

- If a statute gives the President discretion to spend or withhold funds, he may do so.
- But, when a statute unambiguously requires that funds be spent, the President cannot refuse to do so. There is no power to impound funds.

c. Legislative Veto

- _____
- Happens when Congress passes a law reserving to itself the right to disapprove future executive actions by simple resolution
- If Congress wants to override future executive actions, it must _____ (so that the President has an opportunity to veto the new legislation).
- Congress cannot evade the President's guaranteed veto opportunity by passing a law saying that in the future it plans to govern by resolution.

2. Delegation of Powers

- o Congress can delegate its power to administrative agencies, so long as there are **intelligible standards** governing the exercise of that delegated power.
- o Not a demanding test – almost all delegations of legislative powers are upheld.

3. Immunities

a. The President

- Has _____ immunity for official acts
- Has no immunity for acts done _____ to taking office
- Has an _____ privilege not to reveal confidential communications with presidential advisers, but that privilege can be outweighed by a _____ _____ in a criminal prosecution (Nixon)

b. Judges

Judges have absolute immunity for all _____ acts, but may be liable for non-judicial activities.

  c. **Legislators**

- United States Senators and Representatives (not state legislators) are protected by the _____ Clause.

- Senators and Congressmen and their aides *cannot* be _____ or _____ in relation to their _____ acts.

   • The official acts of a federal legislator **cannot** be introduced into evidence.

CHAPTER 6:   THE FEDERAL SYSTEM

A. Federal and State Powers

- Even though federal powers are superior, most federal powers are _____ with those of the states. (On most topics, both Congress and the states have regulatory powers. If there is a conflict, Congress wins.)

- Some powers are exclusively federal. They include the power over foreign relations and the power to coin money.

B. Intergovernmental Immunities

- The federal government is generally _____ from **direct** state regulation or taxation. However, states can tax **indirectly**, such as taxing the income of federal employees.

- States _____ immune from direct federal regulation (for example: pollution regulations, employment laws, etc.).

- State laws cannot shield state officers from federal liability.

- **Exception**: the anti-commandeering principle covered in Chapter 3. States cannot be forced to implement federal programs. The federal government can always use the spending power to bribe states to comply.

C. State Regulation and Taxation of Commerce

1. Privileges and Immunities of State Citizenship under Article IV (Comity Clause)

- Technically, a subject of individual rights, but functionally belongs here because of its similarity to the next subject (Dormant Commerce Clause).

- Forbids serious _____ against _____ individuals, absent substantial justification.

  ■ Does not protect out-of-state _____.

  ■ "Serious discrimination" typically involves **employment**.

- *Rule*: There can be no legal requirement of _____ for _____ employment. States cannot require that you live/reside in the state to work in the state. However, public employment can require residency requirements.

- Examples of unacceptable private employment requirements: Admission to the bar; other occupational licenses.
- Examples of public employment: A city hiring only city residents or requiring a certain percentage of city residents on city construction projects.

- Non-serious discrimination: States can discriminate with regard to recreational opportunities, such as hunting licenses or state park access.

2. Dormant Commerce Clause

- More important than Privileges and Immunities of Article IV because it protects _____ as well as out-of-state individuals.

- "Dormant" describes what the Commerce Clause means in the absence of federal regulation (when the federal commerce power is unexercised).

- **Rule**: In the absence of federal regulation, state regulation of commerce is *valid* so long as:

  1) There is no _____ against out-of-state interests;

  2) The regulation does not _____ interstate commerce; and

  3) The regulation does not apply to wholly extraterritorial activity.

a. No discrimination against out-of-state interests

- Examples include: taxing the out-of-state interest at a higher rate or forbidding sale only of out-of-state products; requiring that manufacturing be performed in-state; limiting privately owned landfills to in-state garbage.

- **Exceptions** to no discrimination against out-of-state interests:

  - **State as Market Participant**—When a state is _____ or _____ goods or services, it can choose to deal with only in-state persons.

    - Examples include: sale of cement produced by state-owned plant only to in-state purchasers; garbage stored in state-owned landfill limited to in-state garbage; law requiring 50% local workforce on state-financed construction projects.

  - **Subsidies**—A state can always choose to subsidize only its own citizens (for example, welfare benefits or in-state college tuition).

  - **Federal Approval**—Remember, the Dormant Commerce Clause applies *only* in the _____ of federal action. If Congress _____ or _____ state regulation of commerce, nothing the state does will violate the Commerce Clause, *even if it discriminates against out-of-state interests.*

  Exam Tip 6: Commonly tested on the MBE

  b. No undue burdens on interstate commerce

   ▪ Non-discriminatory state regulation of commerce is almost always upheld.

   ▪ Only when it is so outrageously costly relative to the benefits of the regulation is a non-discriminatory state regulation struck down as an undue burden on interstate commerce.

   ▪ This is a balancing test, but non-discriminatory regulations are rarely struck down.

  c. No regulation of wholly extraterritorial activity

   ▪ A state may not regulate conduct occurring wholly beyond its borders.

   Example 17: *Connecticut tried to legislate that beer sold in Connecticut could not be sold at a price different from the price of beer sold in other states.*

CHAPTER 7: STATE TAXATION OF INTERSTATE COMMERCE, PREEMPTION, AND RELATIONS AMONG STATES

A. State Taxation of Interstate Commerce

- Generally, the requirements are the same as for any other state regulation of commerce: Discriminatory taxation will be struck down unless Congress _____, and non-discriminatory taxation will be upheld unless it is unduly _____.

  ○ Non-discriminatory taxation is valid if the following **two requirements** are met:

   1) Must be a _____ between the taxing state and the property or activity to be taxed

   Example 18: *A sales tax may be levied on a physically present, in-state seller because there is a substantial nexus.*

   Example 19: *An Internet-based, out-of-state seller with no physical facility in the state—If the state does not have a substantial nexus with the seller, the state cannot impose a sales tax. But, it can impose a use tax on the in-state purchaser for the same dollar amount that the sales tax would have been had the item been purchased from an in-state seller.*

   2) Must be a _____ of tax liability among states

   Example 20: *A state may tax the in-state portion of a corporation's revenue but cannot tax the entire world-wide value of the corporation.*

- Ad Valorem Property Taxes (value-based property taxes)

  ○ Levied on personal property

  ○ Distinguish between two kinds of personal property because they are taxed differently:

   ▪ **Commodities** are the goods that move from state to state.

- States tax all commodities within their borders on a specified date (called *tax day*), but not goods that are merely in transit – the commodities have to come to rest in the state.
- **Rule:** Pay the full tax to every state where goods are stopped for a _____ on tax day. No taxes are due where they are merely _____.

  ▪ **Instrumentalities** are the transportation equipment that moves commodities (railroads, trucks, airplanes, etc.)

  - Each state in which an instrumentality is used can tax the value of that instrumentality.

  Example 21: *A long-haul trucker drives his rig from Maine to California. Every state through which the truck passes can tax the truck itself but each state can only tax a portion of the truck's value, roughly equal to the portion of in-state use. The state of the taxpayer's domicile taxes the full value of the truck, then turns around and gives a credit to every state that asserts taxation when the truck uses its highways. You end up with a scheme of fair apportionment of tax liability among those states with a substantial nexus to the truck. The commodities in the truck cannot be taxed if they are merely passing through; they must stop for a business purpose on tax day.*

B. Preemption

- Federal law preempts (overrides) _____ state law.
- State law _____ preempted simply because it addresses the same subject matter/topic as a federal statute. There must be incompatibility or conflict.

  Example 22: *Federal law provides automobile emissions must be at least 95% pure. California adopts a more stringent requirement requiring CA emissions be 98% pure. Is this state law preempted? No. There is no conflict – you can comply with both of those standards.*

- Preempting the Field: When Congress determines that there should be no state law of any sort in a particular field, then any state law in that area is inconsistent with the federal statute and is preempted. This is **rare**.

C. Relations Among States

- *Interstate compacts* are agreements among states. States can make interstate compacts, but if the compact affects _____ rights, Congress must approve.
- Full Faith and Credit Clause: States don't have to follow other states' laws, but they do have to give full faith and credit to _____ rendered by other states' courts, so long as the rendering court had _____ to render a final judgment on the merits.

CHAPTER 8: STATE ACTION AND PROCEDURAL DUE PROCESS

A. State Action

- The 13th Amendment (outlawing slavery and involuntary servitude) applies directly to private parties and individuals, but it is narrow in its focus.

- Other individual rights apply to states and localities through the _____, which requires state action.

- "State action" means _____ action, whether state or local (for example, a city firing a sheriff is state action; a county denying a permit is state action).

- Most state action is clear, but not always. Government cannot be **significantly involved** in private discrimination.

  o Significant state involvement:

    ▪ Government cannot _____ private discrimination.

    ▪ Government cannot _____ private discrimination.

    ▪ Government cannot _____ a private agreement to discriminate.

    ▪ But, government is **not** required to _____ private discrimination.

  o Generally, the government acts constitutionally so long as its own conduct is neutral and even-handed (for example, trespass laws, liquor licenses for private clubs).

- Anti-Discrimination Statutes

  o State action is required to show a violation of the Constitution.

  o State action is _____ if there is anti-discrimination legislation.

B. Procedural Due Process—the Right to *Notice* and a *Hearing*

1. Consists of two questions:

  1) Is _____, _____, or _____ being taken?

  2) If life, liberty, or property is being taken, what process is due?

2. Breakdown of loss of life, liberty, and property

  o **Life**: death penalty requires procedural due process

  o **Liberty**: physical confinement, probation and parole, physical injury (such as a spanking in school), any restriction on legal rights (including being punished for free speech). Injury to _____ is **not** a loss of liberty.

  o **Property**

    > **Exam Tip 7:** Out of the three, property is the most heavily tested. Most of the questions in this area concern government jobs or benefits.

    ▪ You have a property interest in your government job or benefit whenever you have a _____ to continued enjoyment of the job or benefit.

    ▪ A mere expectation of continued employment or benefit does not suffice.

- Most government benefits are entitlements, and hence property.
- How can you tell whether you have an entitlement to a government job or whether you have a mere expectation of government employment?
  - Government jobs are entitlements only when the government says so—such as by providing a contractual term or discharge only "for cause."

Example 23: *You are hired as the city planner and the boss says, "This job has a term of 5 years. You will not be fired during that 5-year term except for cause." You have a property right in that job for 5 years.*

Example 24: *Barnes was an assistant professor at a state community college. He had a 3-year teaching contract and under state law, 5 years was required for tenure. At the end of 3 years, his contract wasn't renewed, and he sued. What is his strongest argument that he should get notice and a hearing?*

A. He was the best teacher in the school.

B. He was the only teacher not rehired.

C. He was so sure of success that he moved his elderly parents to town to care for them.

D. He had an oral promise of re-employment from the president of the college.

_____ is the answer because the president is acting as the government, and arguably Barnes had an entitlement to continued employment.

What is the strongest argument against Barnes receiving notice and a hearing? Answer: He had a 3-year contract that ended.

- Deprivation: Notice and a hearing are not required when there is an accident. Random negligence by a state employee does not constitute a deprivation of life, liberty, or property (for example, death by a municipal garbage truck). Deprivation requires the **intentional** taking away of life, liberty, or property.

3. **If life, liberty, or property is being taken by the government, what process is due?**

- Procedural due process is variable, and the types of hearings can range from casual to very elaborate.
- To decide what kind of process is due, the courts balance three factors:

1) The _____ at stake (life, liberty, property);

2) The _____ in protecting that interest; and

3) The _____ in efficiency and cost.

- **Timing** of the hearings
  - Sometimes, a hearing must occur before the deprivation.

- Examples include: terminating welfare benefits; non-emergency revocations of driver's licenses.
    - Sometimes, the hearing can occur after the action, so long as the hearing is _____ and _____.
        - Examples include: terminating disability benefits; disciplinary suspension from a public secondary school.
  - Public employees who can be fired only "for cause" must be given some opportunity to be heard _____ to discharge, unless there is a _____ not to keep the employee on the job. If there is a significant reason not to keep a person on the job, then the discharge can come first with a subsequent hearing that is prompt and provides reinstatement with back pay (fair).

    Example 25: *A police officer charged with a crime can be suspended immediately because there is a significant reason not to keep him or her on the job. The hearing can come afterwards, but it must be prompt and provide reinstatement with back pay if the charges are ultimately unfounded.*

CHAPTER 9:   SUBSTANTIVE DUE PROCESS

A. Standards of Review

- Both substantive due process and equal protection have the same three standards of review.

1. Strict Scrutiny

  - Is the law _____ for a _____ government interest?
  - Implicit in strict scrutiny is the requirement for the **least restrictive means**.
  - When strict scrutiny applies, the _____ bears the burden of proof. The government must show that the interest is compelling and the law is necessary to that interest.
  - Applies when there is a _____ classification or a _____ right

2. Intermediate Scrutiny

  - Is the law _____ related to an _____ government interest?
  - Applies to classifications based on _____ and _____
    - While three standards of review are available in both substantive due process and equal protection claims, intermediate scrutiny has only ever been used to decide cases based on equal protection grounds.

3. **Rational Basis**

   o Is the law _____ related to a _____ interest?

   o The _____ bears the burden of proof.

   o Applies to all other cases (residual test)

B. **Fundamental Rights**

   • Triggers the strict scrutiny test under both due process and equal protection

   1. **Due Process versus Equal Protection**

      o If a law denies a fundamental right to **everyone**, it violates _____.

      o If a law denies a fundamental right to **only some**, it violates _____.

   2. **Travel**

      o We have a fundamental right of _____ and settlement.

      o States can impose reasonable residency requirements for _____
      _____ and _____.

         ▪ Most are 30-90 days

         ▪ One year is too long for everything except _____ and
         jurisdiction to _____.

      o All residents have a right to be treated equally. A state cannot have a tax scheme that favors long-term residents over recently arrived residents.

   3. **Voting and Ballot Access**

      o Voting is a fundamental right to all _____ age 18 and over.

         ▪ _____ are unconstitutional because they burden the fundamental right to vote.

         ▪ Short-term (e.g., 30 days) residency requirements are permitted.

         ▪ Congress controls the residency requirements for _____ elections. States control residency requirements for all other elections.

      o Ballot access

         ▪ States can impose requirements for candidates to be listed on a ballot, such as longer residency, filing fees, and nomination petitions, so long as serious candidates can reasonably comply.

         ▪ If the requirements become so onerous that they effectively bar access to the ballot, then they are unconstitutional.

4. **Privacy**

   a. **Marriage**

      There are all sorts of requirements for marriage (e.g., age or restriction on marrying close relatives), but substantial interference with the marriage—including same-sex marriage—is unconstitutional.

   b. **Contraception**

      It is a fundamental right for everyone, whether married or not, to purchase contraceptives.

   c. **Sexual intimacy**

      Perhaps not technically a fundamental right—the Supreme Court found that the government has no _____ in regulating non-commercial sexual intimacy between consenting adults, including same-sex couples.

   d. **Abortion**

      ▪ *Roe v. Wade*: A woman has a right to terminate her pregnancy until viability of the fetus. After that stage, restrictions can apply so long as there are exceptions to preserve the health and life of the mother.

      ▪ States regulate abortion in a variety of ways, but they cannot impose an _____ _____ on the woman's right to terminate her pregnancy.

         • Informed-consent requirements are _____.
         • Twenty-four hour waiting periods are _____.
         • Parental _____ requirements (for minors) are allowed.
         • Parental _____ requirements are generally not allowed.

            o Narrow exception for requirement that an underage female get the consent of a parent or a judge, but requires the judge to give consent if the underage female understands the nature of the act.

         • _____ requirements are not permissible.
         • Government financing of abortion is _____.

   e. **Parental rights**

      ▪ Parents have a fundamental right to raise their children as they see fit, including the choice of religious or private schools.
      ▪ Can lose their rights through abandonment, abuse, or neglect

   f. **Family relations**

      ▪ Includes the right to live together with close relatives

g. **Obscene material**

▪ Fundamental right to read obscene material in the privacy of one's own home.

▪ However, no fundamental right to purchase, sell, import, or distribute such material.

▪ Does not apply to _____

h. **Refusal of medical treatment**

▪ Not clear whether this is a fundamental right, but there is a liberty interest in refusing medical treatment

▪ No right to commit suicide

CHAPTER 10:   EQUAL PROTECTION (RACE, ETHNICITY, AND NATIONAL ORIGIN)

A. General Considerations

- Privileges or Immunities of *National* Citizenship under the 14th Amendment - means nothing today (so **never** the correct answer on the MBE)

  > **Note 2:** Privileges and Immunities of _____ Citizenship Clause in Article 4 (Comity Clause) has a narrow but important meaning. It prohibits serious discrimination against out-of-state individuals, especially in the context of access to the _____ job market, i.e. prohibits requiring those who work in the state to live in the state

- Two Due Process Clauses

  o 5th Amendment applies to the _____ government.

  o 14th Amendment applies to _____ and _____.

- One Equal Protection Clause – found in the 14th Amendment

  o Applies to localities and states

  > **Note 3:** Though no Equal Protection Clause guarantee technically applies to the _____ government, equal protection concepts are applied to the federal government via the Due Process Clause of the 5th Amendment. Therefore, states and localities have both equal protection and due process; for the federal government, equal protection and due process are called Fifth Amendment Due Process.

B. Standards of Review—Same for Due Process and Equal Protection

- Strict scrutiny, i.e., is the law *necessary* for a *compelling* interest?
- Intermediate scrutiny, i.e., is the law _____ related to an _____ government interest?
- Rational basis, i.e., is the law _____ related to a ___ _____ government interest?

  o Rational basis test is generally easily passed. However, recent Supreme Court cases have made exceptions in the field of sexual orientation.

- In the 2003 *Lawrence* case, the Supreme Court struck down laws criminalizing homosexual sodomy using language suggesting the laws did not pass the rational basis test as they reflected prejudice, not a legitimate reason for the laws.
- In the 2013 *Windsor* case, the Court used the same approach in striking down the federal Defense of Marriage Act (DOMA). Court applied a version of the rational basis test "with teeth" suggesting that because the motivation behind the federal DOMA was animus and prejudice, the law was not a rational plan of government.
- More recently, the Court upheld same-sex marriage, although it **did not** state that sexual orientation is a suspect classification.

> **Editor's Note 2:** The Supreme Court in *Obergefell v. Hodges* did in fact state that marriage is a fundamental right.

- Laws against sexual orientation might be struck down as irrational because they are not supported by reasons other than mere prejudice.

C. **Suspect Classifications (Trigger Strict Scrutiny and Arise under Equal Protection)**

- **Race, Ethnicity, or National Origin**—laws that disadvantage minorities will be struck down.

  - Discriminatory _____ is required - For constitutional purposes, a law is a racial classification only if the plaintiffs show it has a discriminatory _____ (not enough to show a disproportionate impact).

    > *Example 26:* Economically restrictive zoning in Arlington Heights—a developer wanted to come in and build a large multi-family housing complex. Developer argued that the 2-acre, single-family zoning ordinance has the effect of restricting the town to wealthy white people; he argued that discriminated against minorities. The Supreme Court said the zoning law was not unconstitutional as racial discrimination unless you can show it was done for the purpose of discriminating against minorities.

    - **Discriminatory purpose**: May be explicit on the face of the statute, or may be proved by a history of discriminatory _____, or by extrinsic evidence about the purposes of those who passed the law.
    - School desegregation: De jure (by law) segregation is unconstitutional. De facto segregation is not (usually by residential housing patterns).

  - Affirmative action

    - It is a racial classification; an effort to benefit a racial or ethnic minority.
    - Triggers _____ and requires a _____ interest
    - **Specific past discrimination**: Affirmative action is valid when it **specifically** corrects past discrimination *by the specific department or agency* now engaged in affirmative action.

      > *Example 27:* New Haven Firefighters case—Nineteen firefighters sued the city of New Haven when they had all scored high enough on a standardized test to

be promoted to management positions. City officials abandoned the test results because minority firefighters had not scored high enough to be considered for these positions, and then the city hired minorities anyway for these spots. The Supreme Court said the city's actions looked like a racially motivated quota and struck it down.

- General societal discrimination does not justify affirmative action.

- Affirmative action is allowed in the context of preferential admissions to colleges and universities

  - Preferential admissions are allowed if _____ to achieve a diverse student body and diversity is essential to the education

    - Must be a strong showing that racial preferences are **essential** to achieving a diverse class.
    - Racial preferences must be "holistic" (can be built into an evaluation if every student is evaluated individually in a holistic way) and flexible.
    - Quotas are not allowed
    - Separate tracks or procedures for minority applicants are not allowed.

  - Preferential admissions not allowed for _____ (though schools may be located and attendance zones created to maximize diversity)

CHAPTER 11: EQUAL PROTECTION (ALIENAGE, GENDER, AND ONE PERSON-ONE VOTE)

A. Suspect Classifications Continued

- **Alienage**—Requirement of U.S. Citizenship

  - Classifications based upon U.S. citizenship are generally suspect classifications that require a compelling interest, but **two important exceptions** to strict scrutiny for alienage apply:

    - **Federal government**

      - Congress has plenary power over citizenship and naturalization.
      - Federal classifications based on U.S. citizenship do **not** trigger strict scrutiny.
      - Federal classifications are valid unless _____ and _____.

    - **State and local participation in government functions**

      - These are jobs that have a particular relevance to the role of government and non-U.S. citizens can be barred from these jobs.
      - States and localities may require U.S. citizenship for participation in government functions, including voting, serving on a jury, and working in any kind of government

law enforcement position (including probation and parole officers), or as a public school teacher.

- o **Rule**: States and localities *cannot* require U.S. citizenship for access to _____ employment or for government _____.

    > ***Example 28:*** *Florida required U.S. citizenship for admission to the Florida bar. Admission to the bar controls private employment as an attorney and therefore triggered strict scrutiny. It was struck down.*

    > ***Example 29:*** *Maryland required U.S. citizenship for Maryland's in-state tuition, a government benefit, a kind of subsidy of in-state students. Basing that subsidy on U.S. citizenship triggers strict scrutiny. The requirement was struck down. However, Maryland could and did validly require* **residency** *for in-state tuition. But Maryland was not entitled to discriminate against lawfully resident, taxpaying members of the Maryland community who were not U.S. citizens.*

    > **Note 4:** Constitutional rights of illegal aliens – *Plyler v. Doe* - Undocumented aliens are not a suspect class. Even so, states cannot deny undocumented children public education.

B. Quasi-Suspect Classifications (Gender and Legitimacy)

- Trigger intermediate scrutiny—is the law _____ related to an _____ government interest?

- **Gender** classifications are almost always **invalid** (e.g., Oklahoma had a law permitting women to legally drink alcohol at a younger age than men).

    - o Permissible examples of gender classifications:

        - ▪ Statutory rape can be gender specific (historically); and
        - ▪ The draft.

- **Legitimacy** (i.e., something depends on whether parents were married at the time of one's birth) laws are almost always **invalid**, especially if punitive in nature.

C. Non-Suspect Classifications (Age and Wealth)

- **Age** discrimination in employment is barred by statute, but it is not a suspect or quasi-suspect classification under the Equal Protection Clause.

    - o Triggers *rational* basis

- **Wealth** is not a suspect or quasi-suspect classification, but the government has to waive filing fees for indigents when charging the fees would deny a _____ right.

    - o Examples include: _____ (because marriage is a fundamental right); transcript for appeal of criminal conviction (because appellate review is a fundamental right); transcript for appeal of termination of parental rights.

D. Fundamental Rights

Some fundamental rights almost always come up under equal protection.

1. Right to travel

2. Right to vote - one person, one vote

- o Requires districts of approximately equal size, i.e. approximately the same number of voters in each
- o Applies whenever you elect representatives by _____

  - ▪ Examples include: U.S. House of Representatives; both houses of a state legislature; local governments when they elect representatives by district.

    - • *Exception*: Special purpose governments—A highly specialized government (e.g., for distribution of water rights) can have a franchise based on that special purpose (e.g., acreage or water entitlements).

3. Gerrymandering

Comes in two varieties—racial and political

a. Racial gerrymandering

- ▪ Vote Dilution: Drawing districts to scatter minorities so that they are not crucial in any one district. If done with a _____, it's unconstitutional.
- ▪ Voting Rights Act: Requires racial gerrymandering to ensure minority success by creating majority-minority districts.

  - • **Rule:** Race may be a factor in drawing district lines, but not the _____ or _____ factor.
  - • Other factors include compactness and observing local, political subdivisions.
  - • A bizarrely-shaped district may be evidence of a predominant racial purpose.

b. Political gerrymandering (drawing districts to hurt one party)

- ▪ Can, in theory, violate equal protection. In practice, it's never struck down.
- ▪ The Supreme Court has not found any judicially manageable standards for implementing that guarantee.
- ▪ A political question (non-justiciable)

CHAPTER 12: PRIVILEGES & IMMUNITIES, TAKINGS, AND PROHIBITED LEGISLATION

A. Privileges & Immunities Clauses Distinguished

Recall that the Privileges & Immunities Clause of *state* citizenship under Article IV prohibits serious discrimination against out-of-state _____, chiefly regarding employment.

B. Takings

- Private property shall not be taken for _____ without _____.

    o **Public use**—basically anything the government wants to do with the property. It need only be _____ related to a _____ public purpose. This includes taking private property to resell to another private owner for purposes of economic development.

    o **Just compensation**—_____ at the time of the taking.

- Taking—this is where the controversy often occurs.

    o Taking versus regulation—If there is a taking of property, compensation is required; if there is a mere _____ on property, compensation is _____, even if the regulation reduces the value of the property.

    o **Economic impact**—The adverse economic impact of the government's action does not necessarily mean there has been a taking (e.g., a new prison built next door to a beautiful, countryside home). Many regulations can dramatically affect the value of property but that does not trigger a right to compensation.

    o **Physical occupation**—This is the key question. If the government physically occupies a private owner's property, then a taking has occurred and it owes just compensation.

        ▪ If the government physically occupies only a tiny portion of your property, it is still a taking.

    o No physical occupation—Generally, no physical occupation means that no taking has occurred.

- Zoning—Not a taking and no compensation required, so long as the zoning advances _____ interests and does not extinguish a fundamental attribute of ownership.

- Regulatory Taking—A zoning regulation can be considered a taking when it leaves **no economically viable use** for the property (rare).

    > *Example 30: Two adjacent beachfront lots were purchased for the purpose of building a vacation home. After the lots were purchased, a new zoning law was passed, which stated that no permanent structure could ever be built on the property for environmental reasons. The Supreme Court said that no economically viable use was left for the owner, so this constitutes a taking and compensation is required.*

- Development permits—Development is often conditioned on "concessions" by the developer, such as building an access road or donating land to a park. Such exactions are valid so long as they can be seen as offsetting the _____ impact of the development.

C. Prohibited Legislation

- Bill of Attainder—A bill of attainder is a _____ punishment imposed without judicial trial and is unconstitutional.
- Ex Post Facto Laws—Unconstitutional to expand criminal liability _____, either by creating a new crime that applies retroactively to past conduct or by _____ the penalty for past conduct.
- Contract Clause—Bars states from legislative impairment of _____ contracts, unless there is an _____ need (something like an emergency).

CHAPTER 13: FREEDOM OF RELIGION

A. Establishment of Religion

1. Three-Part Test of *Lemon v. Kurtzman*:

- o Does the law have a _____ purpose?
- o Does the law have a _____ that neither advances nor inhibits religion?
- o Does the law avoid excessive _____ with religion?

2. Deficiency of *Lemon* Test

- o Exceedingly difficult to apply
- o It once was interpreted to condemn aid to religious primary and secondary schools, but **neutral aid** is now allowed (goes to everyone).
  - The government gives aid to parents and the parents are allowed to send their children to the schools of their choice.
  - The parents are making the decision as to whether a religious school gets the money.
    - The government is not picking and choosing recipients.

3. Endorsement

- o It is a violation of the Establishment Clause for the government to endorse one religion over another and also to endorse religion over _____.
  - But, many endorsements are upheld, such as "In God We Trust" on currency.
- o The Supreme Court wants to prevent _____ endorsement of religion (one that might override individual choice).

- The Establishment Clause prohibits government endorsement of religion in a context that might prove coercive on an individual's conscience.
- Examples:
    - Officially-sponsored school prayer is unconstitutional.
    - Officially-sponsored graduation prayer is unconstitutional.
    - Bible reading is okay, but cannot be inspirational.
    - Display of the Ten Commandments is sometimes okay. It can be displayed for secular purposes (e.g., historical or promoting morals), but not to inspire religious belief.
        - Can teach the Ten Commandments in school as an example of an early legal code.
        - Cannot post the Ten Commandments in a classroom and leave it there every day of the school year – designed to inspire religious belief.
        - Cannot post the Ten Commandments in a _____ if the context makes plain that the purpose is to endorse religious belief.
    - Laws prohibiting teaching evolution have been struck down.
    - Legislative prayer is okay for historical practices.
    - Nativity scenes are okay on public property if there is something else there to dilute the religious message (e.g., menorah, Rudolph).

B. **Free Exercise of Religion**

1. **Religious Belief**

   Protected _____ (entitled to hold any belief)

2. **Religious Conduct**

   o Protected qualifiedly

   - Laws regulating religious conduct because of its religious significance are unconstitutional (i.e., laws aimed at religion).
   - Neutral regulation of conduct: neutral, generally applicable laws can be enforced despite religious objections.
       - No right to accommodation
           - No constitutional right to exemption from neutral, generally applicable regulations of conduct (e.g., *Peyote* case).

       Example 31: Religious Freedom Restoration Act (RFRA) overruled the Peyote decision: even neutral, generally applicable laws could not be enforced against religious objectors unless the government had a compelling interest. Insofar as RFRA applied to state and local governments, the Supreme Court struck it down as beyond federal legislative authority (Congress cannot force states to accommodate religious beliefs). RFRA would not be beyond federal legislative authority insofar as it applied to the federal government's own actions. Can states and localities require a religious accommodation for themselves? Yes.

- **Exception:** "Ministerial exception" – in 2012, the Supreme Court held that the 1st Amendment requires a ministerial exception to employment laws.

  - o Non-discrimination employment laws cannot be applied to _____.
  - o Plaintiff was commissioned minister working as a teacher in a religious school. The school fired her in a plain violation of the Americans with Disabilities Act. She sought reinstatement as provided by the statute.
  - o The Supreme Court held that the 1st Amendment precludes claims concerning the employment relation between a religious institution and its ministers.
  - o The federal government cannot regulate employment relations between a religious institution and its ministers.
  - o The term "minister" was construed **broadly**.

- Campus Access: A state university that allows student groups to meet on campus must allow student religious groups equal access.

CHAPTER 14:   FREEDOM OF EXPRESSION (TIME, PLACE, AND MANNER)

A.   Regulation of the Content of Expression

Content-based regulations trigger _____ and are usually _____.

1.   **Expressive Conduct (a.k.a. Symbolic Speech)**

   - o Laws regulating expressive conduct are upheld if:

     - They further an _____ interest;
     - That interest is _____ to the suppression of expression; and
     - The burden on expression is no greater than necessary.

       Example 32: Laws against flag desecration are _____ because they suppress an expressive type of speech to show disapproval.

       Example 33: Laws against public nudity are _____ because public order must be kept, which is unrelated to speech.

   - o The key: If the government is trying to suppress a message, then the law will be struck down; if the government is trying to pursue an interest unrelated to the suppression of expression, then the law will be upheld.

2.   **Vagueness and Overbreadth**

   - o **Vagueness**: Vague laws are ones that give no clear notice of what is prohibited and thus violate due process.

o **Overbreadth**: Overbroad laws are ones that go too far in regulating speech. These laws burden _____ more speech than is necessary to protect a _____ interest and thus violate the 1st Amendment.

> *Example 34:* *Laws that prohibit all nudity in drive-in movies are overbroad.*

> **Exam Tip 9:** Vagueness and overbreadth are almost always seen together on the bar exam.

3. **Prior Restraints**

   o Are especially disfavored and will be struck down even when other forms of regulation might be upheld

   o Injunctions against speech are almost impossible to get.

B. **Regulation of the Time, Place, or Manner of Expression (Content-neutral)**

   - Apply principally in a _____

   - A public forum is a place traditionally reserved for speech activities. These places include a _____, _____, and _____ around public buildings (but not airports).

   - Only time, place, and manner may be regulated in a public forum. There are **three requirements**:

     1) Content neutral: Must be content neutral on its face and as _____. Also, must not allow executive _____.

        > *Example 35:* *A local D.C. ordinance prohibited picketing within 500 feet of a foreign embassy if the picketing sign brought the foreign government into odium or disrepute. This is plainly content-based and is thus, unconstitutional.*

        > *Example 36:* *Parade permit laws giving permits to first come, first served are constitutional. Parade permit laws giving the chief of police discretion are unconstitutional because the law may not be applied in a content-neutral way.*

     2) Alternative channels of communication must be left open: Time, place, or manner law must be a guideline for speech, not a flat prohibition of speech.

        > *Example 37:* *Laws against amplified sound trucks during the night-time hours are fine. Laws against amplified sound during all times and all places would be struck down.*

     3) Must _____ serve a _____ state interest: Under this test, most content-neutral time, place, or manner regulations are upheld

        - Does not require a compelling interest

- Nonpublic forum
  - This includes all kinds of government property that is not a public forum (e.g., government offices, jails, power plants, military bases, etc.). Here, government has great power. Basically, any _____ regulation of speech will be upheld.
    - Viewpoint discrimination is invalid: One clearly unreasonable kind of regulation would be to discriminate based on viewpoint (e.g., between members of different political parties).
    - Disruption of the functions of government: One should go outside to the public sidewalk surrounding the building since that is a public forum.
- Limited public forum
  - Describes a place that is not a traditional public forum, but that the government chooses to open to all comers (e.g., a municipal theater that anyone can rent)
  - In such areas, only time, place, or manner regulations are allowed, but this is a narrow category.

    Example 38: A school auditorium is not a public forum, limited or otherwise. Just because a school auditorium is open to some speech doesn't mean it has to be open to all.

CHAPTER 15: FREEDOM OF EXPRESSION (CONTENT-BASED RESTRICTIONS ON SPEECH)

A. Regulation of Unprotected and Less Protected Expression

There are some categories of speech that can be regulated because of content.

1. **Obscenity: Defined by the rule of "S"**

   - **Sexy**: Must be erotic; appeal to the prurient interest. (Gore and violence are not legally obscene.)
   - **Society sick**: Must be _____ to the _____ person in the society. The society may be the country as a whole, or a particular state, or a major metropolitan area.
   - **Standards**: Must be defined by the proper standards for determining what is obscene, not vague and/or overbroad.

     Example 39: Tax on films displaying frontal nudity. Not a valid law because frontal nudity is not a good enough standard.

   - **Serious value**: The material must lack serious value. If material has serious value (artistic, scientific, educational, or political), it cannot be held legally obscene. This determination is made by the _____, not the jury, and it must be based on a _____ standard, not a local one.

- o Footnotes on obscenity:
  - Minors: A lesser legal standard can be applied to minors, but the government cannot ban adult speech simply because it would be inappropriate for minors.
  - Child pornography: Can be prohibited whether or not it is legally obscene, and possession can be punished even if it is in the _____.
  - Land use restrictions: Narrowly drawn ordinances can regulate the zoning of adult theaters, but cannot ban them entirely.

2. **Incitement**

   Speech is not protected if it is an incitement to _____ violence.

3. **Fighting words**

   - o Words likely to provoke an immediate _____.
     - Must be aimed/targeted at someone, and that person might hit back.
     - General vulgarity is not enough.
     - In theory, fighting words are _____ protected speech.
     - In fact, all fighting words statutes on the bar exam are unconstitutionally _____ and/or _____ (e.g., laws against "hate speech").

4. **Defamation**

   - o False statements of fact (not opinion) damaging to a person's reputation can be prohibited.
   - o Public officials and public figures can recover for defamation only on proof of _____ or _____ falsity.
   - o Private plaintiffs can recover on proof of _____ falsity.

     > ***Example 40:*** *United States v. Alvarez – The Supreme Court struck down the Stolen Valor Act. The Stolen Valor Act made it a crime to falsely claim receipt of military declaration or medals. The Act was struck down by the Supreme Court as applied to a local politician who lied about receiving the Congressional Medal of Honor. The Justices held that the fact that the statement was a blatant self-serving lie did not exempt it from 1st Amendment protection. The prohibition was content-based and was not supported by one of the five recognized categories of unprotected speech. The statute was unconstitutional.*

5. **Commercial Speech**

   - o Most regulations of commercial speech are _____. So long as the advertising is _____ and _____, it must be allowed.
   - o **Test:** Regulation of commercial speech must directly advance a _____ government interest and be _____ tailored to that interest.
   - o Misleading speech: Misleading commercial speech (unlike political speech) may be prohibited.

B. Government Speech

- The 1st Amendment restrictions basically don't apply to the government as a speaker.
- Government as a speaker is free to express a point of view (e.g., advertising the military).
- The government does not have to accept all monuments donated by a private person simply because it accepts one – when the government is controlling the message, it is entitled to say what it wants.
- But specialty license plates bearing messages requested by purchasers are still government speech, so the government can refuse to issue plates that would be offensive to other citizens.

C. Corporations

Corporations have the same 1st Amendment right to speak as individuals.

CHAPTER 16: REGULATION OF THE MEDIA, REGULATION OF ASSOCIATION, SPEECH BY GOVERNMENT EMPLOYEES, AND CAMPAIGN FINANCE

A. Regulation of the Media

1. No Special Privileges

The press/media have no special privileges. They have the _____ rights as everyone else.

> **Exam Tip 10:** When asked about a law on the media, ask whether that law could be applied to you.

> **Example 41:** *Confidential sources for the media. Does a reporter have a constitutional right to refuse to answer grand jury questions about a confidential source? Think of it in terms of yourself: You won't answer questions because you promised that you wouldn't reveal a confidential source. Can the government force you to talk? Yes, you can be put in jail (held in contempt). The same is true of the media/press.*

> **Example 42:** *Open trials – the press has the right of access to open trials.*

2. Broadcasters

- The only special case is broadcasters.
- Traditionally, because of early limits on the broadcast spectrum, government had greater regulatory authority over broadcasters than over print media or the Internet.

B. Regulation of Association

- Freedom of association: cannot be punished because of political associations.
- Loyalty oaths: Public employees can be required to take a loyalty oath to the Constitution, but most loyalty oaths are struck down as _____ and/or _____.
- Bar membership: States can investigate good character, but they cannot deny admission based on political affiliations.

- Political parties: States cannot require _____ primaries.

C. Speech by Government Employees

- General rule: Government employees cannot be hired or fired based on political _____, political _____, or any act of _____.

  o Can be fired for disrupting the workplace or not doing their jobs

- **Exception:** This general rule does not apply to confidential advisors or policy-making employees (e.g., the President's cabinet officers).

D. Campaign Finance

- The use of money to support a political campaign is _____ and the regulation of that money raises First Amendment issues.

- Contributions versus expenditures:

  o Contributions _____ be regulated, provided that the limits are not _____ low.

  o Direct expenditures in support of a candidate, a campaign, or a political issue _____ be regulated.

    ▪ The rationale is to prevent corruption.

- Independent expenditures versus coordinated expenditures:

  o Independent expenditures *cannot* be regulated.

  o A coordinated expenditure is a disguised contribution (the campaign is in control) and _____ be regulated as contributions can be regulated.

- The constitutional protection of direct independent expenditures applies to corporations, including nonprofits, and unions.

- The Supreme Court has consistently rejected _____ of campaign resources as a valid rationale for restricting campaign expenditures.

> *Example 43:* *Congress passed the Millionaires' Amendment, which basically said that if your opponent spends a lot of his/her own money, then your contribution limit is automatically raised. The Supreme Court struck it down.*

[END OF HANDOUT]

Contracts & Sales

CONTRACTS AND SALES
PROFESSOR GEORGE S. GEIS
UNIVERSITY OF VIRGINIA SCHOOL OF LAW

CHAPTER 1:   INTRODUCTION

A. Introduction

- The MBE emphasizes certain topics over others and covers some ground that is rarely studied in first-year Contracts.

  a. **Has an enforceable contract been formed?**

  b. **Has the contract been performed (or, has the performance been excused)?**

  c. **What are the remedies for breach?**

    - Always come back to these three questions if you get lost or confused.

1. What is a contract?

- A contract is just a _____.
  Look for an agreement plus a special legal basis for enforcing the promise (e.g., bargained-for consideration).

  > *Example 1:*   *I promise to give you $1,000 next week. You say "OK...I accept."*
  > *Is this contract? _____*

- The gateway issue: What universe are you in? The law of contracts and sales spans two parallel universes.

  - Universe One is the _____. We are in this universe whenever a contract deals with real estate or _____.

    > *Example 2:*   *You hire me to mow your lawn. Is this contract governed by common law? _____*

  - Universe Two is Article 2 of the UCC. We are in this universe whenever a contract deals with _____.

    Note 1: The UCC governs all parties who enter a goods contract, not just merchants.

    > *Example 3:*   *You agree to buy five dozen pencils from Staples. Is this contract governed by common law? _____*

    Note 2: The law of contracts is almost exactly the same in both universes, with some key differences often arising on the MBE.

- o Mixed Contracts - What universe are you in if the contract has elements of both services and goods?

   Example 4: You agree to purchase a hot-water heater from Boilermaker Inc. for $1,000. As part of the deal, Boilermaker promises to install the hot water heater in your home. Is this contract governed by the UCC? _____

   - **Rule #1**: The _____ rule. You cannot be in two universes at the same time, so mixed contracts must fall into one class or the other.

      - Exception: _____ contracts - If the agreement is divided into two mini-contracts

   Example 5: You agree to purchase a hot-water heater from Boilermaker Inc. for $950. As part of the deal, Boilermaker promises to install the hot-water heater in your home for an additional $50. Is this latter installation part of the deal governed by the UCC? _____ - Common law now applies.

   - **Rule #2**: The _____ rule. Does a good or a service play a bigger role?

   Example 6: You commission the famous artist Andy Warhol to paint your portrait for $1 million. Does the UCC apply? _____

   Example 7: You commission my mother-in-law, Mickey, to paint your portrait for $10. Does the UCC apply? _____

CHAPTER 2:   MAKING AN OFFER

A. In General

- Has an enforceable contract been formed?
- Four big topics within this question:
   1) Agreement (offer and acceptance)
   2) Consideration (and related theories for when you have to keep your promises)
   3) Defenses to formation (incapacity, duress, etc.)
   4) Statute of Frauds
      - If it helps, "All Contracts Don't Stink"

B. Agreement

- A contract is typically created by agreement. This can be broken down into the offer and the acceptance:
   - o Offer: "Will you go to the football game with me?"

- o Acceptance: "Sure"
- o Counteroffer: "How about we go skating instead?"

1. **Offer**

   - o An offer is a manifestation of a willingness to enter into an agreement (by the offeror) that creates a _____ (in the offeree). (Think of the offer as a caterpillar: cute and fuzzy, but fragile.)

   a. **Creating a Legal Offer**

      - ▪ Offer and acceptance are governed by the _____, which means that outward appearance of words and actions is what matters—not secret intentions.

      - ▪ The key question is whether an offeror displays an objectively serious _____ to be bound.

        Example 8: *I offer to "sell you my Jeep Wrangler for $5,000." But I have my fingers crossed behind my back, and in my mind I'm thinking: "Of course I don't mean it; no way I'll sell the Jeep to you." If you say "OK," do we have a contractual agreement? _____.*

        Note 3: Watch out for situations involving anger or humor—the offeror may not be displaying a serious intent to be bound under the objective test.

        Example 9: *You see me on the side of the road with the hood of my Jeep Wrangler open and wires pulled out everywhere. I kick the side of my Jeep and yell "I'd sell this stupid junker for $5!" You yell back, "I ACCEPT." Do we have a contractual agreement? _____*

      - ▪ Expressions of opinion?

        Example 10: *We are talking causally in the law-school parking lot when I lean against my Jeep Wrangler and ask you, "How much do you think this old thing is worth?" You reply (generously), "I don't know, maybe about $10,000." I say "OK, I accept." Do we have a contractual agreement? _____*

      - ▪ An offer must usually be directed to a specific offeree. In other words, you can't accept an offer unless it is directed at you.

        Example 11: *You hear that there are a lot of good deals to be had on Wall Street. So you walk down through the trading pit, saying "I accept…I accept…I accept." Do you have any contracts with the stock traders? _____*

        Note 4: There is a limited exception here for contest offers or reward offers that promise something to anyone who accomplishes a certain task.

        Example 12: *I've lost my pet cat, Monster, and I take out a newspaper advertisement promising $100 to anyone who finds my cat by this Friday. You*

*see the ad, find Monster, and come by my house on Thursday to collect the
reward. Do we have a contractual agreement?* _____

- How specific must your offer be? Here, we have two slightly different rules for our two different universes:

  - **Common law:** All _____ terms must be covered in the agreement. This typically means parties, subject, price, and quantity.
  - **UCC:** In this universe, the law is more willing to _____ and find a contract, even if the agreement leaves out some key terms. Generally, you need only identify **parties**, **subject**, and **quantity** under the UCC—BUT THE ***PRICE DOES NOT NEED TO BE STATED***!

  Example 13: *Beth offers to pay Seth $50 every week to wash her car each Saturday for the next year. Is this deal covered by the common law? _____ Is it a valid offer? _____; it names the parties, the subject, the price, and the duration (quantity of washes).*

  Example 14: *Beth offers to pay Seth a "fair price" every week to wash her car for the next year. Is this a valid offer? _____*

  Example 15: *Bob offers to buy 500 windshield-wiper blades next week from Sue for $5 each. Is this deal covered by the common law? _____ Is it a valid offer? _____*

  Example 16: *Bob offers to buy 500 windshield-wiper blades next week from Sue for a fair price. Is this a valid offer? _____*

  Example 17: *Bob offers to buy windshield-wiper blades next week from Sue for a fair price. Is this a valid offer? _____ because there is no quantity term.*

  Example 18: *Bob offers to buy "all the windshield wiper blades that I need for the next 10 years" from Sue for a fair price. Is this a valid offer? _____, as a requirements contract.*

- **Requirements contract:** "I don't know how many I need over the next X years, but I promise to buy all of them from you."
- **Output contract:** "I don't know how many I will make over the next X years, but I promise to sell all of them to you."

  - Both requirements and output contracts are specific enough under the UCC, even though they don't state an exact quantity term—they provide a formula for calculation.

o A valid offer must give the power of the acceptance to the other side (i.e., the offeree can simply say "I accept" and know that he has concluded the deal).

Example 19: I tell you that "you'd better decide fast if you want to buy my house, as I expect to have a ton of offers next week." You say "I accept." Is this a contract? _____

Example 20: I place an advertisement in the paper promising "to sell my 1994 Jeep Wrangler for $5,000, first come, first served." You show up at my house waving a check and say "I accept." Is this a contract? _____

CHAPTER 3:   TERMINATING THE OFFER AND IRREVOCABLE OFFERS

A. Terminating the Offer (Squashing the Caterpillar)

- Look for one of six recurring fact patterns on the MBE (but also beware of irrevocable offers):

1. The offeror _____ the offer by express communication to the offeree.

    Example 21: I offer to sell you my house for $100. A split-second later I yell "I revoke." Is there a squashed caterpillar? _____

    Example 22: I offer to sell you my house for $1 million. A day later, I decide that I don't want to move and mutter to myself in my office "Forget it. I revoke that offer." Is there a squashed caterpillar? No, the revocation must be _____ to the offeree.

2. The offeree learns that the offeror has taken an action that is absolutely inconsistent with a continuing ability to contract. This is called a _____ revocation.

    Example 23: I offer to sell you my house for $1 million. A day later, you are talking with Mickey and learn that she bought my house that morning for $1.1 million. You run to my house waving a check and say "I accept." Is this a contract? _____

    Example 24: I offer to sell you my house for $1 million. A day later, you are talking with Mickey and learn that I offered to sell her my house that morning *for $1.1 million. You run to my house waving a check and say "I accept." Is this a contract? _____*

Example 25: *I offer to sell you my signed contracts textbook for $100. A day later, you are talking with Mickey and learn that she bought my signed contracts textbook for $100. You run to my house waving a check and say "I accept." Is this a contract? _____, because there are lots of books available to sell.*

3. **The offeree _____ the offer.**

> **Example 26:** *I offer to sell you my Jeep for $5,000. A split second later, you yell, "NO... I mean YES!" Is there a squashed caterpillar? Yes.*

4. **The offeree makes a _____**

> **Example 27:** *I offer to sell you my Jeep for $5,000. A split second later, you say "I offer to buy it for $4,500." I remain silent. Ten seconds later, you say "OK, OK... I'll buy it for $5,000." Is there a contract? _____ the counteroffer squashes the caterpillar.*

> **Note 5:** Be careful to distinguish a counteroffer from a mere counter-inquiry or indecision.

> **Example 28:** *I offer to sell you my Jeep for $5,000. A split second later, you say "Maybe not; I better check my bank balance." I remain silent. Ten seconds later, you say "OK, OK... I'll buy it for $5,000." Is there a contract? Yes.*

5. **The offeror _____** (As described later, death of one party after the contract has been made does not usually terminate the contract; we're talking here about offers).

6. **A reasonable amount of time passes.**

> **Example 29:** *I offer to sell you 1,000 barrels of oil for $100 each. You remain silent, and I never revoke. Five years later, when the price of oil has jumped to $500, you call me up and accept. Is there a contract? _____*

> **Note 6:** Remember that even if an offer is squashed, the offeror can always throw out a new offer with the exact same terms as before ("revival").

B. **Irrevocable Offers (Caterpillar's "Power Shield")**

- The offeror is normally free to revoke at any time prior to acceptance.

> **Example 30:** *I offer to sell you my house for $1 million, and I promise not to revoke this offer for one week. Five minutes later, I say "Never mind...I revoke the offer." Can you still accept? No.*

- An "irrevocable offer" can arise in four ways.

1. **Option**

> *Example 31:* *I offer to sell you my house for $1 million. You also pay me $100 in exchange for a promise that I will not revoke this offer for one week. Five minutes later, I say "Never mind...I revoke the offer." Can you still accept? _____ What if the $100 will go toward the $1 million purchase price if you exercise the option? _____*

2. **Firm Offer**

- A merchant in the UCC universe can make a firm offer to buy or sell goods (i.e., a binding, free option).

   - A merchant is someone who regularly deals in the type of good at issue. In other words, _____, or a person who holds himself out as having knowledge or skills particular to the goods at issue.

   - Also, for purposes of this rule, a merchant is any business person when the transaction is commercial in nature.

- A firm offer must be written, contain an explicit promise not to revoke, and be signed by the _____.

- How long does it last? Either as long as stated in the offer or for a reasonable time period not to exceed _____ days.

> *Example 32:* *I offer to sell you a contracts textbook for $100 and I promise via a signed writing not to revoke this offer for one week. Five minutes later, I say "Never mind...I revoke the offer." Can you still accept? _____, because Professor Geis is not a merchant.*

> *Example 33:* *Your law-school bookstore offers to sell you a contracts textbook for $100 and it promises via a signed writing not to revoke this offer for one week. Five minutes later, the bookstore says "Never mind...I revoke the offer." Can you still accept? _____*

> *Example 34:* *Your law-school bookstore offers to sell you a contracts textbook for $100. Five minutes later, it says "Never mind...I revoke the offer." Can you still accept? _____*

> *Example 35:* *Your law-school bookstore offers to sell you a contracts textbook for $100 and it promises via a signed writing not to revoke this offer for one week. Ten days later, you stop by the bookstore to accept the offer. Can you still accept? _____, as long as a reasonable amount of time has not squashed the caterpillar. The firm offer has expired and the bookstore may now revoke the offer. However, there is no indication that the bookstore has revoked the offer. The default question is whether a reasonable amount of time has passed (see Example 29).*

3. Offeree has started performance

o A unilateral offer to contract cannot be revoked by the offeror if the offeree has started performance.

- What is a unilateral contract? This arises from a promise that requests acceptance by an _____ of the promisee (versus a return promise of the promisee, which is called a "bilateral contract"). See Example 12, above.

  Example 36: *"I promise to pay you $1,000 if you promise to paint my house."*
  Unilateral or bilateral? _____

  Example 37: *"I promise to pay you $1,000 if you paint my house." Unilateral or bilateral?* _____

o Because a unilateral contract can be accepted only by performance, the law gives the promisee the right to finish.

  Example 38: *I promise $10,000 to the winner of a swim race to Alcatraz Island. The swimmers dive off the dock and are going strong toward the island. When they're about halfway, I stand up on Fisherman's Wharf with my bullhorn and yell "I REVOKE!" Can the winner of the race insist on the prize?* _____ *this is a unilateral contract with part performance.*

  Note 7: The offeree need not complete the performance and can stop at any time.

  Example 39: *You are swimming in the Alcatraz race, but you get tired and swim to a boat. Can I sue you for breach of contract? No; there's no agreement.*

4. Detrimental Reliance

o An offer cannot be revoked if the offeree reasonably and detrimentally relies on the offer in a foreseeable manner.

- Look especially for a general contractor/subcontractor context.
- This is a special variant of the reliance theory of contractual liability (sometimes called "promissory estoppel")

  Example 40: *A builder who is bidding on a law-school building project receives an offer from a subcontractor to supply all of the carpet for $20,000. Armed with this knowledge, the builder offers to renovate the building for $100,000. Before the law school accepts the bid, the subcontractor calls to revoke its carpet offer. Can the general contractor builder still accept the carpet offer from the subcontractor?* _____

CHAPTER 4:   ACCEPTANCE, INCLUDING THE MAILBOX RULE

A. Acceptance

- An acceptance is a manifestation of a willingness to enter into the agreement by the offeree.

1. Acceptance is governed by the _____ test.

   o The starting place here is a famous phrase: "The offeror is master of the offer." This means that the offeree must accept the offer according to the rules of the offer.

> *Example 41:   I offer to sell you my Jeep for $50 and state that in order to accept this offer, you must spring into a handstand, walk across the room to me, and sign this piece of paper. You look at me funny, just stand there, and say "I accept." Is there a contract? _____*

   o Unilateral versus bilateral offers. As master of the offer, the offeror gets to decide which type of offer to make, and the offeree must play by those rules.

> *Example 42:   "I promise to pay you $1,000 if, and only when, you paint my house." You say "I accept." Is there a contract? _____ you haven't done what I said you must do to accept.*

> *Example 43:   Bob sends a letter to Sue, reading "please ship me 500 windshield-wiper blades next week for $5 each." Sue mails back a letter saying "I accept." Unilateral or bilateral offer? Unclear without more information. Is there a contract? _____, under the modern approach.*

> *Example 44:   Bob sends a letter to Sue, reading "please ship me 500 windshield-wiper blades by next week for $5 each." Sue ships 500 wiper blades the next day. Is there a contract? _____*

> **Note 8:   **TRICK**What if the seller tries to accept by shipping the wrong goods? The UCC treats this as *acceptance plus breach.***

> *Example 45:   Bob sends a letter to Sue, reading "please ship me 500 Bosch windshield-wiper blades by next week for $5 each." Sue ships 500 Sloshed wiper blades the next day. Is there a contract? _____ but also a breach.*

B. Other Acceptance Rules

1. The offer must be _____ to the person trying to accept it

You can't accept an offer directed elsewhere. See Example 11, above.

2. Even with an open-to-all offer, you must know about that offer in order to accept it.

> *Example 46:   I've lost my pet cat, Monster, and I take out a newspaper advertisement promising $100 to anyone who finds my cat by this Friday. You never see the ad, but you find Monster roaming near my house and return the*

cat to me. Later, you learn about the reward offer and come by to collect. Do
we have a contractual agreement? _____

3. **You must communicate your acceptance to the other party in order for it to become effective.**

    Example 47: *You offer to buy my contracts textbook for $50. I say "I'll think*
    about it." That night, while I'm alone brushing my teeth, I say to myself "that's
    a good offer... I should really accept that offer... in fact, I do accept that offer
    right now... I accept!" The next morning you call me up and revoke the offer. Is
    there a contract? _____

    o   This requirement of communication can sometimes raise tricky timing issues. This is the
        subject of the _____ rule.

4. **Mailbox rule**

    o   Recall the general rationale behind the mailbox rule: to determine when an acceptance has
        been legally communicated when there is some delay between sending and receiving.
    o   The rule: An acceptance sent by mail is valid when the letter is _____
    o   Does not apply:

        ▪   If the offeree sends something else first (e.g., rejection, counteroffer).
        ▪   To other types of communication (e.g., revocations, rejections).
        ▪   To _____ contracts.
        ▪   It is unclear whether this applies to other media (fax, e-mail, etc.).

        Example 48: *I send you an offer. You mail back your acceptance. I call you*
        before I receive your letter and revoke. Is there a contract? _____

        Example 49: *I send you an offer. You mail back your acceptance. The letter*
        gets lost and never shows up. Is there a contract? _____.

        Example 50: *I send you an offer. You mail back your acceptance. You change*
        your mind and call me up before I receive your letter to reject the offer. Is there
        a contract? _____ unless I detrimentally relied on the rejection.

        Example 51: *I send you an offer. You mail back a rejection. You change your*
        mind and mail back an acceptance a few hours later. Both letters arrive at my
        house on the same day. Is there a contract? It depends on _____
        _____.

5. **Acceptance without communication (by silence)**

    o   There are some exceptions to the requirement that you must communicate an acceptance
        to the offeror. Look for one of the following:

        ▪   Unilateral _____ offers or contests (e.g., the Carbolic Smoke Ball case)

- Unilateral offers in which the parties are geographically close (such that the offeror will see that performance has occurred)
- A _____ of silence serving as acceptance (such that the offeree should reasonably notify the offeror if she does not accept)
- The offeror says that acceptance must come via silence, and the offeree intends to accept the offer by silence

> *Example 52:* *I've lost my pet cat, Monster, and I take out a newspaper advertisement promising $100 to anyone who finds my cat by this Friday. You see the ad, find Monster, and come by my house on Thursday to collect the reward. Can you get the money even though you never communicated your acceptance to me?* _____

> *Example 53:* *Mickey buys her weekly keg of beer by calling up Pabst Blue Ribbon on Monday and leaving a message requesting delivery on Friday. One Monday, she leaves her message as usual, but Pabst does not deliver the keg that Friday. Distraught, Mickey asks if she has a contract for this keg. Does she?* _____

> *Example 54:* *I offer to sell you my Jeep for $500,000, saying "you may accept this offer by remaining silent for five seconds." You stare at me but don't say a word. After five seconds pass, do we have a contract?* _____ *unless you intend to accept.*

6. Implied-in-fact contracts

You can communicate an acceptance without writing or speaking. This communication by gestures or actions is called an "implied-in-fact" contract.

> *Example 55:* *I walk into Cheapcuts, a popular haircut franchise where the service offerings and prices are posted above the cash register. The energetic receptionist offers to put my name in, and I sit down to wait. A haircutter comes forward to call my name; I follow and she cuts my hair. When I walk toward the exit, the receptionist tells me that I owe them $15. Must I pay— even though I never said a single word?* _____
>
> _____

CHAPTER 5:   COUNTEROFFERS AND UCC § 2-207

A. Counteroffer

- The **common law** universe uses the _____ rule.

  o The terms in the acceptance must match the terms of the offer exactly—or it is not an acceptance, but a counteroffer.

- Treat conditional acceptance as just another form of counteroffer. (Look for words like "if," "only if," "on the condition that," "but," etc.)

    Example 56: *I offer to mow your lawn on Saturday for $50. You say, "OK, if you come over on Sunday." Do we have a contract?* _____

B. UCC § 2-207

- The UCC is more forgiving for acceptances that don't match the terms of the offer exactly. It replaces the mirror image rule with § 2-207.
- The main intuition of § 2-207 is that a purported acceptance that does not match the terms of the offer exactly can still count as a legal acceptance in many circumstances.

    o But just because there's been an acceptance, do not assume that all terms in the purported acceptance will govern the contract.

    Note 9: It does not matter whether the parties are merchants for this part of § 2-207.

    Example 57: *I run a business on the side: Geis's Chainsaws. You send me a purchase order requesting a chainsaw for $400. On the back of this form is an indemnification provision saying "seller agrees to indemnify buyer in the event of a lawsuit." I send back a confirming memo that is exactly the same as the purchase order, except for a provision on the back saying "buyer agrees to indemnify seller in the event of a lawsuit." The most likely outcome - we don't ever notice the difference, because nobody ever gets hurt. But it is possible that a dispute arises and one of us tries to back out of the deal. Is there a contract and, if so, which indemnity term, if any, controls.*

- Text of **§ 2-207(1):** "A definite and seasonable expression of acceptance [or a written confirmation] which is sent within a reasonable time operates as an acceptance even though it states terms additional to or different from those offered or agreed upon, unless acceptance is expressly made conditional upon assent to the additional or different terms."

    Example 58: *You send a purchase order requesting acceptance by this Friday. I send back my confirming memo two weeks later. Is there a contract?* _____ *because the purported acceptance is not timely.*

    Example 59: *You send a purchase order. I send back a timely confirming memo saying "Thanks, but I no longer sell chainsaws; however, I have a hand saw which you can have on the same terms." Is there a contract?* _____*, because this is not a definite acceptance of the original offer.*

    Example 60: *You send a purchase order. I send back a timely confirming memo saying "OK, on the condition that you agree to indemnify me against a lawsuit for harm arising from the chainsaw." Do we have a contract?* _____

> *Example 61:* *Same facts as Example 60, but my acceptance letter has a bunch of terms on the back, all of which match yours, except for a clause that says "Buyer agrees to indemnify seller against a lawsuit for harm arising from the chainsaw." Do we have a contract? _____, under § 2-207(1). Unlike #60, in #61 the change was not a major part of the agreement; it was just one term that was changed.*

- The new term in the purported acceptance may control under **§ 2-207(2),** but only if all of the following are true:

  o Both parties are merchants;
  o The new term does not materially alter the deal;
  o The initial offer did not expressly limit acceptance to its terms; and
  o The offeror does not object within a reasonable time to the new term.

- It is very difficult for the new terms in the acceptance to govern the contract.

  > *Example 62:* *Same facts as Example 61. Is my indemnity term part of the contract? _____*

  > *Example 63:* *Does the answer change if the buyer is Lowes? _____ if the indemnification is _____*

- If there is not a real contract but the parties still act as if there is an agreement (for example, by exchanging goods for money), only the terms that both writings agree on become part of the contract, with other terms supplied by the UCC acting as default rules.
- UCC § 2-207 also governs the situation in which two parties have a contract (often a verbal agreement), and one party sends over a confirming memo with additional terms that go further than the earlier agreement. Do these terms come in?
- § 2-207(1): [A definite and seasonable expression of acceptance or] **a written confirmation which is sent within a reasonable time operates as an acceptance** [even though it states terms additional to or different from those offered or agreed upon, unless acceptance is expressly made conditional upon assent to the additional or different terms.]

  > **Note 10:** If you see this fact pattern (early agreement + written confirmation with new terms), work through the same steps as above for § 2-207(2). But recognize that the new terms will very rarely come in.

  > **Editor's Note 1:** Although Professor Geis states that you shouldn't have to worry about the "knock-out" rule, there is a chance that it may appear on the bar exam. The knockout rule applies when there is a contract between merchants and the offer and acceptance contain conflicting terms. See the MBE Contracts and Sales outline for more details.

CHAPTER 6: CONSIDERATION, INCLUDING MODIFICATION AND PREEXISTING DUTY RULE

A. Consideration (And Related Theories) - The "C" in "All Contracts Don't Stink."

1. General Nature of Bargained-For Consideration

o   Consideration in the law means a deal in which the parties exchange promises involving a legal _____

> **Exam Tip 2:** The bar examiners like to test situations in which bargained-for consideration is missing. You can quickly determine whether there is a problem here by asking the following questions:
>
> Who is making the _____ that needs to be supported by law? (That person is the promisor; the other party is the promisee.)
>
> Is there a _____ to the promisor or a _____ to the promisee? (You need just one, not both.)
>
> [**Note:** Most courts find consideration if there is a detriment to the promisee, regardless of whether there was a benefit to the promisor.]
>
> Was this _____? (In other words, did the parties think that they were making a deal when they exchanged promises?)

> ***Example 64:*** *I promise to pay you $1,000 if you don't watch the next season of The Bachelor. You do not watch the show, but I refuse to pay you the money. Who is the promisor? Professor Geis. Who is the promisee? You. Did I benefit from the exchange of promises? Not in a legal sense. Did you incur a legal detriment, even though not watching the show is good for you? _____ Is there bargained-for consideration? _____*

> **Note 11:** Key—Not doing something that you are legally entitled to do is a legal detriment.

o   Gift promises and conditional gifts do **not** count as bargained-for consideration.

> ***Example 65:*** *Every year for Christmas, Mickey gives me a tacky tie, and I give her an ugly sweater. Can she sue me this year if I refuse to give her a present? _____ we are exchanging gifts, not bargaining.*

> ***Example 66:*** *I promise to give you my Jeep if you come to my house to pick it up. Is there bargained-for consideration? _____ I am not bargaining for you to come.*

   ▪   Example 66 is a conditional gift (I would never sue you if you don't come over).

2. Tricks Regarding Consideration

o   **Adequacy of consideration** (nominal consideration): A pretense of consideration is insufficient; there must be some adequacy of consideration.

> ***Example 67:*** *I promise to sell you my Jeep for $1. Is there bargained-for consideration? _____, one dollar is inadequate.*

> **Note 12:** Any difference in economic value between the items exchanged is not grounds for finding that a contract did not exist due to inadequate consideration. As long as the exchanged item has subjective value to the person receiving it, consideration will be adequate.

- o An **illusory promise**: A promisor must clearly commit to the deal or there is no consideration.

    > *Example 68:* *You promise to buy my Jeep for $5,000 on December 1, "if you feel like it." Is there bargained-for consideration? _____*

    - There must be a way for the promisor to breach.
    - Look for situations where one side is not really committing to the deal under the objective test. Look for language like:

        - "I would like to buy your car when I have more money." or
        - "When the economy gets better, I will pay $5,000 for your car."

    - Satisfaction contracts are not illusory. They are real contracts with consideration.

        > *Example 69:* *I promise to pay Mickey $500 if she paints a portrait of my family that meets my satisfaction. She says OK. Is there bargained-for consideration?*
        >
        > _____

    - Output and requirements contracts (see Example 18, above) are not illusory promises

        - There is a way for a party to breach (by requiring the product and purchasing from others or by making the product and selling to others).

- o **Past consideration** is not consideration.

    > *Example 70:* *You are trying to win a race to Alcatraz, when the sharks start to circle. I swing my boat over to pick you up. Grateful, you promise to pay me $500 for the rescue. Is there bargained-for consideration? No.*

- o **Promising not to sue** (settlement of a legal claim) will act as consideration as long as there is an _____ in the validity of the claim and a reasonable basis for that belief.

B. Contract Modification and the Preexisting Duty Rule

1. Common Law

- o Common law has historically followed the preexisting duty rule, which means that a promise to do something that you are already legally obligated to do (by prior contract or otherwise) is not consideration.

    > *Example 71:* *You rent an apartment from Slumlord for one year; the rent is $2,000 per month. Later that year, you start running short on cash, and you both agree to modify the rent to $1,500 per month. Can Slumlord sue you at*

the end of that month for the extra $500? _____, at common law. (There is
no bargained-for consideration for the modification contract.)

- Exceptions include a change in performance, a third party promising to pay, or unforeseen difficulties that would excuse performance.

    Example 72: *Same facts as Example 71, except you agree to re-rent the apartment for another year when the rent is lowered to $1,500 per month. Can Slumlord sue you at the end of that month for the extra $500? No.*

    Example 73: *Same facts as Example 71, except Slumlord's sister (Slumlady) agrees to cover $500 of your monthly rent if you stay in the apartment. Is there bargained-for consideration? Yes.*

- Is promising partial payment for release from a debt obligation binding? The key is to ask whether the debt is currently due and _____. If so, the modification is not binding.

    Example 74: *Mickey owes me $50,000, due today. I promise to release her from this debt if she can pay me at least $1,000. If she does, can I sue her for the other $49,000? _____, because the modification is not valid.*

    Example 75: *Same facts as Example 74, except that the debt is not due until next year. If Mickey accepts the deal and pays me the $1,000 today, can I sue her next year for the other $49,000? _____ because the debt is not currently due.*

2. **Modification under the UCC**

    The UCC universe does not follow the preexisting duty rule. Rather, you should simply ask whether a modification is made in _____. If so, it is binding even _____ new consideration.

    Example 76: *Mickey contracts with Pabst Blue Ribbon to buy her weekly keg of beer for $75. Later in the week, Pabst calls back to say that there is a worker shortage that week, and it can't get her the beer unless she pays $100 (so Pabst can outsource delivery to FedEx). Mickey says, "OK, charge what you must; I need my beer." Is the price modification binding? _____*

    Example 77: *Same facts as Example 76, but Pabst knows that Mickey will do anything for her beer. On Friday morning, Pabst calls to say, "you better pay us $1,000 or we won't deliver your keg this afternoon." Mickey says, "OK, charge what you must." Is the price modification binding? _____*

CHAPTER 7: CONSIDERATION SUBSTITUTES

A. Other Theories of Promissory Liability (Consideration Substitutes)

1. Promissory Estoppel (or Reliance)

o Reliance can arise when one party makes a promise, and the other party relies on that promise to take some action.

o Three key elements for a claim under reliance:

- A promise is made that would be _____ _____ to induce reliance;

- The promisee does indeed take detrimental action in reliance on the promise; and

- _____ can be avoided only by enforcement of the promise.

> *Example 78:* *Grandpa Moneybags promises to pay his granddaughter Katie $100,000 next month so that she doesn't have to work anymore. Katie quits her job. Is this bargained-for consideration? No. Does Grandpa nevertheless have to keep his promise? Maybe yes, under a reliance theory.*

> **Note 13:** Charities do not need to prove detrimental reliance when pursuing a reliance theory to collect on a charitable-gift promise.

- Remember also that reliance was discussed earlier with respect to irrevocable offers in the general contractor/subcontractor context, as a special type of caterpillar "power shield."

2. Quasi-Contract

o Quasi-contract is sometimes called a "contract implied-in-law."

o Think of this as a situation in which you would have made a contract if you could have, but you couldn't. Or, look for a situation in which one party conferred a benefit on another party, and it would be fair to pay for that benefit.

o Quasi-contract elements:

- The plaintiff confers a _____ on the defendant;

- The plaintiff reasonably expected to get paid; and

- It would be unfair to let the defendant keep the benefit without paying (look for an opportunity to decline or a good reason why there was no opportunity to decline).

> *Example 79:* *I am teaching away for this bar review course, when I suddenly grab my chest and keel over with a heart attack. A student rushes out to hire a doctor, who saves my life. Later, that student asks me to pay her back for the doctor's fee. Must I? _____*

Example 80: *I hear about this cool thing called quasi-contract and rush over to paint your house while you are taking the bar exam. When you come home, I stick out my hand and demand a reasonable payment for the paint job. Will I recover? _____*

Note 14: Quasi-contract damages are often limited, as justice requires, to the fair value of the benefit conferred.

- More generally, whenever you see a situation that does not satisfy the normal requirements for a contract but still strikes you as unfair, ask whether quasi-contract might apply.

3. Moral Obligation Plus Subsequent Promise (the "Half Theory")

- A few jurisdictions have some case law suggesting that a moral obligation plus a subsequent promise to pay can be binding. Normally, this would be past consideration and thus nonbinding.

  Example 81: *Recall the facts of Example 70. You are trying to win a race to Alcatraz, when the sharks start to circle. I swing my boat over to pick you up. Grateful, you promise to pay me $500 for the rescue. Is there bargained-for consideration? _____ Might I argue moral obligation plus subsequent promise? _____*

4. The Seal

- Does a seal on a document act as a consideration substitute in most jurisdictions? _____

CHAPTER 8: DEFENSES PART 1: MISUNDERSTANDING, INCAPACITY, AND MISTAKE

A. Defenses to Contract Formation—The "D" in "All Contracts Don't Stink."

- Seven Defenses:

  1) Misunderstanding

  2) Incapacity

  3) Mistake

  4) Fraud/Misrepresentation/Nondisclosure

  5) Duress

  6) Illegality

  7) Unconscionability

1. Misunderstanding

- Look for situations where each party attaches different meanings to the same words. To make out a defense here, you must show that:

1) The parties use a _____ that is open to two or more reasonable interpretations (so the objective test cannot apply);

2) Each side attaches a different meaning to the term; and

3) Neither party knows, or should know, of the confusion.

> ***Example 82:*** *I verbally contract to sell you a bike for "twelve fifty." You think I'm trying to unload the bike by selling it for $12.50. I think you recognize that this is a rare edition bike and you are willing to pay $1,250. Do we have a contract? _____.*

> ***Example 83:*** *Same facts as Example 82, except I know that you would never pay $1,250 for the bike and must think the price is $12.50. Is there a contract? _____. For how much? _____*

2. Incapacity

- o Who lacks the capacity to make a contract?

    - ▪ Minors (under the age of 18)
    - ▪ People who are mentally ill—two standards:
        - • The person cannot understand the nature and consequences of his actions; or
        - • The person cannot act in a _____ _____ in relation to the transaction (if the other side knows this)
    - ▪ Very intoxicated persons (if the other side knows this)

- o The standard changes according to the type of incapacity.

    - ▪ Minors = blanket protection
    - ▪ Intoxicated persons = depends on what the other side knows or should know at the time
    - ▪ Mentally ill = intermediate level of protection

- o What happens if you make a contract with a person who lacks capacity?

    - ▪ The contract is _____ meaning that the incapacitated party can disaffirm
    - ▪ For necessities, the party without capacity must still pay _____ (not necessarily the contract price)
        - • What's a necessity? Something you really need to live, like food, clothing, or shelter
    - ▪ A party without capacity can ratify the deal by keeping the benefits of the contract after capacity is obtained.

Example 84: *Amelia is aged 16 but looks much older. She buys a used airplane for $5,000. The wings fall off as she pulls away from the dealer's lot. Can Amelia get her money back? Yes.*

Example 85: *Same facts as Example 84, except the plane flies OK. Amelia turns 18 and continues to use the plane. Can she get her money back now? No.*

Example 86: *Same facts as Example 84, except Amelia is now 32 and takes LSD prior to buying the plane. She has no idea what she is doing, but witnesses say she seemed perfectly lucid while negotiating and buying the plane. Can Amelia get her money back? No.*

3. **Mistake**

   o A mistake is a belief that is not in accord with a _____ fact.

      Example 87: *Mickey contracts with her stockbroker to buy a share of Google stock for $500. When the price drops to $400 the following month, can she get out of the deal by saying, "I made a mistake; I thought the price was going to go up?" _____*

   o **Mutual mistake** (affecting both parties) lets the adversely affected party rescind if:

      ▪ There is a mistake of fact, existing at the time that the deal is made;

      ▪ The mistake relates to a _____ assumption of the contract and has a material impact on the deal; and

      ▪ The impacted party did not _____ of mistake.

      Example 88: *We are walking along a trail, when I lean down to pick up a shiny rock. "Wow," I say, "look at that diamond. I'll sell it to you for $10,000." You agree and pay me the money but are sad to learn later that the rock is plain quartz. Can you get out of the contract? _____, for mutual mistake.*

      Example 89: *Same facts as Example 88, except I say "Wow look at that shiny rock; I wonder what it is. Well, whatever it is, I'll sell it to you for $10,000." Can you get out of the contract? _____ this is a "compromise of conscious ignorance."*

   o _____ mistake (one party) lets the adversely affected party rescind if:

      ▪ She can prove all of the elements of mutual mistake; **plus**

         • The mistake would make the contract unconscionable; or

         • The other side knew of, had reason to know of, or caused the mistake.

      Example 90: *Mickey decides to move to an annual purchasing model for her beer kegs and solicits 25 brewers for offers. Twenty-four of the brewers quote her prices in the $100,000 to $120,000 range. But one brewer makes a mistake* *about the quantity of kegs she lists and quotes a price of $10,000 for the year's supply. Can Mickey snap up the last deal?* _____

Note 15: Only the adversely affected party can claim the defense.

CHAPTER 9:   DEFENSES PART 2: FRAUD, DURESS, ILLEGALITY, AND UNCONSCIONABILITY

A. Defenses to Contract Formation, Continued

4. Fraud, Misrepresentation, and Nondisclosure

- o A **misrepresentation** is a statement at the time of contracting that is not true. It can be intentional (fraudulent) or accidental.

- o To assert this defense, the party must show:

  - ▪ A misrepresentation of a _____ (not opinion);
  - ▪ That is _____ or fraudulent (intentional); and
  - ▪ That is made under circumstances in which it is justifiable to _____ on the misrepresentation.

    Example 91: Before buying my Jeep Wrangler for $3,000, you ask me how the car runs. I say "it's a great car." In actuality, it only runs on four out of six cylinders, and the radiator leaks. Can you get out of the contract? _____, if this is an opinion.

    Example 92: Same facts as Example 91, except you ask me if the car runs OK, and I say "yes," knowing that it has all the mentioned problems. Can you get out of the contract? _____, due to intentional fraud.

    Example 93: Same facts as Example 92, except I don't know about these problems. Can you get out of the contract? _____, due to material misrepresentation.

    Example 94: Same facts as Example 93, except the only thing wrong with the car is that the cigarette lighter doesn't work. Can you get out of the contract? _____

- o **Fraud in the Execution** - Fraud in the execution is when you trick someone into signing something that she doesn't even know is a contract.

    Example 95: You're walking down the street when you run into Dave Matthews. You ask for his autograph and then laugh when he hands back the paper. If you show that he just signed a contract promising to play music at your birthday party for just a $100 fee, is Dave bound? No, this is fraud in the execution.

- o **Nondisclosure**—The other party doesn't learn the truth about something, but now you just remain quiet.
  - Normally, you need not tell the other side about all material facts related to the deal.
  - But watch out for a special (fiduciary) relationship or active

  _____

  Example 96: *I'm selling my house, but I have a bad termite problem. I hide the ripples in the floor with carpets and put plants on the damaged stairways. You buy the house but soon learn of the termite infestation. Can you get out of the contract for nondisclosure?* _____

5. **Duress**
   - o An improper threat that deprives a party from making a meaningful choice to contract
   - o _____ duress arises when one party makes threats to induce another party to contract (or modify a contract).

   Example 97: *Pabst threatens to breach a contract with Mickey to sell her beer unless Mickey agrees to extend the contract for another year at double the price. Mickey has exhausted her credit with every other brewer and feels that she has no choice but to accede to this threat. Is Mickey bound for the next year?* _____

   - o Undue influence arises when a party puts very intense sales pressure on another party—who often seems weak minded or susceptible to high-pressure sales tactics.

6. **Illegality**
   - o Illegal contracts are unenforceable. But, a contract entered in furtherance of an illegal act (that is not itself illegal) will still be enforced.

   Example 98: *Mobster Tony Soprano agrees to pay Paulie $10,000 to knock off Artie. Is this legally binding as a contract? _____, because it is for an illegal action. If Paulie doesn't knock off Artie, then Tony cannot bring Paulie into court and sue him for breach.*

   Example 99: *Same facts as Example 98. Paulie hires a taxi to drive him over to Artie's restaurant. Can Paulie claim an illegality defense to avoid paying the cab driver? _____*

   - o Typically, the law will just leave the parties where they stand, but there is a modern trend toward allowing less-guilty parties to recover restitution (i.e., get their money back).

   Example 100: *Same facts as Example 99, except Tony pays Paulie the $10,000 up front. If Paulie refuses to perform, can Tony get the money back? _____ The losses will lie where they may.*

o   Contracts against public policy will not be enforced. These are contracting situations that are not formally illegal but present some other policy concern (e.g., a broad exculpatory agreement).

7. Unconscionability

o   This is the ultimate contract defense. Everything seems fine, but a court simply looks at the deal and says, "No, this shocks my conscience. It's unconscionable."

o   Recall the two varieties of unconscionability:

▪   _____ unconscionability: A defect in the bargaining process itself, such as a hidden term (surprise) or an absence of meaningful choice (no other contracting option);

▪   _____ unconscionability: A rip-off in some term of the contract.

o   Some jurisdictions require both varieties to be present before a deal is stuck down; others may act if only one variety is present.

▪   *Example: When you started law school, you signed a license to use Westlaw products. Buried on page 110 of a 235-page contract is a clause in which you agree to pay 25% of your salary for the first 5 years after you graduate law school.*

CHAPTER 10:   STATUTE OF FRAUDS PART 1

A. Statute of Frauds - The "S" in "All Contracts Don't Stink."

•   The Statute of Frauds (SOF) is a barrier that some contracts must meet in order to become "real" (legally binding).

•   The basic goal of the Statute of Frauds is to prevent false assertions about a contract that was never really created.

> *Example 101:*   *I walk up to you one day and say "I'm so glad that you agreed to sell me your house for just $50,000." You stare at me puzzled and reply, "Who are you? We've never met." I laugh and say, "See you in court." Will I win the lawsuit? _____; the Statute of Frauds will bar my claim.*

•   You should always ask two questions here:

5)   Gateway question: Does the Statute of Frauds apply to this transaction? Are we in SOF world?

6)   If so, has the Statute of Frauds been satisfied?

•   Contracts in SOF world require a higher and special form of proof—typically a writing signed by the defendant or some performance on the purported deal.

1. **Is the contract in the Statute of Frauds world?**

   o Recall that the Statute of Frauds applies to only a few types of contracts:

      ▪ Marriage: A contract made in consideration of marriage (like a prenup).
      ▪ Suretyship: A contract promising to guarantee the debt of another.
      ▪ One Year: A contract that by its terms cannot be performed within one year from its making.
      ▪ UCC: Applies to goods contracts for a price of $500 or more
      ▪ Real property: A contract for the sale of an interest in real property.

   o You should think about Lemonheads candy and its mascot: Mr. SOUR (or M. SOUR):

      Example 102: *Mickey buys beer on credit from Pabst, promising to pay $499 at the end of the month for her five kegs. Pabst sues her at the end of the month for failure to pay. Are we in Statute of Frauds world? _____*

      Example 103: *Same facts as Example 102, except Pabst now sues me, claiming that I had offered to pay Mickey's bill if she could not. Are we in Statute of Frauds world? _____, suretyship.*

   o **The Main Purpose Exception**—If the main purpose in agreeing to pay the debt of another is for the surety's own economic advantage, then we are not in Statute of Frauds world.

      Example 104: *Same facts as Example 103, except Pabst sells beer to Mickey that she brings over to my house for weekly parties. Pabst sues me, claiming that I had offered to pay Mickey's bill if she could not. Are we in Statute of Frauds world? _____, because of the main purpose exception.*

   o The one-year rule is interpreted very narrowly; the question is whether there is _____ _____ that the contract could be performed within one year.

      Example 105: *I verbally contract with the mayor of Charlottesville to build an exact replica of the Egyptian pyramids at the edge of town for $50 billion. Are we in Statute of Frauds world? _____ It may be difficult, but it is not impossible to complete the contract within one year.*

      Example 106: *I verbally contract with the mayor of Charlottesville to manage all city elections through 2028 for $50 per election. Are we in Statute of Frauds world? _____*

      Example 107: *I contract on April 1 to hire a 1L student as my RA for three months during her 2L summer. Are we in Statute of Frauds world? _____ The length of the employment is only three months, but it won't even start until after one year from now.*

Example 108: Luke Skywalker hires me to teach him contract law for the rest of his life. Are we in Statute of Frauds world? _____ It is possible that Skywalker could die within one year.

Note 16: All contracts involving real property are not in Statute of Frauds world; only those transferring an interest in the property. Also, leases of less than one year are usually not in Statute of Frauds world.

Example 109: Skywalker hires Chewbacca to build a house on an acre that Skywalker owns on Endor. Is this contract in Statute of Frauds world? _____ It involves land but does not transfer an interest in land.

Example 110: Skywalker agrees to sell his Endor acre to Chewbacca for $5 million. Is this contract in Statute of Frauds world? _____

Example 111: Mickey verbally contracts with Pabst to buy exactly $500 in beer. Are we in Statute of Frauds world? _____, under the UCC part of the SOF.

CHAPTER 11: STATUTE OF FRAUDS PART 2

A. Has the Statute of Frauds been satisfied?

- There are two main ways to satisfy the Statute of Frauds—by _____ and by _____. The exact requirements differ between our parallel universes.

1. Services Contracts

o Full performance of a services contract by either side satisfies the Statute of Frauds.

Example 112: Skywalker verbally agrees to hire Chewbacca to build a house on his Endor property. In exchange, Skywalker will provide "charm lessons" to Chewie for the next three years. Is this contract in Statute of Frauds world? _____ Chewie builds the house, but Skywalker refuses to provide the lessons, asserting a Statute of Frauds defense. Is Skywalker right? _____

o Part performance of a services contract does not satisfy the Statute of Frauds.

2. A writing signed by the party against whom the contract is asserted

o Do you need both signatures on the writing? _____
o Does the writing have to be a formal contract? _____
o But it must cover the fundamental facts by:

- Indicating that a contract has been made;
- Identifying the parties; and
- Containing the essential elements of the deal.

3. **Real Estate**

   o A signed writing will satisfy the Statute of Frauds.

   o But, unlike other service deals, part performance of a real estate contract can satisfy the Statute of Frauds if any two of the following three elements are met:

   1) Possession

   2) Payment

   3) Improvements _____

   > *Example 113: Chewbacca claims that Skywalker agreed to sell his Endor acre for $5 million. There is no signed writing, but Chewie now possesses the land and has erected a nice house by the lake. Is this contract in Statute of Frauds world? _____. Is the Statute of Frauds satisfied? _____.*

4. **Goods**

   o A signed writing will satisfy the Statute of Frauds, but the requirements differ a little under the UCC:

   - There is no need to mention the price;
   - The writing must mention the _____ _____ sold.

   o The contract is only enforceable under the Statute of Frauds for the quantity mentioned.

   > *Example 114: Mickey verbally contracts with Pabst to buy 100 kegs of beer for $75 each. Later, Pabst sends her a signed confirmation order stating that the parties agree to contract for 50 kegs of beer (no price is listed). Even later, Pabst asserts a Statute of Frauds defense and refuses to sell Mickey any beer. Can Mickey satisfy the Statute of Frauds? _____ but only for 50 kegs.*

   o **Part performance** on a goods contract satisfies the Statute of Frauds, but only for the quantity delivered and accepted.

   > *Example 115: Same facts as Example 114, except there is no confirming memo. Mickey changes her mind and decides to order some kegs of Fat Tire beer. Later, Pabst delivers 25 kegs to Mickey, and she eagerly stores the kegs in her basement. Can Pabst satisfy the Statute of Frauds? Yes, but only for the 25 kegs delivered and accepted. Is Mickey contractually obligated to buy the other 75 kegs from Pabst? _____, the Statute of Frauds will bar that claim.*

   o **Custom-made (or specially manufactured) goods** are *exempted* from the Statute of Frauds.

   - The maker can satisfy the Statute of Frauds as soon as it makes a _____ toward the manufacturing of the goods.

> *Example 116: I contract verbally with Brooks Brothers to buy 100 white dress shirts with "GSG" monogrammed on the pocket for $10,000. Brooks Brothers sends me the shirts, but I change my mind and send the shirts back. Can I assert a Statute of Frauds defense if Brooks Brothers sues for the $10,000? No, the custom-goods exception applies.*

- o A **judicial admission**, such as a statement in a pleading or during testimony, satisfies the Statute of Frauds under the UCC.
- o The **failure to object** to a confirming memo within 10 days will satisfy the Statute of Frauds—but only if both parties are _____

  > *Example 117: Mickey verbally contracts with Pabst Blue Ribbon to buy 100 kegs of beer for $7,500. Later, Pabst sends her a signed confirmation memo with all of the material terms. Mickey has changed her mind, crumples up the memo, and throws it in the corner. Ten days later, does Pabst satisfy the Statute of Frauds? _____. Mickey is not a merchant.*

  > *Example 118: Same facts as Example 117, except the buyer is now Whole Foods. Ten days after the memo arrives at Whole Foods, does Pabst satisfy the Statute of Frauds? _____, even though there is no signed writing by Whole Foods.*

5. Miscellaneous Statute of Frauds problems

- o **Agency law:** Do you need a signed writing to authorize an agent to form a contract that is in Statute of Frauds world? _____
  - ▪ This is known as the "_____ rule."

- o **Modification:** Suppose you have a deal that is in Statute of Frauds world, and the Statute of Frauds requirements are met. Now the parties want to modify that deal. Must the modification also satisfy the Statute of Frauds requirements? _____ _____

  - ▪ Ask whether the deal with the alleged modification would be in Statute of Frauds world.
    - • If so, the Statute of Frauds requirements must be met;
    - • If not, there is no Statute of Frauds requirement, even though the initial deal was in Statute of Frauds world

  > *Example 119: Mickey contracts with Pabst to buy five kegs of beer for $500. Later, Pabst sends her a signed confirmation memo with all material terms. Mickey alleges that they later modified the deal to three kegs only for $300. Does she need to supply written proof of this alleged modification? _____ because the modification is not within the SOF world.*

CHAPTER 12:   PERFORMANCE AND THE PAROL-EVIDENCE RULE

A. Second Main Question in Contract Law: Has the contract been performed?

- Four big topics within this question:

    1) **P**arol-evidence rule

    2) **W**arranties

    3) **C**onditions

    4) **E**xcuse of performance obligations (impracticability, frustration of purpose, etc.)

    o   "**P**izza **W**ith **C**rawling **E**scargot"

B. The Parol Evidence Rule (PER) - "P" in "Pizza With Crawling Escargot."

- Step One: Determine what the agreement entails. If you see a written contract that the court finds is the final agreement and **_earlier_** oral or written statements about the same deal, think PER.

    o   Does the PER apply to later written or oral statements about the deal? _____, that's a modification.

    o   Does the PER apply to earlier written documents? _____

- Gateway Question: Have the parties created an integrated writing?

    o   _____ integration means that the contract expresses all terms of the agreement.

    o   _____ integration means that there is a final writing, but some terms are not included.

- How do you distinguish an agreement that is not integrated from one that is completely or partially integrated?

    o   Look for a _____ clause (evidence of complete integration)

        Example 120: _Disney signs a contract with Hugh Grant to make a movie for $2 million. It contains the following language right above the signature line: "This is the entire agreement between the parties. No representations or promises have been made save for those set out in this memorandum." Hugh argues that Disney had verbally promised to provide a free house in Beverly Hills while he was filming, and failed to do so. Can he introduce this evidence? _____

        Example 121: _Same facts as Example 120, except Hugh argues that during the meeting but after the written contract was signed, they verbally agreed that $2 million was not enough and that he would get $3 million. After the meeting, Disney sent Hugh a check for $2 million. Can Hugh introduce evidence that Disney promised to pay Hugh $3 million? _____

o Courts may also ask whether, under the circumstances, an extrinsic term of the agreement would "naturally be omitted" from the writing. If so, it may not violate the parol-evidence rule and can be introduced as evidence if it does not contradict the writing.

> *Example 122: Same facts as Example 120, except Hugh argues that Disney verbally offered him, prior to signing, a sequel part for $5 million. Can he introduce this evidence? Tough call.*

o The UCC universe is more forgiving, presuming that a writing is, at most, only a partial integration—unless the parties would have _____ included a disputed term in the writing.

- Finally, there are some situations in which the parol-evidence rule does not apply to bar earlier evidence.

  o The parol-evidence rule does not bar evidence relevant to a defense against contract formation (duress, mistake, fraud, etc.)

  o Even if a writing is totally integrated, a party can introduce evidence of a _____ _____ deal.

> *Example 123: Same facts as Example 120, except Hugh now argues that Disney verbally offered, prior to signing, to sell him a season pass to Disneyland for $1,000. Can he introduce this evidence? _____*

  o Even if a writing is totally integrated, a party might be able to introduce evidence of a _____ that is designed to interpret an ambiguous term in the final agreement.

> *Example 124: Same facts as Example 120, except the parties disagree over what "movie" means in the contract. Disney believes that Hugh will make "Mrs. Doubtfire 2." Hugh claims that they had verbally agreed that he would make "Driving Miss Daisy 2." Can Hugh introduce this evidence? _____, as long as the term "movie" is sufficiently ambiguous.*

- Recap: Some people confuse the parol-evidence rule with the Statute of Frauds.

  o If the question does not have a signed writing, think _____ _____.

  o If the question does have a signed writing, along with an earlier discussion of the deal, think _____

CHAPTER 13: WARRANTIES AND EXPRESS CONDITIONS

A. Warranties - "W" in "Pizza With Crawling Escargot."

- A warranty is a promise about a term of the contract that explicitly shifts risk to the party making the promise.

  > ***Example 125:*** *I agree to sell you my Jeep for $5,000, but we don't discuss any other term. If the wheel falls off as you drive away, can you get out of the deal? It's uncertain. The buyer would need to argue mistake, duty to disclose, etc. What if I include a warranty that the Jeep will run fine for the next 1,000 miles? _____ you can get out of the deal.*

- Note that you can also _____ all warranties. For example, I might sell the Jeep on an "as is" basis.

1. Express Warranties

- o A promise that affirms or describes the goods and is part of the basis of the bargain is an express warranty unless it is merely the seller's opinion.
- o The use of a sample or model good creates an express warranty that the goods sold will be like the sample.

  > ***Example 126:*** *You walk into an AutoZone store to buy some hubcaps. The clerk shows you some floor samples that are bright gold and says these are our best model. You buy that model of hubcaps but find that they are an ugly yellow color when you pull them out of the box. AutoZone has breached an _____ warranty.*

2. Implied Warranty of Merchantability

- o This warranty is triggered only when the seller is a merchant dealing in the goods at issue.
- o The merchant makes an implied warranty (unless disclaimed) that the goods are fit for

  _____.

  > ***Example 127:*** *: You walk into an AutoZone store to buy some polish for your hubcaps. The clerk waves you over to aisle 12 where you pick up a can of hubcap polish. When you spray it on your hubcaps, they turn an ugly yellow color. AutoZone has breached an implied warranty of*

  _____.

  > ***Example 128:*** *You walk into an AutoZone store and the clerk tells you that their delivery van is for sale. You buy it, but it breaks down the next day. Has AutoZone breached the implied warranty of merchantability? _____ this is a one-off good; AutoZone is not a merchant in vans.*

- o Can a merchant disclaim this warranty? _____ if very clearly done. Look for VERY CONSPICUOUS language that mentions the warranty of merchantability or words like "as is."

3. **Implied Warranty of Fitness for a Particular Purpose**

   o This warranty is triggered when a buyer relies on a seller's expertise to select a special type of good that will be used for a special purpose.

   o The seller makes an implied warranty (unless disclaimed) that the goods will satisfy this special purpose.

   > ***Example 129:*** *Same facts as Example 127, except you can't decide between three different types of hubcap polish. You ask the clerk which one is right for your aluminum-alloy hubcaps, and he picks up a can and says, "THIS is the brand you want." When you spray it on your hubcaps, they turn an ugly yellow color. AutoZone has breached an implied warranty of _____*
   >
   > _____

   o Can a nonmerchant extend this warranty by implication? _____ as long as the buyer relies on any seller's expertise.

   o Can this warranty be disclaimed? _____ if CONSPICUOUS language is used, such as "as is." But, unlike the implied warranty of merchantability, the disclaimer for implied fitness for a particular purpose must be in _____.

B. **Conditions - The "C" in "Pizza With Crawling Escargot."**

   • A condition is another way to shift risk by stating that one party's contractual obligation will kick in only if some future event takes place.

   > ***Example 130:*** *Your rich and eccentric Aunt promises you $5,000 if you pass the bar exam—on the express condition that you study with Barbreeze. You take Themis and easily pass the exam. Must your aunt pay you the $5,000? _____*

   • Like warranties, conditions can be express or implied. By far, the most important implied condition is something called the "constructive condition of exchange."

1. **Express Conditions**

   o Express conditions are created by language in the contract. Look for magic words like "only if," "provided that," "on the condition that," "only in the event that," etc.

   o Express conditions must be _____, unless the condition is somehow excused.

   > ***Example 131:*** *: Mark contracts to work for The Egg House for 10 weeks building a new henhouse for the chickens. The parties agree that Mark will get $10,000 for building the house, along with a bonus of $5,000 awarded on the condition that he shows up every day for work. Mark finishes the henhouse, but he doesn't come to work for the last two days in week 10 because he is really sick. Can Mark collect the $5,000 bonus? _____*

o Recall contracts that have a satisfaction condition. How are these conditions met? It depends on the nature of the performance.

- The preferred approach is to use an objective standard of satisfaction, meaning that if most reasonable people would be satisfied, then the condition is met

- Contracts involving aesthetic taste, such as art or tutoring services, will measure whether any satisfaction conditions are met with a _____ standard. The party can still breach if they claim dissatisfaction in bad faith.

Example 132: : I promise to pay Mickey $500 if she paints a portrait of my family, if the painting meets with my satisfaction. She says OK. After she is finished, the portrait is revealed, and all of the art critics rave over the masterpiece. But I hate it. Must I pay Mickey the $500? _____

o The party receiving the protection of the condition may waive the condition by words or

_____

Example 133: You agree to buy my Jeep for $5,000 on the express condition that you can get a car loan for this amount at an interest rate of 10% or less. You can only get a loan for 12%, but you still want to buy the Jeep. If you waive the financing condition, must I sell you the Jeep? Yes. Can I waive the financing condition? _____

o A condition will also be waived if the other party _____ _____ with or hinders the occurrence of the condition. This will be judged by a good-faith standard.

Example 134: Same facts as Example 133, but you decide that you don't want the Jeep after all. You refuse to provide any documentation to the bank considering your loan and tell the loan officer that you're a lazy deadbeat. Will the financing condition excuse your performance? _____

CHAPTER 14: IMPLIED CONDITIONS, CCE, AND UCC PERFORMANCE RULES

A. The Constructive Condition of Exchange

The Constructive Condition of Exchange ("CCE") says that one party's performance is conditioned on the other side's performance.

Example 135: You agree to buy my Jeep for $5,000 next Friday. That day we meet, but I refuse to sign over the pink slip. Do you have to pay me the $5,000? _____

B. Common-Law Universe

- The CCE need not be satisfied perfectly. The doctrine of substantial performance states that a party will satisfy the CCE if there is not a _____

> **Example 136:** *Shaquille O'Neal hires me to build him a house. I build the doorways all at standard height (6'6") instead of the 8' listed in the contract. Shaquille is mad because he must duck to get from room to room. Has there been substantial performance? _____, this is a material breach, a "big deal."*

- Substantial performance works to satisfy the CCE only if the failure is not _____

  > **Example 137:** *I hire you to build the Geis Towers, a 150-story building in Charlottesville, Virginia, for $100 billion. When you finish, I conduct the final walkthrough and notice that the lobby walls are made of baby blue marble from North Carolina, not dark blue marble from Virginia, as called for in the contract specs. Can I avoid paying you the $100 billion? _____. Assuming the breach was innocent, the CCE has been satisfied.*

  > **Example 138:** *Same facts as Example 137, but our contract includes the following condition: "Geis's payment obligation under this contract is expressly conditioned on the use of Virginia marble in the lobby." Must I pay the $100 billion? _____. This is an express condition, not a constructive condition.*

- If payment needs to be made (because there is only a minor problem) can the nonbreaching party recover **damages** for the deficiency? _____

  o Typically measured as the cost to complete the performance
  o Sometimes damages will be limited to the diminution in market value.

- Can a breaching party who fails to satisfy the CCE due to a **material** breach get paid anything?

  o _____—maybe quasi-contract

- Can a breaching party who fails to satisfy an **express** condition get paid in quasi-contract? Usually not.
- **Divisibility** - If a contract is clearly divisible, then it will be broken down into mini-contracts for the purposes of determining if there has been substantial performance.

  > **Example 139:** *Mickey contracts with Best Buy to install a kegorator in each of the 20 rooms in her house for $2,000. If Best Buy only installs five kegorators before it abandons the job, is this substantial performance? _____ - contract is not divisible - Mickey is paying for the full job.*

  > **Example 140:** *Same facts as Example 139, except Mickey agrees to pay Best Buy $100 for **each** of the 20 kegorators. If Best Buy installs only five kegorators before it abandons the job, can it collect anything on the contract? _____ if divisible: can collect 5 × $100 = $500. (When evaluating substantial performance on a divisible contract, Best Buy can recover on the mini contracts on which it has fully performed.)*

C. UCC Universe: Performance

- The UCC requires _____

  o Exception: The parties **can** contractually change the default rules to include discussion of substantial performance instead of perfect tender.

  o Exception: **Installment contracts** do not have to satisfy "perfect tender."

- Perfect tender has two main obligations:

  o Perfect _____

  o Perfect _____

> **Example 141:** *Mickey contracts for 500 pints of Fireball whiskey for $5,000. Fireball sends Mickey only 495 pints. Is this perfect tender? _____ Mickey can reject all of the whiskey.*

> **Note 17:** Rejection of the goods is not the same as rejection of an offer.

- **Revocation of acceptance**—The buyer may also **revoke an acceptance** of the goods (occurs when the goods seem OK and are accepted at delivery, but a defect is discovered within a reasonable time).

  o *For example, Fireball delivers all 500 pints of the whiskey in the example above, and Mickey stores the bottles in her cellar. A month later, she cracks a bottle to find that it is cola (not whiskey). She can revoke her acceptance and send the bottles back.*

- If the seller **fails to tender perfect goods** and time is left on the contract **or** the seller had reasonable grounds to believe that the buyer would accept a replacement, then the buyer must give the seller a chance to _____.

- Installment contracts—The default method of delivery under the UCC is **one** delivery of the goods

  o But the UCC allows for installment contracts (agreement for delivery in separate lots).

  o The buyer can reject a specific delivery that isn't perfect only when there is a _____ in the installment that cannot be cured.

> **Example 142:** *Same facts as Example 141, except Mickey contracts for 1 pint of Fireball whiskey to be delivered each day at 5:00 p.m. for 500 days. Delivery #345 comes at 5:15 p.m. Can Mickey reject that delivery? _____ (Even though it was not perfect tender, the UCC allows Fireball some leeway because this is an installment contract.)*

1. **Common methods of tender/delivery for goods contracts:**

   o Tender at Seller's place of business—If the goods are tendered at the seller's place of business, then the seller just needs to give the goods to the buyer.

   o _____ contract. [F.O.B. Seller's place of business] If the contract is a shipment contract, then the seller must take three actions to satisfy perfect delivery requirement:

      1) Get the goods to a _____

      2) Make arrangements for _____; and

      3) _____ the buyer.

   o _____ contract [F.O.B. Buyer's place of business], then the seller must get the goods to the **buyer's** business and notify the buyer.

      > *Example 143:* I contract with Brooks Brothers (located in New York) to buy "100 white dress shirts for $10,000 F.O.B. my house in Charlottesville." Has Brooks satisfied its delivery obligation when it gives the shirts to FedEx and sends me an e-mail saying that they are coming? _____ because "F.O.B. my house in Charlottesville" makes this a destination contract.

2. **Risk of Loss Problem**

   o You can recognize a risk of loss problem when there is a **goods** contract followed by **damage** or destruction of the goods **before** the buyer receives them. Who will bear the loss? Seller? Buyer?

      1) Check whether the parties have already dealt with the risk problem in the contract. If so, their agreement will control.

      2) If not, ask whether either party has **breached** (typically another part of the contract).

         • If so, that breaching party bears the risk of loss. Is this true even if the breach is totally unrelated to the delivery damage? _____ If there has been a breach, the breaching party is liable for the risk of loss.

      3) If there is no breach, and the goods are being shipped, then ask what type of delivery contract it was:

         • If it was a **shipment** contract, then the risk of loss during delivery rests with the _____

         • If it was a **destination** contract, then the risk of loss during delivery rests with the _____

4) In all other cases, ask whether the seller is a **merchant.**

- If so, the risk of loss stays with the seller until the buyer _____ the goods.
- If not, the risk of loss moves to the buyer when the seller _____ the goods.

Example 144: I contract with Brooks Brothers to buy "100 white dress shirts for $10,000." Brooks calls to tell me that the shirts are ready, and I can pick them up at the store when I like. That night, the store burns down, and my shirts are destroyed. Do I have to pay for them? _____. (In this risk of loss problem, you continue to the last step in analysis. Seller is a merchant. Therefore, the risk of loss stays with the seller.)

Example 145: Professor Geis contracts with the law-school bookstore to sell 10 used copies of his book for $10 each. He tells the bookstore manager that he has left the books outside his office, so she can get them whenever. That night, a pack of law-review editors steals and burns all of the books. Does the bookstore have to pay for them? _____. Bookstore must pay Professor Geis. (Again, you go through all the steps. Because Professor Geis is not a merchant, the risk of loss moves to the buyer and the bookstore has to pay for the books.)

Exam Tip 5: If you get a risk of loss problem (a **goods** contract followed by **damage** or destruction of the goods **before** the buyer receives them) go through the four-part analysis until you get an answer.

CHAPTER 15: EXCUSES

A. Excuses - "E" in "Pizza With Crawling Escargot."

- There is a clear contract but something has nevertheless happened to prevent one side from having to perform on the contract.

1. Impossibility and impracticability

o Look for these common fact patterns:

- Performance becomes _____ after the contract is formed;
- The subject matter of the contract is _____;
- A services contract with a "special person," and the performing party _____ or is incapacitated;
- BUT, something that just makes performance more expensive than expected will not normally excuse performance. Look for something that hinders the *ability* to perform, not just the *cost* to perform.

Example 146: Mickey contracts with a local tavern, The Whisky Jar, to bartend for one year in exchange for free drinks. If "Prohibition II" is passed, outlawing alcohol consumption in Virginia, must Mickey perform this contract? _____

Example 147: You contract to reroof my house for $10,000, but before you can perform, my house burns down. I insist that our contract requires you to rebuild my house and then reroof it. Am I right? _____

Example 148: You contract to dig a wine cellar for me for $10,000. After you start performing, you hit some big rocks and realize that it will cost you twice as much to finish the job, resulting in a loss on the contract. Are you excused from performing? _____

o   Look for an unforeseeable event in which the non-occurrence of the event was a basic assumption of the contract, and the party seeking discharge was not at fault.

2. Death after a contract

o   Dying does not normally excuse liability on a contract that has been made. The estate will normally be on the hook for any contractual obligations.

Example 149: Old Man Jones finds out that he only has a few more months to live. So he goes out and borrows $1 million from a bank and invests the money in jewelry. When he dies, is his debt contract with the bank excused? _____

o   Ask whether there is something special about the person performing on the contract, such that it makes no sense to continue if they die.

Example 150: You hire the Rolling Stones to play your birthday party next month for $1 million. If, sadly, Mick Jagger dies before the big date, can the rest of the band show up and play for the $1 million? _____ your contractual obligation is excused. Likewise, you can hardly make the full band perform.

3. Frustration of purpose

o   Performance can still occur, but something has happened to undermine the entire reason for the creation of the contract.

o   Note that this is very rare—the event must be extreme and not previously allocated to one of the parties.

Example 151: You are excited for the season opener of your favorite football team's game, especially after paying $2,000 for season tickets. You sit down 20 rows up on the 50-yard line, when right before kickoff, a tall man in an Abe Lincoln hat sits down in front of you. He refuses to remove the hat, and you can't see the game. Can you get out of your contract for the football tickets? _____

Example 152: *You rent an apartment in Chicago at $5,000 for one day because it has a prime view of Wrigley Field, and the Cubs are scheduled to play in the World Series that afternoon. The game is unexpectedly canceled one day before because of an earthquake. Is performance excused due to impossibility? _____ What about being excused for frustration of purpose? _____*

4. **Performance is excused because the initial contract has been modified or canceled**

   o   Can both parties agree to just walk away from a contract? _____ as long as there is some performance remaining from each side. Otherwise, there is no consideration for this modification.

   > *Example 153:* *I contract to sell you my Jeep for $5,000. We meet to swap the money for the pink slip, but both of us want to back out. Can we just say forget it? _____*

   > *Example 154:* *I contract to paint your house for $5,000. After I finish the job, we agree to rescind the deal. Is this valid? _____*

5. **Accord and satisfaction**

   o   The parties to an earlier contract agree that performance will be satisfied instead by the completion of a different performance.

   - The new performance is called the _____
   - The excusing of the initial performance obligation is called the

     _____

     > *Example 155:* *Mickey contracts with Pabst to buy five kegs of beer for $500. Later, she agrees that if Pabst delivers 100 cases of beer, then it does not need to deliver the kegs. If Pabst delivers the cases of beer, can Mickey still sue for the kegs? _____.*

   o   What happens if the accord is not performed? In that case, the other side can sue on either the original obligation or the new promise.

   > *Example 156:* *Same facts as Example 155. If Pabst delivers nothing, then Mickey can sue for the five kegs or the 100 cases.*

6. **Novation**

   o   This arises when BOTH parties agree that a substitute person will take over the contractual obligations.

   - Can one side decide to create a novation by asking someone else to do the work? _____ this is called a "delegation," and will be discussed later.

   o   If there is a valid novation, then the original promisor will be excused from performance.

Example 157: Mickey contracts with Pabst to buy five kegs of beer for $500. Later, both parties agree that Blatz will take over the deal. If Blatz fails to deliver any beer, can Mickey sue Pabst? _____ the novation has excused Pabst.

CHAPTER 16: ANTICIPATORY REPUDIATION; REMEDIES: BASIC CONCEPTS

Third main question in contract law: What are the remedies for breach?

A. Anticipatory Repudiation

- Anticipatory repudiation is closely related to the CCE, but it deals with a slightly different question:

  o What are your remedy options when the other side says he's not going to perform on the contract (repudiates) before the performance is due? Do you still have to go along with your part of the deal and see if he really does breach?

    Example 158: I hire you to build the Geis Towers, a 150-story building in Charlottesville, Virginia, for $100 billion by December 31. On July 31, when you're about half-way finished with the project, I let it slip that I'm broke and never going to pay you the money. Do you have to keep working on the tower? _____, as long as my repudiation is clear and unequivocal.

- If a party clearly and unequivocally repudiates, the nonbreaching party has two options:

  o Treat the repudiation as a breach and sue immediately for damages.

    ▪ But, if you have completed the entire performance and are only waiting for payment, **you cannot sue early.**

  o Ignore the repudiation, demand performance, and see what happens.

    Example 159: Same facts as Example 158. If you decide to sue me for money damages, must you wait until December 31, or can you sue on July 31? You can sue on July 31.

    Example 160: Same facts as Example 159, except you completed the Geis Towers ahead of schedule on June 30. If you decide to sue me for money damages, must you wait until December 31, or can you sue on July 31? You must wait until December 31.

- A party can **retract its** repudiation as long as the other side has not commenced a lawsuit for breach or acted in reliance on the repudiation (by materially changing its position).
- **UCC universe**: Reasonable grounds for insecurity about the other side's performance allows you to demand _____ **of performance.**

o   If the questionable party fails to respond within a reasonable time, then you can treat this as repudiation.

> *Example 161: I agree on January 1 to buy 100 white shirts from Crooks Brothers for $1,000. Half of the money is due on February 1; the balance and the shirts are due March 1. In the middle of January, I see a news exposé about financial trouble at Crooks Brothers, and it fails to return my phone calls. I send a letter demanding adequate assurance of performance on January 15. If it says, "don't worry, we're almost done with the shirts," must I make the $500 February 1 payment? _____ What if it doesn't respond? _____*

B. Money Damages

Money damages are the typical remedy in contract law.

1. Expectation Damages

o   This is the normal way to calculate damages.

o   The goal is to put a party in the same _____ that it would be in if the contract had been performed as promised.

o   Measure expectation damages by comparing the **value of the performance** without the breach to the value of the performance with the breach.

> *Example 162: I hire you to build the Geis Towers, a 150-story building in Charlottesville, Virginia, for $100 billion. You never start the project and tell me that you are breaching the contract. What are my expectation damages if I hire a replacement builder for $110 billion? _____*

> *Example 163: Same facts as Example 162, but the replacement builder costs only $80 billion. What are my expectation damages? _____; I've benefitted from your breach. Do I have to pay you? _____*

o   **UCC universe:** Work through this basic formula to determine any question about expectation damages.

> *Example 164: Buyer breach. Mickey contracts with Pabst to buy a keg of beer for $100. Mickey repudiates the contract, and Pabst sells the keg to a liquor store for $80. What are Pabst's expectation damages? _____*

> *Example 165: Buyer refusal to pay. Mickey contracts with Pabst to buy a keg of beer for $100. Mickey gets the keg but breaches the contract by refusing to pay. The current price for a keg of Pabst has risen to $110. What are Pabst's expectation damages? _____*

> *Example 166: Seller breach. Mickey contracts with Pabst to buy a keg of beer for $100. Pabst fails to deliver the keg, and Mickey has to buy her keg from Blatz for $120. What are Mickey's expectation damages? _____ When*

Pabst refuses to deliver, can Mickey buy a keg of Utopia for $25,000 and sue Pabst for $24,900? _____ cover must be similar.

Example 167: *Seller breach. Mickey contracts with Pabst to buy a keg of beer for $100 (paid up front). When Pabst delivers the keg, it is only half full, but Mickey is desperate to get her keg and keeps the keg. It can be shown that a half keg of Pabst costs $60 at the corner liquor store. What are Mickey's expectation damages? _____*

Example 168: *Same facts as Example 167. Can Mickey send the keg back instead? _____ under the perfect-tender rule.*

CHAPTER 17: EXPECTATION DAMAGES

A. Limits on Expectation Damages

- There are three major limits on the calculation of expectation damages.

1. **Expectation damages must be proven with _____ _____.**

    Example 169: *Will Ferrell decides to run for president and agrees to pay CNN $5 million for ten 30-second advertising slots. CNN forgets to run the ads. Ferrell argues that but for this breach, he would have been elected president, and he sues for the four-year salary of the president. Can he get this as expectation damages? _____ there is too much uncertainty.*

    o Other common fact patterns here include brand new or unproven business ventures, which have trouble proving lost profits from a consistent sales track record.

2. **Unforeseeable consequential damages are not recoverable unless the breaching party had some reason to know about the possibility of these unforeseeable consequential damages (the Hadley rule).**

    o What are consequential damages? You should distinguish two types of damages:

    ▪ **General damages**: The type of losses that almost anyone would suffer from a breach.

    - These include incidental damages, such as the cost of storing rejected goods, or finding a new buyer, or finding a replacement vendor.

    ▪ **Consequential damages**: Losses that are unique or special to this plaintiff.

    Example 170: *I hire FedEx to deliver Super Bowl tickets to a buyer on eBay for $20. FedEx refuses to honor the contract, and I have to pay UPS $50 for rapid delivery to get the tickets there in time. I also use up $5 in gas driving to UPS. What are my expectation damages against FedEx? $50 − $20 + $5 incidental damages= $35.*

Example 171: Same facts as Example 170, except I cannot get another carrier to deliver the tickets in time, and as a result, the buyer doesn't pay me the $2,000 ticket price. Because I bought the tickets for $200, can I sue FedEx for my lost profits of $1,800? _____, this is an unforeseeable consequential damage.

Example 172: Same facts as Example 170, except I also provide FedEx with the exact details of my transaction. Can I now recover my lost profits? _____ unless there are other disclaimers.

3. **The doctrine of mitigation states that a breached-against party must take reasonable steps to reduce damages from breach.**

   Example 173: I agree to pay you $10,000 to fix my roof, which has major holes (I tell you this). You breach the contract. Can I sit in my bed and ring up the cash register every time it rains? _____, I have to hire someone else to do the job.

   o If you refuse to mitigate, the law will calculate damages as if you did mitigate. The defendant bears the burden of proving a mitigation failure.

   Example 174: Same facts as Example 173, but I don't hire a new roofer for several months. My oriental carpets (worth $25,000) are ruined from rain and snow. Eventually, I hire another roofer to do the job for $12,000 and sue you for $25,000 + $2,000 = $27,000. Should I receive this amount? _____ What is my recovery if you can show that there was another roofer able to do the job for $9,000 at the time that you told me of the breach? _____

   o Note that mitigation efforts must be reasonably similar to the original contract.

   Example 175: Shirley MacLaine contracts with MGM to make a movie entitled "Bloomer Girl" for $10 million. MGM decides not to make the movie, but it offers her a replacement part for $10 million in a country-western, "Big Country Big Man." If MacLaine refuses to take the part, can MGM argue that she has failed to mitigate, such that expectation damages are zero? _____ this is not reasonably similar mitigation.

B. **Special Problems That Might Appear on the MBE**

   1. **Lost volume profits (LVP)**

   o If the paying party breaches, then normally the selling party needs to mitigate by reselling the goods or services to another person.

   o But if the seller is a retailer who sells this type of product all the time, the seller can try to argue for LVP.

   Example 176: Outrigger contracts to sell Mickey a speedboat for $15,000 (which cost Outrigger $10,000 to buy from the manufacturer). The following week, Mickey repudiates the sale. The very next day, Will Ferrell walks in to buy the same boat for $15,000. Mickey argues that Outrigger's damages are zero *because it fully mitigated her breach with the sale to Ferrell. Is she right?*

_____ if Outrigger can show that it had plenty of boats to sell and few buyers.

If Outrigger does get LVP, how should these be calculated?

_____

2. **Incomplete performance**

   o   If the paying party breaches in a partially completed building contract, can the builder continue to work on the job? _____, this runs counter to mitigation—it would be "running up the damages."

   o   Accordingly, we need to adjust the recovery price in this special context to take account of the fact that the builder did not need to finish the job.

   o   Use this formula:

      ▪   *Expectation Damages = Contract Price – Amount already Paid – Amount that Would Be Needed to Finish the Job*

         Example 177: *I hire you to build the Geis Towers, a 150-story building in Charlottesville, Virginia, for $100 billion, with $10 billion due every month. You start the project, and I pay you for the first three months. After that, I tell you that I'm repudiating the contract and won't pay another dime. You had expected to build the tower for $85 billion (netting a $15 billion profit), but you have spent only $45 billion thus far. Can you recover the $70 billion balance on the contract price? _____ you didn't do all of the work. What should you get?*

         Expectation damages = $100 billion – $30 billion – $40 billion = $30 billion

         You can also calculate as $45 billion spent + $15 billion profits = $60 billion – $30 billion already paid = $30 billion.

3. **Economic waste and diminution in market value damages**

   o   The normal measure of expectation damages is the cost to complete the job.

         Example 178: *I hire you to build the Geis Towers, a 150-story building in Charlottesville, Virginia, for $100 billion, with $10 billion due each month. You start the project, and I pay you for the first three months, and then you repudiate the contract. I have to pay someone else $80 billion to finish the job. How much can I recover from you under expectation damages? The cost to complete the job: $110 billion – $100 billion = $10 billion.*

   o   But, sometimes using cost-to-complete damages will dramatically overcompensate the plaintiff.

         Example 179: *I hire you to build the Geis Towers, a 150-story building in Charlottesville, Virginia, for $100 billion. When you finish, I'm conducting the* *final walk-through and notice that the lobby walls are made of marble from North Carolina, not marble from Virginia (as called for in the contract specs). I sue you for breach and demand $20 billion (to tear it down) plus $100 billion (to rebuild it with the right marble). Should I get the $120 billion in cost-to-complete damages? _____*

- o Diminution in market value ("DMV")—How much lower is the market value of what you got versus what you wanted?

    - Note that the breaching party must normally have acted in an innocent and unintentional manner for DMV damages.

    Example 180: Same facts as Example 179. If you can show that your use of North Carolina marble was unintentional, what damages must you pay for the breach? DMV, probably zero, or maybe a slight amount if I can show that Virginia marble would increase the market value of the Geis Towers.

CHAPTER 18: OTHER MONEY DAMAGES AND SPECIFIC PERFORMANCE

A. Reliance Damages

- The goal is to put a party in the same economic position that it would be in if the contract had never been created.
- RELIANCE DAMAGES = GROUNDHOG DAY DAMAGES
- Always ask, what loss has the plaintiff incurred that would never have taken place but for the breached contract?

    Example 181: Recall the facts of Example 169, in which Will Ferrell decides to run for president and agrees to pay CNN $5 million for ten 30-second advertising slots. CNN forgets to run the ads. Ferrell cannot recover the four-year salary of the president. Can he get anything under reliance damages? _____, the cost of making all the ads.

- A party _____ recover both expectation and reliance damages; typically, the plaintiff must elect one or the other.

B. Restitution Damages

- The goal is to give the plaintiff an amount equal to the economic benefit that the plaintiff has conferred on the defendant.
- This can sometimes equal reliance damages, but it need not.

    Example 182: Owen Wilson pays $50,000 to Dr. Plastic, a famous surgeon who promises to "make Wilson's nose perfect." Wilson also incurs $20,000 in hospital costs related to this procedure. Dr. Plastic botches the job, and Wilson sues for restitution damages. What does Dr. Plastic owe Wilson?

$_____; the benefit that Owen Wilson conferred upon Dr. Plastic.

Example 183: *Same facts as Example 182, but Wilson sues for reliance damages. What does Dr. Plastic owe Wilson? $50,000 + $20,000 = $70,000.*

Editor's Note 2: Professor Geis misspoke when describing the damages in Example 183. With *reliance* damages, we will rewind time and allow Wilson to recover everything spent in connection with the contract.

Example 184: *Same facts as Example 182, but Wilson sues for expectation damages. How would these be calculated? _____*

_____

C. Liquidated Damages

- These are set out in the contract as an explicitly negotiated amount due upon breach.
- Courts are wary about awarding punitive liquidated damages and will do so only if:
    - o The amount of liquidated damages was reasonable at the time of contracting; and
    - o Actual damages from breach would be uncertain in amount and difficult to prove.

    Example 185: *Same facts as Example 182, but Wilson and Dr. Plastic agreed that the doctor would pay Wilson $500,000 if the operation was a failure. Will these liquidated damages be enforced? _____. What if the liquidated damages were $50 million? _____. This is likely to be viewed as a penalty that will not be enforced.*

D. Punitive Damages

Punitive damages are almost never allowed in contract law. Don't worry about these unless you see a breach that also seems like a tort (e.g., fraud or some other very extreme situation).

E. Specific Performance/Injunction

- Equitable relief, such as specific performance and related injunctions, is the exception, not the norm in contract law.
- This remedy is awarded only when monetary damages are considered inadequate for some reason.
- Specific performance is presumptively available for _____ transactions.

    Example 186: *Hugh Grant contracts to buy a Napa Valley winery for $25 million. If the seller breaches, can Grant get specific performance? _____. What if the seller has already transferred the land to another bona fide purchaser? _____*

- Specific performance is presumptively not available for contracts of personal service.

o   Rarely, a court might grant an injunction prohibiting a breaching party from performing similar services for a competitor for a reasonable period of time/place (the Lumley doctrine).

> ***Example 187:*** *Hugh Grant contracts to make a movie with Disney for $3 million. If Grant breaches, can Disney get specific performance, forcing Grant to act in the movie? _____*

> ***Example 188:*** *Same facts as Example 187. Can Disney get an injunction prohibiting Grant from acting in another Hollywood movie for the next three months? _____ under the Lumley doctrine.*

- Specific performance is available only for **unique goods** like art or custom-made items.

> ***Example 189:*** *You purchased the original Saturday Night Fever dance floor in an auction, but the seller refuses to perform on the contract. Can you get specific performance? _____*

- A **right of reclamation** is an equitable right of an unpaid seller to reclaim goods when credit is extended and the buyer is insolvent. To assert this remedy, the following facts must be present:

o   The buyer is _____ at the time of receipt of the goods;

o   The seller must demand the return of goods within 10 days of receipt (or within a reasonable time if the buyer misrepresented his solvency to the seller); and

o   The buyer still has the goods.

> ***Example 190:*** *Mickey is broke, but she contracts for 500 pints of Fireball whiskey for $5,000 on credit. Fireball sends all 500 pints but learns of Mickey's financial situation and asks for the whiskey back five days later. Must Mickey return the whiskey? _____*

CHAPTER 19:   THIRD-PARTY BENEFICIARIES

- Three main concepts:

    1) Third-party beneficiary contracts

    2) Assignment

    3) Delegation

A. Third-Party Beneficiary Contracts

Whether a third party can sue to enforce a contract made by two other people

1. Identify the parties

o   The **promisor** is the person making the promise that the outsider is trying to sue to enforce.

- o The **promisee** is a contractual counterparty to that promise; this person could presumably enforce the promise but is not doing so.
- o The **third-party beneficiary** is the outsider suing the promisor.

> *Example 191:* Abe agrees to pay Beth $50 if Beth mows Cam's lawn. Beth never shows up, and Cam files a lawsuit against Beth. Who is the promisor? _____ Who is the promisee? _____ Who is the third-party beneficiary? _____

2. Types of third parties

- o The critical issue in a third-party beneficiary contract is whether the third party is an intended or an incidental beneficiary.

   - ▪ _____ beneficiaries have the right to sue.
   - ▪ _____ beneficiaries do not.

- o To determine whether a given third party is an intended or an incidental beneficiary, ask whether the initial counterparties (promisor and promisee) intended to convey enforcement rights to the third party in the event of breach.

> *Example 192:* Same facts as Example 191. Is Cam an intended beneficiary? _____ Can the promisee, Abe, sue Beth? _____

> *Example 193:* Same facts as Example 191. Don lives across the street from Cam, and he has to buy $15 in weed killer when weeds blow over from Cam's yard into Don's yard because Beth didn't mow the lawn. Can Don sue Beth for breach? _____ Don is an incidental beneficiary.

> *Example 194:* Same facts as Example 191. Earl runs a gas station that Beth uses to gas up her lawn mower. Earl would have earned $5 in profits if Beth had performed on her contract with Abe. Can Earl sue Beth for breach? _____ Earl is an incidental beneficiary.

- o A _____ beneficiary arises when the promisee strikes a deal with the promisor in order to repay some earlier debt to the third party. This is a common fact pattern on the bar exam.

> *Example 195:* Cam loaned Abe $500 last month. In satisfaction of this debt, Abe agrees to pay Beth $500 if Beth mows Cam's lawn 10 times. Beth never shows up, and Cam files a lawsuit against Beth. Cam can sue Beth because he is a creditor beneficiary.

- o A donee beneficiary arises when there is no preexisting obligation, but the promisee clearly intends to confer a gift of enforcement on a third party.

> *Example 196:* Abe buys a policy from Bottomless Life Insurance. Under this contract, Abe will pay $500 per year to Bottomless, and Bottomless will pay

$500,000 to Cam when Abe dies. Can Cam sue Bottomless if it fails to pay the

claim? _____ because he is a donee beneficiary.

3. **Revoking third party rights**

o Can the initial counterparties revoke or modify away the third-party's right to enforce the contract?

o Depends on whether the third party knows about the promise and has changed her position in reasonable reliance on the promise. If so, the third party may be able to make out a claim under promissory estoppel. See Example 78.

o A third party will not lose enforcement rights if any of the following facts is true, as these facts cause the right to vest:

▪ The beneficiary _____ on the rights (similar to promissory estoppel);

▪ The beneficiary _____ to the contract/the rights; or

▪ The beneficiary _____ to enforce the contract.

o The promisor can assert any contract defense against the third party that he would be entitled to assert against the promisee.

> **Example 197:** *Abe points a gun at Beth's head and promises to "sell" Beth a contract law casebook if Beth pays $225,000 to Cam. Beth says "OK" but doesn't pay the money to Cam. Would Beth have a contract defense against Abe? _____ duress. Can she assert this defense to avoid having to pay Cam?*
>
> *_____*

CHAPTER 20: ASSIGNMENT AND DELEGATION

A. Assignment

- An assignment is the transfer of rights under a contract. A delegation is the transfer of duties under a contract.

- You can distinguish assignment from a third-party beneficiary contract because you will typically see two steps:

    1) The formation of a contract and

    2) The transfer of the benefits of the contract from an original counterparty to some third party.

- Almost all contractual benefits can be assigned, in whole or in part.

Example 198: I offer to pay you $1,000 to paint my house. Can you assign the offer to Mickey? _____; an offer must be directed at a specific person by the offeror.

Example 199: I offer to pay you $1,000 to paint my house. You accept. Can you assign the $1,000 payment to Mickey such that she can sue me for failure to pay? _____

Note 18: Special terms for the parties in Example 199: Professor Geis is the guarantor; You are the assignor; Mickey is the assignee

Example 200: Same facts as Example 199. Can Mickey sue me for the money if you don't paint the house? _____ All defenses transfer to the assignee.

Example 201: I agree to pay Mickey $1,000 if you paint my house. Mickey is an intended third-party beneficiary.

- If the contract states that rights are not assignable, you need to decide whether the contract invalidates assignments.

  o If the contract just prohibits assignments, then the assigning party has breached the deal when he makes the assignment, but the third party can still recover from the guarantor (i.e., the power to assign persists, even if the right to assign was not present initially).

    Example 202: I agree to pay you $1,000 to paint my house, but the contract states that the rights under this contract are not assignable. You nevertheless assign the $1,000 payment to Mickey. Have you breached? _____. Can Mickey sue me if I don't pay her the money? _____

  o If the contract invalidates assignments, then the third party cannot recover (because there is no power or right to assign).

    Example 203: I agree to pay you $1,000 to paint my house, but the contract states that all purported assignments of rights under this contract are void. You nevertheless assign the $1,000 payment to Mickey. Can Mickey sue me if I don't pay her the money _____

- What happens if someone assigns the same rights twice? The answer depends on whether the assignee has paid consideration for the rights:

  o If the rights are **assigned without consideration**, then the last assignment controls.
  o If the rights are **assigned for consideration**, then the first assignment for consideration will typically hold.

    ▪ **Limited exception**: A later assignment will take priority if the second assignee does not know of the initial assignment and is first to obtain payment or a judgment.

    Example 204: I agree to pay you $1,000 to paint my house. You assign the payment rights to Mickey. You then wise up and assign the payment rights to *your best friend. Can Mickey sue me if I don't pay her the money? _____ Can your best friend sue? _____*

> **Example 205:** *Same facts as Example 204, except Mickey trades you 100 bottles of Fireball whiskey for the assignment of payment rights. You then assign the rights to your best friend. Can Mickey sue me if I don't pay her the money? _____ Can your best friend sue? _____*

B. Delegation

- A delegation of duties occurs when a party to a contract "outsources" her duties under a contract to another party.

- This is generally acceptable, as long as the contract does not prohibit delegation and as long as the other party does not have some special interest in having a specific individual perform.

> **Example 206:** *I agree to pay you $1,000 to paint my house. You delegate your painting obligation to your best friend. Is that OK? _____ You are the delegating party; your friend is the delegatee; I am the obligee.*

> **Example 207:** *If your friend does a lousy job, are you still on the hook for breach? _____ Contrast this outcome with novation, described above in Example 157.*

> **Example 208:** *Same facts as Example 206. Your friend does a great job, and I refuse to pay. Can your friend recover from me? _____; all you have done is transfer the duties, not the benefits. What if you delegated the duties and assigned the rights to your friend? _____ the friend can recover from me.*

- A delegatee is generally not liable for breach unless she receives _____ from the delegating party.

> **Example 209:** *I agree to pay you $1,000 to paint my house. You delegate your painting obligation to your best friend and promise to pay her $800 to do the job. She does a lousy job. We know already that I can sue you. Can I sue your friend? _____ the friend has been paid consideration to do the job. Contrast this with Example 207, in which I cannot sue your friend.*

> **Example 210:** *I commission the famous artist Andy Warhol to paint my family portrait for $1 million. He delegates this duty to Mickey for $50. Is this OK? _____ under the special-person exception.*

> **Note 19:** The bar examiners will often use "assignment" when they are referring to both an assignment and a delegation. Just take the context of the question into account.

CHAPTER 21:   FINAL REVIEW

A. **Which Universe: Common Law or UCC Article 2?**

B. **The Three Big Questions in Contract Law:**

1. **Has an enforceable contract been formed? ("All Contracts Don't Stink")**

2. **Has the contract been performed? ("Pizza With Crawling Escargot")**

3. **What are the remedies for breach? (anticipatory repudiation, money damages, maybe specific performance)**

•   Plus, the after-party (third-party beneficiaries, assignment, delegation)

C. **Hot Topics From Past Exams:**

1. **Rejecting an offer**

2. **Revoking an offer**

3. **Statute of Frauds**

4. **Parol evidence rule**

5. **Warranties**

6. **Rejecting goods**

7. **Money damages**

8. **Third-party beneficiary**

9. **Assignment**

10. **Delegation versus novation**

> **Exam Tip 6:** Remember your DNA twitches.

GOOD LUCK!

[END OF HANDOUT]

Criminal Law

CRIMINAL LAW
PROFESSOR PAMELA S. KARLAN
STANFORD LAW SCHOOL

CHAPTER 1: JURISDICTION AND ACTUS REUS

Before there can be a crime, two things must be present: jurisdiction and actus reus.

A. Jurisdiction

- The United States has the power to criminalize and to prosecute crimes that:

  - Occur _____ ;
  - Occur on _____ and _____ ; or
  - Are committed by United States nationals abroad

- By contrast, the states can only punish crimes having some _____ to the state. For example:

  - A crime that occurs in whole or _____ inside the state
  - Conduct outside the state that involved an _____ to commit a crime inside the state
  - A _____ to commit a crime if an overt act occurred within the state

    > ***Example 1:*** *Doug lives in Delaware and is visiting South Carolina for vacation. In South Carolina, he meets Ken from Kansas in a bar. Doug hires Ken to kill Doug's wife, Vicki. Ken goes to Delaware, kidnaps Vicki, and her body is later found in Pennsylvania where she was killed.*
    >
    > *Can Ken be convicted of murder in Delaware?*
    >
    > *_____ , because part of the crime occurred in Delaware.*
    >
    > *Suppose Ken leaves the bar in South Carolina and rents a car to drive to Delaware. Can Ken be prosecuted for conspiracy to commit murder in South Carolina even if no crime occurred there?*
    >
    > *_____ , because it is a conspiracy and one of the overt acts—renting a car—occurred in South Carolina.*
    >
    > *Can Ken be prosecuted in Kansas?*
    >
    > *_____ , because none of the events connected to the crime occurred in Kansas.*

B. Actus Reus

- No such thing as a "_____" crime. Wanting or hoping to commit a crime is not itself a crime.

1. There must be some _____ in the world

   > **Example 2:** *A thief shoves a gun into the side of a victim and says, "Your money or your life." The shoving of the gun is the actus reus.*

   o The act can be _____.

   > **Example 3:** *A thief walks up to a victim and says, "Give me $100,000 or I will break your mother's legs next week." The act of speaking is the actus reus.*

2. Act must be _____ (i.e., willed by the defendant)

   o An involuntary act does not satisfy the actus reus requirement.

   > **Example 4:** *Steve can't get to sleep because he's worried about the bar exam. His doctor recommends that he take Ambien, a popular sleep medication. One of Ambien's side effects is that users sometimes sleepwalk or eat while not fully awake. One night after taking his Ambien, Steve arises from his bed, sleepwalks into the common area of the dormitory, reaches into the refrigerator, and eats Celia's jar of caviar.*
   >
   > *Can Steve be charged with larceny?*
   >
   > *_____, his taking was not a _____. He was under the influence of a prescription drug.*
   >
   > **Example 5:** *A husband is in bed one night with his wife. In the middle of a dream, the husband rolls over on top of the wife and suffocates her to death.*
   >
   > *Is the husband guilty of homicide?*
   >
   > *_____, the husband did not voluntarily do anything because he was asleep.*

   o "Voluntary" does not necessarily mean the person wanted to do it. It means that he had motor control over the act.

   > **Example 6:** *Tom goes into a store in an attempt to rob the store. He points a pistol at Jerry and says, "Tie up your coworkers or else I'll blow your head off." Jerry, in tying up his coworkers, has committed the actus reus necessary for battery, but he almost certainly will have a defense of duress.*

3. The failure to act can be sufficient actus reus

   o Failure to comply with a _____ duty; such as the failure to file a tax return, failure to register for selective service, etc.

- Failure to act when there is a _____ between the defendant and the victim; e.g., parents' failure to obtain medical attention for their children

- Voluntarily _____ a duty of care that is cast aside

  > *Example 7:* *Anna and her friends are on the beach when they see you drowning. Anna shouts, "I'll save you!" She starts swimming out to you when she looks at her watch and realizes that Mad Men, her favorite TV show, is starting soon. She turns around and swims back to shore. If you drown, can Anna be held criminally liable?*
  >
  > _____, *because Anna started rescuing you and abandoned the rescue.*

- The defendant causes a _____ and fails to mitigate harm to the victim caused by the peril

  - The defendant must be aware that he has made something dangerous.

    - Not enough to be aware that there is a danger

  > *Example 8:* *On the way into the bar exam, you see a student spill his drink all over himself. You notice that he is about to touch a live wire. If you do nothing and let the student get electrocuted, you cannot be held criminally liable. However, if it were your wire and you should have grounded it, you could be held criminally liable.*

  > *Example 9:* *Nancy is a home healthcare worker who cares for an elderly woman named Mona. One evening, while Nancy's friend Dave is visiting Nancy at Mona's house, Mona begins to choke on her dinner. Dave hears Mona choking. Rather than doing anything, he says to Nancy, who is listening to her iPod, "Hey, that old lady is turning blue and gasping. What a hoot!" Nancy decides to wait until the end of a track to check on Mona. Mona chokes to death. Can Dave be charged with any crime related to Mona's death?*
  >
  > _____, *because Dave is just a bystander.*
  >
  > *Can Nancy?*
  >
  > *Yes, because Nancy was in a _____ with Mona.*

CHAPTER 2: MENS REA, TRANSFERRED INTENT, AND MERGER

Exam Tip 1: Mens rea is one of the most important criminal law topics tested on the MBE.

A. Mens Rea—The Common Law States of Mind

1. Specific Intent

o The defendant not only committed the actus reus, but did it for the purpose of causing a particular result

> *Example 10: Burglary is defined as the entering of a dwelling with the intent to commit a felony once inside. You have a suspicion that your neighbor might be a hoarder. One day, you climb into your neighbor's house through a window to look around. Once inside, you happen to see a newspaper from the day that you were born. You take the newspaper and leave the house.*
>
> *Have you committed burglary?*
>
> *_____, because you didn't enter the house with the _____ to commit a felony. Although you committed a crime, you did not commit common law burglary.*

o Memorize the four categories of crimes that are specific intent crimes under the common law. Remember **FIAT!**

   1) **F**_____: On the MBE, the question will expressly state if a defendant is charged with first-degree murder

   2) **I**_____ crimes: "CATS"—conspiracy, attempt, and solicitation

   3) **A**_____ with attempt to commit a battery

   4) **T**_____ offenses: e.g., larceny, embezzlement, forgery, burglary, and robbery

Exam Tip 2: The main reason to memorize the FIAT crimes is that there are some defenses—most notably voluntary intoxication and unreasonable mistake of fact—that are available only for specific-intent crimes.

2. Malice

o I "**AM**" certain there are only two malice crimes: _____ and

   _____

o Malice exists when the defendant acts in reckless disregard of a high degree of harm. The defendant realizes the risk and acts anyway.

> *Example 11: Arson is the malicious burning of the dwelling of another. Lynn is at Paul's house for a Fourth of July cookout. Some of the fireworks seem to be duds, so Lynn tosses them onto the gas grill. Some explode and catch Paul's house on fire. Lynn is charged with arson. At trial, she argues that she didn't want to cause Paul's house to burn down.*

Can Lynn be convicted of arson?

Yes, because arson is not a specific-intent crime. It is enough that Lynn was reckless and engaged in conduct that had a high risk of harm.

3. General Intent

- ○ _____ category
- ○ The defendant intends to commit an act that is in fact unlawful.

  - ▪ The defendant does not need to know the act is unlawful; it is sufficient to intend to perform the act that the law condemns.

- ○ Generally, acts done knowingly, recklessly, or negligently under the Model Penal Code (MPC) are general-intent crimes. Examples include: battery, rape, kidnapping, and false imprisonment.

  > **Exam Tip 3:** General intent crimes most likely to be tested on the MBE include forms of homicide other than murder, such as manslaughter, and battery.

4. Strict Liability

- ○ There is no state of mind requirement; the defendant must merely have committed the act

  1) Statutory/Regulatory offenses

     Example 12: A statute requires that food items be labeled with the expiration date. If a company sells those food items without an expiration date, they've committed a crime under this statute. Even if the company did not intend to sell the food without an expiration date or even if it was an honest mistake, the company is liable under strict liability.

  2) Morals offenses

     Example 13: Humbert is attracted to younger women. He knows the age of consent in his state is 16. He meets Lolita in a bar, where patrons must show ID to enter. Lolita tells Humbert that she is 18 and she suggests they go back to her apartment to have sex. Humbert agrees and they have sex. Later, Humbert is charged with statutory rape, because Lolita is under the age of consent. At trial, Humbert states that he checked her ID and really thought that Lolita was 18. Suppose the judge believes Humbert, can he still be convicted of statutory rape?

     _____, so long as Humbert meant to have sex with Lolita, that is sufficient.

     > **Exam Tip 4:** If an MBE question contains a statute, read it carefully for mens rea language.
     >
     > "Intent to…" = _____ crime

"Knowingly or recklessly...." = _____ crime

No mens rea language = Consider _____

B. **Mens Rea—The Model Penal Code States of Mind**

- The MPC expresses mens rea as: purpose, knowledge, recklessness, and negligence. The MPC also recognizes some strict liability crimes.
- Hierarchy of mental states:

    1) Purpose—highest level of culpability

    2) Knowledge

    3) Recklessness

    4) Negligence—lowest level of culpability

- Look for the mens rea requirement in the statute through words like "knowingly" or "intent to"
- If there is no mens rea language, assume the prosecutor must prove recklessness

1. **Purposely**

   The defendant's conscious objective is to engage in the conduct or to cause a certain result

   > ***Example 14:*** *Patricia raises her gun, points it at Vic, screams "die, you two-timing no-good piece of garbage," and fires, killing him. She has acted purposely.*

2. **Knowingly or willfully**

   Requires that the defendant be _____ that his conduct is of the nature required by the crime and that the _____ is practically certain to occur based on his conduct

   > ***Example 15:*** *Patricia is angry at Vic but can't stand the sight of blood. So she decides to kill Vic by putting arsenic in his coffee Thermos. She knows Vic shares his coffee with his co-worker, Virgil, but she does not care what happens to Virgil. Both men drink the coffee and die. With respect to Vic, Patricia has acted purposely, but with respect to Virgil, she has acted knowingly, since she didn't have the intent that Virgil die, although she knew that the result was practically certain to occur.*

3. **Recklessly**

   Requires the defendant to act with a conscious disregard of a substantial and unjustifiable _____ that constitutes a gross deviation from the standard of conduct of a law-abiding person.

   > ***Example 16:*** *Patricia is a Golden State Warriors fan who lives in downtown Oakland. When the Warriors win their 73d regular season game, she's so*

excited that she takes her semi-automatic gun out of the house and fires several dozen rounds into the air. Several of the rounds hit Vic. She didn't want to hit him, and she actually didn't know he was standing nearby, but she acted recklessly.

4. Negligently

The defendant _____ aware of a substantial and unjustifiable risk and acts in a way that grossly deviates from the standard of care of a reasonable person in the same situation.

C. Transferred Intent Doctrine

- When a defendant has the requisite mens rea for committing a crime directed against Victim A, but actually commits the crime against Victim B, the law _____ the intent from Victim A to Victim B

> *Example 17: Ralph is a professional jewel thief. He is hired to steal a valuable diamond pin from Mrs. Rich at a charity ball. In preparation, Ralph studies her picture from old newspapers. However, Mrs. Rich has had a lot of work done on her face since the picture. At the ball, Ralph approaches Miss Faux, who resembles the picture he studied, believing her to be Mrs. Rich, and steals jewelry from her instead.*
>
> *Can Ralph be charged with larceny—a specific-intent crime—against Miss Faux?*
>
> *_____, he intended to commit larceny; it transfers to Miss Faux.*
>
> *Can he be charged with attempted larceny against Mrs. Rich?*
>
> *_____, because he attempted to commit larceny against her, even if it was Miss Faux.*

> **Note 1:** Transferred intent does not apply to attempted crimes, only to completed crimes.

D. Vicarious liability

- Holds a person or entity liable for an actus reus committed by someone else
- A corporation can be liable for the actions of its high-level employees or the Board of Directors.

    - The MPC requires a specific _____ imposed by law on the corporation, or that high-level officials have _____ or tolerated the act.
    - Both the individual who has the actus reus and mens rea and the corporation for which he works can be held liable.

E. Merger

- A defendant can be convicted of more than one crime arising out of the same act. However, a defendant cannot be convicted of two crimes when the two crimes merge into one. In that case, the defendant can only be convicted of one of the crimes.

- Two categories of merger:

    1) _____ offenses; and

    2) The merger of an _____ and a completed offense

1. Lesser-included offenses:

- o Lesser-included offense: An offense in which each of its elements appears in another offense, but the other offense has something additional

- o Greater-included offense: An offense which includes all elements of the lesser-included offense but requires something additional

- o Think of each element of the offense as a different geometric figure:

    - If the elements of Offense # 1 are a circle and a square,

    - And the elements of Offense # 2 are circle, square, and triangle, then

    - Offense #1 is the _____ offense of Offense #2; Offense #2 is the greater-included offense of Offense #1.

    - Remember: A defendant cannot be convicted of both Offense #1 and Offense #2.

    Example 18: Ralph tries to steal Miss Faux's pin by gently prying it free from her jacket. But she notices Ralph and resists. Ralph then pushes her over and runs off with the jacket. His conduct would satisfy the elements for both larceny and robbery, but since:

    Robbery = _____ + _____ of force

    Larceny is a lesser-included offense of robbery. Robbery is a greater-included offense of larceny. Ralph can be convicted of robbery but not of larceny, because larceny _____ into the robbery.

    Note 2: If there are two separate victims, the crimes against each victim do not merge together.

2. Inchoate and Completed Offenses

- o **Attempt**: A defendant who actually _____ a crime cannot also be convicted of _____ that crime.

    - If you try to commit the crime against Person #1 and actually commit it against Person #2, you can be convicted of both the attempt against Person #1 and the completed crime against Person #2.

- o **Solicitation**: _____ into the completed offense

- If the defendant solicits another person to commit a murder and the other person goes ahead and commits the murder, the defendant is liable for the murder, but not for solicitation as well.

- **Conspiracy** and substantive offenses do not merge!

  - A defendant can be convicted of both _____ to commit a crime and committing the crime itself.

CHAPTER 3: PRINCIPALS, ACCOMPLICES, AIDERS, AND ABETTORS

A. Children

- At common law, children under the age of _____ were never capable of committing a crime
- Children ages _____ were rebuttably presumed to be incapable of committing crimes
- Children at least _____ years old could be charged as adults.

> **Exam Tip 5:** On the MBE, children are more likely to be the victims of crime rather than the perpetrators.

B. Principals

- Defendants whose _____ or _____ form the actus reus of the crime
- Can be more than one principal to a particular crime
- Ask: Who committed the actus reus that gives rise to the offense?

C. Accomplices

- Theory for holding people other than the principal responsible for the crime committed by the principal
- People who _____ the principal either before or during the commission of a crime can be liable as accomplices

  - Must act with the _____ of assisting the principal to commit the crime; bystanders, even approving ones, are not accomplices.

    Example 19: You go to a bar after the exam and a bar fight breaks out. If you applaud during the fight, you are not liable for assault as an accomplice.

- Liable as an accomplice for both the _____ crime and any other _____ crimes that occur in the course of the criminal act

  Example 20: Irving decides to rob a bank. He asks Oscar to drive a getaway car. Irving does not have a gun. Irving then goes to Paul's house and asks to borrow Paul's revolver, telling him he wants to go target shooting. Paul lends him the gun. During the bank robbery, Irving shoots a teller. Oscar takes his share of money from the robbery and buys heroin to sell.

For which crimes can they be convicted?

Irving: _____

Oscar: _____

Paul: _____

> **Editor's Note 1:** Irving and Oscar might also be held liable for conspiracy, discussed below.

- An accomplice can be _____ even if he or she cannot be a principal or even if the principal cannot be convicted

  > **Editor's Note 2:** The modern majority rule is that an accomplice may be convicted of a crime even if the principal is not tried, is not convicted, has been given immunity from prosecution, or is acquitted. However, at common law, the accomplice could be convicted of a crime only if the principal was also previously convicted of the crime. Only a small minority of jurisdictions still subscribes to this approach.

  Example 21: A statute makes it a crime for a public official to take bribes. Mayor Benedict wants to take a bribe, but wants to do it where no one will see. His friend, Claudio, owns a cabin in the woods. Mayor Benedict asks Claudio if he could use his cabin as the location to exchange bribery money. Claudio agrees and offers to chain off the road. Claudio could be guilty of aiding and abetting the bribery as an accomplice. But, he could not be guilty as a principal because he is not a public official.

  Example 22: You assist a 7-year-old child to commit murder. Your little nephew tells you that he really wants to kill his classmate Bobby. You give your nephew a gun to commit it. Your nephew cannot be convicted of murder because he is under the age of 7, but you can be convicted of aiding and abetting as an accomplice.

  > **Editor's Note 3:** The professor misspoke regarding the facts in the above example. In this scenario, you gave your nephew a gun so that he could commit the crime. Your nephew cannot be a principal because he is too young. However, you can be convicted of murder as an accomplice.

  Example 23: If you help a diplomat commit a crime, the diplomat has diplomatic immunity so the diplomat might not be held liable as a principal, but you can still be held liable as an accomplice.

  - **Exception**: A person protected by a _____ cannot be convicted as an accomplice in violating the statute.

Example 24: *If a statute prohibits sex with an underage person, the underage person is not an accomplice to that crime.*

D. Accessories After the Fact

- People who assist the defendant _____ the crime has been committed, e.g., obstruction of justice or harboring a fugitive

    Example 25: *After the bank robbery, Irving asks his accountant for help with laundering the money from the robbery. If the accountant helps Irving, he is not guilty of aiding and abetting the bank robbery, but instead would be guilty of a **separate crime** as an accessory after the fact (e.g., a financial crime).*

E. Aiders / Abettors and Conspiracy

- In addition to accomplice liability for the substantive crime, individuals who aid or abet a defendant to commit a crime may also be guilty of the separate crime of _____ if there was an agreement to commit the crime and an overt act was taken in furtherance of that agreement.

    Example 26: *Recall Example 20, above. Oscar and Irving might also be guilty of conspiracy to commit robbery in addition to the substantive crime of robbery.*

F. Mental States of Accomplices

- **Majority and MPC Approaches**—the accomplice must act with the purpose of promoting or facilitating the commission of the offense; the accomplice must _____ that her acts will assist or encourage the criminal conduct.

- **Minority Approach**—the accomplice is liable if he intentionally or knowingly aids or causes another person to commit an offense.

    o Any voluntary act that actually assists or encourages the principal in a known criminal aim is sufficient for accomplice liability

- **Criminal Facilitation**—under the majority rule, a person who is not guilty of the substantive crime (because he did not act with intent) may nevertheless be guilty of the lesser offense of criminal facilitation for simply assisting

CHAPTER 4:   NEGATING MENS REA

Three categories: Mistake, insanity, and intoxication

A. Mistake

- A defendant claims that some mistake—regarding either facts in the world or the state of the law—negates his _____ and thus he cannot be convicted of a crime for which there is both actus reus and mens rea elements.

1. **Mistakes of Law**

   o   Mistakes about what the law forbids or permits

   o   _____ of the law is no excuse.

   > ***Example 27:*** *The fact that you didn't realize the speed limit was 65 because you thought it was 80 is a mistake of law and is generally not a defense.*

   o   Three potential exceptions:

   1) Reliance on high-level government _____

       •   Relying on your own lawyer's advice does not generally fall into this exception

       > ***Example 28:*** *If a regulation states that something is permitted and you are later prosecuted for that conduct because the regulation was wrong, the regulation might negate the mens rea element.*

   2) Lack of notice

   3) Mistake of law that goes to an element of _____ intent (applies only to the "FIAT" crimes or specific-intent crimes)

       •   For specific-intent crimes, a defendant can argue that his belief that his conduct was legal _____ that element of the offense.

       > ***Example 29:*** *Quentin, a solo practitioner, practices law out of his rented apartment. He drills holes in the wall of his apartment for bookshelves. The landlord tells Quentin to stop drilling and grabs Quentin's drill. Quentin pushes the landlord, causing him to fall and injure his shoulder. Quentin is charged with battery and with the statutory crime of "knowingly damaging the property of another person, [with the intent to deprive that person of the property]." Quentin argues that he thought a tenant was allowed to alter the walls of his apartment as long he had the lease. He argues that he was defending his own property when he pushed the landlord.*

       > *Quentin had the mistaken belief that he was protecting his own property. Is that a defense to a charge of battery? _____, because battery is not a specific-intent crime. He voluntarily applied force to another person and was not entitled to do so.*

       > *Can Quentin's mistake about the property be a defense to violating the statute? _____, Quentin did not knowingly deprive a person of the property because he believed he could alter the walls.*

2. **Mistakes of Fact**

   o   **Key starting point:** Whether the crime is a strict liability crime, a _____ crime, or a _____ crime

a. **Strict Liability:** Mistake of fact is _____ a defense.

  ▪ Must be a voluntary act, but the defendant's state of mind is irrelevant

b. **General Intent:** Mistake of fact is a defense only if the mistake is _____ and it goes to the criminal intent.

  ▪ Remember the transferred intent doctrine: Killing William when a defendant meant to kill Edward is not a mistake of fact

c. **Specific intent:** Mistakes of fact are a defense whether the mistake was reasonable or unreasonable. The only question is whether the defendant held the mistaken belief.

d. **Application**

  Example 30: *Roger is out of town on a business trip and he is very tired. It is dark when Roger rents a car at the airport. He goes to a restaurant, barely noticing what kind of rental car he is driving. After dinner, he gives his ticket to the valet to retrieve his rental car. The valet brings Roger a different car from the one he actually rented. Roger absentmindedly gets into the Porsche and drives off. Roger is charged with larceny (which requires taking away the property of another person with the intent to permanently deprive the other person of the property; a specific-intent crime) and with joyriding (which requires taking the automobile of another person for a short period of time).*

  Can Roger be convicted of larceny if the jury concludes that no reasonable person would confuse an economy car with a Porsche?

  _____. Larceny is a specific-intent crime and specific-intent crimes only require a mistaken belief. He thought he was in his car.

  Can Roger be convicted of joyriding, even if the jury believes that he thought the car was his?

  _____, because the jury concluded that the mistake was unreasonable.

B. **Insanity**

  ● Four different tests:

    1) **M'Naghten:** Defendant either did not know the _____ of the act or did not know that the act was wrong

    Example 31: *A defendant did not realize that he was shooting at a human being; he thought he was shooting at a pumpkin.*

    2) **Irresistible Impulse:** Defendant has a _____ or defect that means the defendant cannot control herself

3) **Durham Rule**: Defendant would not have committed the crime _____ his having a mental disease or defect (rarely used because so defendant-friendly)

4) **Model Penal Code**: Due to a mental disease or defect, the defendant did not have _____ to appreciate the wrongfulness of her acts or to _____ her conduct to the law

> **Note 3:** All four tests require that the defendant have a mental disease or defect. Being a psychopath is not enough to constitute insanity.

- In the majority of jurisdictions, the _____ has the burden of proving insanity either by a preponderance of the evidence or by clear and convincing evidence.

  o Some jurisdictions require the defendant to overcome the presumption of sanity by introducing evidence of insanity, and then the burden of persuasion shifts to the prosecution to prove sanity beyond a reasonable doubt.

C. Intoxication

- Covers alcohol, drugs, and medications
- Can be _____ or involuntary

1. Involuntary intoxication

  o Occurs when a person:

  - Doesn't realize that she received an intoxicating substance (e.g., "date rape" drugs);
  - Is _____ into ingesting a substance; or
  - Has an _____ or unanticipated reaction to a prescription medication.

  o Can be a valid _____ to general intent, specific intent, and malice crimes when it negates the mens rea necessary for those crimes.

2. Voluntary intoxication

  o Occurs when a person _____ ingests the substance, knowing that it was an intoxicant

  o Voluntary intoxication is a defense only to _____-intent crimes (FIAT crimes), and only if it prevented the defendant from forming the mens rea

  - Not a valid defense if the defendant got drunk in order to commit the crime

    Example 32: Terry is a member of a gang. As an initiation rite, she must break into her boyfriend's house and steal one of his mother's shoes. Terry is timid and nervous, so she drinks six shots of bourbon to get her courage up. She's now quite drunk. She then climbs through an open window and begins rummaging around in the mother's closet. She gets one of the mother's pumps and leaves the house. While weaving down the driveway, the mother comes *home and confronts Terry. Terry tries to hit the mother over the head with the shoe. But Terry's hand-eye coordination is not so good, so she misses. Terry then jumps into her car and drives off. Unfortunately, she runs over Ursula and kills her. Suppose Terry is charged with burglary, assault, and vehicular homicide.*

Starting point: She got drunk in order to commit the crime. If she'd simply gotten drunk with friends and then burglarized a house, she could not be convicted of burglary because it is a specific-intent offense. But because she drank in order to commit the burglary, she _____ be convicted, even of the specific-intent crime of burglary.

Assault (with attempt to commit battery) is a specific-intent crime, but it's not the crime she got drunk in order to commit, so if she didn't have the _____ _____, she can't be convicted of assault.

Vehicular homicide: It is not a specific-intent crime, so she's guilty even though she had no desire to run over Ursula.

o Under the MPC, voluntary intoxication is only a defense to crimes for which a material element requires purpose or knowledge and the intoxication prevents the formation of that mental state.

CHAPTER 5:   INCHOATE CRIMES

Note 4: Remember CATS: Conspiracy, Attempt, Solicitation

A. Conspiracy

1. Definitions and Elements

a. Common law conspiracy requires:

- An _____
- Between two or more people
- To commit an _____ act

b. Modern conspiracy statutes

Add a fourth requirement: the _____ requirement

c. Model Penal Code (MPC)

Only the defendant who actually has been charged must actually _____ to commit the unlawful act. The other people with whom the defendant agrees can be undercover agents, for example.

o Agreement can be _____

- Simply _____ a crime is going to occur and doing nothing about it does not turn a bystander into a co-conspirator; there must be an agreement.

  Example 33: *Anna lives in a common law jurisdiction. She agrees with Bob to rob a bank, but she doesn't know that Bob is an undercover police officer. Anna also wants to steal an emerald from a jewelry store in a nearby state, which is an MPC jurisdiction. She asks Ranier for help with stealing the gem from the jewelry store. She doesn't know that Ranier is also an undercover officer.*

  Is Anna guilty of conspiracy to commit bank robbery?

  _____, because there wasn't an actual agreement between 2 people to commit a crime. Anna was the only person agreeing to commit a crime.

  Is Anna guilty of conspiracy to commit larceny?

  _____, because only Anna needs to agree to commit a crime in an MPC jurisdiction.

- **Purpose of the conspiracy:** Unlawful act

  - If what the conspirators agree to do is not a crime, there is no conspiracy even if they think what they're doing is wrong.

    Example 34: *Harry and Sally hear that gray-bellied sapsuckers are exotic birds on the endangered species list and know that someone will pay $10,000 for one of these birds. They know that stealing eggs from endangered species' nests is a crime. Harry and Sally agree to go to the nest of the gray-bellied sapsucker and steal the eggs to sell them. But it turns out that gray-bellied sapsuckers aren't endangered, so it's not actually a crime to catch one. So they are NOT guilty of conspiracy, because what they conspired to do was not a crime—even though they thought it was.*

- **Overt act:** Can be lawful or unlawful, as long as it _____ the conspiracy

  Example 35: *Zacarias Moussaoui and other 9/11 hijackers joined a health club together in Georgia. They did it to build strength so they could overpower the pilots and crew during the hijackings. This is an overt act because it furthered the conspiracy.*

2. **Scope of a Conspiracy**

   - At common law, each co-conspirator can be convicted both of:

   1) Conspiracy; and

   2) All substantive crimes committed by any other conspirator acting in _____ of the conspiracy.

Example 36: Goldie, Frank, and Myrtle all agree to steal goods from a sporting goods store in the mall. Goldie will enter the store to steal the goods, Frank is the lookout, and Myrtle is driving the getaway car. Goldie tells Frank to blow a whistle if a security guard comes by. After Goldie enters the store, Frank panics when he sees a guard and shoves the guard, who falls and breaks his arm. Goldie comes out of the store with the goods, which includes a starter pistol. Myrtle later uses the starter pistol to rob a convenience store. Who is liable for what?

Conspiracy to rob the store:

_____

Battery of the guard:

_____

Robbery of the convenience store:

_____

o Relationships of co-conspirators

- **Chain Conspiracy**: Co-conspirators are engaged in an enterprise consisting of many steps; each participant is liable for the substantive crimes of his co-conspirators

  Example 37: A conspiracy to distribute drugs involves many people in a causal chain (manufacturer—distributer—dealer). The conspirators need not know each other, but they have all agreed to participate in the same conspiracy and each can be held liable (1) for the conspiracy and (2) for the substantive offenses committed along the way.

- **Spoke-Hub Conspiracy:** Involves many people dealing with a central hub; participants are not liable for the substantive crimes of their co-conspirators because each spoke is treated as a separate agreement rather than one larger general agreement

  Example 38: A bank employee agrees to process fraudulent loan applications. This employee would serve as the "hub." Each individual seeking a fraudulent loan is a "spoke." But the spokes are not responsible for the actions of the other spokes.

  Example 39: If many thieves use the same "fence" to sell stolen goods, each robber is responsible for the goods and for conspiracy to sell stolen property, but not for the goods from other robbers.

3. **Withdrawal from a Conspiracy**

   o At **common law**, it's _____ to withdraw from a conspiracy, because the crime is completed the moment the agreement is made.

> *Example 40:* *You and Professor Kramer agree to commit a crime. The next day, she calls and says she no longer wants to participate in the crime. Professor Kramer can still be convicted of conspiracy because you both agreed to commit the crime. But she will not be convicted of the actual crime you both had planned to commit because she has withdrawn.*

- o Under the **federal and MPC rules**, a conspirator can withdraw prior to the commission of any _____ by communicating her intention to withdraw to all other conspirators or by informing _____.

  - ▪ A conspirator who helps to _____ the success of a conspiracy can raise a withdrawal defense even after an overt act has occurred.

    > *Example 41:* *In an MPC jurisdiction, if Professor Kramer withdraws from the conspiracy successfully—either by notifying you or law enforcement—she may not be held liable for conspiracy if the notification was timely enough to thwart the success of the conspiracy.*

- o Even if a defendant cannot withdraw from the conspiracy (e.g., because the notification was not timely), that defendant can limit his liability for substantive crimes committed after he withdraws.

B. Attempt

- Attempt is a _____ crime

1. Requirements

1) Specific intent to commit a particular criminal act; and

2) A _____ step towards perpetrating the crime

  - Moves you down the road towards actually committing the crime

    > *Example 42:* *Waking up and getting dressed on the morning that you plan to embezzle funds from your employer does not constitute a substantial step.*

    > *Example 43:* *Bringing special equipment to the scene of the crime or lying in wait will typically constitute substantial steps.*

- o Attempt is a specific-intent crime always—even when the completed offense is only a _____-intent crime

    > *Example 44:* *Attempted murder is specific-intent crime, but murder is a general-intent crime.*

2. Defenses

- o Defenses for specific-intent crimes can be used as a defense to attempt.

> *Example 45:* *Aaron is standing on an overpass. For a joke, he throws bowling balls onto the highway below. If a bowling ball hits and kills someone, Aaron will be guilty of murder (because he acted with a maligned and depraved heart). But if the ball doesn't hit anyone, Aaron cannot be charged with attempted murder because he lacked the specific intent required to commit murder (i.e., he didn't intend to kill).*

   o Certain defenses like voluntary intoxication and unreasonable mistake of _____ are available even if they wouldn't be available had the crime been completed.

3. Merger

   o Attempt merges into a _____ offense.
   o You _____ be convicted of both attempted murder and murder of the same person in the same episode.
   o You can be convicted of both _____ to commit murder and murder.

C. Solicitation

- Occurs when an individual _____ invites, requests, or commands another person to commit a crime

   o If the person agrees, we have a _____ instead.
   o If the person commits the offense, the solicitation charge will _____ into the completed offense.

> *Example 46:* *Amy offers to pay Doug $1,000 to commit a murder. This is a solicitation. If Doug says yes, this is a conspiracy to commit murder. If Doug actually commits the murder Amy will be guilty of the murder and conspiracy, but not solicitation.*

> **Note 5:** It is an offense simply to ask someone else to commit a crime.

> *Example 47:* *Wallace goes into a bar and offers a guy $10,000 to kill her boss. That is solicitation. If the guy agrees, that is conspiracy to commit murder. If the guy actually kills the boss, Wallace is guilty of both conspiracy and murder.*

> **Note 6:** The solicitation charge merges into the completed offense, but the conspiracy charge does not.

CHAPTER 6:   HOMICIDE

A. In General

1. Definition

   o Homicide: The unlawful _____ of a living human being by another human being

- ▪ Animals: Can't commit a homicide and killing an animal is not a homicide
- ▪ Victim cannot already be dead
- ▪ Suicide is not homicide, but assisting someone to commit suicide can be a homicide.

2. Causation

- o There must be _____ between the defendant's actions and what happened to the victim

  - ▪ **Actual Causation:** Victim would not have died "_____" what the defendant did
  - ▪ **Proximate Causation**: Defendant's act is a _____ cause of the victim's death (death is the natural and probable result of the conduct)

    Example 48: *If a defendant shoots the victim and the victim dies in the hospital because the doctor was negligent, that death is a foreseeable consequence of shooting someone.*

    - • Independent actions by a third person are generally not a foreseeable cause

    Example 49: *Bernie, the defendant, commits securities fraud. One of his victims—who was defrauded of money—commits suicide. Bernie is not the proximate cause of the victim's death, even though he may be viewed as the actual cause.*

    > **Exam Tip 6:** There are three common types of homicides on the bar—first-degree murder, common-law murder, and manslaughter.

3. Consent is Not a Defense to Any Type of Homicide

Assisted suicide is a homicide by the assister.

B. First-Degree Murder

- • Specific-intent crime

  > **Exam Tip 7:** The question will tell you if the case involves first-degree murder. Otherwise, assume that the question involves common-law murder or manslaughter.
  >
  > The question is likely testing the special defenses for specific-intent crimes (FIAT crimes).

C. Common-Law Murder

1. Definition

- o The _____ killing of another human being committed with _____ aforethought
- o Lawful killing of another is not murder (e.g., state execution is not murder)

2. Four Kinds of Malice

a. _____: The defendant acted with the desire that the victim end up dead.

- The intent need not be "premeditated." It can be formed in a second.

b. **Intent to inflict** _____: The defendant intended to hurt the victim badly, and the victim died.

c. _____ **or** _____: The defendant acted with a cavalier disregard for human life and a death resulted.

- The defendant must realize that his conduct is really risky but need not have any intent regarding the outcome of his actions.

    Example 50: *Russian roulette*

d. _____: The death occurred during the commission or attempted commission of a _____ felony

- The "BARRK" felonies—burglary, arson, robbery, rape, and _____
- Deaths caused by other felonies get the label of misdemeanor manslaughter.
- Felony murder can involve:

    a) Someone who _____ the felony

    Example 51: *The defendant attempts to rob the victim and the victim resists. The defendant punches the victim and the victim dies.*

    b) When a bystander is killed during a felony

    Example 52: *You rob a bank and the guard gives chase. You fire your gun at the guard but instead hit a pedestrian on the street.*

    c) Third person killed by the resister or police officers (minority)

    Example 53: *You rob a bank. After robbing the bank, you get into a shootout with the police. If a police officer misses you and shoots a bystander, you are liable in a minority of jurisdictions.*

    - **Majority—agency theory**: A defendant is only responsible for the crimes of the defendant's "agents." Because the victim, police, or third party are not the defendant's agents, the defendant is not responsible for their conduct.

    d) If a co-felon is killed by a resister or a police officer, then the defendant is not guilty of felony murder.

> *Example 54:* *If the defendant is riding with the getaway driver and the police shoots and kills the getaway driver, the defendant is not liable for felony murder.*

> **Exam Tip 8:** If a question just says "murder," assume that it's common law murder, a malice crime. Recall that in malice crimes, an unreasonable mistake of _____ and voluntary intoxication are NOT available defenses.

D. Manslaughter

1. Definition

- All _____ killings of another human being that are not first-degree murder or common-law murder
- Two types: _____ and _____

2. Voluntary Manslaughter

- Occurs when a defendant intends to kill the victim, but his state of mind is less blameworthy than murder

    - Acted in the "_____" or "under extreme emotional disturbance"

- Test to determine if it's murder or manslaughter: Is the situation one in which most people would act without _____ and without time to _____?

    > *Example 55:* *Rufus comes home and finds his wife, Amy, in bed with Luke. Rufus shoots Luke and Amy. This is acting in the heat of passion or heat of the moment. People are not expected to stop, think rationally, and calm down in this situation.*

    > **Note 7:** Hearing about your spouse's affair is not sufficient.

    > *Example 56:* *Frank was sexually abused as a young teenager. Five years later, he testifies at the highly-publicized trial of his abuser and was forced to describe the abuse he had suffered. Several days later, a group of young teenagers surrounded Frank and began taunting him, suggesting that he had "asked for it." Frank lashes out at the group and strangles one of them.*

    > *Would Frank be entitled to a manslaughter instruction? Probably not under the heat of passion defense, but maybe under the emotional disturbance. We need more facts to determine whether it was reasonable to strangle somebody for a taunt.*

3. Involuntary Manslaughter

- A criminally _____ killing or killing of someone while committing a crime other than those covered by felony murder

- o **Misdemeanor manslaughter:** The defendant is engaged in a crime that does not rise to the BARRK level of felony, and as a result of that crime, someone dies
- o A defendant who engages in criminally negligent conduct and causes a death is guilty of involuntary manslaughter (e.g., traffic deaths).

> *Example 57:* *A woman goes jogging with her dogs. A city law makes it a misdemeanor to let a dog off its leash on public property. But the woman ignores the law. While unleashed, one of the woman's dogs attacks and kills a small child. In this situation, the woman may be guilty of involuntary manslaughter, because letting her dog off its leash was the "but-for" cause of the child's death.*

CHAPTER 7: PROPERTY CRIMES

A. Larceny

1. Definition

- o Larceny requires:
  - ▪ Taking
  - ▪ Another person's property
  - ▪ Without his consent (trespassory) and
  - ▪ With the _____ to deprive him of it permanently.

2. Elements

- o **Property**—tangible personal property (e.g., wristwatch, goods sold in a store)
  - ▪ Not intangible property (e.g., copyright) or real property, or services

  > **Note 8:** There are modern "theft of services" statutes that criminalize obtaining a service, e.g., a massage, and then not paying for it. That conduct does not fall under common law larceny.

- o **Taking**—Involves any _____ of property, however slight

  > *Example 58:* *Hank goes into an electronics store to shoplift an MP3 player. He lifts the player off of the counter and heads for the door. Even before he leaves the store, he has satisfied the "taking" element of larceny.*

- o **Trespassory** taking (without consent)

  Consent must be real, not obtained by _____ or _____

  > **Editor's Note 4:** "Lack of consent" is not an element of larceny. The prosecutor must merely show that the taking was wrongful. The defendant can assert consent as an affirmative defense.

- o **Intent**—An intent to deprive the person of the property permanently

- "Borrowing" property, even without the owner's consent, is not larceny as long as you intend to _____.
- If the property is destroyed in your care, you have not committed larceny (e.g., joyriding).

> *Example 59:* *A teenager sees a fancy car with the keys in it. The teen jumps in, thinking he will just drive the car around the block a few times and then return it. But he crashes the car. Is he guilty of larceny?*
>
> *_____, because the teenager intended to give the car back. (Note: he does not get off scot free because there are other crimes, like joyriding, for which he can be convicted.)*

> *Example 60:* *One day before class, you realize that you forgot your textbook. In the law school library, you see someone else's textbook lying on a desk. You borrow the book with the intention of returning it after class. During your class, there is a fire alarm and you leave the book behind. The sprinklers malfunction and start spraying water inside the classroom, ruining the borrowed textbook. Are you guilty of larceny?*
>
> *_____, because you didn't intend to deprive the owner of the textbook permanently.*

- Larceny is a _____ crime. As long as the defendant thinks it's his property—however unreasonably—he is not guilty of larceny.

> *Example 61:* *You take the wrong black umbrella from an umbrella stand in a restaurant. Even if you intend to keep that umbrella forever, you are not guilty of larceny because you were mistaken (this is true even if the mistake was unreasonable).*

3. Embezzlement: A Variation of Larceny

- The defendant starts out having the victim's consent to have the property but commits embezzlement by _____ the property to his own use.

> *Example 62:* *Jake is a teller at King Savings Bank. One day Lou, a depositor at the bank, comes to the window and hands Jake a check, made out to Zach and endorsed over to Lou, for deposit to Lou's account. Jake knows that Lou is an enforcer for an organized crime family, and strongly suspects that Lou obtained Zach's check through force. Believing the check to be ill-gotten gains, Jake instead deposits the check to the account of the Make a Wish Foundation, a local charity.*
>
> *Is Jake guilty of larceny because he stole Lou's check? _____, he had permission.*

Is Jake not guilty of embezzlement because the money was not rightfully Lou's in the first place? _____.

Is Jake not guilty of embezzlement because he didn't keep the money for himself? _____, he converted property he legally obtained for his own purpose.

4. **False Pretenses: Another Variation of Larceny**

The defendant obtains title to someone else's property through an act of

_____.

> ***Example 63:*** *Paying for goods with counterfeit money or a bad check*

5. **Model Penal Code and other Modern Changes**

- o Under the MPC and in many jurisdictions, crimes such as larceny, false pretenses, and embezzlement are treated as a single statutory crime of theft (which includes both tangible and intangible property).

  > **Exam Tip 9:** Be sure to note whether a question wants you to use the MPC definition (i.e., all the theft crimes are treated equivalently) or the common-law definitions (in which case, you must work your way through the elements).

B. **Robbery**

1. **Definition and Elements**

- o Common-law robbery is a simple equation:

  - ▪ Robbery = _____ + _____

- o **Robbery requires**:

  1) Taking;

  2) Another person's property;

  3) Without his consent;

  4) With intent to deprive him of it permanently;

  5) The taking occurs from the victim's person or in his _____; and

  6) Either by violence or putting the victim in fear of _____ physical harm

2. **Extortion: A Variation of Robbery**

Involves threats of _____ harm (including non-physical harm), rather than threats of imminent physical harm

> ***Example 64:*** *Xenia approaches Chris at a party and admires her necklace. Xenia tells Chris, "Give me your necklace or else I'll tell your husband that I saw*

you coming out of a hotel room last weekend with Ben." Chris turns to walk
away and Xenia grabs the necklace, pulling it off Chris's neck.

Of which crimes are Xenia guilty?

Robbery: Yes, because obtained by _____

Extortion: _____, because threat did not do anything

Attempted extortion: _____, threatened to commit larceny, but failed

C. Burglary

1. Definitions

- o **Common-law burglary requires:**
  - ▪ Breaking and
  - ▪ Entering
  - ▪ The _____
  - ▪ Of another
  - ▪ At night
  - ▪ With the specific intent to commit a _____ once inside

- o The common-law elements have been relaxed, so that burglary can now occur in commercial properties or during the day; i.e., **modern law burglary requires:**
  - ▪ Breaking and
  - ▪ Entering
  - ▪ The property
  - ▪ Of another
  - ▪ With the specific intent to commit a felony inside

2. Elements:

- o **Breaking** can involve pushing open or smashing a door or window, or obtaining entry by

  _____

  - ▪ Someone who comes inside another's dwelling with the owner's _____ and then steals something is guilty of larceny (and possibly robbery is he used violence or threat of violence) but not burglary because there was no "breaking."

- o **Entering** involves breaking the plane of the dwelling.

  Example 65: *Sticking your hand through a window constitutes "entering."*

- o A "**dwelling**" at common law is a structure regularly lived in, not a commercial building.
- o **Of another:** Cannot burglarize yourself
- o With the _____ to **commit a felony** once inside.

- The usual felony is larceny, but it could be another felony, such as battery.

Example 66: *Breaking into another's house due to curiosity is not burglary because there is no specific intent to commit a felony once inside.*

Example 67: *Nick has several friends staying at his beach house. One afternoon, he notices that Mary has an expensive diamond watch. She takes it off when she goes to the beach. That evening, while everyone is down at the beach for the sunset, he sneaks back to the house, pries open the kitchen window, enters Mary's bedroom, forces open her jewelry box, and steals the watch. Meanwhile, Quinn, Nick's neighbor, notices the half-open window. He's always wanted to see the inside of Nick's house, but Nick has been very standoffish about inviting him in. Quinn raises the window slightly higher to squeeze into the house. While roaming about the house, he notices Wayne's wallet on the nightstand and takes $250 from the wallet. Nick and Quinn are each charged with burglary.*

Are either of them guilty of burglary?

Nick: Cannot burglarize his own house

Quinn: He did not enter for the purpose of committing a felony

CHAPTER 8: BATTERY, ASSAULT, RAPE, KIDNAPPING, ARSON, AND OTHER CRIMES

A. Battery

1. Definition

- o Unlawful
- o Application of force
- o To another person
- o That causes bodily _____ OR
- o Constitutes an _____ touching

2. Elements

- o **Unlawful**: Consent is a complete defense to battery (e.g., boxing match).
- o **Application of force**: Need not be a great deal of force; the slightest touch can constitute force in some cases
- o Battery is a _____ crime, so voluntary intoxication and _____ mistake of fact are not available defenses.
- o Application of force does not require an actual physical connection between the defendant and the victim (e.g., throwing a rock that hits someone)

B. **Assault (Two Forms)**

1. _____

   o If a defendant has taken a substantial step toward completing a battery but fails, he will be guilty of assault

   o It is a _____ crime because it is an attempt; Specific-intent defenses are available

   > **Note 9:** If there is an actual touching, this form of assault rises to the crime of battery.

2. **Fear of Harm**

   o Intentionally placing another in _____ of imminent bodily harm

   o This form of assault is a _____ crime.

   > *Example 68:* *Thomas has a crush on Ursula. After getting drunk one night, Thomas concludes that Ursula truly loves him. He goes to her room and knocks, but she won't open the door. Thomas breaks it down. Once inside, he tries to kiss Ursula. But she's fast and he's drunk, so she gets away. Thomas falls over and pushes over Isaac—who is also in the room—injuring Isaac.*
   >
   > *Did Thomas commit a battery against Ursula for trying to kiss her?*
   >
   > *_____, because he didn't actually kiss or touch Ursula.*
   >
   > *Is Thomas guilty of attempted battery (assault)?*
   >
   > *_____, if his intoxication prevented him from having the required mens rea.*
   >
   > *Is it a defense to attempted battery that Thomas thought Ursula really wanted to kiss him? As long as the defendant cannot maintain specific intent, he does not have the requisite intent.*
   >
   > *Did Thomas commit a battery against Isaac? _____.*
   >
   > *He also committed assault by breaking down the door because he put them in fear of imminent bodily harm and his voluntary intoxication is not a defense.*

C. **Rape**

1. **Common-law rape requires:**

   o Unlawful

   o Sexual intercourse

   o With a female

   o Against her will by _____ or threat of force

- o Rape is a _____ crime; voluntary intoxication is not a defense.

> **Exam Tip 10:** The MBE will not likely test on common-law rape because the elements have been relaxed or eliminated in most modern statutes.
>
> For example, men can be rape victims today, and rape can occur when the victim is unable to consent even in the absence of force (for example, because she or he is unconscious).
>
> It is more likely that a question about rape will provide a modern rape statute and will ask about potential defenses or elements.

2. Statutory Rape

- o Regulatory morals offense that involves _____ intercourse with a person under the age of _____
- o Statutory rape is a _____ offense, so mistake cannot negate the defendant's guilt if he committed the actus reus.
  - ▪ If a defendant knows that he is having sex, he cannot claim ignorance or mistake about the victim's age.

3. Other sex crimes at common law

> **Exam Tip 11:** These are extremely unlikely to be tested on the bar exam.

- o Adultery: having sex with someone who is not your spouse
- o Fornication: sex between unmarried people
- o Crimes against nature: bestiality
- o Incest: sex between people who are too closely related to one another (the closeness restriction varies among states)
- o Bigamy: strict liability offense of marrying someone while you are still legally married to someone else
- o Seduction: a man tells a woman that he will marry her if she has sex with him

D. Kidnapping

- • **Requires:**
  - o Unlawful
  - o _____ of another person
  - o Against that person's will
  - o Either by _____ or hiding the victim

> *Example 69:* *Olivia and Paula decide to rob a grocery store. There are two people in the store: Alex (a clerk) and Scott (a customer). They tie up Alex and grab Scott and put him into the meat locker. A hostage situation ensues and police eventually get Olivia to release Scott. They are charged with kidnapping Alex and Scott.*

Are they guilty of kidnapping Scott?

_____, because he was confined unlawfully without his consent and he was moved.

Are they guilty of kidnapping Alex? If Alex wasn't moved at all, then they did not commit kidnapping.

E. Arson

1. Definition

- **Common-law arson requires:**

  - _____
  - Burning
  - Of another person's
  - _____

2. Elements

- **Malice**: Intent to act in a way that will cause burning, or is substantially likely to do so
- **Burning**: At common law, there had to be burning (fire) as opposed to an explosion or smoke damage. It also required damage to the structure, not just the contents inside.

  - Under modern statutes, it is arson even if there is no damage to the structure of the building or if the fire was caused by an explosion.

- **Another Person**: At common law, you could not torch your own house.

  - Under modern statutes, burning your own home is arson.

- **Dwelling**: Had to be a dwelling, not another (commercial) structure

  - Under modern statutes, burning down a commercial building is arson.

F. Perjury

- Willful act of _____ promising to tell the truth, either verbally or in writing, about material matters

  - The person must know what they are saying is false, must _____ to say something false, and the falsity must go to a _____ matter.

    > **Example 70:** *Pauline is a called as a witness in a burglary case. She says that she was walking down the street and she saw the defendant break into the victim's house and then come out. It would not be a material falsehood for her to say that just before she saw the defendant, she had been at a friend's house not doing much of anything—when in reality, she was at the friend's house sleeping with her friend's husband. This is not a material falsehood, at least not vis-à-vis the burglary case.*

- **Subornation of Perjury**: A person persuades someone to commit perjury, such as paying someone to testify falsely

G. Bribery

- **Common law**: Corrupt payment of something of value for purposes of influencing an _____ in the discharge of his official duties
- **Modern law**: Allows bribery to be prosecuted even if the person being bribed is not a public official
- Offering a bribe and receiving a bribe are both felonies.
- Recall that a person can be convicted of bribery even if the person could not "be bribed" under the statute

> ***Example 71:*** *If you aid and abet the bribing of a public official by helping the official accept the bribe, you can be guilty of bribery even though you could not receive the bribe and did not offer the bribe.*

CHAPTER 9: DEFENSES

A. Intoxication

- **Ask two questions**:
    1) Was the intoxication involuntary or voluntary?
    2) Is the charged crime a specific-intent crime or a general-intent crime?
    - **Specific-intent crimes (FIAT or MPC statute with "purposely")**: Can use either voluntary or involuntary intoxication as a defense, if the defendant could not maintain the state of mind necessary for the offense
    - **General-intent crimes**: Can use only _____ intoxication as a defense

B. Insanity

- Involves a defendant who, because of a _____ disease or defect, is unable to conform his conduct to the law

C. Mistake of Fact

- What is the _____ required for this crime?
    - General-intent crimes: Only _____ mistakes of fact may be used as a defense.
    - Specific-intent crimes: _____ mistakes of fact are potential defenses, even unreasonable mistakes.

D. Self-Defense

- Two kinds of force:

  - _____ force: Intended or likely to cause death or serious injury (e.g., shooting someone)

  - _____ force: Involves force that is not likely to cause death or serious injury (e.g., pushing another aside, locking a door)

1. Non-deadly force

  - A victim is entitled to use non-deadly force any time he _____ fears _____ unlawful harm

    > *Example 72: In the Thomas and Ursula example, when Thomas tries to kiss her, Ursula can swat his hand away, slap his face, or use another type of non-deadly force.*

2. Deadly force

  - A putative victim is entitled to use deadly force only if he _____ believes that deadly force will be used against him.

    - Under the MPC, a victim can use deadly force if he reasonably believes that the crime involved could result in serious bodily injury.

  - **Retreat**

    - **Majority rule:** Retreat is _____ even when entitled to use deadly force
    - **Minority rule:** _____ retreat rather than using deadly force if safe to do so

      > *Example 73: Jan sees you coming toward her house with a weapon in your hand. In a minority jurisdiction, if she can get inside, lock the door, and call the police, she cannot go upstairs to get her rifle and blow your head off from a window. In a majority jurisdiction, she is not required to retreat and can shoot you.*

    - Even in minority jurisdictions, retreat is never required when the person employing deadly force is in his own home.

      > **Exam Tip 12:** On the MBE, the question will tell you if you are to assume a duty to retreat. Otherwise, assume that you can use deadly force to resist deadly force or another serious crime.

E. Defense of Others

- An individual has the same right to defend other individuals against a criminal that she has to defend herself.

  > *Example 74: You and a friend are walking down the street. Someone approaches your friend and says, "Give me your money or I'm going to shoot*

you." You are entitled to use deadly force to protect your friend, as if you were protecting yourself.

F. Defense of Property

- Right to use only _____ force to protect property

    Example 75: *If you see someone trying to steal your car, you cannot use deadly force to prevent the theft of property.*

    Exam Tip 13: The bar examiners often use a scenario involving deadly force designed to protect property during the owner's absence; e.g., the use of booby traps or spring guns. This is not an appropriate use of force.

G. Duress

- The defendant claims he only committed a crime because he was threatened by a third party and _____ believed that the only way to avoid death or injury to himself or others was to commit the crime.
- In order for duress to be a defense to a crime, there must be a threat of death or serious bodily harm. Mere injury, particularly injury to property, is not sufficient.
- Defense for all crimes other than _____

    Example 76: *Don decides to rob a grocery store. On the way out of the store, he leaps into a passing car driven by Fred, puts a gun to Fred's head, and orders Fred to drive him out of town. "Faster, faster," Don yells. Fred knows that the speed limit is 65, but he cranks the engine up to 90 miles an hour. As a result, he is unable to stop before running over Glenda. Fred is charged with felony murder with respect to Glenda's death.*

    Is Fred guilty?

    _____, he was under duress and killed her while speeding. He did not commit intentional murder.

H. Necessity

- Available in response to _____ forces; i.e., it is the lesser of two evils

    Example 77: *After Hurricane Katrina flooded New Orleans, many people were trapped in the city. One such person is Harold, who is trapped in his house without potable water. He breaks into a neighbor's house looking for drinkable water. Harold could assert a necessity defense, because he could claim that without getting water from his neighbor's house (which was a burglary), he might have died. Thus, breaking into the house was the lesser of two evils.*

GOOD LUCK ON THE EXAM!

[END OF HANDOUT]

Criminal Procedure

CRIMINAL PROCEDURE
PROFESSOR PAMELA S. KARLAN
STANFORD LAW SCHOOL

CHAPTER 1:   **BASIC CONCEPTS, ARRESTS, AND SEIZURES**

A. Basic Principles

- Constitutional protections apply only to _____ action

    > ***Example 1:***   *If parents severely beat a child, they do not violate the Cruel and Unusual Punishments Clause.*

    > ***Example 2:***   *A snoopy neighbor enters your house and steals several things from you—including your marijuana plants. He brings the plants back to his home and calls the government to notify them of what he found. This is not a search.*

- Two important exceptions:

    - Private persons acting as government agents

        > ***Example 3:***   *The government calls your neighbor and asks her to break into your house to look for marijuana plants. This is a search under the Fourth Amendment.*

        > ***Example 4:***   *The government asks one inmate to speak with another inmate in order to get the second inmate to answer some questions. This is an interrogation within the meaning of the Fifth and Sixth Amendments.*

    - Defense counsel (both public and private) are treated as government actors for purposes of the Sixth Amendment with respect to effective assistance of counsel.

B. Arrests and Seizures of Persons

1. In General

- Police can approach anyone in a public place, and unless the encounter escalates to a _____, there is no real constraint on what the police can do and no protection against what they discover (e.g., "tailing" a suspect, canvassing a neighborhood and asking questions).

- **Seizure:** Occurs when an officer, by means of _____ or show of _____ intentionally terminates or restrains the subject's freedom of movement

    - Physical force: grabbing suspect by the arm, shooting a suspect, blocking ability to move

- Show of authority: showing a badge and saying, "Stop!"
- Test: Whether a reasonable person would feel free to _____ the officer

Seizure: Ramming a suspect's car in an attempt to stop the car

Not a seizure: Running over a third party while chasing a suspect (because the officer did not intend to stop the third party)

2. **Types of Seizures**

a. **Stop and Frisk/Terry Stops**

- An officer can stop an individual when the officer has _____ suspicion, based on _____ facts, to believe the suspect is or is about to be engaged in criminal behavior.
- Burden Hierarchy:

Beyond a Reasonable Doubt → Conviction
Probable Cause ("more likely than not") → Arrest
Reasonable Suspicion → Stop

An officer's reasonable mistake of law can give rise to reasonable suspicion

- During a Terry Stop, an officer can pat-down (frisk) a detainee for _____, but cannot frisk for evidence.

If the pat-down reveals objects whose shape makes their identity obvious (i.e., it's obvious that the objects are contraband), the officer can seize those objects.

If _____ develops during a Terry Stop (either because of something the suspect says or because of an object discovered), the officer can then make an arrest.

- Consequences of a stop that is not based on adequate suspicion:

If the initial stop is unlawful, but the officer develops probable cause, any evidence seized during the arrest can be used

> **Example 5:** In Utah v. Strieff, *police were outside of a house where they thought there might be drug activity. Strieff came out of the house and the officers stopped him based merely on a hunch (which is insufficient to support a stop). During the stop, the police ran a warrant check which revealed a warrant for Strieff's arrest. During a search incident to arrest, the officer discovered drugs.*

- If the arrest itself had been unlawful, evidence seized during a search incident to arrest would likely be suppressed at trial.

b. Traffic stops

- Officers must have reasonable suspicion to stop a car

Once there is lawful stop, officers may pat-down the occupants for weapons

- Checkpoints—Officers do not need reasonable suspicion to stop drivers if they pull over everyone.

c. Arrests

- There must be _____ to believe that the arrested individual has committed a crime.

Can be with or without an arrest _____

- Pretext arrest: As long as the police have probable cause to believe an individual committed a crime, they may arrest that individual even if their real motive is based on a different crime that is not supported by probable cause.

    Example 6:   *Undercover officers are walking the streets of D.C. looking for illegal drug activity. They see a man driving a car—he appears nervous and somewhat suspicious. He then makes a turn without using his turn signal. Police can pull over this driver because he failed to use his turn signal—even though they were really concerned about drug activity. They did not have probable cause to stop him for the drugs, but he could be pulled over because they had probable cause to believe that he committed some crime.*

d. Warrants

- Authorizes an officer to arrest a particular person
- An arrest warrant is issued by a _____ and detached magistrate based on a finding of _____ to believe that the named individual has committed a particular crime.
- The warrant must name the person and identify the _____
- Allows officers to enter an individual's home to arrest that individual

    - An arrest warrant alone does not authorize officers to enter a third party's home or business to arrest the individual
    - Officers must also have a search warrant to search the premises for the individual (or meet an exception to the warrant requirement)

- Absent an arrest warrant, officers can arrest someone inside a dwelling if:

    a) There are exigent circumstances (felony hot pursuit or danger to others), or

    b) There is _____ to enter.

e. **Warrantless arrests**

- An officer can arrest an individual without a warrant in a public place, either for a crime committed in the officer's _____ or based on probable cause to believe the individual committed a _____

If the crime was not committed in the officer's presence, the officer can make an arrest only for a felony

> ***Example 7:*** *You just robbed a bank (a felony) and fled the scene. An officer arrives and a witness describes you to the officer. The officer walks around the area and notices you because you perfectly match the suspect's description. The officer can arrest you because he has probable cause.*

- An illegal arrest does not prevent prosecution for the crime. But, it may result in the exclusion of evidence

C. **Searches Incident to Arrest**

- A lawful arrest permits the arresting officers to make a contemporaneous search of the person arrested and the immediate _____ to:

  o Protect officers from _____ or other dangers; and

  o To prevent the _____ or concealment of evidence

- Any evidence discovered during a search incident to a lawful arrest can be used against the person arrested.

- **Arrest on the street:** Can search the suspect and his _____

- **Arrest at home:** Can search the suspect and his immediate arrest area

- **Arrest in a car**: May search _____ compartment of a vehicle as long as the person/suspect still has _____ to the vehicle at the time

  - Officers cannot arrest a suspect and put him in the back of the squad car and then go back and conduct a search of the car

    > **Editor's Note 1:** Note that if it is reasonable to believe that the vehicle contains evidence of the offense of the arrest, such a search would be proper, even though the suspect would no longer pose a threat to the officers.

- Inventory searches—When the police arrest a driver and impound his car, it may be searched for inventory purposes.

- Special rule for cellphones—officers may seize a cellphone during an arrest and check the phone for dangers, but police need a warrant to search the phone's digital information

  > **Exam Tip 1:** Determine whether the arrest was legal, either based on a warrant or on probable cause to believe the crime was committed. If the arrest was legal, there is a presumption that the officer can conduct the search and use the evidence. If the arrest was illegal, there is a presumption that any fruits of the arrest will be suppressed.

CHAPTER 2:   SEARCHES

Exam Tip 2: "Searches" is a topic that is often tested.

A. **What is a "Search"?**

- Occurs when _____conduct violates a reasonable

  _____ of privacy

- **Government:** Must be government conduct (e.g., it is not a search if your mother or private employer goes through your things)

  o   Can occur with physical intrusion upon private property

      Example 8:   The police bring a drug-sniffing dog onto your porch, or place a GPS device on your car

  o   But, a search can occur without a physical intrusion

      Example 9:   The defendant was growing marijuana in his basement and used grow lamps. A government agent set up a thermal imaging device on the public street and found that the basement was unusually warm. The agent used this information to obtain a search warrant. The use of the thermal imaging device was a search in violation of the defendant's reasonable expectation of privacy.

      ▪   Using some types of **technology** constitute a search, but dog sniffs from a public street do not.

- **Reasonable expectation of privacy:**

  o   Places where we do have an expectation of privacy against the government:

      ▪   Homes

      ▪   _____

      ▪   Offices

      ▪   Backyard of your home (curtilage)

      ▪   Luggage

  o   Places where we do not have an expectation of privacy against the government:

      ▪   Public streets

      ▪   Open fields (even if they're private property with right to flyovers)

      ▪   Garbage cans left out in the street

      ▪   _____ property

      Example 10: Quentin goes into the dressing room of a men's store and hides a valuable leather belt in his underwear. Wendy, a store security guard monitoring a hidden camera in the dressing room, sees Quentin. As Quentin is leaving the store, Wendy grabs him, handcuffs him, thrusts her hands into his pants, and grabs the belt. Wendy calls the police and Quentin is subsequently charged with larceny. He argues that the belt should be excluded from evidence because the search violated his constitutional rights. What result?

This was not an unconstitutional search because Wendy was not a government agent. She was a private security guard for the store.

Exam Tip 3: Be careful in determining whether there was government action and whether the defendant had a reasonable expectation of privacy.

B. The Warrant Requirement

- Generally, the government needs a warrant to conduct a search if there is a reasonable expectation of privacy. Three requirements:

    1) A search warrant must be issued by a neutral magistrate

    2) Must be based on probable cause to believe that the items sought are
    _____, instrumentalities, or _____ of crime

    Example 11:   There has been a bank robbery. The loot that was stolen from the bank is the fruit of the crime; the gun used to commit the robbery is an instrumentality of the crime; the bloody shirt the robber wore is evidence of the crime.

    3) Must describe the _____ and _____ to be searched with particularity

- If a warrant does not meet the above requirements, the warrant is _____, and the items seized pursuant to the warrant will be _____ from the prosecution's case-in-chief.

- Wiretapping constitutes a search

    o Must have probable cause and a warrant
    o Must specifically identify whose conversations are to be intercepted
    o Must include an end date for the warrant

C. Exceptions to the Warrant Requirement

- There are seven major exceptions; think of them as seven _____ from the warrant requirement:

    o Exigent circumstances
    o Search incident to arrest
    o Consent
    o Automobiles
    o Plain view
    o Evidence obtained from administrative searches
    o Stop and frisk

1. **Exigent Circumstances**

   o Officers are entitled to secure premises (i.e., prevent people from moving things) while they obtain a warrant, but sometimes this is not sufficient.

   o If officers are in "hot pursuit" or _____, they may conduct a search without getting a warrant first (i.e., emergency situations).

   > **Example 12:** A woman runs out of a building and tells an officer that there is a man inside with a bomb who is threatening to blow everyone up. The officer may enter the building and search without first obtaining a warrant.

   > **Example 13:** If officers believe that a suspect dropped a weapon in a place where a small child might pick it up, officers may look for the weapon without first obtaining a warrant.

   o This exception does not apply when police create the exigency.

   o Absent exigent circumstances, police need a warrant for a DUI blood draw

2. **Search Incident to Lawful Arrest**

   o If the arrest was lawful, a search warrant is unnecessary.

   o Scope—limited to the immediate area around the individual

   o Automobile—arrestee must be within reach of the passenger compartment for that to be searched

   o DNA—samples may be collected as part of search incident to arrest

   o Cellphones—cannot search digital contents

3. **Consent**

   o A defendant can consent to a search.

   o Consent does **not** require the officer to _____ the subject of his right to refuse. (e.g., "Mind if I look in that ….?")

   o **Third Parties**

   ▪ A third party with _____ authority can allow a search.

   > **Example 14:** You give your bags to a friend and say, "Please hold my knapsack while I run into the library for a second." A police officer approaches your friend and asks to look in the knapsack. If your friend agrees, the officer need not obtain your consent to search the knapsack because the friend had apparent control over the property.

   ▪ Officers cannot search over the objection of a present occupant. (*Georgia v. Randolph*)

   ▪ However, officers can search if the suspect is not present and the other occupant consents. (*Fernandez v. California*)

4. **Automobiles**

o Recall that police are allowed to conduct a warrantless search of an automobile incident to arrest if the arrestee is within reach of the passenger compartment and to conduct an inventory search of an impounded vehicle.

o In addition, if police have **probable cause** to believe an automobile contains _____, they can search those parts of the vehicle (including containers) that might contain contraband, even without an arrest

> ***Example 15:*** *If police have probable cause to believe that there are drugs in a car, they may search the parts of the car (and containers in the car) that might contain the drugs. (might be the whole car)*

> ***Example 16:*** *If police believe that there are submachine guns in a car, they may search the trunk and passenger compartment. They cannot search inside a wallet or lipstick container or in other areas or containers where they could not reasonably expect to find the contraband.*

5. **Plain View**

o If police are _____ present, they can seize any item in "plain view" (or "plain smell"), even if that item was not named in the warrant.

> ***Example 17:*** *If police are legally present in a house and they smell marijuana, they can seize the marijuana. If they see stolen goods, they may seize the stolen goods.*

o Officers cannot open drawers, turn items over, or move anything

6. **Evidence Obtained From Administrative Searches**

o Police do not need search warrants to conduct administrative searches.

o Two kinds:

1) Administrative warrants

Do not require _____ (such as fire or health inspections of a building).

2) Warrantless administrative searches

Used to ensure compliance with various administrative regulations
Examples:

 Airplane boarding areas
 International borders
 Highly regulated industries (liquor stores, gun shops, etc.)
 Searches of students in public schools
 Special needs searches; e.g., drug testing of railroad employees after an accident

Roadblocks for drunk driving or seeking information

7. Stop and Frisk

o   Terry stops (covered in Chapter 1), merely require reasonable suspicion

CHAPTER 3: INTERROGATIONS

A. The Fifth Amendment

*   Provides, among other things, that no person shall be _____ in any criminal case to be a witness against himself

1. Scope of the Privilege

o   Applies to _____, not corporations or unions

> ***Example 18:*** *A custodian of a corporation's records may not claim the privilege because the records would incriminate him—the records belong to the corporation.*

o   Applies to _____ evidence, not physical evidence

> ***Example 19:*** *Fifth Amendment protection does not apply to blood tests or handwriting exemplars*

o   Applies to testimony that would be a link in the chain leading to prosecution or conviction

▪   As long as there is reason to believe the testimony might lead to future criminal prosecution, you are entitled to invoke the Fifth Amendment

> ***Example 20:*** *Lara is a witness in a bank robbery case. When asked if she saw the suspect rob the bank, Lara can refuse to answer the question if by answering, she would somehow incriminate herself. Suppose Lara was a law enforcement officer and was supposed to be watching another suspect at the time of the robbery. By admitting that she was at the bank, she might incriminate herself with regard to theft of government services.*

o   If someone is given immunity for their statements, they cannot continue to refuse to answer

2. Statements Made By an Individual

o   Must be made by the individual to the _____

> ***Example 21:*** *Jana comes home and tells her parents that she just robbed a bank. The government can force her parents to testify about what Jana said to them. She would have no Fifth Amendment protection.*

> *Example 22:* *Remember that other privileges or protections may apply via evidence law. Suppose that after robbing the bank, Jana had an appointment with her doctor and told him about the bank robbery because she was feeling anxious and wanted some tranquilizers. Those statements are protected by the doctor-patient privilege.*

- o Key starting point for the privilege against self-incrimination: *Miranda v. Arizona*
    - ▪ Statements made as a result of _____ _____ are inadmissible unless they are accompanied by procedural safeguards (i.e., you receive the *Miranda* warnings first)
    - ▪ "Custodial": The person being questioned has been arrested or is otherwise not _____ (e.g., in the back of a police cruiser).
        - • If not in custody, no warning is required. Any statement (or silence) can be used.
        - • Someone who is already imprisoned is not necessarily treated as "in custody" for purposes of custodial interrogation. The prisoner is not "in custody" if he is free to be taken back to his cell.
    - ▪ "Interrogation": Involves either the official asking questions or engaging in other words or _____ that police know or should know will elicit a response

    Does not include volunteered statements, but does include induced statements
    Does not include _____ booking questions

3. **Miranda Warnings**
   - o Before conducting custodial interrogations, the police must inform the suspect:
       - ▪ She has the right to remain _____ ;
       - ▪ Any statement she makes may be used against her in court;
       - ▪ She has the right to consult an attorney and to have the attorney present during questioning; and
       - ▪ She has the right to have an attorney appointed if she cannot afford one.
   - o Interrogators must ask whether the defendant _____ the rights
       - ▪ I.e., Defendant understands English, can hear, and actually heard what was said
   - o No magic words: As long as the substance of the Miranda warnings is communicated, it will be sufficient
   - o The police must cease questioning if either of the following occurs:
       - ▪ **Invoking the right to remain silent**

       If a defendant says she does not want to talk, the interrogation must _____.
       The right must be affirmatively invoked; it is not enough to just remain silent.

After a _____ period of time, police can go back to the suspect, give warnings again, and seek to talk to her.

- **Invoking the right to counsel**

Right must be affirmatively invoked: "I want a lawyer." It is not enough to say, "I think I should talk to somebody," or "I want to talk to my… (Parents, doctor, etc.)"

If the right to counsel is invoked, all questioning must stop until either:

    i) The lawyer is present, or

    ii) The defendant affirmatively _____ contact with police. Police cannot generally go back to the defendant.

Police do not have to tell the defendant that a lawyer is trying to reach her if the defendant does not ask for the lawyer.

4. **The Public Safety Exception**

    o When public safety is at risk, the police do not have to give Miranda warnings before questioning.

> *Example 23:* *If there is a ticking time-bomb in a grocery store, the police need not give Miranda warnings before questioning people. Or if police are called to a school and told that a man planted a bomb inside, they can arrest the man because they have probable cause and can question him about the bomb's whereabouts before giving Miranda warnings.*

5. **Interrogation Tactics**

    o The confession must be _____

    o Statements obtained by _____, even after warnings, are inadmissible.

> *Example 24:* *"We will prosecute you," is not a threat. "We will beat you up," and "We will go and arrest your children," are threats.*

    o Confessions can be the product of _____

> *Example 25:* *It is permissible to tell a suspect (who was caught on video wearing a mask) that police have the capability to peel off the stocking mask through photo-technology.*

> *Example 26:* *Police can also use the colander and copy machine "lie detector."*

B. **Consequences of Fifth Amendment Violations**

- Two categories:

    o Statements obtained involuntarily

    o Statements obtained in violation of Miranda

1. **Involuntarily Obtained Statements**

   o An involuntarily obtained statement is _____ admissible against a defendant.

      Example 27: *Police may never put a gun to a suspect's head and say, "Confess or die." Any incriminating statement made by the suspect is inadmissible.*

   o Whether to overturn a conviction depends on the harmless error standard.

   o Evidence obtained as the result of an involuntary statement (e.g., "Tell us where the body is buried" while a suspect is at gunpoint) is fruit of the poisonous tree and is _____ inadmissible.

2. **Miranda Violation Statements**

   o A statement obtained in violation of Miranda is inadmissible in the prosecution's case in chief, but can be admitted in order to _____the defendant to challenge his credibility.

   o Evidence obtained as a result of a voluntary statement taken in violation of Miranda is _____

CHAPTER 4: THE SIXTH AMENDMENT RIGHT TO COUNSEL; IDENTIFICATION PROCEDURES

A. The Sixth Amendment

In addition to the Fifth Amendment right to counsel for custodial interrogations (covered in the *Miranda* discussion), the Sixth Amendment explicitly provides a criminal defendant with "the _____ of counsel for his defense."

1. **Sixth Amendment Right to Counsel vs. Fifth Amendment Miranda Right**

   o **How is it invoked?** Automatically attaches once there has been an indictment, information, or other formal charges and exists unless a defendant knowingly and intelligently _____ the right.

      ▪ By contrast, the Fifth Amendment right (protected by *Miranda*) must be affirmatively invoked by the defendant.

      Example 28: *You are arrested and brought to the police station. Unless you ask for a lawyer after getting Mirandized, you will not get one. But if you are charged in court, you get an attorney unless you affirmatively waive the right to counsel.*

   o **To what charges does the right apply?** The Sixth Amendment right to counsel is offense-specific. A defendant has a Sixth Amendment right to counsel only with regard to the offenses for which he has actually been _____ (and any lesser-included offenses).

- With respect to unrelated charges, the defendant can be questioned, either expressly or through undercover government means

  Example 29: *You are charged with burglary so you have a Sixth Amendment right to counsel regarding that burglary and a lesser included offense, such as larceny. But police can still question you about an unrelated robbery for which you have not been charged.*

- Applies whether you are in _____ or not

  - By contrast, the Fifth Amendment *Miranda* right applies to custodial interrogation for any charge, but not to non-custodial interrogation.

2. **When Does the Sixth Amendment Right to Counsel Apply?**

- Applies to all _____ prosecutions and to any misdemeanor prosecutions in which jail time or suspended jail sentence is imposed.

  Example 30: *If you are charged with a misdemeanor and are not sentenced to any jail time, you do not have a Sixth Amendment right to counsel.*

- Applies to all _____ stages of the prosecution

  - Examples of critical stages:

  Hearings
  Post-indictment lineups
  Post-indictment interrogations
  All parts of the trial process, including guilty pleas, sentencing, and appeals as of right

  - Examples of non-critical stages are:

  Investigative lineups (pre-indictment)
  Witnesses looking at photo arrays
  Discretionary appeals and post-conviction (habeas) proceedings

B. **Identification Procedures**

1. **Types of Procedures**

- There are two kinds of identification procedures: _____ and
_____

  - **Photo arrays**: Neither the defendant nor his lawyer has the right to be _____, but police must turn over the array to the defendant.
  - **Pre-indictment lineups**: Defendant has no right to counsel.
  - **Post-indictment lineups**: Defendant has a right to have _____ present.
    - If that right is violated, then evidence that the witness identified the defendant at the lineup must be excluded.

2. **Admissibility**

   o **Lineup evidence at trial**

      ▪ If the defendant moves to suppress evidence that a witness picked the defendant out of a lineup, the court will consider whether the lineup was _____ _____.

      ▪ If it was, the court can exclude the testimony.

   o **In-court identification**

      ▪ The prosecution must establish by _____ evidence that the witness would have identified the defendant even without the suggestive lineup in order to allow the in-court identification.

      Example 31: *Ingrid is charged with art theft. The prosecution alleges that she stole a small but valuable sculpture from an art gallery by putting it into a large shopping bag. The police ask Oscar, who works at the gallery, to view a photo array of five potential perpetrators. Ingrid is the only blonde-haired woman in the array and she appears quite a bit younger than the others. Oscar identifies Ingrid. The police then place Ingrid in a lineup. Preeta, another gallery employee, views the lineup. The Assistant D.A. asks Preeta, "Do you see the person who walked out of the gallery with a large shopping bag?" Preeta says no, but adds that she "saw the third person from the left" – Ingrid – "reach into a lady's pocket and steal her wallet." The A.D.A. knows that another patron at the gallery, Sarah, had filed a complaint with the police that her pocket had been picked on the day of the alleged sculpture heist. So the A.D.A. obtains a search warrant for Ingrid's house, and the police find Sarah's wallet. Ingrid is now charged with larceny against Sarah as well as art theft. Which of the following statements about the use of evidence are true?*

      A) The wallet is inadmissible at Ingrid's trial for larceny because Ingrid's lawyer was not present at the lineup. True or False? _____

      B) Oscar's identification is inadmissible at Ingrid's trial for art theft because Ingrid's lawyer was not present at the photo array. True or False? _____

CHAPTER 5: THE EXCLUSIONARY RULE AND ITS EXCEPTIONS

> **Exam Tip 4:** This is one of the most important Criminal Procedure topics on the MBE.

- **Rule**: Illegally obtained evidence, either _____ evidence obtained by an illegal search or a statement obtained through an illegal _____, is inadmissible at the criminal trial of the person whose rights were violated.

- The Exclusionary Rule applies at _____ and not to pretrial proceedings (e.g., grand jury proceedings).

A. Standing

- The violation must have been of the _____ rights, and not someone else's rights.

    Example 32: *Police enter Ellen's house without a warrant and while there, they find a photograph of Robert holding a sawed-off shotgun. Robert would have no standing to object to introduction of the photograph at his trial for possessing an illegal weapon, since it was Ellen's Fourth Amendment rights that were violated.*

    Example 33: *Lucy is arrested but police do not give her Miranda warnings. If she makes a statement that she robbed a bank with you, you cannot suppress her statements at your trial (because it was a violation of Lucy's rights, not your rights).*

- One slight qualification: If the driver of a car is arrested without probable cause, passengers are deemed to have been seized as well, so they _____ challenge the constitutionality of the stop.

B. The Exclusionary Rule

- **Definition:** Evidence obtained in violation of the _____, _____, or _____ Amendments cannot be introduced at trial to prove a defendant's guilt.

    o _____ of the Poisonous Tree: The exclusionary rule applies not only to the evidence obtained in violation of the Constitution, but also to evidence obtained as a result of the initial violation.

    Example 34: *Police illegally search your house and find a safe deposit box key. They take the key to the bank, look inside the deposit box, and find some incriminating items. Those items are considered fruit of the poisonous tree, because but for the first illegal search, they would not have found the items in the safe deposit box.*

- **5½ Exceptions**

    o **Knock and announce:** Officers executing an arrest warrant at a residence are required to knock and request admission.

    ▪ But, if they fail to do so, and discover evidence, that evidence is _____.

    o **Inevitable discovery:** If the evidence would have been discovered anyway through _____ means, it will be admissible.

> *Example 35:* *Officer Thomas was searching Ulysses' house without probable cause. Officer Young, who had probable cause, was in the process of acquiring a search warrant.*

- o **Independent source:** Relevant evidence discovered on the basis of an independent source will be admissible.
- o **Attenuation in the causal chain:** _____ _____ events and the passage of time can remove the taint of the unconstitutional conduct

> *Example 36:* *An officer unlawfully discovered some betting slips in a flower shop. He told a second officer what he had seen. This second officer then spoke with a former employee of the flower shop who admitted that a bookmaking operation was run out of the shop. Here, there were enough steps in the chain of causation that the evidence gained from talking to that former employee need not be suppressed.*

> *Example 37:* In Utah v. Strieff, *police were watching a house with a suspected drug operation. They decided to stop and question the next person who left the house. The police stopped and questioned Mr. Strieff without adequate suspicion to do so. During the course of questioning, the officers discovered an outstanding arrest warrant for an unrelated event. The officer arrested Mr. Strieff and conducted a search incident to the arrest. During the search, the officer found drugs. The Court held that there was attenuation between finding the drugs and the initial illegal stop. The arrest was lawful and that was sufficient to remove the taint and admit the evidence.*

> **Note 1:** If the officers question a defendant without warning him and then in midstream warn him and continue the interrogation, the causal chain has not been broken.

- o **Good faith**
  - ▪ Biggest of the exceptions to the exclusionary rule
  - ▪ It applies to officers who rely on either:
    - a) An existing law that was later declared unconstitutional, or
    - b) A warrant that, while facially valid, is later found to be defective.
  - ▪ If officers are acting in good faith reliance, they are entitled to use the evidence that was obtained.
  - ▪ Officers can rely on a warrant unless:
    - • The warrant was obtained by _____
    - • The warrant was obtained in _____ on an unacceptably bare-bones affidavit (defective on its face)
    - • The magistrate wholly abandoned his judicial role

- o **(Half) Exception**—Isolated _____ by law enforcement personnel does not necessarily trigger the exclusionary rule.

  - To trigger the exclusionary rule, police conduct must be sufficiently deliberate so that exclusion could meaningfully _____ it.

    Example 38: In Herring v. United States, *Herring went to a police station to pick up his truck which had been impounded. At the station, an officer who was familiar with Herring asked the clerk to see if there was an arrest warrant for him. There was not. The officer then asked her to call the next county and ask whether there was a warrant there for Herring. The clerk said there was. The officers pulled Herring over after he left the police station without probable cause, arrested him, and conducted a search incident to arrest. They found some incriminating information. In the meantime, the clerk discovered that there was no longer a valid warrant for Herring's arrest. Mr. Herring moved to suppress the evidence on the grounds that he was arrested without probable cause and without a warrant. The Supreme Court held that the good faith exception should apply—even though the police may have been negligent.*

- **Key Points**

  - o Remember that suppression is an issue only after you conclude that there has been a _____ in the first place.

    - Fourth Amendment: Was there a search? Was there a seizure? If yes, was there probable cause?
    - Fifth Amendment: Was there a Fifth Amendment interrogation violation? Was the defendant in custody? Was there an interrogation? Was the defendant given warnings? Did he invoke his rights?
    - Sixth Amendment: Did the Sixth Amendment right to counsel attach? Was this a critical stage?

  - o If there was a violation, ask whether the exclusionary rule applies to that kind of violation.
  - o Then ask whether one of the _____ to the exclusionary rule makes the evidence admissible anyway.
  - o If the question involves whether a conviction should be overturned (rather than simply whether the evidence should be suppressed), apply the harmless error rule:

    - Ask, if this piece of evidence had not been admitted, would it make a difference to the outcome?

CHAPTER 6: PRETRIAL PROCEDURES

A. The Initiation of Charges

- Under the Fifth Amendment's Presentment Clause, all federal felony charges must be initiated by _____ by a grand jury unless the defendant waives indictment.

  o An indictment is a finding that there is _____ to believe the defendant committed the crimes charged.

- The Fifth Amendment Presentment Clause has not been incorporated to the states, so the states have the choice of whether to proceed by grand jury indictment or by

  _____

  o If proceeding by information, there must be a preliminary hearing before a neutral judge to determine whether there is probable cause.

B. Proceedings before the Grand Jury

- Grand juries can consider evidence that was obtained _____ and _____ evidence in deciding whether there is probable cause to indict.
- **Prosecutors** have no duty to present _____ evidence to the grand jury.
- **Defendants** do not have the right to testify before the grand jury or to call witnesses.
- **Witnesses** do not have the right to _____ within the grand jury room, although they can leave the grand jury room to consult with their lawyers.
- Grand jury proceedings are held in _____
- The grand jury does not have to be _____

C. Competence to Stand Trial

- Test: Whether the defendant comprehends the _____of the proceedings against him and can _____ his lawyer in defending the case
- If a defendant is competent to stand trial, he is also competent to plead guilty and waive the right to trial

D. Bail

- The Eighth Amendment forbids the setting of _____ bail, but does not state outright that bail must be offered pending trial.

  o **General rule:** Bail is available unless the defendant poses either a flight risk or a _____ to the community.

  o There is a presumption in favor of release pending trial.

  o Courts can impose pretrial release conditions on defendants, such as house arrest, avoidance of particular people, or reporting requirements

  o There is a presumption against release after conviction, pending appeal.

E. Guilty Pleas

- The majority of defendants do not go to trial: the charges are either dismissed or the defendant pleads guilty

- When a defendant pleads guilty, he _____ various trial rights, such as the right to put the prosecution to its proof, to confront and produce witnesses, to trial by jury, to challenge the introduction of evidence, to appeal if there is a conviction.

- For a guilty plea to be valid, the defendant must _____ and _____ waive these rights. This is accomplished through plea allocution, where the judge:

    o Informs the defendant of his rights and ensures that the defendant understands those rights
    o Informs the defendant of the possible sentences
    o Informs the defendant of immigration consequences (although the judge is not required to inform the defendant of all collateral consequences, such as difficulty getting student loans)
    o Makes sure there is a factual basis for the plea
    o Determines that the plea did not result from _____, coercion, threats, or promises

- If a defendant challenges his plea agreement and succeeds in reopening the case, the prosecution can reinstate charges that it had dropped.

- The defendant is entitled to _____ assistance from counsel in the plea bargaining process.

CHAPTER 7:   THE TRIAL PROCESS

A. The Jury

1. Defendant's Right to a Jury Trial

    o The Sixth Amendment provides a right to jury trial for all _____ offenses, for which the authorized punishment is more than _____ months.

    > **Note 2:** The Sixth Amendment right to *counsel* attaches in misdemeanor cases only if a sentence of incarceration is actually imposed.

2. Jury Size

    o **Federal:** A jury in a federal criminal case must have _____ members and must decide the case _____
    o **States:** States can use juries of _____ or more in criminal cases. Juries do not have to be _____ (though a six-person jury must be unanimous).

3. Jury Selection

    o Begins with a venire or jury pool

- Must represent a fair _____ of the community from which no distinctive group is excluded.

- The petit or petty jury is selected through the process of voir dire.

    - Two ways to remove potential jurors: challenges _____ or peremptory challenges.

        - The actual jury that is seated must be impartial, but it does not have to reflect a fair cross-section of the community.

    - **For-cause challenges:** Used to ensure an impartial jury

        - Jurors can be removed for cause when they reveal something that will prevent them from being impartial and deliberating _____ (e.g., if a juror knows one of the parties or the victim; if a juror has a general belief that prevents him from being impartial)

        - There is _____ to the number of challenges for cause.

    - **Peremptory challenges:** Can generally be made for anything, including hunches

        - Exception (Batson doctrine): Neither side can challenge jurors on the basis of race or _____

        - Each side is statutorily limited in the number of peremptory challenges.

B. **Speedy and Public Trial Rights**

1. **Speedy Trial Rights**

    - Defendants can be injured by the passage of time between an alleged crime and their trial
    - Statutes of limitations give defendants repose.

        - Statutes of limitations normally begin to run when the crime was committed.
        - For continuing offenses, the statute of limitations does not begin to run until the end of the offense (e.g., a conspiracy starts on the day of agreement but continues until the conspiracy's purpose has been achieved or abandoned).

        Example 39: *In January 2003, Pam entered into a conspiracy to distribute drugs. The conspiracy continued until 2007. The statute of limitations begins to run from 2007, not 2003.*

    - Two constitutional provisions that protect against delay:

        - The _____ protects against pre-accusation delay. It's relatively toothless, as long as the limitations period has not run.
        - The _____ Clause of the Sixth Amendment protects defendants against delay that occurs between the time of arrest or indictment (whichever comes first) and the time of trial.

- A court faced with a Speedy Trial Clause claim looks at four factors:

    1) Length of the delay

    2) _____ for the delay

    3) Whether the defendant _____ to a speedy trial

    4) _____ to the defendant

2. Public Trial Rights

- The Sixth Amendment and First Amendment, taken together, protect the rights of the defendant (Sixth) and the public (First) to attend public trials.

- Courts do have some discretion to close particular proceedings if there is a substantial likelihood of _____

3. The Confrontation Clause

- The Sixth Amendment guarantees defendants the right to _____ the witnesses against them, as well as the right to compulsory process to produce their own witnesses.

- *Crawford Doctrine*

    - If a statement is _____ (i.e., made under circumstances which would lead a reasonable person to believe that the statement would be used at a later trial), then the Sixth Amendment bars admission of the statement if:

        - The declarant is _____ and
        - The defendant had no prior _____ to cross-examine the witness.

        Example 40: *In* Melendez-Diaz v. Massachusetts*, the prosecution tried to admit a forensic report into evidence without calling the forensic analyst who prepared the report as a witness. The Court determined that the defendant was entitled to cross-examine the analyst and so, the report was inadmissible without that opportunity.*

    - For non-testimonial statements, look to the rules of evidence.

- *Bruton Category*

    - A defendant's own statements are always _____ against him. This is true even if the defendant does not testify at trial.

    - If there are co-defendants, a non-testifying co-defendant's statements are _____ against the co-defendant.

Example 41: Pam and her brother Peter are on trial for robbing a bank. During the investigation, Pam said, "It's true, I drove the getaway car. But Peter talked me into the whole thing and Peter is the one who held the gun to the teller's head." Pam's statement is admissible against her, but the statement also incriminates Peter. They go to trial together. If Pam takes the stand, Peter may of course cross-examine her about the statement, and there's no Confrontation Clause problem. But if Pam doesn't testify, the statement could still be used against Pam, the statement becomes inadmissible against Peter because he cannot cross-examine Pam. (Courts have been required to redact or alter the confession so that it no longer refers to the non-testifying co-defendant.)

- **Defendant's right to present witnesses:** The defendant has the right to testify on his own behalf. He also has the right to compulsory process to obtain witnesses in his defense.

4. Burden of Proof

- The prosecution must prove every element of the crime beyond a _____ doubt

- Distinguish elements of the crime from affirmative defenses

  - The government can place the burden of proof with regard to affirmative defenses on _____

- Affirmative defenses can include insanity, self-defense, entrapment, or mistake.

CHAPTER 8: RESPONSIBILITIES OF JUDGES, PROSECUTORS, AND DEFENSE COUNSEL

A. Judges

- The Due Process Clause requires that judges possess neither actual nor _____ bias.

- Actual bias consists of interests that would impair the judge's _____

  Example 42: A judge who got paid for issuing search warrants only when he issued the search warrant was considered "actually" biased, per the Supreme Court, because, in effect, he only got paid for finding against the suspect.

  Example 43: A justice was deciding an appeal. The justice had been a district attorney in the jurisdiction when the death penalty was imposed and had approved the death sentence. It violated Due Process for the justice to sit on the case because it might hinder his impartiality.

B. Prosecutors

1. Four Prosecutorial Duties

a. Brady doctrine: Must turn over all material _____ evidence to the defense; includes two types of evidence:

1) Evidence that tends to show that the defendant is not guilty of the crimes charged

   Example 44: Two witnesses to a bank robbery described the suspect as a white, middle-aged, Jewish woman wearing a double strand of pearls, a pink top, and a black suit. However, several other witnesses described the robber as a six-foot-five Samoan male wearing flip-flops and a sarong. The prosecutor is obligated to turn over all of this information to the defense, as it suggests that the suspect described by the first two witnesses may not have committed the crime.

2) Evidence that would enable the defense to _____ the credibility of prosecution witnesses

   Example 45: The prosecutor must disclose if one of the government's witnesses is testifying because the prosecutor promised to drop charges against the witness.

   Example 46: If one of the witnesses in the bank robbery example above first described the robber as a tall Samoan male but later said it was a short white woman, this must be disclosed to the defense. This allows defense counsel to impeach that witness by questioning his credibility.

   - Evidence is _____ if disclosure could change the outcome of the proceeding.
   - *Brady* material includes inconclusive lab reports, witness descriptions that do not match the defendant, cooperation agreements with witnesses, etc.

     • Evidence within the control of the government (including the police)

b. A prosecutor may not knowingly present _____ testimony

c. A prosecutor may not contact (or direct others to contact) a defendant outside the presence of his _____ (i.e., cannot violate the defendant's Sixth Amendment right to counsel).

d. A prosecutor may not comment on a defendant's _____ to testify at trial or make unfair remarks about the defendant to the jury (i.e., cannot violate the defendant's Fifth Amendment right to remain silent).

   - A prosecutor may, however, comment on a defendant's silence before his *Miranda* rights attached.

2. **Prosecutorial Misconduct**

   o Prosecutorial misconduct that has a reasonable possibility of affecting the verdict may require a _____ or reversal of a conviction.

   o Other forms of prosecutorial misconduct may result in discipline to prosecutor but generally do not result in any consequence for a defendant.

C. Defense Counsel

   • The Supreme Court has held that the Sixth Amendment not only guarantees defendants the right to the assistance of counsel, it also guarantees them _____ assistance of counsel at all _____ stages of prosecution (from the time they are charged through the end of any appeals as of right).

1. **Conflicts of Interest**

   o Joint representation can lead to a conflict of interest

      ▪ For instance, co-defendants represented at the same trial by the same lawyer can create a conflict of interest

      ▪ If there is an actual conflict, the judge must _____ the defendants that joint representation is a risk

   o If a conflict of interest actually affects counsel's behavior, there is a _____ of prejudice. The defendant is not required to show actual innocence in order to obtain a new trial.

   > *Example 47:* *Harry and Sally are represented by the same lawyer at trial. Because he represents them both, the lawyer decides not to cross-examine a particular witness because the testimony could be damaging to Sally. Harry need not show that the cross-examination by itself would have changed the outcome. He only needs to show an actual effect on the lawyer's behavior.*

2. **Effective Assistance**

   o The Supreme Court has developed a two-part test (the Strickland test) for assessing whether a defendant was denied effective assistance: Performance and Prejudice

      ▪ **Performance:** Did defense counsel's performance fall below the wide range of _____ conduct that lawyers might engage in?

   > *Example 48:* *The defendant shot the victim in the buttocks and was charged with assault with intent to kill, attempted murder. The defendant's lawyer told him that he would be acquitted if he went to trial because the elements of the crime of attempted murder could only be satisfied if the victim was shot above the waist. Here, the lawyer got the law totally wrong. Shooting at someone is enough to show intent to kill.*

- **Prejudice:** There is a _____ probability that, had counsel performed effectively, the result would have been different.

  Example 49: *In this jurisdiction, suppression motions must be brought no later than thirty days before trial. The defendant's lawyer fails to bring the motion in time, filing it three days before trial. The judge denies the motion. There is clearly a failure of performance. But if the evidence had been seized legally, the lawyer's failure to file a timely motion would not have resulted in a different outcome. This would not be ineffective assistance because the defendant was not prejudiced.*

  - Cases that go to trial: Defendant must show that there was a reasonable probability that he would not have been _____ if the lawyer had done a proper job.
  - Guilty pleas: Defendant must show that he would not have pleaded guilty if his lawyer had not given him bad advice or performed ineffectively

  o If a defendant is denied effective assistance of counsel, either at trial or in the guilty plea process, his conviction must be reversed because the defendant has already shown that he was prejudiced.

3. **Choice of Counsel**

   o Defendants who can afford retained counsel are entitled to the counsel of their choice as long as the lawyer is:

   - Properly _____ in the jurisdiction (including pro hac vice rules);
   - Available for _____; and
   - No conflict or other reason to disqualify the lawyer

   o A defendant who is denied the retained counsel of his choice is entitled to have his conviction _____ regardless of whether the lawyer who actually represented him at trial provided effective assistance of counsel.

   o Indigent defendants: _____ to appointment of the lawyer of your choice

   - As long as they receive competent assistance at trial, they have received all the Constitution guarantees them.

4. **Proceeding Pro Se**

   o Defendants are entitled to _____ the right to counsel and to represent themselves.

   o The competence standard for waiving counsel is the same standard for pleading guilty.

- A defendant who proceeds pro se does not have a constitutional right to a "back-up" lawyer.

CHAPTER 9: SENTENCING AND POST-TRIAL PROCEDURES

- There are three primary constitutional provisions that regulate sentencing:
  - The Cruel and Unusual Punishments Clause of the Eighth Amendment;
  - The Double Jeopardy Clause of the Fifth Amendment; and
  - The Apprendi line of cases under the Sixth Amendment

A. The Cruel and Unusual Punishment Clause

1. Length of Prison Sentences

- The Supreme Court has given the government free rein to authorize virtually any length sentence for virtually _____

  Example 50: *Life sentences without parole for recidivists are constitutional, even if the offense that results in the life sentence is a minor crime.*

- Exception: Juveniles cannot be sentenced to life without parole for non-homicide crimes and mandatory LWOP cannot apply.

  Exam Tip 5: This is very unlikely to be tested because the details involved are too case-specific.

2. Capital Punishment

- The death penalty can be imposed in cases only when the victim _____.
  - It is constitutionally disproportionate to apply the death penalty in non-homicide cases.
- The death penalty cannot be imposed on:
  - Defendants who were under the age of _____ when they committed the crime
  - Defendants who suffer from mental retardation
  - Defendants who are _____ at the time of execution
- The state must provide a variety of special safeguards before executing a defendant, including a bifurcated trial process, the opportunity to present mitigating evidence, and a process that sufficiently narrows the class of death-sentence eligible offenses.

  Exam Tip 6: The states' death penalty procedures are sufficiently distinct from one another that it seems unlikely that the MBE will test on those procedures themselves.

3. Other Types of Sentences or Punishments

- The Eighth Amendment also prohibits the imposition of cruel or unusual/degrading punishments.

- o You must have been convicted of a _____ for the Eighth Amendment to apply.

   > *Example 51:* *Torturing a suspect to get the suspect to confess violates the Fifth and Fourteenth Amendment Due Process Clauses, but it does not violate the Cruel and Unusual Punishment Clause.*

- o Courts have extended this Eighth Amendment protection to prison conditions (e.g., overcrowding).

   > **Exam Tip 7:** The law here is so fact-specific and complicated that it's unlikely to be on an MBE question.

B. The Double Jeopardy Clause

- • Provides three separate protections:

   - o Protection against prosecution for the same offense after _____

   - o Protection against prosecution for the same offense after _____

   - o Protection against _____ prosecutions or punishments for the same offense

- • Ask: (A) What counts as the "same offense"? (B) Has jeopardy attached and has it been completed?

1. Defining the "Same Offense"

   > *Example 52:* *You are prosecuted for and acquitted of a homicide. If the government finds more or new evidence, you cannot be prosecuted again.*

   > *Example 53:* *You are prosecuted and convicted of larceny and sentenced to three years in jail. The prosecutor cannot prosecute you again in an attempt to get a longer sentence.*

   - o **The Blockburger test:** Ask whether each statutory provision requires proof of an element that the other does not

      > *Example 54:* *Offense #1 = A + B and Offense #2 = A + C (These are separate offenses and you can be prosecuted and punished for both.)*

      > *Larceny = (taking the property of another) + (intent to permanently deprive)*

      > *Conspiracy to commit larceny = (agreement to take property)*

      > *Example 55:* *Offense #1 = A + B and Offense #2 = A + B + C*

      > *These are not separate offenses; Offense #1 is a _____ offense.*

      > *Larceny = (taking the property of another) + (intent to permanently deprive)*

Robbery = (taking the property of another) + (intent to permanently deprive) +
(use or threat of force)

If you are prosecuted for and convicted of larceny, you cannot be indicted and
prosecuted for robbery in the same episode.

- o **Two warnings about the same offense test:**

  - ▪ Offenses with different _____ are separate offenses for double jeopardy purposes. Killing two victims with one shot can be prosecuted as two separate crimes.

    Example 56: *Isaac shoots his gun and the bullet goes through Cain and hits Abel. He has committed two offenses. He can be tried for murdering Cain, and regardless of the outcome, he can be tried for murdering Abel as well.*

  - ▪ Separate Sovereigns Rule: If two different sovereigns have jurisdiction over the crime committed (e.g., a state and the U.S. or two different states), they can each try the defendant separately. The Double Jeopardy Clause does not bar a defendant from being tried, convicted, and punished in both jurisdictions.

  - ▪ Charged v. punished: A defendant can be charged and tried for an offense and a lesser-included offense at the same trial, but the defendant can only be _____ for one offense

2. **The Attachment and End of Jeopardy**

   - o Jeopardy attaches when a _____ is sworn in or, in a bench trial, when the _____ is sworn in.

     - ▪ Before the trial begins, the prosecutor can add, drop, or change the charges against a defendant without Double Jeopardy problems.

   - o **Acquittal:** If the jury acquits the defendant, it is the _____ of the case and the defendant cannot be _____ by the same jurisdiction for the same offense.

     - ▪ The prosecution cannot _____ from an acquittal.

   - o **Conviction:** If the jury convicts the defendant and he either does not appeal or his conviction is affirmed, that is the end of jeopardy and he cannot be retried by the same jurisdiction for the same offense.

     - ▪ If the jury convicts the defendant, and he appeals and gets the conviction reversed, he can be retried unless the reversal was based on a finding of _____ evidence.

   - o **Mistrial:** Two kinds of mistrials

     - ▪ Manifest necessity: Defendant _____ be retried (occurs when e.g., the jury is deadlocked or defense counsel engages in misconduct)

- No manifest necessity: Defendant _____ be retried by that jurisdiction

C. The Apprendi Doctrine (Sixth Amendment)

- The Sixth Amendment right to a jury trial prohibits judges from _____ criminal sentences beyond the statutory maximums based on facts other than those decided by the jury beyond a reasonable doubt.

- Two components:

    o All the facts necessary to authorize a particular sentence must be found by a _____

    o All the facts necessary to authorize a particular sentence must be found _____

- Many statutes give the judge wide discretion to sentence the defendant

    Example 57: *A statute states that a defendant convicted of robbery can be sentenced between 5 and 10 years' imprisonment. The judge has discretion within this range.*

    Example 58: *A statute states that the maximum sentence for robbery is 8 years, but if the victim was unusually vulnerable, the sentence can be doubled. A jury would have to find beyond a reasonable doubt that the victim was unusually vulnerable in order to enhance the sentence.*

- Exception: Sentence enhancement based on prior _____ convictions need not be found by a jury.

BEST OF LUCK!

[END OF HANDOUT]

Evidence

MBE EVIDENCE
PROFESSOR DAVID SCHOTT
UNIVERSITY OF DENVER STURM COLLEGE OF LAW

> **Editor's Note 1:** The distribution of Evidence questions on the MBE has changed since Professor Schott recorded this lecture. The breakdown is now as follows:
>
> 1/3 - Relevance (approx. 8-9 questions)
> 1/4 - Presentation of Evidence (approx. 6-7 questions)
> 1/4 - Hearsay (approx. 6-7 questions)
> 1/6 - Everything else (approx. 3-4 questions)

CHAPTER 1:   INTRODUCTION AND PRESENTATION OF EVIDENCE

A. FACTUAL SCENARIO TO BE USED THROUGHOUT THE LECTURE - The assassination of Abraham Lincoln on April 14, 1865

- President Lincoln was watching a play called *"Our American Cousin"* at Ford's Theatre in Washington, D.C.

    o   He was accompanied by his wife, Mary Todd Lincoln, in the President's box, as well as Major Henry Rathbone and his fiancée, Clara Harris.

    o   History tells us that the assassin was John Wilkes Booth.

    o   Booth shot Lincoln in the back of the head with a one-shot, blue-smoke Derringer.

- After Booth shot the President, he leapt over the balcony and onto the stage, which was about 15 or 20 feet below.

    o   He caught his spur on the bunting or draping of the President's box.

    o   He hit the stage oddly, shattered his leg, stood up, held up a knife, and yelled *"Sic semper tyrannus,"* which is Latin for "thus to tyrants."

- President Lincoln died the next morning, April 15, 1865

    o   Co-conspirators in the crime were Mary Surratt, John Surratt, George Atzerodt, David Herold, and Dr. Samuel Mudd.

    o   Secretary of War Edwin Stanton was in charge of investigating the assassination.

    o   John Wilkes Booth was killed about two weeks later on April 26, 1865, at Garret's Farm.

    o   His journal and his Derringer were found on his person.

B. Presentation of Evidence

- On the MBE, the Federal Rules of Evidence (FRE) govern. They apply to civil, criminal, district court, appeals, bankruptcy cases, etc.

- FRE do not apply to grand jury proceedings, criminal procedures re search warrants, preliminary examinations, rendition, extradition, _____, sentencing, probation.

C. The Role of the Judge and the Jury

- The jury is the trier of _____; the judge is the trier of _____ (and the trier of fact in a bench trial).
- The judge determines what evidence the jury can weigh and evaluate; the judge determines the _____ of a witness and of evidence; the judge determines if a witness is _____ and if any _____ apply.
- The jury determines the _____ assigned to that evidence. (FRE 104)

> *Example 1:* *An audience member testifies as an eyewitness. However, the witness was not wearing his glasses at the theater. Judge would determine whether the witness was _____ to testify about what he claims to have seen while not wearing his glasses. The jury would then determine what weight and credibility to apply to the witness' testimony.*

D. Challenges to Rulings on Evidence (FRE 103)

- A party may challenge an evidentiary ruling as erroneous if:
  - The error affects a _____ right of a party, and
  - The party _____ the judge of the error.
- There are two ways to call the court's attention to the error—_____ and offer of proof.

  1. **Objection or Motion to Strike** - Used if evidence is being admitted (preventative measure)
     - Counsel must provide the _____ for an objection.

       Example 2: *"Objection. Your Honor, that is speculation."*

  2. **Offer of Proof** - If evidence is excluded, counsel must preserve the potential evidence for the appellate court.
     - Counsel must explain the _____ and the _____ of the testimony.

- Consequence of definitive ruling - Once a judge has made a _____ ruling, there is no need to _____ the objection.
- Challenge if no party objects
  - An attorney need not make an objection and may still appeal when the _____ applies (FRE 103).
    - The error is so _____ that an objection is not necessary.
    - A _____ right is affected.

Example 3: *If in a closing argument the prosecutor tells the jury that the defendant invoked his right to remain silent when he was arrested, the defense need not object based on the Plain Error Rule because the prosecution violated the Constitutional rights of the defendant.*

- o Evidence may be let in for limited admissibility.

Example 4: *The audience member may testify that he heard someone yell "sic semper tyrannus." This statement cannot be offered to show who said it or what the statement means. But it might be offered to show that the speaker knew Latin.*

E. The Rule of Completeness (FRE 106)

- Applies when a party introduces a writing or recorded statement in part

    - An adverse party may compel the introduction of an omitted portion of the writing or statement

        - Usually based on _____

Example 5: *A reply letter written by Wilkes Booth stating "Yes, let's kill him" is entered into evidence. Defense counsel may say, "Objection. Your Honor, pursuant to the Rule of Completeness, we ask that the original letter also be entered into evidence." The original letter provides the context for the reply letter.*

Example 6: *The prosecution attempts to enter only 7 of 9 voicemails left by the Defendant. Defense counsel may object pursuant to the Rule of Completeness to include the remaining 2 voicemails for fairness. Again, about putting things into context.*

- Opposing counsel can wait until cross-examination to bring in the omitted portion.

CHAPTER 2:   MODE OF PRESENTATION

A. Judicial Notice (FRE 201)

- The court's acceptance of a _____ as true without requiring formal _____

    - o Only applies to adjudicative facts, not legislative facts

Example 7: *The fact that April 14, 1865 was a Friday is an adjudicative fact. The court can take judicial notice of this fact.*

Example 8: *The exception to the common-law marital privilege is a legislative fact. The court cannot take judicial notice of this fact. The court must hear evidence to determine if that privilege exists.*

- o Multiple witness testimony is not sufficient for judicial notice.
- o Adjudicative facts cannot be subject to _____ dispute. They must be _____known, although not by everyone.
- o Judge cannot take judicial notice based solely on the _____ personal knowledge

    Example 9: *A judge cannot take judicial notice of the fact that it was raining on a particular day based on his memory of that day.*

- o Fact must be _____ and readily determinable
- o Must be from a source that cannot be _____ questioned

    Example 10: *A calendar is a source that cannot be reasonably questioned with regard to what day of the week a particular date falls on.*

- Procedure

    - o A party can ask a court to judicially notice a fact _____ during the trial; or on appeal.
    - o Usually upon motion by a party - but Court can take judicial notice _____
    - o Exception: Court may not take judicial notice against a _____ _____ for the first time on appeal
    - o Court must take judicial notice if:

        - Requested
        - Necessary information is given to court

    - o The opposing party has the right to _____ to judicial notice and be heard.

        Example 11: *The prosecution presents the calendar to the court and asks that the court take judicial notice of the fact that April 14, 1865 was a Friday. The court takes judicial notice of that fact. Defense counsel may object and ask for the opportunity to be heard regarding this fact.*

- **Effect of Judicial Notice**

    - o ***Civil*** juries _____ accept that fact as true. (FRE 201)
    - o ***Criminal*** juries _____ accept that fact as true.

B. The Mode and Order of Presentation of Evidence (FRE 611)

1. Trial Process

- o The prosecution (or the plaintiff) goes first and presents its case-in-chief.
- o The defendant then presents his case-in-chief.
- o After the defense rests, the prosecution (or the plaintiff) gets to present rebuttal witnesses.
- o Judicial control - A judge may question, or even call, a witness.

2. **Examination of Witnesses**

   a. **The scope of cross-examination is limited to two things:**

   ▪ The scope of direct; and

   ▪ _____

      • Credibility is _____ at issue.
      • The defendant does not _____ his 5th Amendment privilege by answering preliminary questions

3. Form of Questions

   a. **Leading Questions: Suggest the _____ in the question**

   ▪ General Rule - _____ on direct
   ▪ Exceptions

      • _____ questions
      • A witness who has trouble communicating (i.e., a child).
      • Adverse or _____ witness on direct.

      Example 12: *"What is the color of the sky?" Is this leading?*

      _____

      Example 13: *"The color of the sky was blue, right?" Is this leading?*

      _____

      Example 14: *"Is the color of the sky blue?" Is this leading?*

      _____

      Example 15: *"Your name is Major Rathbone?" "You are a Major in the Union Army?" "You were at Ford's Theater on April 14th?" "Your fiancé at the time was Clara Harris?" These are all permitted foundational questions.*

   ▪ General Rule -There are _____ on the use of leading questions on cross-examination

      Note 1: One way to avoid asking a leading question is to break it down so that it is a "who, what, where, when, or why" question. For example, "**What** color was the sky?"

   b. **Improper Questions**

      1) _____ **Questions: Require multiple answers**

      Example 16: *"Mr. Booth, you were an actor, you were at Ford's Theater on the night of April 14th, you had rented a horse, and you shot President Lincoln?"*

2) **Questions that Assume** _____ **Not in Evidence**

Example 17: *"Major Rathbone, after John Wilkes Booth killed President Lincoln with a blue-smoke Derringer, you lunged at him?" Assumes facts not in evidence. Must lay foundation first.*

3) Argumentative Questions: Intended to provoke an _____

Example 18: *"Mr. Booth, when did you start being a murderous rebel?"*

4) **Questions that call for a** _____ **or opinion not qualified to give**

Example 19: *"Major Rathbone, how did Mrs. Lincoln feel after her husband was shot?"*

5) **Repetitive Questions: Have been asked and** _____

Note 2: Remember that if opposing counsel asks a series of questions on direct, one is still able to explore that on cross.

4. **Exclusion of Witnesses (Rule 615)**

   o Witnesses shall be excluded or sequestered:

   - Upon the motion of a party; or
   - Upon the court's own motion

   o Prevents contamination

   o Exceptions who may not be excluded

   - A party
     - Only one party in a criminal case (the defendant)
   - An officer or employee who is the _____ of a corporation
   - _____ or _____ witnesses
   - Victims

CHAPTER 3:   BURDENS AND PRESUMPTIONS; RELEVANCE

A. Burdens

- Burdens of proof -The burden of _____ and the burden of _____

1. **The Burden of Production (prima facie case)**

   - The party with this burden must present enough evidence that the trier of fact could infer that each alleged fact had been proved.

2. **The Burden of Persuasion** (standard of proof)

- Degree to which legally sufficient evidence must be presented
- This burden does NOT shift.

  - **Civil case** – by a _____ of the evidence

    - More likely than not that a fact which the plaintiff is presenting is true
    - Exception: Fraud claim - clear and convincing evidence

  - **Criminal case** - Beyond a reasonable _____.

    - Prosecution must prove every element of every count beyond a reasonable doubt

B. Presumptions

- A conclusion that the trier _____regarding an underlying fact

  Example 20: *The defendant is charged with murder. A presumption arises that the victim is dead if the person has been missing for more than seven years.*

- Two types

  - _____

    - May be overcome if _____ is presented
    - If no contrary evidence is presented, a judge _____instruct the jury to accept the presumption
    - Shifts the burden of production to other side, but _____the burden of persuasion

  - Conclusive (irrebuttable) – may not be challenged – treated like a rule of _____

    Example 21: *A child under four years of age lacks the ability to form the intent necessary to commit an intentional tort. This is a conclusive presumption. No contrary evidence is permitted.*

C. Relevance (FRE 401, 402, and 403)

- All relevant evidence is admissible, unless it is excluded by:

  - Rule
  - Law
  - Constitutional provision

- What does it mean for evidence to be relevant? It must be both _____ and _____.

  o **Probative -** Evidence that has any _____ to make a fact more or less _____ than it would be without that evidence.

  o **Material -** It is a fact of _____ in determining the action

    Example 22: *The fact that John Wilkes Booth was raised in the south is both probative and material to show his motive for killing President Lincoln.*

  o **Sufficiency -** Evidence need not prove by itself an element. A single piece of evidence must be individually relevant, but does not need to be individually sufficient to prove the element.
    - "A brick is not a wall" i.e., evidence is admissible if it is only a single brick.

- **Direct vs. Circumstantial Evidence**

  o **Direct -** Evidence that is identical to the factual proposition it is offered to prove

    Example 23: *An _____ account. "I saw John Wilkes Booth put a gun to Lincoln's head and pull the trigger."*

    Note 5: Conviction without direct evidence - A defendant can be convicted solely upon circumstantial evidence.

  o **Circumstantial -** Evidence that _____ proves a factual proposition through _____

    Example 24: *You go to bed tonight and there is no snow on the ground. When you wake up in the morning, there are six inches of snow on the ground. Though you did not see it snow, circumstantially it is reasonable for you to conclude that it snowed during the night.*

    Example 25: *You go home tonight and park your car in front of your house. When you wake up in the morning, your car is gone. Can you conclude your car was stolen? Perhaps. Maybe your car was towed or you forgot to put on the emergency brake, and the car rolled down the street. Maybe you have a 16-year-old kid who decided to buy Mom and Dad donuts and coffee for breakfast.*

    Example 26: *An audience member at Ford's Theater did not see John Wilkes Booth shoot President Lincoln. But, he heard the shot, looked up at the viewing box, and saw John Wilkes Booth holding a gun with smoke coming out of it.*

  POP QUIZ: Can circumstantial evidence be more probative than direct evidence?

    Example 27: *It would be more persuasive to show that a one-shot, blue-smoke Derringer was found in John Wilkes Booth's backpack when he was arrested than to present an eyewitness who says, "I saw John Wilkes Booth jump from the balcony to the stage. But I wasn't wearing my eyeglasses, and I'm pretty much blind without them."*

- **FRE 403 Exclusion of Relevant Evidence -** Relevant evidence may be excluded if its probative value is _____ outweighed by the danger of:
  - Unfair _____
  - Confusing the issues
  - Misleading the _____
  - Undue delay, waste of time
  - Needless presentation of _____ evidence.
    - The key is that these dangers *substantially* outweigh the probative value

      Example 28: *The prosecution wants to present 28 pictures of Abraham Lincoln's dead body to the jury. Defense counsel may object to the unfair prejudice all 28 photos will create.*

- When the relevance of evidence depends on the existence of another fact, it is admissible if sufficient proof of the other fact is introduced. Standard is by a preponderance of evidence.

  Example 29: *Mary Todd Lincoln hears someone yell, "Sic semper tyrannus," but she does not know who it is. Someone else could testify that they saw John Wilkes Booth yell that. The relevance and admissibility of Mary Todd Lincoln's testimony is dependent upon the other witness' testimony.*

- What if irrelevant evidence is admitted?
  - Curative admission - The court may allow additional irrelevant evidence in to rebut the irrelevant evidence.

    Example 30: *John Wilkes Booth deposited $10,000 into an account the day before he assassinated President Lincoln. The court may allow the defense to present evidence that John Wilkes Booth just signed a deal with Paramount.*

  - Whether an objection was timely is a factor in determining whether to allow a cure.
- Foundation - You must lay a foundation for relevant evidence.

  Example 31: *Authentication of a photo. "Do you recognize what I placed in front of you?" "What is this?" "Does this fairly and accurately represent what Ford's Theater looked like on the evening of the assassination?" The attorney can then seek to introduce the photo into evidence.*

  - The failure of the proponent of the evidence to establish that foundation may be challenged by an objection for lack of proper foundation.

CHAPTER 4: CHARACTER EVIDENCE (PART 1)

A. Character Evidence (FRE 404-406 re defendant and victim, 607-609 re witnesses)

- General information about a person's behavior

    Example 32: *A person is violent. A person is a reckless driver. He's a bad parent.*

- General rule - _____ to prove conduct in conformity.
    - Propensity purposes

        Example 33: *The opposing party tries to offer evidence that John Wilkes Booth is a violent and angry person and therefore, he killed President Lincoln. Just because he is violent does not mean he killed the president. Such evidence is inadmissible.*

B. Evidence of Defendant's Character

- **Civil Cases:** (FRE 404)

    - _____ to prove conforming conduct

        - Acted in accordance with the alleged character trait

            Example 34: *A plaintiff cannot produce evidence that the defendant is a reckless driver to prove that the defendant drove recklessly on the day in question.*

            Example 35: *Mary Todd Lincoln later sues John Wilkes Booth in civil court. She cannot call George Atzerodt to the stand and ask him to testify that John Wilkes Booth was violent, and therefore he killed Abraham Lincoln.*

    - *Exceptions*

        - Admissible if character is an _____ element of a claim or defense
        - When character is "at issue" in the case

            Example 36: *Character is most commonly an essential element in defamation, negligent hiring, negligent entrustment, child custody, etc.*

            Example 37: *Mary Todd Lincoln sues Ford's Theater for negligent hiring and supervision of security personnel. Evidence that the security personnel regularly slept on the job may be admissible.*

            Example 38: *A plaintiff sues a business for negligent hiring after an employee assaulted the plaintiff. Evidence that the employee had been fired twice for violent behavior may be admissible.*

- **Criminal Cases** FRE 404(a)

    o RULE: The prosecution _____ introduce evidence of a defendant's **bad character** to prove that the defendant has a **propensity** to have committed the crime in question.

    > ***Example 39:*** *The prosecution may not present evidence that John Wilkes Booth is violent to show that he acted violently on the day of the assassination.*

    o *Exception:* The defendant may present _____ _____ that is inconsistent with the type of crime that is being charged.

    > ***Example 40:*** *The defense may present evidence that John Wilkes Booth was non-violent.*

    - Must be pertinent to the crime charged

    > ***Example 41:*** *The defense could not present evidence that Booth was a clean person or a good speller. That is not consistent with the crime charged.*

    o Form of evidence

    - Must be through reputation in the community or _____ testimony

    > ***Example 42:*** *Booth's fiancée could testify that Booth had a reputation in the theater community for being non-violent.*

    > ***Example 43:*** *The prosecution may introduce negative character evidence to rebut the defendant's evidence, i.e. after the defendant "opens the door." If John Wilkes Booth presents evidence that he is non-violent, the prosecution can then present evidence that he is violent.*

    - Must relate to the _____ character trait

    o The defendant does not "open the door" to the prosecution's attack simply by _____, or testifying.

    > ***Example 44:*** *John Wilkes Booth testifies at the criminal trial. He is never asked about his character for peacefulness on direct examination. Therefore, he did not open the door to the issue of his character for nonviolence. The prosecution cannot introduce Booth's character for violence either in cross-examination or by other evidence.*

C. **Evidence of Victim's Character**

- A criminal defendant may introduce evidence of the victim's character that is relevant to one of the _____ asserted.

    > ***Example 45:*** *John Wilkes Booth claims that Abraham Lincoln attacked him. This gives defense counsel the opportunity to present evidence claiming that Lincoln was violent.*

- Form -Defendant can use _____ or _____ evidence
- The prosecution can offer good character evidence only after the defendant has _____ the victim's character.

CHAPTER 5:   CHARACTER EVIDENCE (PART 2)

A. Character Evidence; Crimes or Other Acts (FRE 404(b))

- Prior bad act is _____ to prove conforming conduct (propensity)

  Example 46: Prosecution cannot attempt to show that John Wilkes Booth previously attacked a man to prove that Booth attacked the President on April 14th.

  o   A prior act refers to a specific instance of conduct as opposed to a general character trait.

- Exceptions - Prior acts are not admissible to show propensity, but are admissible to show:

  - _____
  - Opportunity
  - _____
  - Intent
  - Lack of _____
  - Preparation
  - Common Plan
  - Knowledge
  - Absence of _____

- Remember MIMIC: **M**otive, **I**ntent, Absence of **M**istake, **I**dentity, **C**ommon Plan

  Example 47: There is evidence that John Wilkes Booth drilled a hole in order to peer into the President's box. The prosecution seeks to introduce evidence that John Wilkes Booth previously attacked a man and before that attack, he drilled a hole in the man's office in order to look inside. The defense will object that this is improper character evidence. The prosecution can respond that the evidence is offered to show common plan or preparation, not propensity.

o Prosecution must give the defense _____ _____of its intent to use a prior act at trial

o Introduction of Prior Bad Acts

- **Civil Cases**: when character evidence is admissible (an element of a claim or defense), it may be proved by:

  - Reputation
  - _____ or
  - Specific instances of conduct

  Example 48: *Mary Todd Lincoln sues Booth in civil court for wrongful death, and seeks to introduce evidence that Booth previously attacked a man in the viewing box at Ford's Theatre. This is admissible if the court has deemed the character evidence is admissible due to a claim or defense.*

- **Criminal Cases**: when character evidence is admissible ("opened the door"), it may be proved by:

  - Reputation or
  - Opinion

- Specific instances of conduct are _____

  - **Exceptions**

    o Prosecution may use character evidence to prove something other than propensity - **MIMIC**

    Example 49: *John Wilkes Booth's fiancée testifies that Booth was a very peaceful, non-violent man. The prosecution can use opinion or reputation evidence to rebut the evidence that he was a non-violent man. The prosecution cannot present evidence of a prior attack in the box, because it is a specific instance of conduct. However, the prosecution may use evidence of the prior attack for MIMIC.*

    o May be used to **cross-examine a character witness**

    Example 50: *John Wilkes Booth's fiancée testifies that Booth was a very peaceful, non-violent man. The prosecution can cross-examine her on Booth's previous attack of a man in that viewing box.*

    Note 8: Evidence of prior bad acts is especially vulnerable to Rule 403 challenge (Exclusionary Rule): when the probative value is substantially outweighed by unfair prejudice.

B. **Habit and Routine Practice Evidence (FRE 406)**

- Habit refers to the act of a person

- Routine practice refers to the acts of an organization
- Evidence of a person's habit or the routine practice of an organization is _____ to prove conduct in conformity on a particular occasion (propensity).

> *Example 51:* *During his acting career, John Wilkes Booth entered Ford's Theater through the tunnel under the stage. The prosecution might present evidence that Booth always used the tunnel. The prosecution may show that using the tunnel was Booth's habit and so, he used the tunnel on the day of the assassination.*

- May be admitted without _____ or an eyewitness

> **Exam Tip 1:** Habit is more specific than character evidence. On the MBE, words like "always" or "every time" generally refer to _____, whereas words like "often" or "frequently" are more likely to imply character evidence.

C. Summing Up

- FRE 404 (a) – prohibits bad character evidence _____ being used for propensity purposes
- FRE 404 (b) – generally prohibits a specific prior _____ unless it is for _____
    - Specific instances of prior conduct are allowed in _____ cases if an element or a defense
    - Specific instances of prior conduct are allowed in _____ of a character witness

CHAPTER 6: WITNESSES (PART 1)

A. Competence (FRE 601)

- Every witness is _____ competent unless proven otherwise. (FRE 601)
    - Questions about mental competence go to the _____ not admissibility of a witness's testimony.

> **Note 9:** In diversity cases, witness competence is determined by state law.

1. Non –expert (lay) witnesses must have _____.
They cannot speculate or hypothesize. (Rule 602)

> **Note 10:** Expert witnesses can speculate or hypothesize.

> *Example 52:* *Eyewitness at Ford's Theater must have some basis for his testimony, e.g., "I saw Booth," or "I heard Booth."*

2. **Witnesses must take an _____ or affirmation. (FRE 603)**

   o To impress a duty of conscience on the witness.

   o Interpreters must also take an oath. (Rule 604)

3. **Judges as Witnesses: (FRE 605)**

   o May not testify in trial over which she presides

   o No objection required (plain error)

4. **Jurors as Witnesses: (FRE 606)**

   o **At trial** may not testify as witness at trial in front of their co-jurors

      Example 53: Juror may need to testify if there is bribery of a juror or a juror has failed to follow the court's instructions. The juror may testify outside the presence of the other jurors.

      ▪ Opposing counsel must be given the opportunity to object outside the presence of the jury.

   o **After the trial** may not testify about:

      ▪ Statements made _____

      ▪ Effect of anything on a particular juror's vote and

      ▪ Any juror's _____ processes

   o **After the trial** juror **may** testify about

      ▪ _____ prejudicial information was brought in (e.g., newspapers)

      ▪ Outside improper influences (e.g., threats)

      ▪ _____ in entering the verdict on the form

         • Does not extend to mistakes about the consequences of the verdict

• Child as Witness

   o _____ decides competency (no bright-line rule)

   o Factors:

      ▪ Intelligence

      ▪ Ability to distinguish between truth and falsehood.

      ▪ Understanding importance of telling the truth

B. **Dead Man Statutes**

   Exam Tip 2: MBE has tested on this in the past.

• Does not apply in a _____ case

- Common Law: A party that has a _____ in a civil case is prohibited from testifying about a _____ or transaction with a dead person whose estate is a party to that suit, and the alleged communication is adverse to the estate.

    Example 54: Mary Todd Lincoln sued John Wilkes Booth in civil court for wrongful death of Abraham Lincoln. Booth cannot quote Abraham Lincoln in this civil suit brought on behalf of Lincoln's estate if the alleged communication Booth had with Lincoln while he was alive is _____ to Abraham Lincoln's estate.

- Federal Law: NO Dead Man's Statute restriction (but Dead Man's Statute restriction can apply if state law applies to a federal case)

    Exam Tip 3: On the MBE, the Dead Man's Statute will only apply if the question explicitly says that state law applies and the state has a Dead Man's Statute in effect.

C. Impeachment

Witness may be impeached by calling witness's credibility into question

- **Bases for challenging credibility**

    o Bias

    o Character for untruthfulness

    o Inability to perceive what they are testifying about

    o Prior inconsistent statements

    o Another contradictory witness or evidence

    Note 11: Any party can impeach a witness, even the party calling the witness.

1. Witness's Character for Truthfulness

a. How can you impeach a witness's character for truthfulness?

- _____
- Opinion
- _____

b. Truthful character evidence: Credibility may not be _____ until it has first been attacked.

Example 55: Prosecution cannot put George Atzerodt on the stand and ask on direct, "Are you honest?" "Do you tell the truth?" This is bolstering.

Note 12: Attacking a witness' bias is NOT attacking his truthfulness

Example 56: Mary Todd Lincoln is on the stand and on cross-examination she is asked, "You loved Abraham Lincoln?" "You want revenge?" This is not an attack

on her truthfulness. These are questions about her bias, not an attack on truthfulness.

c. Specific instances of conduct

- Extrinsic evidence of specific instances of untruthful conduct is generally not admissible to attack a witness's truthfulness. However, on _____, specific instances can be asked about if it's regarding truthfulness of (i) the witness or (ii) another witness about whose character the witness being cross-examined has testified.

> **Editor's Note 2:** The professor misspoke when he spoke about attacking the witness's "untruthfulness."

Example 57: George Atzerodt lied on his job application. I am not allowed to bring in the job application to show that he lied. However, on cross, I can ask him about the job application. If he denies lying, I cannot bring in the extrinsic evidence.

- Limits on cross-examination regarding specific instances of conduct:

  - Must have a good-faith belief in prior misconduct
  - May not cross-examine a witness about an _____

    - May cross-examine about the underlying conduct that led to the arrest

Example 58: George Atzerodt was arrested for writing bad checks. I cannot ask, "You were arrested for check kiting, correct?" However, I can ask, "You cashed checks in someone else's name, correct?"

    - Extrinsic evidence generally cannot be used to _____ that specific instance of untruthfulness.
    - Discussion of consequences is also prohibited

Example 59: The bad check may be asked about but may not be introduced to show George Atzerodt cashed checks in someone else's name. The check is extrinsic evidence of the underlying conduct.

    - Extrinsic evidence of specific conduct can be used to impeach on _____, e.g. bias.

Example 60: I cannot bring in the forged check unless, for example, it's brought in to show bias against Booth. George Atzerodt forged John Wilkes Booth's name on a bad check and was caught. The bad check may be introduced to show George Atzerodt's bias.

    - When the foundation for the extrinsic evidence (e.g., the check) is established through the witness being impeached, it is possible that the extrinsic evidence might be admissible to impeach the witness's character for truthfulness.

- **Privilege against self-incrimination:** By testifying on another matter, a witness _____ waive the privilege against self-incrimination for testimony relating only to the witness' character (FRE 608(b)).

2. **Criminal Convictions: FRE 609**

   General Rule: _____ of a prior crime is a possible basis for impeaching a witness's character for truthfulness. The rule is subject to limitations.

   a. **Crimes involving dishonesty or false statement - Any prior conviction is admissible, subject to a 10-year restriction, whether a misdemeanor or a felony and regardless of the punishment**

      - Crimes of dishonesty: Fraud, _____, embezzlement, and false pretenses
      - NOT crimes of dishonesty: _____ rape, and assault

           Example 61: George Atzerodt testifies for the prosecution. Five years earlier, he was convicted of check kiting. Is this admissible? _____. Whether misdemeanor or felony, it's within the 10 year restriction and it's a crime of dishonesty.

   b. **Crimes that do not involve dishonesty**

      - Subject to 10-year limitation
      - Rule: Admissible, but only if the crime is punishable by _____ or imprisonment for more than _____, i.e., a felony

      Example 62:   Atzerodt testifies that he was convicted five years ago for assault. It would be inadmissible if the imprisonment was for less than one year.

      1) If witness is the criminal defendant and crime is not crime of dishonesty

         Example 63: John Wilkes Booth testifies. He was convicted five years ago for assault. Even if he was imprisoned for more than one year, the prosecution must pass the FRE 403 test; must prove that the probative value of the evidence outweighs the risk of unfair prejudice

         - Admissible if its probative value outweighs the potential prejudicial effect to that defendant. (FRE 609(a)(1)(b))

      2) Witnesses other than the criminal defendant

         - General Rule: Evidence _____. To exclude, burden is on opposing counsel to overcome the FRE 403 challenge

   c. **Convictions more than 10 years old**

      - If more than 10 years has elapsed since conviction or release (whichever is later):

- Conviction is admissible _____ if the party offering the evidence shows that probative value of the conviction substantially outweighs the risk of unfair prejudice; and
- Proponent gives reasonable _____ of the intent to use the evidence to opposing counsel

d. **Conviction evidence [FRE 609(c)] NOT admissible if:**

- Pardoned
- Annulled
- Later found innocent
- Rehabilitated

e. **Juvenile Convictions**

Not admissible to impeach _____

- If witness is not defendant – admissible if offered to impeach truthfulness and if:
  - Offered in a _____ case
  - Would be admissible if an adult conviction would be admissible; and
  - Admitting evidence is necessary for fair determination of guilt or innocence

  Note 13: A criminal defendant can use a witness's juvenile conviction to impeach by showing bias.

f. **Manner of Proof - Can prove prior convictions by:**

- Witness's admission on cross or direct or
- _____ evidence (the record of the conviction)

g. **Pendency of an appeal has _____ effect on impeachment. Evidence of pending appeal is also admissible.**

CHAPTER 7: WITNESSES (PART 2)

A. Impeaching a Witness

1. Prior Inconsistent Statement

- _____ be used to impeach
- Prior inconsistent statement does not need to be a _____ statement

  Example 64: *George Atzerodt testifies that he never said that he wanted to kill Abraham Lincoln. Any prior statements that he made to the contrary would be admissible to impeach him.*

- An attorney does not need to show the prior statement to the witness, but must show it to opposing counsel if requested. (FRE 613)

- o Extrinsic evidence may only be introduced if the witness is given the opportunity to
  _____ the prior inconsistent statement.
  - ▪ This opportunity to explain or deny does not need to take place _____
    the statement is admitted.

    *Example 65: George Atzerodt testified that he never said he wanted to kill
    Abraham Lincoln. The defense presents evidence of Atzerodt's prior inconsistent
    statement through another witness. The prosecution cannot object on the
    grounds that Atzerodt has not been given the opportunity to explain or deny the
    statement because Atzerodt can be recalled and given that opportunity later.*

  - ▪ Exceptions: No opportunity need be given to explain or deny if:
    - • Impeaching a hearsay declarant
    - • Admission of a _____ (FRE 801(b)(2))
  - ▪ Extrinsic evidence of a prior inconsistent statement cannot be used to impeach a
    witness regarding a _____ (i.e., irrelevant) matter.

2. **Bias (always relevant)**
   - o Bases:
     - ▪ Witness has a relationship to the party or victim (e.g., Mary Todd Lincoln)
     - ▪ Witness has an interest in the _____ of a case
     - ▪ Witness has an interest in testifying

       *Example 66: George Atzerodt cut a deal with the prosecution in exchange for
       his testimony.*
   - o Foundation must be laid before _____ may be introduced.

     > **Exam Tip 4:** MBE questions normally test bias in the context of a witness who
     > is employed by a party or a witness who has cut a deal with the prosecution.

3. **Sensory Competence**
   - o May be impeached by showing witness has a deficiency in ability to perceive, _____
     or relate information

     *Example 67: An audience member who did not have his glasses on when he
     saw a man jump from the balcony onto the stage – can be impeached for lack of
     sensory competence.*

4. **Impeaching a Hearsay Declarant (FRE 806)**

   *Example 68: George Atzerodt is on the stand. He quotes Mary Surratt as
   saying, "John Wilkes Booth ran out of here." Mary may be attacked by any
   evidence that might have been admitted if she had in fact testified.   Mary
   Surratt had previously written a note to Booth saying, "I've never seen you*

running out of Ford's Theater." That note may be admitted against her hearsay
statement for impeachment purposes.

- o May be impeached by any evidence that would have been admissible had the declarant testified
- o Similar impeachment treatment is given to a non-hearsay statements by a co-conspirator, agent, or authorized spokesperson.

5. **Rehabilitation - A witness who has been impeached can be rehabilitated. FRE 801(d)(1)(b).**

- o Explanation on redirect
- o By reputation or opinion evidence with regard to character for truthfulness (if the witness's character was attacked)
- o By a prior _____ statement offered to rebut a charge that the witness lied

6. **Religious Opinions and Beliefs**

- o _____ to attack or support a witness's credibility

   Example 69: *If John Wilkes Booth was a Quaker, the defense cannot put him on the stand to testify that he is a Quaker, and therefore he tells the truth.*

- o Exception: May be used to show _____ or interest

   Example 70: *A religious sect is a party to the lawsuit. The court may permit you to ask a question about the religious beliefs of the witness, if it shows bias.*

7. **Contradictory Evidence**

- o A witness may be impeached by evidence that is contradictory to the witness's testimony

   Example 71: *The plaintiff is suing the defendant for damage to his car as a result of an accident. The defendant may introduce the plaintiff's record of car insurance to show that the plaintiff's car was damaged in a previous accident.*

8. **Collateral Issues**

- o General Rule: May not impeach the credibility of a witness by introducing _____evidence on a collateral matter

   Example 72: *The defendant is charged with assault. The prosecution witness says the victim was wearing a plaid shirt. The defendant cannot call another witness to testify that the victim was wearing a striped shirt.*

B. **Present Recollection Refreshed**

- • A witness may examine _____ item (document, photo, apple) to refresh the witness's present recollection.
- • The witness may not use the object or item while testifying (i.e., read from document)

- The item is not introduced into evidence (by _____ counsel).

> ***Example 73:*** *Mary Todd Lincoln is on the stand and cannot remember what play she was watching on the night of the assassination. The attorney can show her the playbill and ask if her memory was refreshed. The attorney can then take the playbill from her and ask, "What was the play you were watching on the night of the assassination?" The playbill does not go into evidence.*

- Opposing counsel's options (FRE 612)

  o Right to _____ the refreshing item

  o Opposing counsel can introduce the item into evidence (usually for impeachment purposes)

  o In a criminal case, if the prosecution does not produce the evidence, the court may strike the testimony and declare a mistrial.

C. Past Recollection Recorded

- A memorandum or record regarding a matter about which a witness _____ _____, but now has insufficient recollection upon which to testify

> ***Example 74:*** *Mary Todd Lincoln kept a diary about what happened right after the assassination. On the stand, she has insufficient recollection of the night her husband was murdered. But she once did have knowledge of it and made a record of it. Her diary record may be admissible as a hearsay exception, but only admissible as an exhibit if offered by opposing counsel. (The attorney offering the information is allowed to read the contents of the diary to the jury. Opposing counsel may introduce the diary as an exhibit.)*

- Difference between present recollection refreshed and past recorded recollection:

  o The item used to ***refresh*** the witness's present memory is usually NOT admitted into evidence.

  o The document used as a ***recorded recollection*** may be admitted into evidence.

D. Opinion Testimony

1. Lay Witnesses (FRE 701)

  o Generally, may not testify about an _____

  o Opinion testimony is allowed if it is a _____ impression.

> ***Example 75:*** *A lay witness may testify about intoxication, the speed of a car, the apparent emotions of someone (i.e., someone is crying).*

  - Opinion must be based on _____ and
  - Must be helpful to _____ the understanding of a fact at issue
  - Cannot be scientific, technical, or _____ in nature

Example 76: *A lay witness could testify as to how far Booth jumped to the stage.*

Example 77: *Major Rathbone could testify to the apparent emotions of Mary Todd Lincoln.*

2. Expert Witnesses (FRE 702)

a. Subject matter of testimony

- Before an expert witness can testify, the court must find that subject matter of the testimony is:

    - Reliable: Scientific, technical, or _____and

    - Relevant: Will help the trier of fact understand evidence or a fact

b. Qualified expert

- To be qualified to testify as an expert, witness must show

1) Witness is qualified by possessing knowledge, skill, experience, training, or
   _____

2) Testimony is based on sufficient _____

3) Testimony is the product of _____ principles and methods (reasonably relied upon by experts in the field, although underlying data need not be admissible);

4) Witness _____those principles and methods to the facts of the case

    Example 78: *Fingerprint analysis was first developed around 1858. Widespread use of the analysis began in the 1870s. The assassination of Abraham Lincoln occurred in 1865, so the principles and methods may not have been reasonably relied upon by experts at that time because the field was so new.*

- Experts must also possess a_____ in their opinion.

c. Ultimate Issue FRE 704

- An expert may give an opinion on an ultimate issue (including a defendant's state of mind)

- Exception - An expert _____given an opinion on whether a criminal defendant had the requisite _____ for the crime charged

Example 79: *An expert could say the John Wilkes Booth was an angry man. However, the expert could not testify that Booth had the requisite mental state of premeditation.*

    d. **Basis of an Expert's Opinion**

- Personal observations
- Data that was provided

  - Expert may base his opinion on pictures, reports, or other analysis
  - If underlying facts are inadmissible, expert's opinion may still be admissible if experts in the field would rely on that data

    o The proponent may disclose the underlying facts to the jury if their probative value in helping the jury evaluate the opinion substantially outweighs their prejudicial effect.
    o The expert need not disclose the underlying data before giving an opinion.
    o On cross-examination, the expert may be required to disclose those underlying facts.

  Example 80: *The prosecution calls an expert in fingerprint analysis who testifies that the prints on the door to the box match John Wilkes Booth's prints. On cross-examination, defense counsel can ask what data the expert relied upon.*

- Can use hypotheticals to elicit an expert opinion but they are not required

    e. **Court-Appointed Experts**

- Court may appoint an expert
- Court must inform expert of _____
- Expert must advise both parties of findings
- Each party may _____ a court-appointed expert

    f. **Interpreters are subject to the same rules as expert witnesses**

CHAPTER 8: TANGIBLE EVIDENCE

Tangible evidence is any evidence not presented as oral or verbal _____

    Example 81: *Documentary evidence: Letters, contracts*

    Example 82: *Physical evidence: Guns, knives, clothing, videotapes*

A. Authentication

All tangible evidence must be authenticated. Authentication is showing that an object is what it is claimed to be.

1. **Authenticating Physical Evidence FRE 901**

   a. _____ of the witness who has familiarity with the object

      Example 83: *George Atzerodt states, "That is John Wilkes Booth's derringer."*

   b. Using _____ characteristics

      Example 84: *Booth had his initials engraved on his derringer.*

      Example 85: *Electronic documents can be identified by their meta-data.*

   c. By _____

      Example 86: *Blood samples or drug samples*

      ▪ Witness must verify whereabouts from time evidence was collected until trial

   d. **Reproductions FRE 901**

      Example 87: *Photographs, diagrams, maps, movies*

      ▪ A witness who has personal knowledge must testify that it _____ _____ what it is claimed to represent.

   e. **X-Rays or Electrocardiograms (PMOC)**

      1) Accurate _____

      2) Machine was working properly

      3) Qualified _____ and

      4) Show chain of _____

2. **Documentary Evidence**

   o **Common Methods of Authenticating Documentary Evidence**

      1) _____ (parties agree)

      2) Testimony of an _____; or

         Example 88: *David Herold traveled with John Wilkes Booth. He testifies that the diary belongs to Booth, and he saw Booth writing in it.*

      3) _____ verification

   o **Types of Documentary Evidence**

      ▪ **Ancient Documents**

         i) More than _____ years old;

         ii) In a condition that is unlikely to create suspicion about its authenticity; and

iii) Found in a place it would _____ be found.

Example 89: *A letter written on papyrus that is thought to be written by Pharaoh is found in the basement of Wal-Mart. This creates suspicion and is not found in a place it would likely be found.*

- **Public Records**
  - Recorded or _____ in a public office as authorized by law; or
  - The document is from the office where items of that kind are kept.
- **Reply Letter Doctrine**
  - Written _____ to an original communication; and
  - Unlikely it was forged by someone else
- **Handwriting Verification**

  i. _____ - Expert witness or the trier of fact compares the writing in question with another writing that has been proven to be genuine.

  ii. A non-expert witness with personal knowledge of the handwriting who recognizes the handwriting

Example 90: *David Herold needs to have original knowledge of what John Wilkes Booth's handwriting looks like before litigation.*

> **Note 14:** A non-expert witness cannot have become familiar with the handwriting for litigation purposes.

- **Self-Authenticating Documents do NOT require extrinsic proof of authenticity**

  i. Public documents bearing a seal

  ii. Certified copies of public records

  iii. Official publications issued by a _____ authority

  iv. Newspapers or periodicals;

  v. _____ inscriptions (e.g., a label)

  vi. Notarized or acknowledged documents

  vii. Commercial paper

  viii. Documents declared by _____ to be authentic

  ix. Records of regularly conducted business activity

> **Editor's Note 3:** 'The business records need to be certified by a custodian of the records.
>
> **Note 15:** Although most self-authenticating documents do not require advance notice, records of regularly conducted business activity do require advance notice provided to opposing counsel.

- Attesting Witness - Testimony of attesting witness is generally not required to authenticate a document

3. Oral Statements

o Voice Identification

- Any person who has heard the voice at _____

- Even if made for purpose of _____

- Makes no difference whether mechanical, electronic, or live

Example 91: *An audience member heard John Wilkes Booth yell. Then, she stands outside the window of his jail cell to hear him talk. Her testimony is admissible as identification of Booth's voice.*

o A party to a **telephone conversation** may authenticate statements made during that conversation by testifying that:

i. He recognized the speaker's voice;

ii. The speaker _____ that only a particular person would have known;

Example 92: *George Atzerodt testifies to a telephone conversation with John Wilkes Booth. If Booth states facts that only Booth could know, that could be authentication that it was in fact Booth on the phone.*

iii. The caller dialed the number that was believed to be the speaker's and the speaker _____ himself upon answering; or

iv. The caller dialed a _____ and spoke to the person about regular business.

B. Best Evidence Rule (FRE 1001)

> **Exam Tip 5:** The Best Evidence Rule is frequently a wrong answer on the MBE.
>
> The Best Evidence Rule (Original document rule) ONLY applies when the material terms of a writing are at issue or if a witness is relying on the writing _____. So, beware of a fact pattern in which the witness is not relying on the document while testifying. Beware of a fact pattern in which the witness is relying on a writing but for an _____matter.

1. In General

o Applies to writings, recordings, photographs, electronic documents, X-rays, and videos

o Applies when

- The _____ of a writing are at issue; or

- A witness is relying on the document when testifying.

> **Note 16:** The Best Evidence Rule does NOT require a party to present the most _____ evidence; nor does it require that the document be presented if the witness can testify without it

Example 93: *Clara Harris wrote down her observations immediately after the shooting. She can testify about the event, even though a writing exists, if she can testify about the document without it.*

2. **Contents "at issue"**

    o   A document is being used as _____of an event

    o   The document has _____ effect (e.g., a will or contract) or

    o   The witness is testifying based on the facts learned in the writing

3. **Original**

    o   An original of a writing or recording includes any counterpart intended to have the same _____as the original

        Example 94: *A printout of electronically stored information*

        Example 95: *A negative or print of a photograph*

4. **Exceptions**

    o   A duplicate is admissible if produced _____unless

        ▪   A genuine question of authenticity of the original arises; or

        ▪   _____ to admit the duplicate (e.g., a partial copy)

            Note 17: A handwritten copy of an original is not a duplicate and Is only admissible when the original or duplicate is _____, destroyed, or in the possession of an adversary who fails to produce it.

    o   Original Unavailable - Original Not Required and Duplicate Will Suffice

        ▪   All originals _____or destroyed

        ▪   Original could not be obtained through any judicial process

        ▪   Party against whom it is being offered is in control of it and fails to produce it when they had notice the writing was needed at trial; or

        ▪   _____matter

    o   Copies of Public Records

        ▪   Must be _____or

        ▪   If non-certified, there must be testimony by someone who saw the original

        ▪   If no copies available, court may allow other means to prove the issue

    o   Summaries or a Chart of an Original

        ▪   Allowed if proponent makes originals or duplicates available for copy and examination

        ▪   By court order

    o   Admission by a Party FRE 1007

- Can be a substitute if the contents of a writing, recording, or photograph are proven by _____ of the party against whom it is being offered

    o Role of Court FRE 1008

        ▪ Generally, Court determines whether Best Evidence Rule has been satisfied

C. Parol Evidence Rule (PER)

- Exclusionary rule that relates to _____ contracts
- Assumes that a written contract represents the _____ agreement
- Complete Integration: PER applies and _____ extrinsic evidence is allowed at trial
- Partial Integration: If the document contains some _____ of the terms, extrinsic evidence is allowed at trial and PER would not apply.

CHAPTER 9: PRIVILEGES (PART 1)

1. In General

- Definition: When there is potential evidence, but an individual has the right to hold the evidence secret and cannot be forced to provide the information
- The FRE contain_____ specific privilege provisions; _____ law applies

> **Exam Tip 6:** In federal question cases, privileges are determined under federal common law, pursuant to Rule 501 of the Federal Rules of Evidence. In diversity or supplemental claims in which a state's substantive laws apply, that state's law determines whether a privilege applies.

- A claim of privilege applies at _____stages of a case [FRE 1101]

2. Confidential Communication

    o For a communication to be privileged it must be _____

        ▪ Overheard by an unwanted third party = privilege _____ because it is not confidential

        ▪ Exceptions - privilege not destroyed

            ▪ If third party is _____ eavesdropper

            ▪ If party's presence is _____(e.g., translator)

    o Holder may waive privilege

        ▪ If holder fails to _____assert it

        ▪ _____

        ▪ Contractual waiver

> **Note 18:** Wrongful disclosure without holder's _____is not a waiver.

3. Spousal Privilege

Two distinct privileges: Spousal _____ and confidential marital communications

1) Spousal Immunity: a spouse is immune from testifying against husband or wife

   Example 96: *John Wilkes Booth is married. His wife cannot be forced to testify against him because she has spousal immunity.*

2) Confidential Marital Communication: prevents a spouse from being able to testify about something that was said _____ the marriage

a. Spousal Immunity

- *General Rule:* A criminal defendant's spouse may not be called as a witness by the _____ to testify against the defendant.

- A married person may not be _____ _____ to testify against her spouse in any _____ proceeding, including a grand jury.
  - It does not matter who the defendant is.

  Example 97: *David Herold's wife is called to testify in Booth's trial. The spousal immunity privilege applies even though Herold is not the defendant.*

- Holder of the privilege
  - **Federal court** and a **majority** of the states: _____ holds privilege and may choose to testify

  Example 98: *John Wilkes Booth's spouse, the witness spouse*

  - **Minority** of states: _____ holds the privilege. May prevent spouse from testifying, even if witness spouse wants to testify

  Example 99: *John Wilkes Booth, the party spouse*

- Period of the privilege
  - Applies to testimony about events occurring _____ and _____ the marriage

- Time limit to assert
  - Only _____ the marriage
  - Expires on _____ or annulment.

b. Confidential Marital Communication

- A communication made between spouses _____ is privileged.

Example 100: John Wilkes Booth says to his wife, "I am going to kill Abraham Lincoln." This is considered a confidential marital communication.

- Holder

  - Majority – Holder is _____

Example 101: In federal court spousal immunity - Mrs. Booth holds the privilege and can choose to testify against her husband John Wilkes Booth. She can waive her spousal immunity to testify and take the stand. However, Booth can object and invoke the confidential marital communication privilege if Mrs. Booth attempts to testify to a statement Booth made to her in confidence during their marriage.

- Scope of the privilege
  - Only applies to communications made _____ the marriage.
  - Applies to both _____ and criminal cases.
- Time limit to assert

  - Extends _____ end of the marriage.

c. Exceptions

- Neither spousal privilege applies

  - When one spouse is _____ the other spouse
  - When one spouse is charged with crime is against the other spouse
  - When one spouse is charged with crime is against the children of _____spouse

4. Attorney-Client Privilege

a. Elements

1) Confidential

   - Communication must be _____to be confidential
   - Third party present = generally _____ the privilege.
   - Exception: Client representatives do not destroy the privilege

2) Communication

   - Communication must be for _____ or representation.

     o Even if no legal advice is given and no representation occurs, statements made by the potential client can be privileged.

Example 102: *John Wilkes Booth is seeking legal advice and tells an attorney his story. Even if the attorney does not give legal advice or Booth does not retain the attorney, attorney-client privilege still attaches.*

- Not privileged
    - o Fee arrangement
    - o Identity of client
    - o Underlying facts of employment
    - o Statement made to an attorney who is acting in _____

Example 103: *The attorney is a tax preparer and acting in that capacity. Or, the attorney is the chief operations officer and general counsel of a corporation and acting on behalf of the corporation. Statement is not privileged if made to an attorney who is acting in another capacity.*

- Corporate Clients
    - o Some states limit the privilege only to the control group members of the corporation (i.e., directors and officers)
    - o Federal law: Non-control group communications can be privileged if they are communicating within their employment duties and for the purpose of seeking legal advice for the corporation.

3) Holder

- The _____ holds the privilege; only the client can _____ the privilege.

    - The attorney must _____ the privilege on the client's behalf.
    - The privilege exists until it is waived and survives the client's _____

b. **Exceptions**

The attorney-client privilege does not exist in the following situations:

- Communications made to enable or aid commission of what client knew or should have known was a _____ or fraud.
- Communication re disputes between attorney and client (e.g., malpractice)
- Communication between two parties who claim the same _____client
- Communications between co-clients of the same attorney who are now adverse

    Note 19: Attorney documents do not fall under attorney-client privilege—Work-product doctrine

c. **Effect of Disclosure on Waiver - FRE 502 (litigation related disclosures)**

- FRE do not generally address common law privileges. But FRE 502 addresses litigation-related disclosures of protected information.

- Inadvertent disclosure - No waiver of privilege in a federal proceeding if holder

  - Took reasonable steps to _____ disclosure; and
  - Took reasonable steps to _____ disclosure.

- Intentional disclosure – limitation on scope of waiver – in a federal proceeding

  - Acts as a waiver of the privilege
  - Extends to _____ information if:

    - Both sets of information concern the same subject; and
    - Fairness requires disclosure of both

- Disclosure in a **state proceeding** does not act as a waiver in a later federal proceeding if:

  - Would not have been a waiver in federal courts; or
  - Was not a disclosure under state law

- Federal court must apply most protective law

■ Court order: A federal court may order that disclosure of a privileged communication is not a waiver for later proceedings

■ Parties' Agreement: The parties' agreement regarding disclosure only binds the parties, unless it is incorporated into a court order

CHAPTER 10: PRIVILEGES (PART 2) AND OTHER POLICY EXCLUSIONS

A. Privileges (cont.)

1. Physician-Patient Privilege

- Not privileged under common law
- Most states protect by _____, so long as communication is for

  _____
- _____ holds the privilege; only patient can waive
- Situations where the privilege does NOT exist:

  1) Information was acquired for reasons other than treatment

     Example 104: John Wilkes Booth goes to the doctor and says, "I have the measles, and I'm looking to kill Lincoln," the latter half of the statement is not privileged.

  2) Patient's physical condition is _____ in the case

     Example 105: A plaintiff is suing for damages for injuries from a car accident. Statements made to the plaintiff's doctor regarding those injuries are not privileged because those injuries are at issue in the case.

3) Communication was made as part of the commission of a _____ or tort

4) A dispute exists between the physician and the patient

5) The patient contractually agreed to _____ the privilege

6) A case is brought in federal court and state law does not apply.

- What if an attorney sends a client to a doctor? Communication is not privileged unless _____ is being contemplated.

> *Example 106:* JWB said to Dr. Mudd, "I broke my leg when I shot the president. I need you to fix my leg to escape." This statement is not privileged because it relates to the commission of a crime or tort.

2. Psychotherapist-Patient Privilege

- Federal courts and most states recognize this privilege.
- Made between a psychiatrist, psychologist, or licensed social worker and a patient
- _____ holds privilege, but psychotherapist must assert in patient's absence
- This privilege does NOT exist if:

1) Patient's _____ is at issue

2) Communication was part of a court-ordered exam

3) Case is a _____ proceeding against the patient

- The psychotherapist-patient privilege is more widely recognized than the doctor-patient privilege.

3. Self-Incrimination

- *5th Amendment Protection* - Allows a witness to refuse to give testimony that may tend to incriminate him

  ▪ Only covers _____, not prior statements.

  ▪ Does not apply to _____ characteristics or mannerisms

  ▪ Holder: Human beings – not ____ _____ or other organizations

- Comment

  ▪ Criminal case: A prosecutor _____ comment on a defendant's failure to take the stand or suggest that the jury should draw a negative inference therefrom.

  ▪ Civil case: Opposing counsel _____ask the jury to draw negative inferences from a witness's claim of privilege.

- ○ Immunity
  - ▪ A witness may be compelled to provide incriminating testimony if the government grants him _____ from prosecution.
    - • Transactional immunity: Protection regards entire transaction
    - • Use immunity: Protection only covers the compelled statements.

    Note 20: The government is constitutionally required to offer "use" immunity, which prohibits only the use of the compelled testimony against the witness.

    Example 107: David Herold can be compelled to testify at Booth's trial without violating the 5th Amendment if the government offers him use immunity. Use immunity protects Herold from being prosecuted based on statements he makes about aiding and abetting Booth. Use immunity does not protect Herold from his other actions as a co-conspirator or other statements he makes during his testimony.

  - ▪ Exceptions
    - • If the government does prosecute the witness, government has the burden to show in a later proceeding that compelled testimony did not provide an investigative lead to the prosecution.
    - • No privilege if witness's danger of incrimination has been removed (i.e., acquittal or conviction)

4. **Clergy-Penitent**

- ○ A confidential communication made by a penitent to a member of the clergy is privileged.
- ○ Holder? _____ holds the privilege; clergy member asserts

5. **Accountant-Client**

- ○ Not available at common law
- ○ Many jurisdictions recognize this privilege by statute
- ○ Operates similarly to the attorney-client privilege

6. **Professional Journalist**

- ○ No federal privilege protecting a journalist's source of information
- ○ Some states have enacted statutes extending protection to journalists.

7. **Governmental Privileges**

- ○ The government, at all levels, is privileged against disclosing the identity of an _____ in a criminal case and the communication of official information by or to public officials.

B. **Public Policy Exclusions**

- **Subsequent Remedial Measures (FRE 407)**

  o Prohibits admission of measures taken after injury or harm that make future injury less likely

  o Inadmissible to prove _____, a defective product or design, or culpable conduct.

  > *Example 108: Mary Todd Lincoln is suing Ford's Theater for inadequate security and locks. After the assassination, but before trial, Ford fixes the locks and adds security bars. The fact that he did that is not admissible to prove that Ford was negligent or that he was culpable.*

  o Admissible to show ownership/control of the property or for_____

  > *Example 109: Mary Todd Lincoln is suing Ford's Theater for inadequate security and locks. Ford denies that he owns the theater. Evidence that Ford fixed the locks and added security bars could be offered for impeachment or to show ownership.*

- **Compromise Offers or Negotiations (FRE 408)**

  o Offers, conduct, or statements made during negotiations are_____ to prove a disputed claim, an amount, or for impeachment

  o Exceptions

    ▪ Negotiations with governmental agencies (e.g., IRS) are admissible in a later _____ case

    ▪ Admissible to prove bias, _____, obstruction, or to negate a claim of delay

    Note 21: Evidence discussed in a negotiation is not protected from admission.

  o A compromise is not admissible on behalf of any party (who participated in the compromise negotiations). If there are multiple parties and one settles, the agreement _____ admissible.

- **Offers to Pay Medical Expenses (FRE 409)**

  o _____ to prove liability for plaintiff's injuries

  o Any _____ or statements that accompany the payment or the offer to pay would be admissible

- **Plea Negotiations (FRE 410)**

  o Applies in civil and criminal trials

  o The following are inadmissible against the defendant:

    ▪ Withdrawn _____

    ▪ Pleas of nolo contendere (no contest)

- Statements made while negotiating with the D.A.
- Statements made during _____ proceedings

o Exceptions

- Pleas or negotiation statements are admissible if _____ dictates
- Perjury hearings

o Waiver - Defendant may waive if the waiver is _____ and _____

- **Liability Insurance (FRE 411)**

  o Evidence of insurance or lack of insurance is _____ to prove negligence or wrongful conduct.

  o Admissible if it goes to agency, _____, control, or witness bias and prejudice.

- **Sexual Conduct**

  a. **Victim's Conduct**

  - Rape Shield Law

    - Victim's sexual behavior or predisposition is _____ in any civil or criminal proceeding involving sexual misconduct.
    - Cannot be used for impeachment or for substantive purposes

      o Sexual behavior: Intercourse, diseases, use of contraception, etc.
      o Predisposition: The way a person dresses, speech, lifestyle, etc.

    - Exceptions in Criminal Cases

      o In a criminal case, sexual behavior of the victim can be used to prove source of semen or source of injury
      o Used to prove victim's _____
      o If offered by the prosecution

      Note 22: Opinion or reputation testimony is not admissible.

      o Evidence is allowed if exclusion would violate _____ rights of defendant

    - Exceptions in Civil Cases

      o Victim's reputation is only admissible if victim places it in controversy
      o Victim's sexual behavior is admissible if the _____ substantially outweighs any unfair prejudice

      Note 23: The probative value must be proven by the defendant.

- - Restriction on this evidence only applies if the party is a victim of sexual misconduct

    Example 110: In a defamation case, there is no restriction on admission of the victim's sexual behavior.

  - Procedure

    - Notice requirement for intent to use the evidence - At least _____ days before trial

  b. **Defendant's Conduct**

  - In a criminal case, evidence of defendant's other sexual assault is_____ when defendant is accused of committing sexual assault, rape, or child molestation
  - This evidence can be used for propensity
  - Court has discretion under 403 balance test to exclude the evidence
  - Not limited to convictions – can include _____ and unreported incidents
  - No time restriction
  - Notice requirement - At least _____ days before trial

CHAPTER 11: HEARSAY

A. Overview

> **Editor's Note 4:**   While hearsay questions historically have comprised 1/3 of the Evidence questions on the MBE, they now account for only 1/4 of the questions.

- Definition: An out-of-court statement that is offered to prove the truth of the

  _____.

  > **Note 24:** Four rules deal with hearsay: FRE 801, 802, 803, and 804.

  o General Rule: Hearsay is inadmissible (FRE 802)

  - Unless authorized by federal statute, a rule of evidence, or the Supreme Court.

  o FRE 801: What is not hearsay
  o FRE 803 & 804: Exceptions to Hearsay

  Example 111: Yesterday, you look up at the sky and say, "The sky is blue today." Today, you are brought into court and asked, "What did you say yesterday?" You respond, "Yesterday, I said the sky was blue." This is an out-of-court statement. If it is being offered in court to show that the sky was blue yesterday, it is hearsay.

- Three Categories of Hearsay
  - Living (FRE 801) - Not hearsay (not offered for the truth of the matter asserted OR designated as non-hearsay by the rules)
  - Dead (FRE 802) - Hearsay is inadmissible
  - Undead (FRE 803 and 804) Exceptions
    - These statements should be hearsay (offered for truth of matter asserted).
    - The rules have brought them back to life.

      Example 112: Same facts as above: Today I testify that yesterday I said, "The sky is blue today!" If offered for the truth of the matter asserted (the sky was in fact blue) it is inadmissible hearsay (dead). However, counsel may argue a hearsay exception applies, allowing the statement to be admissible.

    - Rule 804: Declarant must be _____ in order for out-of-court statement to come in
    - Rule 803: Declarant's availability as a witness is_____

      Example 113: Instead of calling me to testify about what I said to my wife yesterday, my wife is called to the stand. She is asked what I said to her yesterday. Her answer is still hearsay if offered for the truth of the matter asserted: the sky was blue. Counsel may still argue an exception applies. However, if the exception comes from FRE 804, counsel would also have to show that I (the declarant) am unavailable to testify.

      Example 114: Co-conspirator John Surratt is not testifying. Can someone take the stand and quote John Surratt? Under 803, it does not matter if John is available. However, if the witness wants to quote him under 804, that party must meet one of the requirements in the rule.

  - Living [FRE 801]
    - Out-of-court statements that are offered for the truth of the matter asserted that are NOT hearsay (exclusions)

      Example 115: Opposing counsel says, "Objection your honor, hearsay." My response using an exception under 803 or 804 is, "Your honor, this is hearsay. But this out of court statement falls under an exception." My response using an exclusion under 801 is, "Your honor, this is an out of court statement and we are offering it for the truth of the matter asserted, but it is not hearsay pursuant to an 801 exclusion."

    - Statements that are not offered for the truth of the matter asserted [801(c)]

      Example 116: David Herold testifies, "I told the police that John Wilkes Booth was hiding in the barn." If offered to prove that JWB was in fact hiding in the barn it is inadmissible hearsay. However, if it is offered to prove the effect the statement had on the police, then that is not hearsay.

- Impeachment of Prior Statement or Identification [FRE 801(d)]

  Example 117: *Clara Harris testifies that she did not see the shooter's face, but she did hear his voice. She states that the shooter said, "The sky is blue today!" and then a gun went off. She testifies that she knows the shooter was John Wilkes Booth because she recognized his voice. This statement is not being offered to show that the sky was blue. The statement is being offered for identification purposes, and is admissible.*

- Admissions of a party opponent [FRE 801(d)(2)]

B. What is Hearsay? [FRE 801 (a)-(c)]

- Hearsay: A statement made by a declarant other than while testifying at trial that is offered for the truth of the matter asserted.

  Example 118: *John Wilkes Booth (declarant) yells, "Sic semper tyrannus!" The prosecution has George Atzerodt on the stand. If the prosecution is offering this statement to prove that Booth could yell, is it hearsay? _____ _____.*

  Example 119: *If the statement is offered to prove that John Wilkes Booth was the speaker, is it hearsay? _____ _____.*

  Example 120: *If it is used to prove that John Wilkes Booth intended to shoot Abraham Lincoln, is it hearsay? _____ _____.*

  Example 121: *Instead of yelling, "sic semper tyrannus!" Booth yelled, "I just shot Abraham Lincoln!"_____ _____.*

  Example 122: *Major Rathbone yelled, "en vino veritas."*

      a. *If offered to prove he was angry:*
  _____.

      b. *If offered to prove he could yell:*
  _____.

      c. *If offered for vocal recognition:*
  _____.

      d. *If offered to prove that boozers tell the truth:* _____.

- Declarant must be a _____

- o Not hearsay

    - ▪ A dog bark

    - ▪ An automatically generated time stamp on a fax

    - ▪ A printout of electronic telephonic tracing equipment

    - ▪ Raw data from a forensic lab machine

        > **Note 25:** A witness's statement quoting himself outside of court while in court _____ be hearsay

- The statement must be an assertion. It may be:

    - o _____

    - o Written

    - o _____ conduct, if intended as an assertion, e.g., nodding, thumbs up, pointing

        > *Example 123:* *John Wilkes Booth testifies and says he asked George Atzerodt, "Did you kill Abraham Lincoln?" Atzerodt responded by nodding and smiling. The nod is an assertion.*

- Statements that are not offered to prove the truth of the matter asserted are

    _____.

    > *Example 124:* *John Wilkes Booth testifies that George Atzerodt said, "I just killed the President!" If this statement is to show that Atzerodt knows English, it is not hearsay.*

    - o Questions are NOT hearsay – there is no matter being asserted

        > **Exam Tip 7:** A statement that is not hearsay is not automatically admissible. It may be inadmissible if it falls under a privilege, is improper character evidence, or fails the 403 test.

    - o Not offered to prove the truth of the matter asserted

        - ▪ Legally operative fact - A statement offered to prove that the statement itself was made, regardless of its truth

            > *Example 125:* *Outside of court, George Atzerodt says, "John Wilkes Booth has an STD." In a slander action, this is offered to show that Atzerodt actually made the statement. Not to prove the fact that JWB has an STD.*

        - ▪ To show the _____ on the _____

            > *Example 126:* *George Atzerodt testifies that he told JWB "there will be a guard at the front door of the theater." It is being offered to show why JWB used the back door. It is not being offered to prove the truth of the matter asserted. It is being offered to show the effect on the listener.*

- A statement offered to show the declarant's _____ or state of mind

  Example 127: *John Wilkes Booth testifies that the night before the assassination, George Atzerodt said, "I am Henry VIII, I am!" This might be offered to show Atzerodt's mental state.*

- Impeachment: Not being offered for the truth, but to impeach

  Example 128: *George Atzerodt testifies that he has never had any ill will toward the President. John Wilkes Booth can then take the stand and say, "Atzerodt told me on April the 14th, 'I have much ill will toward the President.'" This is not being offered to show that Atzerodt has ill will toward the President, but rather to show that he has said contradictory things.*

- **Multiple Hearsay** [FRE 805]

  o Hearsay within hearsay
  o May be admissible
  o Both levels of hearsay must fall within an exception

    Example 129: *A police officer testifies at trial and says, "George Atzerodt ran up to me right after the shooting in a very excited state. He yelled, 'John Wilkes Booth just told me that he was going to kill the President tonight!'" Two levels of hearsay: (1) what Booth said to Atzerodt; and (2) what Atzerodt said to the police officer. If both of those statements can overcome hearsay, the statement is admissible. Booth's statement is an admission of a party opponent (if offered by the prosecution). Atzerodt's statement to the police officer is an excited utterance.*

CHAPTER 12: NON-HEARSAY

A. The Living: What is not hearsay under FRE 801(d)

Exclusions - Out of court statements offered for the truth of the matter asserted. These statements would qualify as hearsay, but are admissible because Rule 801 treats them as non-hearsay.

1. **Prior Statements - The declarant must be testifying at trial; and the declarant must be subject to cross-examination**

   a. **Prior Inconsistent Statements [801(d)(1)]**

   - Admissible as _____ evidence if:

     - Previously made under penalty of perjury; (deposition, prior trial) and
     - Inconsistent with the present testimony being given at trial

- Not previously given under oath = can only be offered for_____ purposes, not for the substance of what was previously said

    Example 130: Booth testifies that George Atzerodt previously said, "I killed Abraham Lincoln." If this statement was made under oath and subject to cross-examination, it can be offered to prove that Atzerodt killed Lincoln, the substance of the statement. If the statement was not made under oath, it can only be offered to impeach Atzerodt.

b. Prior Consistent Statements [801(d)(1)]

- Only admissible to _____ a charge or claim that the declarant is fabricating or has recent motive to fabricate the statement in court

    - Is admissible, regardless of whether made under oath or not
    - The prior consistent statement must have been made before the declarant had reason to fabricate the statement

    Example 131: George Atzerodt testifies that he never wanted to kill Abraham Lincoln. Previously, he told people that he did not want to kill Lincoln. This statement is admissible. The prosecution can only offer this statement once the defense has tried to show that Atzerodt has previously made an inconsistent statement.

    Example 132: Atzerodt took a plea deal in exchange for his testimony. The prior consistent statement must have been made before Atzerodt took the deal, i.e. before he had motive to fabricate.

c. Prior Statements of Identification [801(d)(1)]

- A previous out-of-court identification of a person after seeing them, e.g., in a lineup or photo array, is admissible as _____ evidence.

    Exam Tip 8: Be aware of fact patterns involving prior out-of-court identifications by a witness who is *not* testifying at this current trial (and is therefore not subject to cross-examination). This rule cannot apply and those out-of-court identification statements are not admissible if, for instance, the witness is dead or otherwise unavailable for trial.

2. Party Admissions [FRE 801(d)(2)]

Note 26: *Who* the declarant is is key here.

o A prior out-of-court statement made by a _____ (or representative) to the current litigation that is offered by the _____ party against that party is not hearsay.

Note 27: In criminal prosecutions, there is only one party: the defendant. Therefore, because the government is not a party, out-of-court statements of a government representative (e.g., a police detective) cannot be overcome by saying they are an admission of a party opponent.

Example 133: George Atzerodt testifies that John Wilkes Booth said, "I'm a Libra!" Because JWB is a party, this statement is admissible as a statement by a party opponent, even though it is not against Booth's interest. It is not hearsay because the defendant said it and the opponent is offering it.

o   An opposing party's statement need not have been against the party's interest at the time that it was made.

o   The statement may be admitted even if it is not based on personal knowledge or within the party's normal _____ of knowledge.

a. **Judicial Admissions - Admissible if made:**

■   During discovery process

■   By stipulation

■   During a proceeding

■   Unless they are _____

Note 28: Withdrawn Guilty Plea - Not admissible in subsequent proceeding as a statement by a party opponent

b. **Adoptive Admission**

■   A statement made by another person (not the party) that a party expressly or impliedly _____ as his own can be used in court.

■   Silence is considered an adoptive admission if:

•   The party was _____ and heard and understood the statement;

•   The party had the _____ and opportunity to _____ it; and

•   A _____ person who is similarly situated would have denied the statement.

Example 134: Mary Surratt is testifying for the prosecution. She says, "All of us were sitting around the house and my son said, 'John Wilkes Booth is going to be the one to kill Abraham Lincoln.'" If Booth was present, he heard and understood the statement, he had the opportunity and ability to deny it, a reasonable person would have denied it, and he did not deny it, the statement qualifies as an adoptive admission, and is admissible for the truth against Booth.

c. **Vicarious Admission**

■   An out-of-court statement made by one person that may be imputed to an opposing party based upon certain relationships between the parties

- A statement made by an _____ or agent qualifies as an opposing party's statement if:

  - Made within scope of employment; and
  - During the course of the relationship

- A statement made by an _____ speaker
- Co-Conspirator Admission - A statement made by a co-conspirator is admissible if it is made during and in _____ of the conspiracy.

  - A statement made after arrest would not be made in furtherance of the conspiracy, so not admissible of a co-conspirator

  Example 135: George Atzerodt testifies that David Herold said, "I have a Derringer you can use, John Wilkes Booth." This statement is admissible as a co-conspirator's admission.

CHAPTER 13: HEARSAY EXCEPTIONS (PART 1)

- The Undead: Although hearsay is generally inadmissible, the FRE identify some situations in which hearsay is allowed.
- FRE 804 provides exceptions to hearsay when **necessity** requires the statements because declarant is unavailable
- FRE 803 provides exceptions to hearsay when the statements are **inherently trustworthy.**

A. Exceptions That Apply ONLY If the Declarant Is Unavailable (FRE 804)

- **"Unavailable"**

  1) Exempt on the grounds of _____ (e.g., spousal immunity)

  2) Refuses to testify, despite a court order

  3) Lacks _____ of the subject matter of the statement

  Example 136: The prosecution wants to quote Mary Todd Lincoln. However, she does not remember anything she said. The prosecution can show that she is unavailable.

  4) Unable to testify due to death, infirmity, or physical or mental _____

  5) Absent and cannot be subpoenaed or otherwise made to appear

  Note 29: A declarant is not deemed unavailable if the proponent of the declarant's statement is responsible for the declarant's unavailability in order to prevent the declarant from testifying.

Example 137: *Booth wants to use a statement Herold made in the woods. Booth on the stand wants to claim Herold said, "I killed Abraham Lincoln." Booth cannot use Herold's statement if Herold is missing because of something Booth had done. If Booth had imprisoned Herold in a cave, Booth cannot argue that Herold is unavailable because he caused Herold's unavailability.*

- **The Five Unavailable Declarant Exceptions**

    1. **Former Testimony**

        ▪ Testimony will be admissible if:
            - The declarant is unavailable;
            - The statement was prior testimony given at a _____ hearing or deposition; **and**
        ▪ The opposing party had an opportunity and_____ _____ to develop the testimony through cross- or direct examination.

        Example 138: *The prosecution is attempting to use Mary Todd Lincoln's statement at trial. They are claiming she is unavailable due to mental disability following a nervous breakdown. Mary Todd Lincoln previously testified at a deposition, and John Wilkes Booth's counsel was present and had a chance to cross-examine her. Additionally, they had a similar basis or motive in developing her testimony. The statement is admissible.*

        Example 139: *Mary Todd Lincoln was deposed in a different case and Booth's counsel was not present. The statement is not admissible because Booth did not have an opportunity to cross-examine her.*

        ▪ Prior testimony at a _____ does NOT qualify as former testimony (opposing counsel was not present)

    2. **Dying Declarations**

        ▪ Statement will be admissible at trial if:
            - The declarant is unavailable and
            - The declarant believed her death was _____when she made the statement and
            - The statement pertains to the _____ or the circumstances of her death.

        Note 30: The declarant need not actually die; must only believe death is imminent

        Note 31: Only available in homicide and civil cases

Example 140: David Herold died of natural causes. On his death bed he said he killed Abraham Lincoln. Is this statement admissible?

_____

_____

3. Statements Against Interest

- Statement is admissible if:
  - The declarant is unavailable
  - The statement is against the declarant's_____ and
  - A _____ person would not have made the statement unless he believed it was true
- "Against self-interest"
  - Pecuniary or proprietary interest; or
  - Exposes declarant to _____or _____ liability
    - Criminal liability: Must have corroborating evidence that clearly indicates the trustworthiness of the out-of-court statement

  Note 32: Contrast **statement of opposing party** which does not require the statement to be against the party's self-interest.

  Example 141: John Wilkes Booth wants to quote David Herold as saying, "I killed Abraham Lincoln." When the police found Herold, he had a one-shot, blue-smoke Derringer. This is corroborating evidence. Booth can use Herold's statement because it was against his interest and there is corroborating evidence.

4. Statement of Personal or Family History

A statement concerning the unavailable declarant's own birth, adoption, marriage, divorce, etc., is not excluded.

5. Declarant Unavailable Due to Wrongdoing (Forfeiture Against Wrongdoing Exception)

Example 142: John Wilkes Booth causes David Herold to be unavailable. Booth cannot object if the prosecution attempts to use David Herold's out-of-court statement against JWB. Herold's out-of-court statement is, "I saw John Wilkes Booth kill Abraham Lincoln." Herold is unavailable because JWB locked him in a cave. If JWB objects to this statement, it would be admissible under the forfeiture against wrongdoing exception.

- A statement that is offered against a party who is wrongfully responsible for the declarant's unavailability is admissible.

  Note 33: The act that made the witness unavailable need not be criminal (e.g., sending someone on a world cruise). It must be deliberate (or acquiesced to) with the intent to prevent the witness from testifying.

CHAPTER 14: HEARSAY EXCEPTIONS (PART 2)

A. Exceptions Where Declarant's Availability Is Immaterial (FRE 803)

- o FRE 804 provides exceptions to hearsay when necessity requires the statements because the declarant is unavailable.
- o FRE 803 provides exceptions to hearsay when the statements are inherently trustworthy.

1. Present Sense Impression

- o A statement describing or explaining an event or condition that is made while or immediately after the declarant perceived the event.

   Example 143: Clara Harris takes the stand and testifies, "Moments after the shooting, there was a woman in the audience who said, 'I just saw John Wilkes Booth shoot President Lincoln.'" Is this admissible as a present sense impression?

   _____

   _____

   Example 144: Clara Harris is in line for the bathroom when she hears a commotion back in the theatre. She cannot see what is going on, so the lady near her describes what she sees, "John Wilkes Booth is jumping off the balcony, he's running across the stage with a knife." Is this statement admissible as a present sense impression?

   _____

   _____

2. Excited Utterance

- o A statement made about a _____ event or condition while the declarant is under the stress of excitement caused by the event.

   - The statement must relate to the event, but the declarant need not be a participant in the event – can be a bystander

   Example 145: The radio announcer who was describing the Hindenburg event. Someone could quote this man and offer it for the truth of the matter asserted.

   Example 146: Major Rathbone testifies that an usher at Ford's Theater came rushing up to him five minutes after the shooting and said, panting, "I saw John Wilkes Booth shoot President Lincoln!" Is Major Rathbone allowed to quote the man?

   _____

   _____

   Exam Tip 9: Look for facts indicating that the out-of-court declarant is still under the stress or excitement of the event, e.g., panting.

- o Different from present sense impression:
    - Present sense impression must be a description of the event
    - Excited utterance need only _____ the event

        Example 147: *You are on the phone with your girlfriend who is at Ford's Theater. She says, "I am watching JWB jump from the balcony." This is a present sense impression.*

        Example 148: *A man runs up to you ten minutes later and says, "I'm having a fit from seeing John Wilkes Booth shoot the President!" This is an excited utterance because he was still under the stress of the event.*

3. **Statements of Mental, Emotional, or Physical Condition**

    - o A statement of a declarant's _____ state of mind, emotional, sensory, or physical condition used to show the declarant acted in conformity therewith
    - o State of mind

        - Present intent
        - _____
        - Plan

            Example 149: *John Wilkes Booth is on the stand. He is testifying about something David Herold said. Booth says that Herold said, "I'm so angry, I'm going to kill that scalawag Abraham Lincoln." Is this admissible for the truth of the matter asserted? _____. It displays Herold's then-existing state of mind – motive or present intent*

            Note 34: Not admissible if it is about a memory, a past belief, or a past state of mind

            Example 150: *John Wilkes Booth cannot testify that David Herold said, "I was really angry at President Lincoln last week."*

            Exam Tip 10: Do not confuse the state of mind exception with **circumstantial** evidence of the declarant's state of mind (not hearsay). To meet the state of mind exception, the statement must be offered to prove that the declarant acted in accordance with the stated intent (i.e., Herold tried to kill the President).

    - o Physical condition

        - Used to prove that the condition existed
        - Cannot be used to prove the cause of the condition

            Example 151: *John Wilkes Booth could testify, "The morning after the assassination, David Herold said to me, "My leg is killing me." However, JWB* *cannot testify that David Herold said, "My leg is killing me from jumping off the balcony at Ford's Theater last night." This goes to the cause of the condition.*

4. Statements Made for Purposes of Medical Diagnosis or Treatment

- An out-of-court statement is admissible if it is made for medical diagnosis or treatment.
- Can include statements of past or present _____.
- Also admissible if it goes to the _____of the injury

   Example 152: Booth calls Dr. Samuel Mudd. Dr. Mudd could testify about Booth's statement, "I broke my leg trying to stop George Atzerodt from shooting the President and I fell off the balcony."

   - Note that Booth is calling Samuel Mudd and so is not a party opponent - cannot admit Dr. Mudd's testimony re Booth's statement under the party opponent exception.

   Note 35: A statement that falls within this hearsay exception still may be inadmissible if it is protected by the physician-patient privilege.

- Admissible if:

   - Made to a physician or other medical personnel or even to a family member, as long as the statement is made for the purpose of treatment or diagnosis.
   - Made to a physician consulted only for the purpose of enabling the physician to testify at trial
   - The statement need not necessarily be made by the patient, so long as it is made for the purpose of medical diagnosis or treatment.

      - Admissibility depends on relationship between declarant and the patient - the closer the relationship the more the statement is trusted
      - The court assesses the probative value of the statement

   Example 153: JWB's mother was with John Wilkes Booth when he went to see Dr. Mudd. John Wilkes Booth was so tired he couldn't talk so Mrs. Booth made statements about his treatment.

CHAPTER 15: HEARSAY EXCEPTIONS (PART 3); CONSTITUTIONAL LIMITATIONS

A. Exceptions Where Declarant's Availability Is Immaterial (cont.) (FRE 803)

1. Recorded Recollection

- The record is read into evidence because the witness cannot recall the event or information
- Requirements

   - The record is about a matter the witness once _____ about
   - The record was _____ or adopted by the witness when the matter was fresh in his mind;

- The record accurately _____ the witness's knowledge; and
- The witness now cannot ____ _____ the events well enough to testify, even after consulting the writing while on the stand.

   Example 154: Mary Todd Lincoln had a diary. She went home immediately after the shooting and wrote about the assassination. Now, she cannot recall the event, even after she reads her diary entry. This would possibly qualify for admission under the recorded recollection exception.

- The record may _____ into evidence. However, the proponent cannot enter the record as an exhibit. Only the _____can introduce it as an exhibit.

   Note 36: Contrast with **present recollection refreshed** which allows a witness to consult an item to refresh her memory. The witness cannot use the item while testifying and the item is NOT admitted into evidence.

2. **Business Records**

- A record is not excluded as hearsay if:

   - Record is kept in the course of _____ business activity
   - The making of the record was a _____ of the activity and
   - The record was made at or near the time that someone by someone with knowledge.

   Example 155: A receptionist who logs calls as they come in. This log is admissible under the business records exception.

   Note 37: Distinguish from Recorded Recollection: the business records exception does not require the witness to be unable to recall the events.

- Authentication

   - By the _____
   - Qualified witness
   - Records may be self-authenticated

- May be deemed inadmissible if the source or the preparation of the information appears to lack trustworthiness

   Example 156: The records were prepared in anticipation of litigation. These may not be considered trustworthy because the person who prepared the records may have wanted to mischaracterize things.

- Examples of business records

   - Medical records, as long as they relate to diagnosis or treatment
   - Police reports

- But witness statements within police reports are *not* admissible under this rule (although they may be admissible under another exception).

  o Absence of a Record

    ▪ May be admissible to prove the event did _____ occur
    ▪ Admissible if a record is _____ kept for that type of matter

    Example 157: *Mary Todd Lincoln sues Ford's Theater for improper locks and poor security. There is a maintenance and security log. Mary Todd Lincoln could offer the log to show that on the night of the assassination, there were no entries showing that the security guards made their rounds that night.*

3. **Public Records**

   o Applies to a record or a statement of a public office or agency that sets out

     ▪ The _____ of office or agency **or**
     ▪ ____ _____ of a person who has a duty to report that observation (except for observations of a law enforcement officer in a criminal case) or
     ▪ Factual findings of a legal investigation in a _____ case, or in a criminal case if it is against the government

   o May exclude if the source of information or other aspects indicate a lack of trustworthiness
   o Absence of a Record

     ▪ If public officer usually keeps a record and no record exists, that _____is admissible to show that the matter did not occur

   o Records of vital statistics

     ▪ Record of death, birth, marriage, etc.
     ▪ Not excluded if event is reported to a legal office in accordance with a legal duty

4. **Learned Treatise**

   o Statement in a treatise, periodical, pamphlet, etc.
   o Not excluded

     ▪ If an expert _____ on statement during direct or expert was cross-examined on it; and
     ▪ If publication is established as a reliable authority

       • By expert
       • By another expert
       • By judicial notice

     ▪ If admitted, statement is _____ into evidence; the publication is NOT admitted as an exhibit

5. **Judgment of a Previous Conviction**

    o   Not excluded if:

        ▪   Judgment was entered after trial or a guilty plea (does not include nolo contendere/no contest);

        ▪   Punishable by _____ or imprisonment greater than one year; and

        ▪   The evidence is offered to prove any fact essential to sustain the judgment

            Example 158: Traffic conviction less than one year. Not admissible to prove driver's negligence.

6. **Other Exceptions Enumerated under FRE 803**

    o   Records of religious organizations regarding personal or family history

    o   Marriage and baptismal certificates

    o   Family records (e.g., family Bible)

    o   Records of documents affecting an interest in property

    o   Ancient documents (authenticated documents in existence at least _____ years)

    o   Market reports

    o   Reputation concerning personal or family history, boundaries, general history, or character

    o   Judgments regarding proof of matters of personal, family, or general history if the matter was essential to the judgment and could be proved by evidence of reputation

B. **Residual Exception/Catch-All Exception (FRE 807)**

    •   This is an exception for a statement that is not otherwise covered by any of the rules.

    •   A hearsay statement may be admissible under this exception if:

        1) Equivalent circumstantial guarantees of _____

        2) It is offered as evidence of a _____ fact

        3) It is more _____ than any other evidence on the point and

        4) Admitting the hearsay statement will best serve the purpose of the FRE and the interests of justice.

    •   Reasonable notice must be given to opposing counsel of the intent to use this

C. **Constitutional Limitations – Hearsay Evidence Restrictions**

    1. **6th Amendment - Confrontation Clause and Hearsay Evidence**

        ▪   A **testimonial statement** is admissible against a criminal defendant only if:

            •   Declarant is _____; and

            •   Defendant had an opportunity to _____ the declarant prior to trial

- **Testimonial Statement**
  - A statement made to police during the course of questioning with the primary purpose of enabling police to provide assistance to someone is not testimonial and would probably be admissible.
  - A statement is testimonial if it is made during a police interrogation with the primary purpose of using the statement in a criminal prosecution (e.g. ascertaining past criminal conduct).

  Example 159: Statement was made to police during questioning, but purpose was to help an injured person. This is not considered testimonial.

  Example 160: Major Rathbone is laying there right after being stabbed. The police officer bends down and Mahor Rathbone says, "It was Booth." You have a pretty good argument that this is not testimonial.

  Example 161: A statement made to the police during questioning to ascertain past criminal conduct is considered testimonial.

- **Unavailable**
  - To use a testimonial statement and overcome the hearsay, the prosecution must show the defendant _____ the declarant's unavailability and the defendant did it with the _____ to make the declarant unavailable.

2. 14th Amendment: Due Process Clause

- May prevent application of a hearsay rule when the rule would restrict the defendant's ability to mount a defense.

D. Constitutional Limitations - Face-to-Face Confrontation

- The Confrontation Clause generally requires a face-to-face confrontation between the defendant and a witness in court.

  Example 162: The defendant can force a child witness who is a victim of a sex offense to step out from behind a screen to testify.

- Exception - When there is an important public interest, such as _____ a child

  Example 163: A child witness is the victim of a sex crime. The child can testify via one-way, closed-circuit television if the court finds the child would suffer serious emotional distress if the child was forced to testify in open court.

CHAPTER 16:   REVIEW QUESTIONS (PART 1)

A.   PRESENTATION OF EVIDENCE

1.   Who decides whether evidence is admissible, the judge or the jury? _____

2.   Once evidence is admitted, who determines issues of weight or credibility? _____

3.   On appeal, what must you show in order to predicate error on a trial court's evidentiary ruling?

   - _____ of a party was affected; and
   - Court was _____ of the error at the time

4.   What are the ways to notify the trial court of an error and thus preserve issue for appeal?

   - _____
   - _____

5.   What is judicial notice?

   Court's acceptance of a fact as true _____ requiring proof

6.   What sorts of adjudicative facts are subject to judicial notice?

   - Facts _____ within the jurisdiction; or
   - Can be _____ by a source whose accuracy cannot be questioned

7.   What is the effect of judicial notice in a civil case?

   Jury instructed to _____ it

8.   What is the effect of judicial notice taken in a criminal case?

   Jury _____ accept it

B.   FORM OF QUESTIONS, BURDENS, AND PRESUMPTIONS

1.   What is a leading question?

   One that _____ within the question

2.   When are leading questions generally permissible on direct examination?

   - _____ matters
   - Witnesses who have_____ (e.g., a child)
   - _____ or hostile witnesses

3.   What does the phrase "burden of production" mean?

   Necessity of producing evidence _____ to get your case to the jury

4.   What does the phrase "burden of persuasion" mean?

   Persuading _____ that you should win your case

5. What is a "rebuttable presumption?"

Shifts the _____ and requires the

_____ to offer counterproof

C. RELEVANCE

1. What is the standard or test for determining whether evidence is relevant?

Evidence is relevant if it makes any fact of import _____
than it is without the evidence.

2. Under what circumstances can the court exclude relevant evidence under Rule 403?

_____ is _____

_____ by _____ (e.g., unfair prejudice,

misleading the jury)

3. What is character evidence?

Proof of a trait or _____ as a way of proving that the
person probably acted in that manner on a particular occasion (a.k.a. propensity)

4. For what purpose is character evidence not admissible in civil cases?

To prove _____ with that character trait

> ***Example 164:*** *The defendant is a fast driver. This evidence is not admissible to*
> *prove the defendant drove fast on the day of the collision.*

5. If character evidence is admissible as evidence in a case, what form(s) may it take?

- _____;
- _____; and
- _____

D. CHARACTER EVIDENCE IN CRIMINAL CASES AND PRIOR BAD ACTS

1. What does it mean to say that character evidence is offered to prove "propensity?"

That a person _____ because
they are that kind of person

> ***Example 165:*** *He is mean, so I bet he killed Abraham Lincoln.*

2. When is evidence of a crime victim's character admissible to prove propensity?

When introduced by a _____ as a relevant trait

> ***Example 166:*** *John Wilkes Booth claims self-defense, and wants to introduce*
> *evidence that Abraham Lincoln was a violent, fighting person. This is admissible*
> *evidence of the victim's character.*

3. When is evidence of a criminal defendant's character admissible to prove propensity?

When the _____

> **Example 167:** *John Wilkes Booth took the stand and said he is a peaceful, non-political person. He opened the door, allowing the prosecution to introduce evidence of his character for violence.*

4. If a defendant offers proof of an alleged victim's character or propensity for violence, may the prosecution offer evidence of the defendant's character or propensity to commit fraud?

_____

_____

5. If character evidence is admissible in a criminal case to prove propensity, what form(s) may it take?

- _____; or

- _____;

- But not _____

6. For what purposes may the prosecution introduce evidence of a criminal defendant's prior crimes?

To prove something other than _____. (Remember MIMIC)

7. What is the difference between character evidence and habit evidence (which is admissible under Rule 406)?

Habit evidence is more _____ and _____

E. WITNESSES: IMPEACHMENT

1. Is it permissible to "impeach" a witness regarding bad character for untruthfulness?

_____

2. If evidence of bad character for untruthfulness is admissible, what form(s) may it take?

_____ or _____

3. Under what circumstances may evidence be offered of a witness's good character for truthfulness?

Only if the character for truthfulness has been _____

4. Under what circumstances may a witness be impeached on cross-examination about prior bad acts?

Discretion of the court, if _____

_____

5. May a witness be impeached by having another witness describe the first witness's prior bad acts?

_____. Reputation or opinion evidence only. Prior bad acts on _____ _____ of the first witness only. Cannot be proven through _____

6. What two sorts of criminal convictions may be used to impeach a witness?

   • _____

   • _____

7. How does the standard for allowing or disallowing impeachment differ regarding these two types of criminal convictions used for impeachment?

   • Dishonesty: _____

   • Serious crime: subject to a _____

8. How are criminal defendants treated differently from other witnesses in regard to impeachment by proof of prior criminal convictions?

   • Most witnesses: must prove that the _____ is _____ by danger of _____.

   • Criminal defendants: _____ must _____ the risk of _____

9. Is it necessary to give the witness an opportunity to explain or deny a prior inconsistent statement before impeaching a witness with that the statement?

   _____

10. May prior inconsistent statements generally be proven with extrinsic evidence?

    _____

11. What techniques may be used to rehabilitate a witness who has been impeached?

    • Character evidence of _____ may be presented

    • Introduce _____

    • Allow witness to _____ on cross-examination

12. What is the difference between present recollection refreshed and past recollection recorded?

Present recollection refreshed: showing the witness something to _____ _____ so he can testify from _____.

Past recollection recorded: _____ something the _____ instead of testifying from memory because the witness _____ enough details to testify

13. Is an adverse party permitted to inspect documents used to refresh a witness's memory?

   _____

14. May an adverse party introduce into evidence documents used to refresh a witness's memory?

   _____

F. OPINION TESTIMONY

1. Under what circumstances may an expert witness testify?

   When _____ will
   _____ the trier of fact

2. Under *Daubert* and Rule 702, what requirements must expert testimony meet?

   - Witness is _____ as an expert
   - Testimony is based on sufficient _____
   - Testimony is the product of reliable principles and methods
   - Witness applied the principles and methods _____ to the facts
   - Witness possesses a reasonable degree of certainty in her opinion

3. In general, may an expert witness offer an opinion on an ultimate issue in the case?

   _____

4. Under what circumstances will an expert witness be precluded from opining on an ultimate issue?

   Opinion about whether a defendant in a criminal case had the _____
   _____ for a crime or defense

G. BEST EVIDENCE RULE

1. What sort of evidence is generally excluded by the best evidence rule?

   Testimony about the _____

2. If an accurate video recording of a car accident were available, would it violate the best evidence rule for a party to call a witness to describe the accident, rather than introducing the videotape?

   _____

3. When might a photocopy or carbon copy be considered the "original" under the best evidence rule?

   Any copy meant to have the _____

H. PRIVILEGES

1. What are the two forms of spousal privilege?

- _____

- _____

2. May the spousal immunity privilege be invoked regarding testimony about events that occurred *before* the defendant spouse and the witness spouse were married?

   _____

3. What is protected by the confidential marital communications privilege?

   Confidential communications made _____

4. May the confidential marital communications privilege be invoked after a divorce?

   _____

5. What are the key exceptions to the confidential marital communications privilege?

   - Lawsuits _____

   - When one spouse is accused of a _____

     _____ or their children

6. What are the essential elements of the attorney-client privilege?

   _____ between a lawyer and a client

   for the purpose of _____

7. Identify two central exceptions to the coverage of the attorney-client privilege:

   - Future _____

   - Disputes between _____

8. Under state laws recognizing a physician-patient privilege, what limitations are common?

   - Does not exist if acquired for

     _____;

   - _____ purpose;

   - Dispute between _____

9. What limits attach to the psychotherapist-patient privilege?

   - _____ as physician-patient privilege

   - Does not apply if part of a _____ or

     _____

10. May the privilege against self-incrimination be invoked in a civil case?

    _____

I. **PUBLIC POLICY EXCLUSIONS**

   1. For what purpose is evidence of liability insurance NOT admissible?

To prove _____

2. For what purpose is evidence of subsequent remedial measures NOT admissible?

    • To show _____
    • To show a product was _____
    • To show a product had a _____

3. For what purposes is evidence of subsequent remedial measures admissible?

    _____, _____, or
    _____ (if controverted)

4. For what purposes is evidence of an offer to settle a case admissible?

    _____

5. Under what circumstances will statements made during plea bargain negotiations be admissible?

    If _____ of the statement have been introduced by the
    _____, the _____ can introduce
    other portions as necessary to provide _____

6. When will evidence of a victim's past sexual behavior be admissible in a criminal case?

    • Source of _____ or _____
    • _____ with defendant
    • As the _____ requires

7. When will evidence of a victim's past sexual behavior be admissible in a civil case?
    If the _____
    the risk of harm to the victim or prejudice to any party

CHAPTER 17:   REVIEW QUESTIONS (PART 2)

A. HEARSAY

1. What is the basic definition of hearsay?

    An _____ or conduct intended as an assertion
    offered to prove the _____
    _____.

    > *Example 168:* *I said to my wife yesterday, "The sky is blue." If it is being offered*
    > *to prove that the sky was blue yesterday, it is hearsay.*

2. May nonverbal conduct be considered hearsay?

    _____, if intended as an _____

3. What uses might there be for a statement other than to prove the truth of the matter asserted?

   • _____

   • _____

   • Circumstantial evidence of _____

4. If the statement, "I will shoot you, if you do not give me that horse," were offered to prove duress on the part of the thief, would it be objectionable as hearsay?

   _____

5. If the statement by a person lending a car, "Be careful, my brakes are bad," were offered to prove that the car borrower was comparatively negligent or had assumed the risk, would it be hearsay?

   _____

6. What is "multiple hearsay" and what must be shown to render it admissible?

   • _____

   • Each _____ must fit within an _____
     _____

   > **Example 169:** *Secretary of War Stanton testifies and quotes George Atzerodt, who was quoting John Wilkes Booth. There are two levels of hearsay. The statements of John Wilkes Booth are an admission of a party opponent. Stanton's testimony is admissible if Atzerodt's statement fits within an exception or exclusion.*

7. The three categories of prior statements that are defined as not hearsay by Rule 801(d)(1) all share one common threshold requirement or element. What is that threshold requirement?

   The declarant must _____
   _____

8. What sorts of prior inconsistent statements are defined as not hearsay by rule 801(d)(1)(A), and thus may be used not merely to impeach a witness, but as proof of what they assert?

   Made _____ at a _____
   _____

9. Will a prior consistent statement made subsequent to the alleged improper motive or influence qualify as not hearsay under rule 801(d)(1)(B)?

   _____

10. What other sorts of statements are defined as not hearsay under rule 801(d)(2)?

    Statements made _____

B. HEARSAY EXCEPTIONS (DECLARANT UNAVAILABLE)

1. What five hearsay exceptions require a showing that the declarant is unavailable to testify?

   - 804(b)(1): Former _____
   - 804(b)(2): _____ declaration
   - 804(b)(3): Statement _____
   - 804(b)(4): Personal or family history
   - 804(b)(6): _____ by wrongdoing

2. What are the five ways in which a declarant can be shown to be unavailable under Rule 804(a)?

   - 804(a)(1): _____
   - 804(a)(2): _____
   - 804(a)(3): _____
   - 804(a)(4): _____
   - 804(a)(5): _____ and cannot be _____

3. Under Rule 804(b)(1) [the "former testimony" exception], what must be shown in order for the former testimony to be admissible?

   - The declarant _____ at a proceeding; and
   - The party against whom the testimony is being offered had _____ _____ to develop the testimony by _____.

4. What are the elements of the "dying declaration" hearsay exception under Rule 804(b)(2)?

   - Declarant believed _____
   - Declarant believed that _____
   - Statement concerned _____ _____

5. What is the difference between a statement against interest and a party admission?

   Statement against interest does not have to be _____

6. What would be the consequence under Rules 804(a) and 804(b) if a party was to threaten a witness and frighten the witness into being unwilling to testify?

- Party who frightened witness _____ claim that the witness was _____ ;
- _____ could introduce _____
  _____

C. HEARSAY EXCEPTIONS (DECLARANT'S AVAILABILITY IMMATERIAL)

1. If a witness were to testify, "My wife saw the shooting, and then called me and told me John Wilkes Booth was the shooter," would that be admissible as a present sense impression under Rule 803(1)?

   _____

2. What sorts of statements are admissible as excited utterances under Rule 803(2)?

   Statements that relate to _____ _____ made _____ of the exciting event

3. If a witness were to testify, "The plaintiff told me on Tuesday that his leg was sore because the defendant kicked him the week before," how would a court treat that testimony under Rule 803(3) [the exception for statements of mental, emotional, or, physical condition]?

   o _____ part about _____
   o _____ part about _____

4. If a witness were to testify, "Atzerodt told me he was planning to go to Washington, D.C.," would that be admissible under the state of mind exception of Rule 803(3) to prove that he went to D.C.?

   _____

5. What must be shown in order for a statement to qualify under the Rule 803(4) exception for statements for purposes of medical diagnosis or treatment?

   Made for purposes of _____

6. If a plaintiff visits a doctor not for treatment, but in order for that doctor to diagnosis his condition for purposes of testifying for the plaintiff as an expert at trial, will those statements still be admissible under Rule 803(4)?

   _____

7. If a declarant said to his doctor, "I was run over by a white horse," will that statement be admissible under the Rule 803(4) exception for statements for purposes of medical diagnosis or treatment?

   _____ about the hose being white. Being run over by a horse is admissible.

8. What is the difference between a past recollection recorded and a present recollection refreshed?

- Past recollection recorded: _____ to the hearsay rule applies if you want to _____ to the jury

- Present recollection refreshed: used to _____ so he can _____

9. What must be shown in order to render a document admissible under the past recollection recorded exception (Rule 803(5))?

- Record concerns a matter about which the witness once had_____

- Witness _____ at the time the _____;

- Record was _____;

- Witness does not now have _____ to testify _____

10. What must be demonstrated to show that a document qualifies as admissible under the business records exception of Rule 803(6)?

It was created in the _____ of a regularly conducted business activity by_____.

Example 170: Medical records, phone log made by a receptionist, etc.

11. If an accident report were created primarily for purposes of preparing for possible litigation, would it qualify under the business records exception of Rule 803(6)?

_____

12. Under what circumstances may a court exclude a document otherwise fitting under Rule 803(6)?

Circumstances indicate _____

13. May a party attempt to show that an act or event did not occur by the absence of an entry in a record?

_____

14. What limitation applies to statements in public records by law enforcement of "matters observed" under Rule 803(8)(B)?

Cannot be used against _____

15. Under what circumstances may statements in a scientific, historical, or medical treatise or periodical be admissible under Rule 803(18)?

- Established as a _____; and

- _____

D. CONSTITUTIONAL LIMITATIONS TO THE HEARSAY RULE

1. On what two Constitutional grounds might hearsay evidence be challenged?

    - _____

    - _____

2. What is the source of the requirement that an accused be confronted with witnesses against him?

    _____

3. What sorts of out-of-court statements will violate the confrontation rights of an accused if offered against him in a criminal trial?

    _____

4. What makes a statement "testimonial" under Confrontation Clause case law?

    Made under circumstances that indicate it was likely to be used in a

    _____

5. Will statements made for the purpose of seeking emergency help be considered testimonial under the Confrontation Clause?

    _____

6. What must be shown before a testimonial statement may be introduced against a defendant?

    - _____

    - Defendant had

    _____

7. If a witness is unavailable because the defendant killed him, will that necessarily render the witness's prior statements admissible?

    _____; only if for purpose of preventing testimony. The defendant must have acted with the intent to prevent the witness from testifying for the hearsay statement to be admissible.

[END OF HANDOUT]

Real Property

REAL PROPERTY
PROFESSOR ZACHARY A. KRAMER
ARIZONA STATE UNIVERSITY – SANDRA DAY O'CONNOR COLLEGE OF LAW

CHAPTER 1:   OWNERSHIP

A. Basics

- Different ways property can be transferred (i.e., alienated):

    1) _____

        Example 1:   *Oliver sells his home to Anna for $325,000.*

    2) _____

        Example 2:   *Oliver gives his lucky pen to Anna, "in the hope that it will bring her as much luck as it has brought him."*

    3) _____

        Example 3:   *Oliver dies in a tragic fishing accident. In his will he gives his stamp collection to his wife Anna.*

        When is this gift effective? At Oliver's _____.

        Note 1: Gifts in a will are effective when the decedent dies.

    4) _____

        Example 4:   *Oliver dies without a will. He is survived solely by his wife, Anna, who is his _____ at law (i.e., a person who survives the decedent and takes by intestate succession).*

B. Estates in Land

- Ownership interests: divided in time between _____ interests and future interests

    o Key distinction is timing of _____

        Example 5:   *Oliver transfers Blackacre "to Anna for life, then to Ben."*

        Who has the right to possession presently? _____
        Who has the right to possession in the future? _____

        Example 6:   *Oliver transfers Blackacre to Anna once she passes the bar exam.*
        Who has the right to possession presently? _____
        Who has the right to possession in the future? _____

    o Someone must be in possession of the property at all times.

C. Fee Simple

- Fee simple is the _____ possessory estate
- Why is it the largest? Capable of _____

  o Inheritable: Upon the owner's death, the owner can pass it by will or by intestate succession; can also be transferred by gift or sale during owner's life.

    Example 7: *O transfers land to A. A has a fee simple absolute. A dies without a will. B is A's only heir. B then has a fee simple. B dies without a will, leaving C. C has a fee simple.*

- To create a fee simple:

  o Look for magic words: "_____"

    ▪ But these words are *not* required: "O to A" and "O to A and his heirs" are the same thing.

  o Watch out for ambiguous grants. If ambiguous, it creates a _____.

    Example 8: *Oliver conveys Blackacre" to Anna forever." What does Anna have?* _____

- Fee simple absolute is the default estate. There is a presumption that the grantor conveys the most that he or she has.
- Don't be fooled by words of _____ or _____.

    Example 9: *Oliver conveys Blackacre "to Anna, my hope and wish being that on her death, Anna will give the property to her son, Ben."*
    What interest does Anna have? _____
    What interest does Ben have? _____

    Note 2: Precatory words such as "my hope and wish" are not enough to show actual intent.

- No future interest associated with a fee simple

  o Capable of _____

CHAPTER 2:   DEFEASIBLE FEES

A. Defeasible Fees

- May be _____ by the occurrence of an event
- Capable of lasting forever but also of being terminated early
- Condition will _____ the fee simple

B. Fee Simple Determinable

- Limited by specific _____ language

> *Example 1:* Oliver conveys Blackacre "to Anna _____
> the land is used as a farm."

- Examples of durational language include:

  - "_____ the land is used as a farm"
  - "_____ its use as a farm"
  - "_____ it is no longer used as a farm"

  > **Note 3:** The fee simple lasts while the period is in play (e.g., while used as a farm), but as soon as the period ends (e.g., when the land is no longer used as a farm), the fee simple ends.

C. Fee Simple Subject to Condition Subsequent

- Limited by specific _____ language

  > *Example 2:* Oliver conveys Blackacre "to Anna, _____ the land isn't farmed, Oliver may re-enter and re-take the property."

- Examples of conditional language include:

  - "_____ the land isn't farmed."
  - "_____ the land isn't farmed."

- Focus on the language to the grantor: suggests that the grantor must exercise a right in order to take possession.

  > *Example 3:* Oliver conveys Blackacre "to Anna, but if the land isn't farmed, Oliver may re-enter and re-take the property." When, if ever, is Oliver entitled to possession? _____

D. Future Interests Associated With Those Two Defeasible Fees

- **Possibility of Reverter:** Future interest held by a _____ following a _____
  _____

  - Interest vests _____ after the durational period ends

    > *Example 4:* Oliver conveys Blackacre "to Anna and her heirs, so long as the land is used as a public park." What future interest does Oliver have? Oliver has a
    > _____. If the land isn't used as a park, the interest vests in Oliver as a fee simple because it reverts back to the grantor.

- **Right of Entry:** Future interest held by the _____ following a _____
  _____

  - Does not vest automatically; it must be _____

    > *Example 5:* Oliver conveys Blackacre "to Anna and her heirs, but if the land is not used as a public park, Oliver can re-enter and re-take." Oliver has a _____

_____. In order for Oliver's interest to become possessory, Oliver must exercise the right of entry and reclaim the interest.

Note 4: The right of entry is also known as the power of termination.

E. Fee Simple Subject to Executory Interest

- Will end upon the happening of an event and the future interest will vest in a _____ (i.e., someone other than the grantor)
- Held by another _____ and not the grantor

> **Example 6:** Oliver conveys Blackacre "to Anna and her heirs, but if liquor is served on the premises, then to Ben and his heirs."
>
> Anna has a _____.
>
> Ben has an _____. If liquor is ever served, Ben will divest Anna of her interest and hold a fee simple.
>
> **Note 5:** Look to who holds the future interest to distinguish a fee simple subject to executory interest (third party holds) from a fee simple subject to a condition subsequent (grantor holds).

F. Executory Interest

- Future interest that will _____, or terminate, an earlier interest
- Word for terminating a prior interest is to _____

> **Example 7:** Oliver conveys Blackacre "to Anna and her heirs, but if liquor is served on the premises, then to Ben and his heirs."
>
> Ben has an executory interest. Why? Because Ben will divest Anna's interest if _____. Whose interest is being divested? _____

- **Problem 1:** Oliver conveys Blackacre "to Anna."

  Anna has a _____.

  Oliver has _____.

  > **Note 6:** Always presume a party conveys the most that it has to convey.

- **Problem 2:** Oliver conveys Blackacre "to Anna while the land is used for school purposes."

  Anna has a _____.

  Oliver has a _____.

- **Problem 3:** Oliver conveys Blackacre "to Anna while the land is used for school purposes, then to Ben."

  Anna has a _____.

  Ben has an _____.

Oliver has _____.

- **Problem 4:** *Oliver conveys Blackacre "to Anna, but if Anna gets a pet, Oliver may re-enter and re-take."*

  Anna has a _____.

  Oliver has a _____.

CHAPTER 3:   THE LIFE ESTATE

A. Definition

- Present estate that is _____ by a _____
- Whose life?

  > **Example 1:** *Oliver conveys Blackacre "to Anna for life."*
  > *This life estate is measured against _____ life.*

  > **Example 2:** *Oliver conveys Blackacre "to Anna for Ben's life." Anna's life estate is measured against _____ life. This is known as a life estate pur autre vie (meaning measured against the life of someone else).*

B. Creation

- Magic words to create a life estate are "_____"
- If ambiguous, look for the grantor's intent to create an estate that will end _____ _____

  > **Example 3:** *"To A to live in your house." Some argue that this language creates a fee simple for A. Others argue that this language creates a life estate. Both arguments have merit. Resolve based on whether it should be inheritable or limited just for the person while they are alive.*

C. Termination

- Ends naturally when the measuring life _____
  - Transferable

    > **Example 4:** *Oliver conveys Blackacre "to Anna for life." Anna later transfers her interest to Ben. When will Ben's interest terminate? _____*

- Can a life tenant (of a life estate measured by the life tenant's life) pass the property by will?
  - _____, the life estate ends at tenant's death
- Can a life tenant (of a life estate measured by the life tenant's life) pass the property by intestate succession?
  - _____, the life estate ends at life tenant's death

Example 5: Oliver conveys Blackacre "to Anna for life." Anna dies, leaving her son Ben as her sole heir. Does Ben inherit Anna's life estate? _____, Anna's interest ended on her death.

D. Future Interests Following a Life Estate

- If possession of the land goes back to the *grantor* after the life estate ends, then the grantor retains a _____.

    Example 6: Oliver conveys Blackacre "to Anna for life." Oliver retains a reversion. Upon Anna's death, Oliver takes the property in _____.

- If possession of the land goes to a *third party* (transferee) after the life estate ends, then the third party takes a _____.

    Example 7: Oliver conveys Blackacre "to Anna for life, then to Ben." During Anna's life, Ben has a _____. What happens when Anna dies? Ben takes possession in _____. Oliver has _____ because Anna has the present interest (life estate) and Ben has the future interest.

E. Waste

- Comes into play when more than one party has an interest in the same piece of real property

    Example 8: Oliver conveys Blackacre "to Anna for life." Anna has been dumping hazardous materials onto the property, which have caused serious damage to Blackacre. The doctrine of waste gives Oliver a claim to stop Anna from injuring the land. Why? _____ _____

- Three kinds of waste:

    1) _____ waste: Waste caused by _____ conduct, which causes a _____ in value.

    Example 9: Dumping hazardous materials on the property

    2) _____ waste: Waste caused by _____ toward the property, which causes a _____ in value.

    Example 10: Harm caused to property through tenant's failure to take action after a storm

    3) _____ waste: Special situation where life tenant or other person in possession _____ the use of the property and actually _____ the value of the property.

    Example 11: Renovation of a house, construction of a dam, fixing a fence

- Not unique to estates and future interests
- Situations where the doctrine of waste applies include:
  - Landlord vs. Tenant
  - Co-tenant out of possession vs. Tenant in possession (concurrent estates)
  - Mortgagee (bank/lender) vs. Mortgagor (borrower)

> **Exam Tip 1: How to Spot a Waste Problem**
>
> 1. Do multiple parties have simultaneous interests, (e.g., life tenant, remainder, future interests, Landlord vs. Tenant)?
>
> 2.   Is there a change in the value of the property due to the actions/inactions of the party in possession?
>
> 3.   Will the waste substantially change the interest taken by the party out of possession?

CHAPTER 4:   FUTURE INTERESTS

A. Remainders

- A remainder is a future interest that follows what present possessory estate? _____
  - A remainder _____ follow a vested fee simple. Why? A future interest following a vested fee simple would have to divest the prior interest (the fee simple) but a remainder does not function that way because it instead waits for the prior interest to end.
- Can be _____ or _____
- RAP generally applies only to _____ remainders
  - **Vested Remainder**—An interest that is:
    1) Given to an _____ grantee (i.e., someone who can be identified); *and*
    2) Not subject to a _____ (i.e., there is no condition that must be satisfied in order for the interest to vest)
       - If the remainder fails either 1 or 2, it is a _____ remainder.

       Example 1:   *Oliver conveys Blackacre "to Anna for life, then to Ben."*
       What does Anna have? _____
       Is Ben an ascertainable grantee? _____
       Is there a condition precedent? _____
       Ben has a _____ *remainder.*

       > **Note 7:**   If the holder of a vested remainder dies, the interest passes to the holder's heirs.

       Example 2:   *Oliver conveys Blackacre "to A for life, then to A's firstborn grandchild."* *At the time of the conveyance, A does not have any grandchildren.*

What interest does the firstborn grandchild have? _____

Is the firstborn grandchild an ascertainable grantee? _____

The firstborn grandchild has what type of remainder? A _____ *remainder.*

> **Note 8:** If a contingent remainder does not vest before it becomes possessory (e.g., A does not have any grandchildren before A dies), the grantor has a reversion.

Example 3: Oliver conveys Blackacre "to Anna for life, then to Ben if Ben survives Anna." What kind of remainder does Ben have?

Is Ben an ascertainable grantee? _____

Is there a condition precedent? _____

Ben has a _____ *remainder.*

Oliver has a _____ .

B. Class Gifts - Vested Subject to Open

- Vested subject to open is:

  - Vested remainder in a _____; and
  - Full class membership is _____

    - At least one person in the class must be vested for it to be vested subject to open; if no one in the class has vested, the remainder is contingent.
    - When all members of a class are identified, the class is _____

      Example 4: Oliver conveys Blackacre "to Anna for life, then to Anna's children *who reach 21.*" Anna has three kids—Ben is 25, Carmen is 18, and David is 15. What is Ben's interest? _____

      _____

      Why is it subject to open? Because we do not know who else will reach 21 and make it in the class.

      When will we know when the class closes and who the class members are?
      _____ .

      If and when more of Anna's children reach 21, they will partially divest Ben.

      > **Note 9:** In property law, it is presumed a party can have a child at any time before the party's death, regardless of age.

      Watch out! *At least one member of the class must be vested. If no one in the class is vested, then the remainder is* _____ . *Here, if Ben was 20 instead of 25, his remainder would be contingent.*

- RAP applies to a vested remainder subject to open.

- o **Rule of Convenience:** A class-closing mechanism to avoid application of _____ _____ to a class gift.
- o If the grant does not have an express closing date, the Rule of Convenience closes the class when any member of the class becomes entitled to _____.

> ***Example 5:*** *Oliver conveys "to Anna for life, then to Ben's children." Ben has one child. When will this class close under the rule of convenience?* _____ _____

C. Special Cases

- • **Doctrine of Worthier Title:** Prevents against remainders in _____ heirs
  - o Creates presumption in a reversion to the grantor

> ***Example 6:*** *Oliver conveys "to Anna for life, then to my heirs." What future interest does Oliver retain under the Doctrine of Worthier Title?* _____

- • **Rule in Shelley's Case:** Prevents against remainders in _____ heirs
  - o Uses doctrine of merger to create a fee simple

> ***Example 7:*** *Oliver conveys "to Anna for life, then to Anna's heirs." What estate does Anna have under the Rule in Shelley's case?* _____

D. Executory Interests

- • Subject to the Rule Against Perpetuities ("RAP")
- • Definition: Future interest in a _____ that _____ (i.e., divests) a prior _____ interest
  - o Two kinds of executory interests:
    - ▪ **Springing Executory Interest:** Divests _____
    - ▪ **Shifting Executory Interest:** Divests prior _____

> ***Example 8:*** *Oliver conveys Blackacre "to Anna for life, then to Ben one year after Anna's death."*
>
> *What interest does Anna have?* _____
> *What happens immediately after Anna's death?* _____ _____
>
> *Whose interest does Ben divest?* _____
> *What interest does Ben have?* _____

> ***Example 9:*** *Oliver conveys Blackacre "to Anna, but if the land is used for commercial purposes, to Ben."*

What interest does Anna have? _____

Under what condition will Ben take the property? _____

_____

Whose interest does Ben divest? _____

What interest does Ben have? _____

Example 10: *Oliver conveys Blackacre "to Anna after she is admitted to the bar."*

What interest does Anna have? _____

Whose interest does Anna divest? _____

What interest does Oliver have? Fee simple subject to executory interest

Exam Tip 2: Count the parties

If there are **two parties** (Grantor + Grantee), it is most likely a **springing** executory interest because the grantee will divest the grantor.

If there are **three parties** (Grantor + Grantee + Grantee), it is most likely a **shifting** executory interest because a grantee will divest another grantee (the executory interest will shift from one grantee to another).

CHAPTER 5: THE RULE AGAINST PERPETUITIES (RAP)

A. What is going on here?

- Three questions to set the RAP context:

  1) Why do we have such a silly rule?

     - Parental desire to keep property in family but distrust of children vs. court's concern over tying up property endlessly

     - Prevents _____ vesting

  2) What's the goal of the rule? _____

     - Operates like a statute of limitations for contingent future interests.

  3) Why 21 years?

     - Protect property from children's foolishness

     - Allows property to be tied up for "a life in being plus 21 years"

B. Method - When, What, Who?

- **When:** Identifying when the interests are created

  o Inter vivos transfers: Interests created at time of _____

  o Devise (will): Interests created at _____ not when the will is drafted

- **What:** Determine if interests created are subject to RAP

o RAP applies to:

- _____

- _____

- _____ , if not closed by rule of convenience

o Does not apply to vested remainders unless subject to open

- **Who:** Identify the relevant and, if applicable, validating lives

  o Relevant life: Person who affects vesting, usually mentioned or implied by the grant (e.g., prior life tenant, the parent where a conveyance is made to a child)

  o Validating life: Person who tells us whether or not the interest vests within the perpetuities period (lifetime plus 21 years)

  - Must have been _____ when the interests were created

  - Can validate her own interest

  - If no validating life, then interest is _____ and we strike it from grant; if there is a validating life, the interest is good

- **"When, what, who?" Application**

  Example 1: Oliver conveys Blackacre "to Anna, but if the land is ever used as a business during Anna's lifetime, to Ben."

  When: Interests created _____

  What: Interest subject to RAP is _____

  Who: Lives in being at the creation of the interest are _____ and _____

  Validating life? Will we know 21 years after either of their lives whether this interest will vest or not? _____

  _____.

  Result: RAP is not violated. Ben's executory interest is valid.

  Example 2: Professor Kramer conveys "$1000 to my Themis students who are admitted to the bar." (Not a binding contract!)

  When: Interests created _____

  What: Interest subject to RAP is _____

  Who: Lives in being at the creation of the interest are _____

  and _____.

  Validating life? Will we know 21 years after someone's death whether this interest vests or not? _____

  _____

  Result: RAP is not violated. Students' executory interests are valid. No change.

  Note 10: The RAP is not about what ends up happening but is only focused on certainty and whether an interest will either vest or fail within the period.

C. RAP Violations

- We ~~strike out~~ the violating interest, as if the interest was never created in the first place.

> **Example 3:** Oliver conveys "to Anna for life, then to Anna's first child who reaches the age of 22." This conveyance _____ RAP. It is a contingent remainder, and possible for the contingent remainder in Anna's first child to vest more than 21 years after Anna's life. Anna's first child, even if alive, is not a validating life because the child could die.
>
> Result—Strike the offending interest: Oliver conveys to Anna for Life, ~~then to Anna's first child who reaches the age of 22~~.
> Anna's interest: _____
> Oliver interest: _____
> First child's interest: _____

> **Example 4:** Oliver conveys "to Anna so long as the property is used as a farm, then to Ben." Anna has a fee simple subject to an executory limitation and Ben has an executory interest. This conveyance _____ RAP. It is possible that Ben's executory interest will vest more than 21 years after Anna's or Ben's death.
>
> Result—Strike the offending interest: Oliver conveys to Anna so long as the property is used as a farm, ~~then to Ben~~.
> Anna's interest: _____
> Oliver interest: _____
> Ben's interest: _____

> **Example 5:** Oliver conveys "to my grandchildren who reach 21." Oliver has two children, Anna and Ben, and three grandchildren under the age of 21. This conveyance _____ RAP. It is possible that Oliver could have another child—call her Carmen—who gives birth to a grandchild after Oliver, Anna, and Ben have died. This grandchild will not reach age 21 until more than 21 years after the deaths of the measuring lives (Carmen is not a validating life because she was not in existence when the interest was created).
>
> Result—Strike the offending interest: ~~Oliver conveys to my grandchildren who reach 21~~.
>
> Oliver interest: _____
> Grandchildren's interests: _____

CHAPTER 6:   THE RULE AGAINST PERPETUITIES (RAP)—SPECIAL CASES

A. RAP and Class Gifts

- **Special Rule:** If the gift to any member of the class is void under RAP, then the gift is void as to all members of the class. The gift is "bad as to one, bad as to all." (The "**all or nothing**" rule.)

   > ***Example 1:***   *Oliver conveys "to Anna for life, then to her children who reach 25." At the time of the conveyance, Anna's son Ben is 26 and her daughter Carmen is 18.*
   >
   > *Who are members of the class? _____*
   > *Has any class member vested? _____*
   > *Is the class closed? _____*

   - Remember: Living people have the nasty habit of breeding. Property law assumes that anyone who is alive can still have children.

      > *Does the gift survive RAP? _____. Anna could have another kid (call her Dana) after the conveyance. Dana can't be a validating life. Dana could vest more than 21 years after Anna, Ben, and Carmen's death.*
      > *What happens to Ben's interest? _____*
      >
      > *Result—Strike the offending interest: Oliver conveys to Anna for life, ~~then to her children who reach 25~~.*
      >
      > *Anna's interest: _____*
      > *Oliver interest: _____*
      > *Children, including Ben who is vested, have _____*

B. Rule of Convenience

- Can save a class gift from being _____ under RAP

- For purposes of avoiding RAP, the class closes as soon as a member of the class is entitled to _____.

   > ***Example 2:***   *Oliver conveys "to Anna for life, then to Anna's grandchildren." Anna has one grandchild, Ben. It is possible that other grandchildren will be born more than 21 years after Anna or Ben's death. Without the Rule of Convenience, the gift to Ben is _____ under RAP. With the Rule of Convenience, Ben will take _____. When Anna dies, class treated as _____.*

C. Exceptions to the Class Gift Rule (when "all or nothing" rule does not apply)

- Two exceptions:

   1) Transfers of a specific _____ to each class member, and

2) Transfers to a _____ that vests at a _____ time, e.g., "to the children of B, and upon the death of each, to that child's issue"

D. Exceptions to RAP

1) RAP does not apply to a gift from one _____ to another _____.

- The gift to alternate charity is not subject to RAP

Example 3: *Oliver conveys Blackacre "to the Donald McRonald House so long as the property is used to support cancer patients and their families, then to the Glaser Elizabeth Pediatric AIDS Fund."*

The AIDS Fund's executory interest, which normally would violate RAP, is valid because RAP does not apply to charity-to-charity gifts.

2) RAP does not apply to _____ held by a current tenant to purchase a fee interest in the leasehold property.

E. "Wait and See" Approach

- The traditional RAP has been softened by reform (e.g., Uniform Statutory Rule Against Perpetuities). The most common modern approach is to "wait and see" if an interest subject to RAP vests within the perpetuities period. Some of these states changed the vesting period to 90 years.

> **Exam Tip 3:** The bar exam still tests the traditional RAP though you should be aware of the modern "wait and see" approach.

F. Cy Pres

- An equitable doctrine (borrowed from the law of trusts) that allows a court to _____ a transfer to avoid RAP.

CHAPTER 7: CONCURRENT ESTATES

A. Basics

- Definition: Ownership or possession of real property by _____ persons simultaneously

> *Example 1:* *Oliver conveys Blackacre "to Anna and Ben and their heirs."*
> *Anna and Ben are concurrent owners of Blackacre.*

- Basic Rule: Concurrent owners each have right to use/possess the _____ property

  o Exception: Concurrent owners can contract out of the basic rule.

- Three kinds of concurrent ownership/concurrent estates:

  1) _____

2) _____ and

3) _____.

B. Tenancy in Common

- Default concurrent interest

    o Any conveyance to more than one person is presumed to be a tenancy in common.

- Concurrent owners have _____
  interests in the property

    > *Example 2:* Oliver conveys Blackacre "in equal shares to Anna and Ben."
    > Their interests are separate *because they have* _____ *shares in*
    > Blackacre. Their interests are undivided *because Blackacre is not physically*
    > divided; Anna and Ben each have a right to _____ the
    > _____ of Blackacre.

- No right of survivorship

    o Each co-tenant can transfer the property freely at death as well as during life.

    > *Example 3:* Oliver conveys Blackacre "in equal shares to Anna, Ben, and
    > Carmen." Anna conveys her interest to Amy. Ben dies and his will gives his
    > entire estate to his son Brad. Who owns Blackacre?
    > Amy has a _____ interest in Blackacre. Brad has a _____ interest in
    > Blackacre. Carmen has a _____ interest in Blackacre.

C. Joint Tenancy

- Defining characteristic is the right of _____, whereby the surviving joint
  tenant(s) automatically take the deceased tenant's interest

    > *Example 4:* Oliver conveys Blackacre "to Anna and Ben as joint tenants with a
    > right of survivorship." Anna dies in a tragic hunting accident. Anna's will leaves
    > everything to her daughter Amy. Who owns Blackacre and why? _____
    > _____

- How do you create a joint tenancy?

    o Grantor must make a _____ of intent, PLUS

    o Must be _____, e.g., "as joint tenants with a right
      of survivorship"

D. Four Unities [PITT]

- To create a joint tenancy, four unities must be in place:

    1) _____: Requires every joint tenant have an equal right to
       possess the whole of the property

2) _____: Joint tenants must have an _____ share of the same _____ of interest.

Example 5: *Anna and Ben own Blackacre as joint tenants. Each has a 50% share and each owns the property in fee simple—equal shares, same interests.*

3) _____: Joint tenants must receive their interests at the same time.

4) _____: Joint tenants must receive their interests in the same _____ of title.

Example 6: *Oliver's will leaves Blackacre "to Anna and Ben as joint tenants with a right of survivorship." The will further provides that Anna takes a 1/3 interest and Ben takes a 2/3 interest. Are the four unities present?*

Possession: _____

Interest: _____

_____

Time: _____

Title: _____

This conveyance would create a _____.

E. Severance

- If any of the unities are severed, i.e., _____, then the joint tenancy is terminated and turns into a _____.

- Common situations:

  o ***Inter vivos transfer:*** Transfer during life will _____ the right of survivorship and convert the estate into a tenancy in common

Example 7: *Anna, Ben, and Carmen own Blackacre as joint tenants. Anna transfers her share to Amy. What effect on the joint tenancy?*

Amy's interest: _____

Ben and Carmen's interests: _____

- o *Mortgages:* A joint tenant grants a mortgage interest in the joint tenancy to a creditor. Does the mortgage sever the joint tenancy?

    - **Majority:** Most jurisdictions follow a _____ theory. The mortgage is treated as a lien and does _____ destroy joint tenancy.
    - **Minority:** A minority of jurisdictions follow a _____ theory. The mortgage _____ title and the tenancy between the joint tenants and creditor is converted into a tenancy in common.

- o *Leases:* A joint tenant leases her share in the property to a tenant. Does the lease sever the joint tenancy? Jurisdictions are split.

    - Some jurisdictions hold that the lease _____ the joint tenancy.
    - Other jurisdictions treat the lease as a _____ suspension of the joint tenancy.

F. Tenancy by the Entirety

- Joint tenancy between _____

    - o Marriage is fifth unity (sometimes called the unity of person)

- Has right of _____
- Tenants by the entirety _____ alienate or encumber their shares without the consent of their spouse.
- Magic words: Property conveyed "as tenants by the entirety, with a right of survivorship"
- If grant is ambiguous, courts presume property is held as joint tenants or as tenants in common.

CHAPTER 8:   RIGHTS AND OBLIGATIONS OF CONCURRENT OWNERS

A. Possession and Use

- **General Rule:** Each co-tenant has right to possess _____ of the property, regardless of that co-tenant's share and regardless of the type of co-tenancy

    - o Exception: Co-tenants have entered into an agreement to the contrary

        Example 1: *Anna and Ben are tenants in common in Blackacre. Anna owns a 2/3 share and Ben owns a 1/3 share. Ben is in sole possession of Blackacre. They have no agreement as to possession.*
        Question 1: Can Ben occupy the whole of the property? _____
        _____

        Question 2: Is Ben an adverse possessor? _____
        _____

Question 3: Does one co-tenant owe the other a duty to pay rent? _____ a co-tenant in possession _____ required to pay rent to co-tenants out of possession.

- **Ouster:** Co-tenant in possession denies another co-tenant _____ to the property (e.g., one tenant changes the locks)

  o Remedies for the ousted tenant:

  ▪ Get an _____ granting access to the property, and/or

  ▪ Recover _____ for the value of the use while the co-tenant was unable to access the property

B. **Third Party Rents and Operating Expenses**

- **Rent:** Received from a third party's possession of the property, minus operating expenses, are divided based on _____ of each co-tenant

  Example 2:   Anna and Ben own Blackacre as tenants in common. Anna has a 10% interest and Ben has a 90% interest in Blackacre. Carmen is renting Blackacre for $1000 a month. Each month, Anna is entitled to $_____ of Carmen's rent, while Ben is entitled to $_____ of Carmen's rent. The outcome would differ if Carmen was renting from one co-tenant and the other co-tenant was also in possession.

- **Operating Expenses:** Necessary charges, such as taxes or mortgage interest payments

  o Divided based on _____ interests of each co-tenant

  o A co-tenant can collect _____ from the other co-tenants for payments in excess of her share of the operating expenses.

- **Repairs:** There is _____ right to reimbursement from co-tenants for necessary repairs. However, the co-tenant who makes the repairs can get credit in a partition action.

- **Improvements:** There is _____ right to reimbursement for improvements. However, the co-tenant who makes the improvements can get credit in a partition action.

C. **Partition**

- Equitable remedy available to all holders of a tenancy in common or a _____. It is a _____ right. Tenants by the entirety do _____ have the unilateral right to partition.

- Effect of a partition action is that the court will divide the property into _____ _____.

- Courts have a preference for a _____ division; i.e., a partition in kind.

  o Court will order a partition by sale if the physical partition is:

  ▪ _____ (e.g., land has complicated terrain); *or*

- ▪ _____

  o Proceeds from a partition by sale are divided among the co-tenants based on their ownership interests.

    Example 3: *Anna and Ben own a condo unit as tenants in common, each with a 50% share in the property. Anna sues for partition. What kind of partition will the court order?* _____

    _____

- • Co-tenants can agree not to partition. Such an agreement is enforceable, provided:

  o Agreement is _____, and
  o Time limitation is _____

CHAPTER 9:   SPECIAL ISSUES – DISCRIMINATION & CHOICE OF LAW (CONFLICT OF LAWS)

A. Discrimination

- • The Fair Housing Act (FHA) prohibits discrimination in the _____, _____, and _____ of dwellings (homes, apartments, etc.). It also prohibits _____ that states a discriminatory preference.

  o **Who's covered?** Primary focus is on _____ residential housing
  o **Who's not covered?** There are **two exemptions** from the FHA:

    - ▪ Single-family housing that is sold or rented _____
    - ▪ Owner-occupied buildings with four or less units ("Ms. Murphy's Boarding House")

  o **Who's protected?**

    - ▪ **Protected traits:** Race, color, religion, national origin, sex, disability, and familial status

      - • Sex refers to gender discrimination, but does not include sexual orientation.
      - • Familial status means families that have _____ or someone is pregnant

        - o Special exemptions for senior living (e.g., seniors-only communities)

      - • Disability provision mandates reasonable accommodations for the disabled (e.g., ramp)

  o **What's prohibited?**

    - ▪ Refusing to _____, _____ or _____ a dwelling
    - ▪ Requiring different rents
    - ▪ Falsely denying that a unit is available
    - ▪ Providing different services to facilities

      - • Exception: When making a reasonable accommodation for a disabled tenant

- Stating a discriminatory preference in an advertisement

    Note 15: There are no exemptions when advertising a dwelling for sale or rent, even if the party is otherwise exempt from the FHA provisions when selling or renting a dwelling.

  o **Intent:** FHA allows for both intent (disparate _____) and effect (disparate _____) cases

  o **Causation:** Prohibited behavior must be linked to the protected basis

    Example 1: *Larry advertises an available one-bedroom unit in one of his apartment buildings. Two applicants apply for the unit—Sally, a black woman who works as a nurse, and Tim, a white male student at Acme University. Both filled out an application and, after running credit and background checks, Larry rented the unit to Tim. Did Larry violate the Fair Housing Act?* _____

    _____

    Example 2: *Jenny puts the following advertisement in the local paper: "One-bedroom unit apartment available. Perfect bachelor pad. Hot tub and other amenities. Close to bus line, bars, and grocery. Utilities not included. Call Jenny, 867-5309. No creepers." Does the advertisement violate the Fair Housing Act?* _____, *the statement "perfect bachelor pad" states a discriminatory preference based on sex and familial status.*

    Note: *The unlawful act is the advertisement itself. Jenny has violated the Act even if she does not otherwise engage in discriminatory behavior.*

B. Conflict of Laws

- **Basic Rule**: In cases about property, controlling law is based upon where the property is _____, **(law of the situs).**

- *Why do you care about this*? Law of the situs is the baseline choice of law rule in a property dispute that involves more than one state, e.g., the parties to the suit are in different states.

- *When do you care about this*? In many testable issues involving property:

  o Foreclosure
  o Land contract dispute
  o Equitable interests (e.g. trust property)
  o Intestate succession
  o Interpreting conveyances

- *When do you ignore the basic rule*?

  o If the instrument in question _____ an applicable jurisdiction
  o In cases involving _____, specifically with respect to classifying property as marital or separate, the domicile of the party may override the law of the situs

o In mortgage cases, where the mortgage documents require repayment be made in another state

CHAPTER 10:   LANDLORD AND TENANT—THE TENANCIES

A. Lease

- Creates both a _____ interest and a _____ interest
- Landlord-tenant law is a mix of contract law and property law.

B. Tenancies

- Four types of estates that can govern the landlord-tenant relationship, i.e., tenancies

    1) _____

    2) _____

    3) _____

    4) _____

- You want to know two things:

    o How is each created?

    o How is each terminated?

C. Tenancy for Years

- **Definition:** Measured by a fixed and ascertainable amount of time

    Example 1:   *Larry leases Blackacre to Tara for two years.*

    Note: It need not be measured in years. It can be for _____ length of time.

    Example 2:   *Larry leases Blackacre to Tara for two weeks. This is a tenancy for years.*

- **Creation:** What is required to create a tenancy for years?

    o An agreement by the _____ and the _____.

      ▪ Purpose is to demonstrate _____

    o If the term is longer than one year, then the agreement must be in _____ because of the Statute of Frauds.

- **Termination:** How is a tenancy for years terminated?

    o At the end of the term: Termination occurs _____ upon the expiration of the term

      ▪ Is notice required to terminate? _____ (unless the lease requires it)

- Before the term is over:
    - Tenant _____ the lease, or
    - The tenant or the landlord commits a _____ of the lease, e.g., tenant fails to pay rent.

D. **Periodic Tenancy**

- **Definition:** Estate that is _____ and _____ for a set period of time (e.g., a month-to-month lease, a year-to-year lease)

    - Renews _____ at end of each period until one party gives notice of termination

- **Creation:** Parties must intend to create a periodic tenancy

    - Intent can be _____ (e.g., a signed lease) or _____ (e.g., payment of rent)

        Example 3: *Larry and Tara did not execute a formal lease agreement. Every month, however, Tara pays rent and Larry accepts the payment. This will create a periodic tenancy by implication.*

- **Termination:** Renews automatically until proper notice is given

    - Proper notice means the terminating party gives notice before the _____ of what will be the _____. Most jurisdictions require written notice of termination.
    - Notice is effective the _____ day of the period.

        Example 4: *Larry leased Blackacre to Tara on a month-to-month basis. Tara gives notice of termination on January 15th. When is termination effective?*

        _____.

E. **Tenancy at Will**

- **Definition:** May be terminated by either _____ or _____ at any time, for any reason
- **Creation:** Can be created by express agreement or by implication
- **Termination:** Can be terminated by either party without _____

    - If agreement gives only the landlord the right to terminate at will, the tenant _____ _____.
    - If agreement gives only the tenant the right to terminate at will, the landlord _____ _____.
    - If the landlord dies, does that terminate the tenancy at will? _____ _____. This is not true for the tenancy for years or the periodic tenancy.
    - Similarly, if the tenant dies, the tenancy at will is terminated.

F. Tenancy at Sufferance

- **Definition:** Created when a tenant _____ after the lease has ended

  o Temporary tenancy that exists before the landlord either _____ the prior tenant or _____ the property to the prior tenant (creates a new tenancy with the holdover tenant)

- Terms of the _____ lease control if a new tenancy is created
- **Creation:** Distinguish between a tenancy at will and a tenancy at sufferance:

  o Tenancy at will: Created by _____ of the landlord and tenant

  o Tenancy at sufferance: Created by _____ of the _____ alone

- **Termination:** Consider three ways to terminate:

  o The tenant voluntarily _____

  o The landlord _____ the tenant

  o The landlord _____ to the tenant

CHAPTER 11: LANDLORD AND TENANT—TENANT'S DUTIES

A. The Gist

- The tenant has two basic duties:

  1) _____ and

  2) _____

B. Duty to Pay Rent

- Duty arises because of the contractual relationship between the landlord and tenant (i.e., the lease)

  o Three situations when duty to pay rent is suspended:

  1) Premises are _____, so long as the tenant didn't cause the damage

  2) The landlord completely or partially _____ the tenant

    - Complete eviction: removal of tenant from the entire property
    - Partial eviction: removal of tenant from a portion of the property

  3) The landlord _____ the lease

- Particularly concerned with breaches of the implied covenant of quiet enjoyment and the implied warranty of habitability

  o **Implied Covenant of Quiet Enjoyment:** The tenant can withhold rent when the landlord takes actions that make the premises wholly or substantially _____ for their intended purposes, and the tenant is _____ evicted.

- **Constructive Eviction**—four elements:

    i) Premises were _____ for their intended purposes (i.e., breach of the covenant of quiet enjoyment);

    ii) The tenant _____ landlord of the problem;

    iii) The landlord _____ correct the problem; and

    iv) The tenant _____ the premises after a _____ amount of time has passed.

    Example 1: *The Scott Michael Paper Company rents office space from Landlord. Due to poor construction, the office floods whenever it rains. The first time the office floods, the Company notifies Landlord and explains that it will no longer pay rent. The next day, the Company rents a new space and moves its belongings. Is the Company liable to Landlord for rent? Why? _____, because the Company _____ prematurely; it did not give Landlord the opportunity to fix the problem. Note that Landlord had breached the covenant of quiet enjoyment and the Company did give the landlord notice of the problem.*

- **Implied Warranty of Habitability ("IWH"):** The landlord has an obligation to maintain the property such that it is suitable for **residential** use. We are concerned with conditions that threaten tenant _____ and _____.

    - Background Points

        - The tenant _____ waive habitability protection.
        - The landlord's failure to comply with applicable _____ codes constitutes a breach.
        - Applies to _____ properties, usually multi-family buildings; not to commercial leases
        - IWH and Rent: If premises are not habitable, tenant may:

            o _____ to pay rent;

            o _____ the defect and _____ costs against the rent; or

            o _____ against eviction

            Note 16: If the tenant chooses to withhold rent, tenant must: (i) _____ the landlord of the problem; and (ii) give the landlord a _____ _____ to correct the problem.

            Note 17: Unlike quiet enjoyment and constructive eviction, IWH does _____ require the tenant to vacate the premises.

    Example 2: *Tara rents an apartment from Larry. The apartment is in a bad state—there is no hot water, ants and roaches are getting in, there is mold growing in the bathroom, and the security light over Tara's door is inoperable.*

Tara has repeatedly notified Larry of the problems to no avail. Can Tara
withhold rent? _____, because Larry has breached IWH and failed to correct
the problems.

C. Duty to Avoid Waste

- The duty to avoid waste is a background rule; it does not have to be _____ in a lease in order to apply.

- The tenant has a duty not to commit _____ (voluntary) waste or _____ (neglectful) waste.

- A tenant may make changes to the property that _____ the property's value ("ameliorative waste"). Landlords usually require permission before a tenant can make the change.

    > **Note 18:** A landlord can put a provision in the lease prohibiting the tenant from making improvements to the property.

- **Duty to Repair**: In a residential lease, the _____ is presumed to be responsible for repairs. The tenant must _____ the landlord of any needed repairs.

    > **Note 19:** The landlord is not responsible to make repairs caused by the tenant's actions.
    >
    > **Note 20:** In a commercial lease, the landlord can place the duty to repair on the tenant.

CHAPTER 12: LANDLORD AND TENANT—LANDLORD'S DUTIES

A. Duty to Mitigate Damages

- If the tenant abandons the property early or is evicted by landlord, does the landlord have an obligation to mitigate damages by re-renting the property?

    o **Majority Rule:** The landlord must make _____ to re-rent the property.

    - The landlord must treat leasehold as if it was _____, that is, like any other property she would try to rent, e.g., advertise, allow for viewings.

    - If the landlord does not make diligent efforts to mitigate, tenant is _____ from the obligation to continue paying rent.

    - If the landlord does seek to mitigate, landlord is entitled to the difference between the _____ and the _____ from the replacement tenant.

    - The landlord does not have to accept an unacceptable replacement tenant.

    o **Minority Rule:** The landlord does not have to mitigate damages. The minority rule is more common in cases involving _____.

Example 1: Larry rents a studio apartment to Tara at $2000 per month for a one-year term. Tara abandons the apartment after a month in search of a cheaper apartment. Larry does nothing until the one-year term is up. In a majority jurisdiction, can Larry recover damages from Tara? _____

_____

Example 2: Instead, assume Larry advertised as normal but was only able to find a tenant who was willing to pay $1000 for the studio apartment. In a majority jurisdiction, can Larry collect the remaining half from Tara? _____

_____

B. Holdover Tenant

- How can the landlord deal with the holdover?

    o Can _____ the holdover tenant; or

    o Can _____ with the tenant by treating the holdover tenant as a _____ tenant

        ▪ The landlord will continue the relationship by accepting _____.

            • Amount of rent: Rent amount under the old lease is the amount due

                o Exception: The landlord can impose a _____ rent if the landlord had informed the tenant of the increase prior to the expiration of the old lease.

C. Duty to Deliver Possession

- **Majority Rule:** The landlord must deliver _____ possession of the leasehold premises. This means _____ possession of the property.

- **Minority Rule:** The landlord only required to deliver _____ possession.

    Note 21: The difference between actual and legal possession is of particular importance with holdover tenant issues and the obligation to the new tenant.

D. Conditions of Leased Premises

- The landlord cannot deny the tenant **quiet enjoyment**. In practice, quiet enjoyment is violated when the landlord, or someone connected to the landlord, renders the premises unsuitable for the intended purpose.

    o The landlord *must* control:

        ▪ _____, such as a lobby, hallway, or laundry room

        ▪ _____-like behavior of other tenants (Remember: Don't touch the stinky wall!)

    o The landlord *does not have to* control:

        ▪ Off-premises actions of _____ that are beyond the landlord's control, (e.g., the noisy bar across the street)

- In a residential lease, the landlord must provide _____ premises.

    Example 3: *Larry is the landlord for an apartment building. The lock on the front door of the building is broken and, although tenants have complained, Larry has not fixed it. Young hooligans have been vandalizing the lobby hallway of the building. Tara, a tenant in the building, is injured by a piece of debris left in the hallway by one of the hooligans. Has Larry breached his obligation to Tara? _____, because the damage took place in a _____, which is under Larry's control.*

- If a tenant complains about conditions, the landlord cannot retaliate by evicting the tenant.

CHAPTER 13: LANDLORD AND TENANT—TORT LIABILITY & TRANSFERS

A. Tort Liability

- The tenant owes a _____. This extends to invitees, licensees, and foreseeable trespassers.
- The landlord's liability to invitees, licensees, and foreseeable trespassers is as follows:

    o Responsible in negligence for _____ (hidden) defects about which the tenant has not been warned

    o Responsible for _____ completed by the landlord (or the landlord's agent) negligently

    o Responsible for negligence that causes injuries in _____ areas of the property

    Example 1: *Larry rents a studio apartment in a large building to Tara. When Tara moved in, Larry warned her that there was a loose beam in the floor of the hallway in her apartment. Shortly after moving in, Tara tripped on the loose beam and fractured her ankle. Is Larry liable for her injuries? _____*

    _____

    Example 2: *Tara noticed that the building's back door had a broken hinge, causing it to slam shut quicker than most would expect it to. Tara informed Larry about the door. Larry sent a handyman to fix the door, but the handyman ended up making the door worse. Tara smashed her fingers in the door. Is Larry liable for her injuries? _____, because the landlord's agent undertook to repair the door, but the repair was faulty.*

    Editor's Note 1: The above rule reflects the common law. The modern approach is to hold landlords to a general duty of reasonable care.

B. The Basics of Transfers – Subleases and Assignments

- Who's who? Three parties:

    1) Landlord: _____

2) Tenant: _____

3) Subsequent tenant: _____

- **Assignment** is a _____ transfer of the tenant's remaining term.
- **Sublease** is a transfer for _____ the entire duration of the lease.

> *Example 3:* *Larry rents a studio apartment to Tara and the lease is set to end on August 14th. Tara decides to move to Belgium for the summer so she transfers her lease to Sally Theresa. Tara will re-take possession from Sally Theresa on August 1st. Is the transfer to Sally Theresa an assignment or a sublease?* _____

> **Exam Tip 4:** If the tenant retains a reversionary interest in the leasehold, the transfer is a sublease.

C. Responsibility for Rent

- In an assignment, the landlord can collect rent from:

  o _____ (because of **privity of contract**), or

  o _____ (because of **privity of estate**)

- In a sublease, the landlord can collect rent from:

  o _____ (because of **privity of contract and estate**)

  - Subtenant only has rent obligations to the original tenant

    > *Example 4:* *Larry rents a studio apartment to Tara and the lease is set to end on August 14th. Tara decides to move to Belgium for the summer so she transfers her lease to Sally Theresa. Tara will re-take possession from Sally Theresa on August 1st. Larry doesn't receive rent during the summer months. Can he try to get rent from Sally Theresa?* _____ _____. *He can only collect rent from* _____.

D. Permission

> **Editor's Note 2:** Absent language to the contrary, a lease may be freely assigned or sublet. If the lease terms require permission of the landlord before a tenant may transfer her interest, but are silent as to the applicable standard, the rules below apply:

- Issue: Can the landlord deny permission to a transfer of the lease?

  o **Majority Rule:** A landlord may deny permission to a transfer only for a _____ _____.

  o **Minority Rule:** A landlord may deny permission _____, which means for any reason or no reason at all.

- **Transferring a landlord's interest**: A landlord does not need the tenant's permission before transferring her interest. The new landlord is bound by terms of the existing lease.

Example 5: Larry rented a one-bedroom house to Tara at $1000 per month for a one-year term. The lease included a covenant that Larry would shovel the snow and take care of the lawn maintenance. A few months into Tara's tenancy, Larry decided to move to Tahiti, so he transferred his interest in the property to Lucy. Lucy contacted Tara to inform her that her rent would go up to $1200 per month and that Tara was now responsible for snow removal and lawn care.

Question 1: Did Larry need Tara's permission before transferring to Lucy? _____

_____

Question 2: Can Lucy change the terms of Tara's lease? _____

_____

CHAPTER 14: LAND SALE CONTRACTS – THE BASICS, STATUTE OF FRAUDS & MARKETABLE TITLE

Exam Tip 5: Expect questions on the MBE in this area. The land sale contract is one of the most heavily tested subjects in real property.

A. Who's Who?

- Seller: Owner looking to unload property
- Buyer: Sucker looking to get stuck with a money pit
- Broker (or real estate agent): An intermediary between buyer and seller

  - Listing agent: The agent who assists the seller in promoting and selling the property
  - Seller's agent: A sub-agent for the listing agent who helps find buyers

  Note: In most cases, the listing and seller's agent share the commission. The agent who shows you property is working for the seller.

  - Buyer's agent: The broker who serves as the representative of the buyer. Will receive commission similar to seller's agent fee
  - Dual agent: Represents both buyer and seller (many states forbid dual agency)

B. Framework

- **Two stages** to land transactions:

  - _____ stage (where parties negotiate terms)
  - _____ stage (where parties transfer property)

- Liability is controlled by the stage:

  - Contract stage: Any liability must be based on a _____ provision
  - Deed stage: Any liability must be based on a _____ warranty

- **Doctrine of Merger:** Covenants under the contract are _____ into the deed and any remedy will flow from the deed.

C. **Statute of Frauds**

- Land sale contracts are subject to the Statute of Frauds.
- Three requirements:

1. Must be _____;
2. Must be signed by the party to be charged; and
3. Must include _____

   ▪ Essential terms?

      • _____ (i.e., the seller and the buyer)
      • _____; and
      • _____ (e.g., money, financing)

D. **Exceptions to the Statute of Frauds**

- Two main exceptions:

  ○ _____
  ○ _____ (also called estoppel)

- **Part Performance:** Partial performance by either the seller or the buyer is treated as evidence that the contract existed.

  ○ Look for acts of performance, such as:

     ▪ _____ of all or part of the purchase price;
     ▪ _____ by the purchaser; or
     ▪ _____ by the purchaser

- **Detrimental Reliance:** An estoppel doctrine that applies where a party has _____ _____ on the contract and would suffer hardship if the contract is not enforced.

Example 1: Paul orally agrees to purchase Sandy's home for $75,000. Paul sends Sandy a check for the home, then proceeds to move into the new house, sell his old house, buy new furniture, and hire a contractor to make repairs. Weeks later, Sandy returns the check and demands that Paul leave the house. Can Paul enforce the contract? _____, despite the absence of a written contract, under both the _____ and the detrimental reliance exceptions to the Statute of Frauds.

E. Marketable Title

- **_Every_** land sale contract includes an implied covenant of marketable title.

  - What is marketable title? Title that is free from an _____ risk of litigation
  - Examples of defects in title that would render title unmarketable:

    - Title acquired by adverse possession that hasn't been quieted
    - Private encumbrances, e.g., mortgage, covenant, easement
    - Violation of a zoning ordinance

      Note 23: Defect in title must be cured or fixed _____, at which point the contract and deed merge and the deed controls.

- In judging whether title is unmarketable, the standard is that of a _____ buyer.
- If the seller cannot deliver marketable title, the buyer's remedy is _____ of the contract.

  > **_Example 2:_** Sadie contracts to sell a condo to Benson in the Hilly Flats community. A title search on Hilly Flats reveals two covenants. The first says that condos in Hilly Flats "cannot be transferred to Non-Caucasians." The second says, "No pets can reside anywhere in Hilly Flats condos."
  >
  > Can Benson rescind the contract because of the racially-restrictive covenant? _____. This covenant is not enforceable under the Fair Housing Act or the 14th Amendment of the Constitution. Thus there is no risk of litigation.
  >
  > What about the "no pets" covenant? _____. The covenant is an encumbrance that would prevent Benson from having a pet (potential enforcer of the covenant: neighbors or HOA) or from eventually selling to anyone with a pet.

CHAPTER 15:   LAND SALE CONTRACTS – PERFORMANCE AND REMEDIES

A. Delays

- Basic rule: _Unless_ the contract or parties notify, time is not of the essence.
- Why does this matter? If time is _not_ of the essence, failure to close on the date set for close may be a breach of the contract, but is _____ grounds for rescission of the contract.
- Specific performance is still available.

B. Implied Warranty of Fitness or Suitability

- Applies to defects in _____

  - In most jurisdictions, both the initial homeowner-purchaser and subsequent purchasers may recover damages. In other jurisdictions, only the original buyer can enforce this warranty.
  - Generally, suit for breach of this warranty must be brought within a _____ time after discovery of the defect. (Some jurisdictions have a statutory time period.)

C. **Duty to Disclose Defects**

- Most jurisdictions impose a duty on the seller to disclose to the buyer all known, physical and _____ defects.

    o Concerned with _____ or hidden defects

    o Material defect must _____ the value of the home, health and safety of its occupants, or the desirability of the home

    o General disclaimers (e.g., "as is") will not satisfy the seller's duty to disclose.

D. **Merger**

After closing, obligations contained in the contract are merged into the deed. If there was something important in the contract that was not in the deed, the cause of action is lost because the deed controls after closing.

E. **Seller's Remedies on Breach by Buyer**

- Remedies available to the seller?

    o _____: Measure is the difference between the contract price and _____ _____

    o _____: Seller can sell the property to someone else

    o _____

F. **Buyer's Remedies on Breach by Seller**

- Remedies available to the buyer?

    o _____: Measure is the difference between _____ and market value on the date of breach

        ▪ What if the seller breaches but acted in good faith? Buyer can only recover _____ _____

    o _____: Returns payments to the buyer and cancels the contract

    o _____

    > **Note 24:** Buyers and sellers must choose between damages and specific performance—can't have both remedies.

G. **Equitable Conversion and Risk of Loss**

- Issue: Who bears the risk of loss if there is damage to or destruction of the property?

- **Majority Rule:** The _____ holds equitable title during the period between the _____ of the contract and the closing and _____ of the deed.

    o Buyer is responsible for any damage to the property that happens during that period.

    o As holder of legal title, seller has a right to possess the property.

- **Minority Rule:** Place the risk of loss on the _____ until the closing and delivery of deed.

Example 1: Sadie and Benson agree that Sadie will sell Benson Banana Acre. Two days before Sadie and Benson are set to close on Banana Acre, an epic storm blows through town and crushes Banana Acre, reducing it to rubble. Who is responsible for the damage to Banana Acre?

In a majority jurisdiction? _____ . As the holder of _____ title, he bears the risk of loss.

In a minority jurisdiction? _____ , as seller, bears the risk of loss.

CHAPTER 16:   ADVERSE POSSESSION

A. The Gist

- The doctrine of adverse possession allows a person in unlawful _____ to acquire good title to a piece of property. Until the person acquires good title, the person is a _____.

- When a person acquires title by adverse possession, the new title relates back to the date of the person's entry onto the property. There is no transfer of title from the former owner.

- Property owned by the government _____ be adversely possessed.

- Two basic rationales for the doctrine of adverse possession:

  - _____ the true owner for sleeping on her rights, and
  - Rewarding adverse possessor for _____ good title

B. The Elements

- Four elements:

  1) _____ for statutory period

  2) _____ and _____

  3) _____ and

  4) _____

1. Continuous

  - Three phases:

  1) Entry phase: When the adverse possessor _____ the land; required to trigger the applicable statute of limitations

  2) End phase: When the statute of limitations _____ ; now, the adverse possessor is the legal owner of the property by operation of law

  3) Middle phase: When the adverse possessor makes _____ of the property, between the entry and end phases

- o The continuous requirement is not literal. Seasonal or infrequent use may suffice if the use is _____ with the type of property being possessed (e.g., a vacation home, land at a summer camp).
- o **Tacking:** If the adverse possessor cannot satisfy the continuity requirement on her own, she can tack on her predecessor's time on the property to satisfy the statute of _____.

  > *Example 1:* Anderson takes possession of Tony's property and lives there for five years. Anderson later "sells" his interest in the property to Annie, who takes possession and lives there for three years. The statute of limitations is seven years. Can Annie satisfy the continuous requirement? Yes, by tacking on Anderson's time of possession. Note: Annie and Anderson are in _____.

  - ▪ To tack the time of adverse possession of a prior adverse possessor, the current adverse possessor must be _____ with the prior adverse possessor. Privity is an exchange of some sort between the adverse possessors.

- o **Disabilities:** The statute of limitations will not run against a true owner who has a disability at the time the adverse possession begins. Common examples of disabilities include _____, _____, or _____.

  - ▪ The disability must exist when the trespasser enters the property.

- o **Interruptions:** A true owner can interrupt the adverse possession period by _____ the adverse possessor. This will stop the adverse possession clock.

2. **Open and Notorious**

- An adverse possessor's use must be open and notorious.

  - o Use must be such that it would put a _____ on notice of the adverse use.

    - ▪ I.e., the use cannot be hidden; the trespasser must use the property as if she was the true owner

    Example 2: Tony owns Blackacre but has never visited it. Annie trespasses on Blackacre and begins living there. To conceal her trespass, Annie only goes out at night and never uses lights. Would Annie's use be open and notorious? _____, because it is designed to avoid detection.

3. **Hostile**

- o "Hostile" does not mean unpleasant. Possession must be _____ to the owner's interest. It is a claim of competing title.

Example 3: *I invite my friend to stay at my house while I'm out of town. Is my friend's use hostile? _____, the use is _____.*

- o **Majority Rule:** Does not inquire into the adverse possessor's state of mind
- o **Minority Rule:** Inquires into the adverse possessor's state of mind

    - ▪ Two camps:

        - • **Good Faith:** Some jurisdictions require that the adverse possessor thinks the land is unowned or that she is the rightful owner. This is adverse possession based on a _____.
        - • **Bad Faith:** Other jurisdictions require that the adverse possessor tries to acquire title to the property by adverse possession. This is adverse possession based on an _____.

Example 4: *Trevor buys Blackacre from Charlie for $200,000 cash. Trevor didn't know that the deed was fraudulent and Charlie didn't own the rights to Blackacre. Trevor takes possession of Blackacre and begins farming it. Was Trevor's use hostile?*

In a majority jurisdiction? _____, state of mind is irrelevant and Trevor's use is adverse to the true owner's interest.

In a good faith jurisdiction? _____, Trevor mistakenly believed he had acquired good title from Charlie.

In a bad faith jurisdiction? _____, since it was based on mistake, Trevor's possession was not an aggressive trespass.

4. Exclusive

- o An adverse possessor _____ share possession with the true owner.
- o If two people possess the property together, can they both acquire title by adverse possession? _____, they acquire title as _____.

C. Scope of Possession

- • Traces the legal boundaries of the property

    - o Exception—Constructive adverse possession: Adverse possessor enters under _____ _____ from an invalid instrument (e.g., fraudulent deed) and occupies a portion of the property described in the instrument. The adverse possessor is in actual possession of the occupied land and constructive possession of remaining land described in the deed.

        Example 5: *A fraudulent deed states that a buyer purchases all ten acres of a piece of property. When the tenant moves onto the property, she only occupies one acre. Here, the tenant entered under color of title and occupied one acre (i.e., was in actual possession of one acre). But because ten acres are described in the deed, the tenant is in constructive possession of the remaining nine acres.*

- Includes rights to _____, unless those rights already belong to a third party
- Easements can also be acquired by adverse possession (or prescription).

    Example 6: *Annie regularly crosses Tony's land to reach the main road, which she has done consistently for over ten years. The jurisdiction has a ten-year statute of limitations. Annie can acquire an easement by adverse possession (prescription). Has Annie acquired title to Tony's land? _____, she has only acquired the right to _____ his land (use rights), not to possess it (ownership).*

CHAPTER 17: DEEEDS (AND A TASTE OF RECORDING)

A. What's What?

- Deed – Basics: A deed is a legal instrument that transfers ownership of real property.
- For a deed to be valid, it must be _____ and _____. The delivery requirement houses the issue of intent.

    o **Delivery**: The controlling question is whether the grantor had the _____ to transfer the property

    ▪ **Note 1:** _____ transfer of a deed is not required.

    Example 1: *Garrett executes a deed conveying Blackacre to Barbara. Garrett learns that Barbara is out of the country when he tries to deliver the deed to her. So he calls her and says "Great news! I conveyed you Blackacre. You're the new owner." Has the deed been delivered? _____, because the phone call manifests the necessary intent to make an immediate transfer of Blackacre.*

    ▪ **Note 2:** Be on the lookout for situations where delivery is incomplete or seemingly revocable.

    Example 2: *Garrett asks his attorney to transfer a deed for Blackacre to Barbara "in two months' time, unless I change my mind before then." Has the deed been delivered? _____, because Garrett can change his mind before the date of delivery.*

    ▪ **Note 3:** Remember that the grantor can make proper delivery to an _____

    Example 3: *Garrett gives a deed to an escrow agent with clear instructions to deliver it to Barbara. Has proper delivery been made? _____*

    o **Acceptance** is generally presumed provided the gift is for value.

Example 4: *Garrett conveys a deed to Blackacre to Barbara. A day later, Barbara changes her mind about Blackacre and says she doesn't want it. Has Barbara accepted the deed? _____. What must Barbara do if she doesn't want the property anymore? _____*

_____

B. Who's Who?

- Brokers *can* be involved in land sale contracts so long as they do not _____

   - **Permissible**: Most states permit real estate agents and brokers to prepare a contract of sale
   - **Impermissible**: Real estate agents cannot usually draft a legal document like a deed or mortgage.
   - Keep in mind we are looking for the exercise of legal _____ and whether the broker or non-lawyer is giving legal advice.

C. Contents of a Deed

- A valid deed must identify the _____ _____ (i.e., grantor and grantee) and it must be signed by the _____. (Statute of Frauds).
- A valid deed must include _____.

   - A granting clause can include any words that evidence a _____ intent to transfer.

- A valid deed must include a _____ description of the property.

   - Does the description have to be a legal description? _____

      - Can it be based on monuments or physical attributes of the property? _____
      - Can extrinsic evidence be admitted to clarify an ambiguous description? _____

D. Execution

- **Signature**: As a general matter, the _____ signature is required for execution to be effective.

   - Is the grantee required to sign too? _____.
   - Must the deed be witnessed or notarized? _____.
   - What if the signature is forged? The deed is _____, even if purchaser is by a BFP.

- **Agents**: A principal can appoint an agent to execute a deed.

   Equal Dignities Rule: If the agent is required to sign (e.g., execute a deed), then the agency relationship must be _____.

E. Recording - The Basics

- What does it mean to record? _____
- What is the purpose of recording? Put the world on notice that you own the property.
- Does recording affect the validity of a deed? _____, a deed is valid at delivery.

- If they don't affect validity, what's the big deal with recording statutes? We're concerned about

_____ .

> *Example 5:* *Garrett conveys Blackacre to Barbara. Later, Garrett conveys*
> *Blackacre to Sandy without informing her about the prior deed to Barbara.*
> *Who is the subsequent purchaser? _____ . The purpose of a recording*
> *statute is to mediate conflicts between first and subsequent purchasers, in this*
> *example, Barbara and Sandy.*

F. Common-Law Recording Rule

- A deed does _____ have to be recorded to be valid!

- The baseline for recording problems is the common-law rule. It follows the "first in _____,
first in _____" principle; i.e., under the common-law rule, the first grantee to receive a
deed wins.

    Note 1: Every state has a recording statute that _____ the common-law rule to
    give priority to certain deeds when there are competing claims to title.

    Note 2: In the absence of a recording statute, the common-law rule controls.

    > *Example 6:* *Garrett sells his property to three people. First to Barbara, then*
    > *to Candace, and finally to Darla. All three are claiming title. Who has title at*
    > *common law? _____ . Why? Because she was _____ .*

CHAPTER 18: RECORDING ACTS

A. Scope of Recording Acts

- What's what? What types of interests are covered?

    - _____
    - _____
    - _____
    - _____
    - _____ affecting title
    - Other instruments creating an interest in land, such as _____ or

    _____

    > **Note 25:** Title by adverse possession is NOT covered. Recording statutes do not
    > cover interests created by operation of law.

- Who's protected? Who is covered by recording acts? _____

    > **Note 26:** The term "purchaser" means someone who has acquired an interest
    > in land.

- Unprotected Persons: Who is not covered by recording acts? Grantees who acquire title by _____, _____, or _____ are not protected by recording acts.

  Why not? The policy behind recording acts is that we want to protect those who make economic investments by purchasing property.

B. Notice

- The concept of notice is crucial in applying two of the three recording acts.
- Three kinds of notice

  1) _____ notice - when the subsequent grantee has real, personal knowledge of a prior interest

  2) _____ notice (i.e., record notice) - when prior interest is recorded

  3) _____ notice - when a reasonable investigation would have disclosed the existence of prior claims

     - **Helpful hint about inquiry notice:** There are two common situations where a subsequent grantee will be put on inquiry notice:

       ○ **Dude on the land**: When there is someone else _____ _____ the land; had the subsequent grantee investigated the land, he would have discovered the person in possession.

       ○ **Mentioned interest**: When there is an interest mentioned in the deed to some other transaction; had the subsequent grantee inquired, he would have discovered the interest.

     Example 1: *Garrett's deed to Barbara references an easement from Garrett to Jones. Any subsequent purchaser in Garrett's chain of title will be charged with knowledge of the easement.*

     Exam Tip 8: Of the three types of recording acts, notice statutes and race-notice statutes are most heavily tested on the MBE.

C. Race Statutes

- Rule: First to _____ wins, even if the subsequent purchaser had notice of a prior, unrecorded conveyance
- Key language: "First recorded" or "First to record"

D. Notice Statutes

- Rule: Subsequent purchaser wins if she buys without _____ of a prior, unrecorded conveyance.
- Key language: "In good faith" or "Without notice"

E. Race-Notice Statutes

- Rule: Subsequent purchaser wins if two requirements are met:

1) Purchase _____ notice of a prior unrecorded conveyance; and

2) _____

- Key language: "In good faith" or "Without notice" **plus** "First duly recorded" or "First recorded"

F. Name that Statute

Example 2: No conveyance or mortgage of real property shall be good against subsequent purchasers for value and without notice unless the same be first recorded according to law. This is a _____ statute.

Example 3: No conveyance or mortgage of real property shall be good against subsequent purchasers for value unless the same be first recorded according to law. This is a _____ statute.

Example 4: No conveyance or mortgage of real property shall be good against subsequent purchasers for value and without notice unless the same be recorded according to law. This is a _____ statute.

G. Application

Example 5: Oliver owns Blackacre. Oliver conveys Blackacre to Anna, who does not record. Oliver later conveys Blackacre to Benny for $200,000. Benny does not know about the deed to Anna. Benny records. Anna then records.

Who wins in a "race" state? _____, because _____

Who wins in a "notice" state? _____, because _____
_____

Who wins in a "race-notice" state? _____, because _____
_____

Example 6: Blackacre is located in a state that has the following statute: "No conveyance or mortgage of real property shall be good against subsequent purchasers for value unless first duly recorded in good faith." Oliver sold Blackacre to Anna, who did not record. Later, Oliver conveyed Blackacre to Benny for valuable consideration. Benny did not know of the prior conveyance. Anna recorded. Then Benny recorded.

What kind of recording act is it? _____

Who owns Blackacre? _____, because _____

Example 7: Oliver owns Blackacre, which he conveys to Anna for $100,000. Anna does not record. Weeks later, Oliver offers Benny Blackacre for $15,000. Before buying it, Benny inspects Blackacre and sees Anna working in the garden on the property. Benny goes ahead with the purchase and records his deed.

Who wins in a "race" state? _____, because _____

Who wins in a "notice" state? _____, because _____
_____

Who wins in a "race-notice" state? _____, because
_____

> **Example 8:** *Oliver owns Blackacre. Oliver conveys Blackacre to Anna for $100,000. Anna does not record. Weeks later, Oliver makes a gift of Blackacre to his nephew Benny. Benny does not know about the prior conveyance to Anna. Benny does not record. Anna records.*
>
> *Is Benny covered by the Recording act? _____, because _____*
> _____
>
> *What rule controls? _____.*
>
> *Who wins? _____.*

H. Special Rules

- **Shelter Rule:** A person who takes from a bona fide purchaser protected by the recording act has the _____ rights as his grantor.

  > **Example 9:** *Oliver sells Blackacre to Anna, who does not record. Later, Oliver sells Blackacre to Benny. Benny has no knowledge of the prior conveyance. Carter is interested in buying Blackacre from Benny, though Carter is aware of the prior transfer to Anna. Benny sells to Carter. The state is a "notice" state.*
  >
  > *Does Carter have good title? _____. Even though Carter had notice of the prior conveyance, Carter stands _____, who did not have notice of the conveyance to Anna.*

- **Estoppel by Deed:** Arises when a grantor conveys land the grantor does not _____

  o If a grantor subsequently acquires title to the land, the grantor is _____ from trying to repossess on grounds that he didn't have title when he made the original conveyance.

CHAPTER 19: DEEDS; WILLS & TRUSTS, RESTRAINTS ON ALIENATION

A. Deed

- **Reminder**: After closing, the land sale contract is merged into the deed. Any liability must arise out of the _____, not the contract.
- **Three kinds of deeds**:

  ▪ _____ deed

- _____ deed
- _____ deed

B. Particulars

1. **General Warranty Deed:** Provides the _____ amount of title protection; grantor warrants title against _____ defects, ***even if the grantor did not cause the defects***

   o The **six implied covenants** in the general warranty deed:

      - *Present Covenants*

         • **Covenant of seisin**: Warrants that the deed _____ the land in question

         • **Covenant of the right to convey:** Warrants that the grantor (i.e., the seller) has the _____ to convey the property

         • **Covenant against encumbrances:** Warrants that there are no _____ encumbrances on the property that could limit its value

      - *Future Covenants*

         • **Covenant of quiet enjoyment**: Grantor promises that grantee's _____ will not be disturbed by a third-party claim

         • **Covenant of warranty**: Grantor promises to defend against future claims of _____ by a third party.

         • **Covenant of further assurances**: Grantor promises to fix future title problems

2. **Special Warranty Deed:** The grantor warrants against defects only caused by the _____. This type of deed provides a lesser amount of title protection than a general warranty deed.

   o It includes the same six covenants as a general warranty deed, but they only apply to the acts (or omissions) of the _____.

3. **Quitclaim Deed:** The grantor makes _____ as to the health of the title. This type of deed provides the least amount of title protection.

   o Often used in tax sales and intra-family disputes (e.g., divorces)

      Example 1: Sadie transfers a quitclaim deed for Banana Acre to Benson for $25,000. After taking possession, Benson discovers a bunch of his neighbors using paths on his property. He learns from them that Sadie had granted a right-of-way easement across Banana Acre, which she did not disclose to Benson. Does Benson have a claim against Sadie for failing to disclose the easements? _____. Because she used a quitclaim deed, Sadie made no warranties as to the state of the title.

Example 2: Instead, assume that Sadie had transferred a special warranty deed. Would Benson have a claim against Sadie for failing to disclose the easements? _____. Sadie breached the covenant _____ _____.

Example 3: Instead, assume that Benson discovered that a prior owner, rather than Sadie, had granted the easements across Banana Acre. Sadie still conveyed a special warranty deed. Would Benson have a claim against Sadie for failing to disclose the easements? _____. Sadie only warranted against defects that she herself created.

C. Breach and Remedies

- Breach of the *present* covenants occurs at the _____
- Breach of the *future* covenants occurs _____ the conveyance, once there is interference with possession
- Remedies: Damages

D. Wills

- Real property can be transferred by _____.
- Guiding principle in the interpretation of wills is the testator's _____.
- If a person dies without a will, his estate is distributed by _____. This is a default estate plan created by the legislature.

  o **Who's Who**:

  - **Heirs**: People who take a decedent's _____ estate. In order to be an heir you have to survive the dead person who dies without a will.
  - **Devisee**: A person who takes a devise by will (alternative terms is legatee).
  - **Decedent**: Dead guy
  - **Testator**: Dead guy who _____

  o **What's What**:

  - **Escheat**: If a decedent dies without a will and without heirs, the decedent's property goes to the state.
  - **Ademption**: Devise of property that fails (or "adeems") because it is not in the testator's estate _____.

    - Basic rule: The gift fails and the intended recipient gets nothing
    - Satisfaction: If the testator gives the intended beneficiary the promised gift _____, the beneficiary keeps the gift ("ademption by satisfaction").

  - **Lapse & Anti-Lapse**

    - **Lapse**: The intended beneficiary predeceases (dies before) the testator. Traditionally, the gift fails and would fall to the residuary gift.

- **Anti-Lapse**: Every state has an anti-lapse statute to prevent a gift from failing because an intended recipient predeceased the testator.

  - The statute replaces the intended beneficiary with a family member (e.g., the children of the beneficiary) who _____ of their parent and take the gift on their behalf.
  - Why? The purpose is to favor the testator's intent and have the gift go to the person's family rather than to no one at all or to the residuary gift.

E. Trusts

- Definition: Device for managing property with bifurcated ownership. One person (_____) owns property (legal title) for the benefit of another person (_____) who holds equitable title.

  - **Charitable Trust**: Trust designed to benefit the public and is charitable in nature
  - **Private Trust**: Trust designed to satisfy some legal purpose by giving property to a person or group for the benefit of another person or group.

- **Who's who?**

  - **Settlor**: Person who _____ the trust
  - **Beneficiary**: Person who _____ from the trust

    - Holds equitable title (no obligations and all of the benefit)
    - Has standing to enforce the trust

  - **Trustee**: Person (can be an entity) who _____ the trust property and holds _____ title)

- **What's what?**

  - **Res**: Property that is subject to the trust. Generally, a trust must contain property.
  - **Bifurcated transfer**: Ownership is divided

    - Giving someone _____ title to act as the owner (trustee)
    - Giving someone _____ title to benefit from that ownership (beneficiary)

      Example 4: *Sam wants to save money to pay for his son Ben's education. Sam executes the following deed: "I convey $100,000 to my friend Todd for the benefit of Ben's education." The deed creates a trust.*

      Who is the settlor? _____. Who is the trustee? _____. Who is the beneficiary? _____. Who has legal title? _____. Who has equitable title? _____.

F. **Restraints on Alienation**

- A restriction on _____

- Where do we see these restrictions?

  o Inter vivos grant of an estate smaller than a fee simple

  o Devise of an estate smaller than a fee simple

  o Co-tenant agreement

  o Covenants that run with the land

- Rules about restraints

  o Absolute restraint on alienation is _____.

  o Partial restraint is valid if it is for a _____ and a _____
  _____.

  o A restriction on the **use** of property is generally permissible (e.g., covenants).

- What's the effect of the restraint on alienation?

  o If the restraint is valid, any attempt to alienate the property will be _____.

  o If the restraint is invalid, the restraint is rejected and the property can be _____
  in violation of the restraint.

CHAPTER 20:   MORTGAGES

A. **Basics**

- What is a mortgage? A _____ device used to secure payment of a _____.

  ▪ Two component parts:

    • _____: Borrower's promise to repay the loan/debt

    • _____: Instrument that provides security to the note

      o Put the two parts together: If the borrower defaults on the loan, then the lender
      can force a foreclosure sale to satisfy the outstanding debt.

      o Big picture: Lender lends money (with interest) to someone who wants to
      purchase a home. Lender takes an interest in the home as security. When loan
      is paid, everybody benefits.   But, if payments are not made, the lender will
      foreclose on its interest and force a sale of the home to satisfy the debt.

- **Who's who**?

  ▪ Mortgagor: _____

  ▪ Mortgagee: _____

- Two kinds of mortgages:
  - **Purchase money mortgage**: Person takes out a loan for the purpose of _____ _____
  - **Future advance mortgage**: A _____ used for home equity, construction, business, and commercial loans (often referred to as a "second mortgage")

    Example 1: Bonnie takes out a $100,000 mortgage from America's Bank to buy a home. Years later, she takes out a $25,000 second mortgage from Village Bank to renovate her kitchen. Now both America's Bank and Village Bank have an interest in Bonnie's home. She now has two separate mortgages to pay out. Two different lenders have an interest in her property that could be foreclosed on.

B. **Lien States vs. Title States**
  - **Majority ("Lien States")**: Treats a mortgage as a lien that _____ _____ a joint tenancy
  - **Minority ("Title States")**: A mortgage _____ a joint tenancy and converts it into a tenancy in common

    > **Exam Tip 9:** This is an ideal exam question. Encompasses two areas of study - concurrent ownership and security devices (mortgages).

C. **Alternatives to Mortgages - Equitable Mortgages**
  1. _____
     - Operates like a mortgage but uses a trustee to hold title for the benefit of the lender (beneficiary of the trust receiving the payments)
  2. _____ **land contract**
     - Seller finances the purchase; seller retains title until the buyer makes final payment on an installment plan
     - Traditional rule: If the buyer breaches (misses a payment), the seller keeps the installment payments made and the property.
     - Modern approaches: States are trying to assist defaulting buyers
       - Some treat installment contracts as a _____, requiring the seller to foreclose
       - Some give the buyer the equitable right of redemption to stop a foreclosure sale
       - Some allow the seller to retain ownership, but require some _____ for what's been paid.

3. _____ deed

- Mortgagor (borrower) transfers the _____ for the property instead of conveying a security interest in exchange for the loan.

  - If this is a mortgage disguised as a sale, the borrower must prove a mortgage-like agreement by _____ evidence, i.e. that there was an obligation created prior to or contemporaneously with the transfer.
  - Parol evidence is admissible to make this showing.
  - Statute of Frauds _____ bar oral evidence about the agreement.

4. Conditional sale and repurchase

- Owner sells property to the lender who leases the property back to the owner in exchange for a loan. Lender gives the owner the option to repurchase, after the loan is paid off.

D. Transfers

1. By Mortgagor/Borrower

   a. Liability of mortgagor/borrower

   - Mortgagor may transfer the property by deed (selling), by will, or by intestate succession.
   - Mortgagor remains _____ after the transfer unless:
     - Lender/mortgagee releases by mortgagor; or
     - Lender _____ the transferee's (buyer/new owner) obligation
   - **Due-on-sale clause**: Lender has option to demand immediate full payment upon transfer. Think of this as an _____ clause that allows the lender to speed up the payment when the property is _____.
   - **Due-on-encumbrance clause**: Acceleration when mortgagor obtains a _____ mortgage or otherwise encumbers the property.

   b. Liability of subsequent transferee

   - **Assumes the mortgage**
     - Upon default, if the transferee (buyer) assumes the mortgage, the transferee is _____ liable for the mortgage.
     - _____ the original mortgagor and the transferee are liable upon default.
     - In most jurisdictions, the assumption agreement does **not** need to be _____.
   - **Takes "subject to" mortgage**
     - Transferee is _____ personally liable upon default.

- If the deed is silent or ambiguous as to liability, transferee/buyer is considered to have taken title _____ the mortgage.

2. **Transfer by Mortgagee/Lender**

> **Editor's Note 4:** The professor misspoke when introducing this section as transfer by the "mortgagor"

> *Example 2: Bonnie takes out a $250,000 mortgage from Local Bank to buy a home. Local Bank assigns the note and mortgage to America's Bank. Despite this transfer, Bonnie still must make her mortgage payments. The payments will go to America's Bank.*

> *Special Situation #1 - Local Bank transfers the note but not the mortgage. The rule is that the mortgage _____ the note.*

> *Special Situation #2 - Local Bank transfers the mortgage but not the note. The transfer is either (i) _____ because the note is the evidence of the debt, or (ii) the note and mortgage are considered a single entity, thus the note follows the mortgage.*

CHAPTER 21:   FORECLOSURE

A. Pre-Foreclosure Rights and Duties

- When can the mortgagee/lender take possession?

  o **Lien theory state** - Mortgagee/lender _____ take possession prior to foreclosure because lender has a _____ until foreclosure is complete. Mortgagor is owner up until foreclosure.

  o **Title theory state** - Lender technically has the right, as the _____, to possess the property at any time.

  o **Intermediate title theory state** - Minority of jurisdictions modify the title theory - the mortgagor retains title until _____, at which point the lender can take possession.

- **Waste**

  o Homeowner cannot commit waste that will impair the lender's security interest.

  o Affirmative waste, voluntary waste, and permissive waste are more of a concern than ameliorative waste (improvements).

- **Equity of redemption**

  o A common law right held by the mortgagor to _____ and prevent foreclosure upon the full payment of the debt.

  o Mortgagor must exercise the right of equity of redemption _____ the foreclosure sale.

Example 1: Bonnie takes out a $350,000 mortgage to buy a condo. She misses a considerable number of payments and the bank initiates a foreclosure sale on account of Bonnie's default. Bonnie can _____ the foreclosure under the equity of redemption if she can repay the debt in full _____ the foreclosure sale.

- o **Deed in lieu of foreclosure**: Rather than face foreclosure, mortgagor can convey the property to the lender in exchange for releasing her from any outstanding debt.
- o **"Clogging" the equity of redemption**: Homeowner gives up their right to stop the foreclosure sale. A mortgagor may waive the right to redeem. Courts hate clogging because they don't want homeowner's to give up their equity of redemption.

B. Foreclosure Methods

- **What's what?** A foreclosure is a _____ of an asset to pay off a debt.
- **Notice**: Mortgagee must give notice _____ foreclosing.
- **Two methods**:
    - ▪ **Judicial Sale**: Sale under the supervision of a _____
    - ▪ **Power of Sale** (Private Sale): Sale is held by the _____
    - o Either way, proceeds of the sale are used to pay off the debt.
    - o Excess proceeds will be used to satisfy other _____
- **Deficiency**: Is the mortgagor responsible if the sale produces less than the mortgagor owes? _____. In that situation, the court can issue a _____ judgment for the remaining balance.

    Example 2: Bonnie takes out a $200,000 mortgage from America's Bank to buy a home. She defaults on the loan and the home is foreclosed upon and sold for $100,000. The remaining debt, including principal and interest, is $175,000. What happens to the proceeds of the sale? The bank will take the $100,000 and get a _____ judgment against Bonnie for the remaining $_____.

C. Priorities

- **General Rule**:
    - ▪ **Senior interests**: Interests acquired _____ the interest that is being foreclosed. They survive the foreclosure.
    - ▪ **Junior interests**: Interests acquired _____ the interest that is being foreclosed. They are extinguished by the foreclosure.
    - ▪ **First in time rule**: Surviving debts are satisfied _____.

    Note 28: Classify the interest as either senior or junior and then apply the rule to determine whether the interest survives foreclosure.

- **Exceptions** to chronological "first in time" rule:

  1) **Purchase-money mortgage exception** – The purchase money mortgage has priority over mortgages and liens created by or against the purchaser/mortgagor _____ the purchaser/mortgagor's acquisition of the property.

     Example 3:   A purchase-money mortgage would have priority over a judgment lien that pre-dates the purchase of the property.

  2) **Recording act exception** - A senior mortgage may sometimes not get recorded. A junior mortgage that satisfies the requirements of the state recording act _____ take priority over the unrecorded senior mortgage.

     Example 4: America's Bank is foreclosing on its mortgage on Blueberry Acre. America's Bank never recorded its mortgage interest. Village Bank has a later (junior) mortgage on Blueberry Acre. At the time of the execution, Village Bank was not aware of the earlier interest. The jurisdiction follows a notice rule for recording. Because it took its interest without knowledge (notice) of the senior interest, Village Bank's junior interest will take priority.

  3) **Subordination agreement between mortgagees** - A senior mortgagee can _____ to subordinate its interest to a junior interest.

  4) **Mortgage modifications** - A senior mortgagee who enters into an agreement with the mortgagor/landowner to modify the mortgage by making it _____ burdensome subordinates its interest, but _____ as to the modification. The original mortgage will otherwise remain superior.

  5) **Future-advances mortgages** - Line of credit. See MBE Real Property outline at V.E.2.

D. **Effects of Foreclosure**

  - **Mortgagor:** Foreclosure _____the mortgagor's interest in the property.

    o **Exception**: _____ redemption - Some states allow the mortgagor to redeem the property even *after* the foreclosure sale. A statute enables the homeowner to _____ the foreclosure. It ends the purchaser's title and restores title to the homeowner.

      Example 5: Bonnie purchased a home for $350,000. Bonnie can't afford to make payments and defaults. Polly purchases the home at a foreclosure sale. Normally, at that point, Polly would become the rightful owner of the house and Bonnie's interest would be extinguished. In a state with statutory redemption, however, Bonnie can _____ the subsequent sale to Polly, provided she satisfies the statute.

Note 29: Absent statutory redemption, the purchaser of property at a foreclosure sale takes the property *free and clear* of any junior mortgage and *subject to* any senior mortgage.

- **Purchaser**: Purchaser of property at a foreclosure sale takes the property _____ of any junior mortgage and subject to any senior mortgage; BUT:

  - The purchase may be subject to the mortgagor's statutory right of redemption, if one exists.

- **Senior interests**: Rights of senior interests are generally not affected by the foreclosure sale.
- **Junior interests**: Rights of junior interests are generally _____.

CHAPTER 22:   EASEMENTS, PART I

A. Basics

- **Definition:** Right held by one person to make _____ of another person's land
- **Servient estate:** Land _____ by the easement
- **Dominant estate:** Land _____ by the easement

    > *Example 1:*   *Sissy has an easement to cross Dominic's property to reach the highway.   Who has the dominant estate? _____*
    > *Who has the servient estate? _____*

- **Affirmative easement:** Holder has the right to _____ on someone else's property

    > *Example 2:*   *Eddie has an easement to cross Sue's land to reach the highway.*

- **Negative easement:** The holder has the right to _____ someone from doing something on her land

    > *Example 3:*   *Eddie has an easement that entitles him to prevent Sue from growing her bamboo to a height that blocks Eddie's windows.*

- **Easement appurtenant:** Easement is tied to the _____ of the land.

    > *Example 4:*   *Eddie and Sue are neighbors. Eddie has the right to cross Sue's land to reach the highway. Who has the dominant estate? _____. Who has the servient estate? _____.*

    Note 30: An easement appurtenant is fully transferable. Goes with the land.

- **Easement in gross:** Easement benefits the holder _____.

    > *Example 5:*   *Sue has a lovely pool. Eddie is an avid swimmer but doesn't have a pool. Sue gives Eddie an easement so he can use her pool. It does not matter where Eddie lives. It benefits him personally.*

    Note 31: In an easement in gross, there is no dominant estate, only a servient estate.

Note 32: Traditionally, easements in gross were not transferable, but now courts allow the easement to be transferred if there is intent for it to be transferable.

B. Creating an Easement

- Two methods:

  - _____ easement
  - _____ easement

C. Express Easements

- An express easement is subject to the Statute of Frauds. Thus it must be in _____.
- Can be created by a _____
- Can also be created by _____. An easement by reservation is created when a grantor conveys land but reserves an easement right in the land for the grantor's use and benefit.

  > *Example 6:* *Fddie conveys Blackacre to Sue. In the deed, Eddie "reserves the right to cross Blackacre to reach the lake."*

- **Remember:**

  - Express easements are subject to _____ statutes.
  - A _____ easement must be express; it cannot be created by implication. Why? Implied easements arise out of circumstances and a negative right will rarely be created by circumstances.

D. Implied Easements (Easements by Operation of Law; Non-express Easements)

Exam Tip 10: Expect a question on the MBE on implied easements.

- Implied easements are informal; they arise out of factual circumstances.
- They _____ transferable
- They are **not** subject to the Statute of Frauds
- They are **not** subject to recording statutes, *unless* the subsequent purchaser had _____ of the easement.
- Four kinds:

  - Easement by _____
  - Easement by _____ (easement by prior use)
  - Easement by _____
  - Easement by _____

E. Implied Easement by Necessity

- An easement by necessity is created only when property is virtually _____. For example, when the property is landlocked; there is no road or access without crossing another's land.

- **Conditions that must be met**:

  1) **Common Ownership:** Dominant and servient estates were owned _____ by one person; and

  2) **Necessity at Severance:** When the estates were severed into two separate estates (severance), one of the properties became virtually useless without an easement.

- "Necessity" in a strict sense
- Ends when it is _____

> ***Example 7:*** *Donna owns Purple Acre. She divides the property, selling the west portion to Wayne, and keeping the east portion for herself. When he purchased the property, Wayne asked Donna if he could cross her land because it was more convenient than using the road that abuts the north side of his property. Does Wayne have an easement by necessity? _____, because inconvenience is not enough.*

CHAPTER 23: EASEMENTS, PART II

A. Implied Easement by Implication

- **What is it?** An easement by implication is created by an existing use on a property.
- **Conditions that must be met**:

  1) **Common Ownership**: A large estate owned by one owner

  2) **Before Severance**: The owner of the large tract uses the land as if there's an easement on it. We call this a _____. It's "quasi" because an owner can't have an easement over her own land.

  > ***Example 1:*** *Olivia owns Blackacre. Her house is on the west side of the tract and she crosses the east side of the tract to reach the highway.*

  3) **After Severance**: Use must be _____ and _____ at the time of severance.

  4) **Necessity**: Use must be _____ necessary to the dominant estate's use and enjoyment.

  > **Note 33:** "_____" necessary is a lesser standard than "strictly" necessary.

  > ***Example 2:*** *Olivia owns Blackacre. She lived on the west side of the property and regularly crossed to the east side to reach the well. She did not have indoor plumbing in her home. She sold the east half (with the well) to Sam, but the deed did not reserve an express easement over Sam's property for Olivia to access the well. Olivia kept crossing Sam's property to fetch water until Sam*

demanded that she stop. Has Olivia acquired an easement by implication?
_____

B. Implied Easement by Prescription

- **What is it**? It's like acquiring an easement by _____
- **Important differences:**
    - Adverse possession is about possession, whereas an easement by prescription concerns _____, not possession.
    - Elements are the same as adverse possession, except _____.

C. Implied Easement by Estoppel

- **Creation**

    1) **Permission**: Starts with a _____ e.g., the first neighbor permits the second neighbor to use her land

    2) **Reliance**: Continues when the second neighbor relies on the first neighbor's promise

        - Reliance must be reasonable and in good faith
        - Look for facts where the second neighbor _____ money in reliance on the first neighbor's promise (e.g., made improvements to the easement)

    3) **Permission withdrawn**: Finally, the first neighbor withdraws permission.

- **Result**: If reliance was _____ to the second neighbor, the first neighbor is _____ from withdrawing permission, in effect creating an easement.

    > **Example 3:** *Olivia and Sam are neighbors. Olivia gives Sam permission to use the roadway across her property to reach Sam's property. Based on this promise, Sam uses the roadway to construct a cabin on his property. After building the cabin and paving the roadway, Olivia blocks the roadway and tells Sam he is trespassing. Can Olivia prevent Sam from using the road?* _____, *because he has acquired an easement by estoppel.*

D. Scope

- Depends on the type of easement
- **Express Easements:** Determined by the _____ of the easement when it was created

    - **Ambiguous Terms**: If the terms are ambiguous, the court considers the _____ of the original parties as to the _____ of the easement.
    - **Changes in use:** Changes in use of an easement are tested under a _____ standard. Presume the parties contemplated both its current use and its future use, which means the future use of an easement must be reasonably _____.
    - **Trespass**: If the use exceeds the scope, the dominant tenant is trespassing on the servient estate.

> ***Example 4:*** *Oliver gave Mary an easement to take walks along the forest on his property. After years of strolling on the property, Mary has begun riding her motorcycle on the path across Oliver's property. Can Oliver eject her from the path? _____, because Mary's current use was not _____ _____ when they created the easement. Her current use burdens the scope.*

- o **Watch out!** Be on the lookout for fact patterns where a person has an easement to cross another's land and the holder of the easement seeks to redevelop or subdivide the property to add many new holders.

  - ▪ Considerations:

    - • Can the easement be transferred to the new holders of the estate?
    - • Was the new use an ordinary foreseeable development?

- o **Also note:** Holder of the dominant estate is not entitled to use the easement to access property acquired after the easement is created (cannot "GLOM").

- • **Implied Easements:** Determined by the nature of the _____ or _____

E. Duty to Maintain

- • Who has the duty to maintain the property subject to an easement? The _____ of the easement

  - o **Exception**: Parties can agree otherwise.

F. Termination

1. Release

- o The holder of the easement _____ releases it. The release must be in _____, because it is subject to the Statute of Frauds.

2. Merger

- o An easement is terminated if the owner of the easement acquires fee title to the underlying estate. The easement _____ into the title.

  > ***Example 5:*** *Jose has an easement that gives him a right to cross Jenny's land to reach the river. Later Jose purchases Jenny's land. Is Jose's easement terminated? _____, the dominant and servient estates have merged. Jose cannot have an easement on his own property.*

3. Abandonment

- o Owner acts in an affirmative way that shows a clear intent to relinquish the right

  - ▪ Requires more than non-use or statements
  - ▪ Usually need _____ plus an _____ demonstrating intent to abandon

Example 6: *Rancher gives Shepherd an easement to use a path on his property so that Shepherd's sheep can get to the river to drink. Fed up with country living, Shepherd sells his flock and moves to New York City with plans never to return. Has Shepherd abandoned his easement? _____, because Shepherd no longer uses the path and has taken acts (i.e., selling his sheep, moving to New York) that demonstrate his intent to abandon the easement.*

4. **Prescription**

   o   Holder fails to protect against a trespasser for the statutory period

   > *Example 7:* *Millhouse has an easement to use the path along Lulu's property. Lulu hates Millhouse and no longer wants him on her property. She puts up a fence to block Millhouse's access to the path. If the path is blocked for the statutory period, will Millhouse's easement be terminated? _____, Lulu's action prevented Millhouse from exercising his easement rights.*

5. **Sale to a bona fide purchaser**

6. **Estoppel**

   o   Servient owner changes position to his _____ in _____ on statements/conduct of the easement holder that the easement is abandoned

   > *Example 8:* *Horace has an easement to use the road on Grace's property. Horace tells Grace that he is not going to use the road anymore. Grace hires a landscape designer who begins work to turn the path into a giant topiary garden. After the garden is half built, Horace demands that Grace reinstate the path for his use. Was the easement terminated? _____, Grace reasonably relied on Horace's statement.*

7. **End of Necessity**

   o   An easement by necessity lasts as long as the easement is _____. If it is no longer necessary, the easement ends.

G. **Not Easements**

   •   Distinguish an easement from two other interests

   o   **Profit:** Right to enter _____ and remove a specific _____ _____, e.g., oil, gas, timber

      ▪   **Note:** Operate similarly to easements, but profits cannot be created by _____.

   o   **License:** A _____ to use another's land; e.g., a ticket to a sporting event, the permission you give to a plumber to come into your house

      ▪   **Remember:** Easements are not revocable but licenses are revocable.

CHAPTER 24: REAL COVENANTS

A. The Gist

- **What is it?** A promise concerning the use of the land that _____ to successors to the promise

  Example 1: Oliver conveys a neighboring property to Caleb. In the deed, Oliver and Caleb agree to paint their houses white. This agreement is governed by contract law.

  Example 2: Compare: Caleb later conveys his property to Gertrude, who intends to paint her house yellow. Contract law doesn't answer the question of whether Oliver can enforce the agreement against Gertrude, but property law does.

- When an agreement binds a successor, it "_____."

  - Benefit of the covenant is the ability to _____ the covenant.
  - Burden of the covenant is being _____ to it, bound by it.

    Example 3: Oliver conveyed property to Caleb and they both agreed to paint their houses white. When Caleb conveys to Gertrude, who intends to paint her house yellow, Oliver wants to stop Gertrude from breaching the covenant. Are we running the benefit or the burden to Gertrude? _____. The burden running from Caleb to Gertrude will prevent her from breaching the covenant.

B. Requirements to Run

- Five elements:

  1) _____

  2) _____

  3) _____

  4) _____

  5) _____

C. Writing

- Subject to the Statute of Frauds so it must be _____

  Note 34: Real covenants can be recorded. Are they subject to recording acts? _____

D. Intent

- To bind a successor, the _____ must intend for the covenant to run with the land.

E. Touch and Concern

- Must touch and concern the land in order to run
- Benefit or burden of the covenant must affect both parties as owners of the land

    o **Negative Covenants:** A restriction on use will usually touch and concern because they restrict what you can do with your land. Watch out for promises that are unenforceable such as covenants not to compete or discriminatory covenants, as these do not touch and concern.

    o **Affirmative Covenant:** Covenant to pay money, e.g., homeowners association fees. Traditionally, such fees did not touch and concern, but the modern trend is to say that these fees do _____.

F. Notice

- What kind of notice is required to run a real covenant? Either _____ notice or _____ (i.e., record) notice

    o Inquiry notice may suffice for an equitable servitude.

G. Horizontal Privity

- To **run the burden** to a successor, the _____ to the promise must have been in horizontal privity.
- Horizontal privity refers to _____, where the estate and covenant are contained in the same instrument (e.g., the deed).

    o **Helpful Hint:** Look for a _____ of property between the original parties that contains a covenant in it. (Key - horizontal privity - look for the original parties to the agreement.)

        Example 4: *Oliver owns Blackacre and Whiteacre. He conveys Whiteacre to Caleb. The deed says "Oliver and Caleb promise to use their property for residential purposes only." Are Caleb and Oliver in horizontal privity?* _____ *Why?* _____

        _____

        _____

H. Vertical Privity

- Vertical privity refers to the relationship between the original party to the agreement and his/her _____ to the property.
- To **run the burden** of the covenant to the successor, the successor must take the original party's _____ interest. This is called strict vertical privity.

- To **run the benefit** of the covenant to the successor, the successor need only take an interest that is _____ of the original party's estate. This is called relaxed vertical privity.

> ***Example 5:*** *Oliver and Caleb have in their deeds to Blackacre and Whiteacre a promise not to build a shed on their properties. Oliver conveys his fee simple interest to Marsha, who plans to build a shed on the property. Can Caleb recover against Marsha? Ask first if you're running the benefit or the burden and then what kind of vertical privity is needed. Here we're running the _____. To run the burden you need _____ vertical privity. So here, because Marsha took Oliver's fee simple interest (strict vertical privity) we have enough to run the burden, provided there is horizontal privity.*
>
> ***Example 6:*** *Would there still have been vertical privity if Oliver had conveyed a life estate to Marsha? _____, because she took an interest carved out of the fee simple interest rather than the whole fee simple interest.*

> **Exam Tip 12:** Ask yourself a series of questions –
>
> (i) Identify whether you are running the benefit or the burden;
>
> (ii) If it is the benefit, you need relaxed vertical privity and you don't care about horizontal privity;
>
> (iii) If it is the burden, you need horizontal privity and strict vertical privity.

I. Remedy

- The remedy for a breach of a real covenant is _____.

CHAPTER 25: EQUITABLE SERVITUDES

- Two ways to bind a successor to an original party's promise: (1) real covenant; (2) equitable servitude, but an equitable servitude has an easier standard to meet and the remedy differs.

A. The Gist

- Operates like a real covenant but with _____ requirements
- To bind a successor:

    1) It must be _____.

    2) Must have been _____ to run with the land (same standard as a real covenant);

    3) Must _____ the land (same standard as a real covenant);

    4) Successor must have _____ (actual, record, or _____);

- *No privity requirement*
- The remedy for a breach is _____.

B. Implied Reciprocal Servitude

- It is a kind of equitable servitude that is implied and need NOT be in writing
- Usually comes up in _____ communities (condo, subdivision)
- How are they created?

  o Developer must _____ to create a covenant (i.e., promise) on _____ plots in the subdivision;

  o Promises must be _____ (i.e., benefits and burdens each and every parcel equally);

  o Must be _____ rather than positive (i.e., it must be a restriction on owner's use);

  o Successor must be on _____ of the restriction (at least *inquiry* notice); and

  o Must be a _____

  > **Example 1:** *Developer Joe Schmo has an idea for a community. He buys the land and writes up a master plan for the community. He begins conveying the property, including a restriction that your house must be painted white. However, some of the later transfers do not include a "white house" covenant. One of the new owners does not have the "white house" covenant expressed in their deed and this owner wants to paint the house turquoise. This owner will not find a "white house" covenant in her chain of title.*
  >
  > *Should the owner be bound by a restriction that wasn't in her deed? Though the owner had neither record nor actual notice, the owner may be on _____ notice. Why? Looking around every house is painted white. Even though the restriction is not in the deed, it may be implied - an exception to the requirement that the promise needs to be in writing. It is an implied reciprocal servitude.*

  - To prove there is a **common plan**, look for:

    - A (recorded) map of the community showing the common scheme
    - Marketing or advertisements of the community
    - Oral or written mention that the lots are burdened by common restriction

C. Termination

- Terminates as an easement does, i.e. merger, release, etc.

D. Changed Circumstances Doctrine

- Look for situations where the restriction no longer _____ due to _____ changes in the surrounding area since the restriction was put in place.

  o **Critical question:** Does the property subject to the restriction still retain some benefit from the restriction?

Example 2: *The houses in the Hilly Flats subdivision all have restrictions against commercial use. When Hilly Flats was developed, the surrounding neighborhoods were exclusively residential. In the following years, commercial properties developed adjacent to Hilly Flats, though there are no commercial properties within the subdivision itself. Henry wants to open a business on his property within Hilly Flats. His neighbor opposes it, seeking to have the servitude enforced.*

Will the court continue to enforce it? Most likely, _____. Although there is change outside the community, there have not been changed circumstances inside the community, so residents still benefit from the restriction (e.g., noise, traffic). Change outside the community is not sufficient to terminate.

E. Equitable Defenses

- Equitable defenses are available, including unclean hands (Plaintiff not acting in good faith) and laches (unreasonable delay).

CHAPTER 26:   COMMON INTEREST COMMUNITIES; FIXTURES

A. Common Interest Communities

- **What are we talking about**? Real estate development in which individual units/lots are burdened by a covenant to pay dues to an association. The association:

  o **Services**: Maintains grounds, provides facilities, etc.

  o **Enforces the covenants**: The association is the heavy when your neighbor breaks the rules

- **Three types**:

  o **Owners' Associations**: Where property owners belong and pay dues to an association or board

  o **Condominiums**: Where individual units are owned outright, but common areas are owned collectively as _____

  o **Cooperatives**: Property is owned by a corporation (made up of residents/shareholders) that leases individual units to shareholders (residents)

- **Governance**

  o **Declaration**: The governing documents that outline the controlling covenants and restrictions, as well as the particulars about the association or board

    Note: Rules laid out in declaration are valid so long as they are not _____, against public policy, or _____

  o **Powers**: The board has general powers to manage the common property and administer the residents. For example:

- Assessments/Fees
- Manage and maintain the common property (e.g., clubhouse, gym)
- Enforce rules
- Create new rules
  - Basic test: A new rule must be reasonably related to further a _____ purpose of the association (think rational basis test)

- **Duties**
  - To the community: The association must deal fairly with members of the community
    - Good faith
    - Prudence
    - Ordinary care
    - Business Judgment Rule controls (board is shielded from honest but _____ business decisions)

B. Fixtures

- **What is it?** Tangible _____ property that is _____ to _____ property in a manner that is treated as part of the real property (e.g., a wall or a bridge; the materials used to make a wall or a bridge)

- **Making Improvements:**
  - A fee simple owner of property is free to make improvements to the property, including fixtures, subject to governmental land use regulations.
  - Holders of a life estate or tenants, by contrast, are limited by the doctrine of _____.

    Example 1:   *Anita is the fee simple owner of Apple Acre. Sick of buying eggs every week, Anita decides to build a large chicken coop in her backyard. The municipality has no restrictions against landowners keeping farm animals on their property. Can Anita make the improvement? _____, she is a fee simple owner and there are no governmental restrictions against her doing so.*

    Example 2:   *Ray is the life tenant on Iowa Acre, a corn farm. After hearing a mysterious voice, Ray plows under his corn field and builds a baseball field. Should Ray be worried about a claim by the future interest holder? _____, Ray's action could be considered waste.*

- **Removal:** The _____ of real property is generally entitled to the chattel, unless the seller reserves in the _____ the right to keep the chattel.

  - **Life tenants and tenants**: Presumption is that they can remove fixtures unless doing so would _____ the property

- **Trespassers**
  - Old Rule: Trespassers could never remove any fixtures or improvements that they installed.
  - New Rule: Modern/majority rule is that trespassers can remove an improvement, or at least recover the value added to the property, so long as they acted in _____.

    Example 3: Terry rents an apartment from Leo. Terry installs special lights that she uses to grow orchids. The lights, which hang on a stand and are not permanently affixed to the property, and can be removed with ease. The lease does not contain a provision about improvements or fixtures. Leo is eager to keep the lights on the property, hoping to repurpose them to be fancy patio lights. Can Terry remove the lights at the end of the lease? Yes. Removing the lights will not cause permanent damage to the property.

    Example 4: Archibald takes possession of Cotton Acre, thinking he is the rightful owner. During his three year stay on Cotton Acre, Archibald repaired the barn and built a shed for farm equipment. Butch, the rightful owner of Cotton Acre, discovers Archibald and demands that he leave Cotton Acre at once. Archibald agrees, but insists that Butch pay him the value of the shed Archibald built. Will Archibald recover the value of the shed? _____, (in a modern jurisdiction) because Archibald improved Cotton Acre _____.

CHAPTER 27: LAND USE

A. Zoning Basics

- **What are we talking about?** State and local governments may regulate the use of land through zoning laws. Zoning laws are enacted for the _____ and _____ of the community.
  - States have authority to zone through _____
  - Local governments get power to zone through specific enabling acts

- **Objective:** Segregate _____ from being developed in the same area (e.g., residential vs. commercial and industrial)
  - **Cumulative Zoning:** The traditional approach in which residential use is permitted everywhere, commercial use is restricted to some areas with industrial use allowed in the fewest areas.
  - **Mutually-Exclusive Zoning:** Some jurisdictions have developed an approach where only one type of use is permitted by zone.

B. Nonconforming Uses

- Two situations:

  - **Existing Nonconforming Properties**: When zoning is changed and a structure does not satisfy the zone's requirements, it is called a "nonconforming use."

    - The goal of the property owner is to get the nonconforming use _____ in.
    - **Vested Rights**: If the project is in process when the change happens, the developer must have the proper building permits by the time the ordinance _____. The developer must also demonstrate the project was in _____.
    - What if...?

      - Owner wants to expand the nonconforming use? This is generally _____ allowed.
      - The nonconforming owner switches to another nonconforming use? _____.
      - The nonconforming owner transfer the property to a new owner? _____.

  - **Post-ordinance Nonconforming Properties:** When the property owner requests a change *after* the zoning ordinance is in place.

    - **Variance**: Owner applies for a variance, essentially permission to violate the rules.

      - **Use Variance**: Obtain the right to use property in a manner not permitted by zoning

        Example 1: *Otis wants to open a café in a residential neighborhood. To support his case, he argues that there is already a smattering of small businesses in the neighborhood, that his cafe won't increase the burden on the neighborhood traffic patterns, and that his café will make the neighborhood more desirable. The argument is about the use and trying to make it consistent with the existing neighborhood.*

      - **Area Variance**: Focuses on restrictions concerning property development.

        Example 2: *Amanda wants to build a fence around her property. Her plan is to follow the natural tree line surrounding her property. One spot of the proposed fence, on the west side of her property, will slightly encroach on the City's utility right of way. Amanda argues that the encroachment is slight and that diverting from the tree line will be unsightly.*

    - **Standard**: The person applying for a variance must show ALL of the following:

      - Compliance would create _____;
      - The hardship arises from circumstances _____ to the property;
      - The owner did not create the hardship;
      - The variance is in keeping with the _____ of the ordinance; and
      - The variance will not cause substantial harm to the general welfare.

C. Nuisance

- **Private Nuisance:** A _____ and _____ interference with another individual's use or enjoyment of his property

    o **Substantial:** One that would be offensive, inconvenient, or _____ to an _____ person in the community

    o **Unreasonable:** The _____ outweighs the _____ of the defendant's actions

- **Public Nuisance:** Unreasonable interference with the health, _____, or _____ rights of the community.

    o Private Party: Must show that she suffered a _____ kind of harm than the rest of the community

- **Remedies:** Usual remedy is _____

    o If money damages are inadequate or unavailable, court can impose _____ _____ .

D. Water Rights

- Two basic approaches:

1. Riparian Rights

    o Doctrine of riparian rights holds that landowners who _____ a waterway own the rights to the waterway. The right depends upon whether the landowner is located near the water.

    o Riparians share the right to _____ of the water, such that one riparian is liable to another for interference with the other's use.

2. Prior Appropriation

    o **First in Time, First in Right:** _____ to use the water, regardless of where their land is located, has the rights to the water.

    o **Beneficial Use:** In a prior appropriation jurisdiction, the user must put the water to a beneficial use. Any _____ use satisfies this standard.

E. Support Rights

- **Lateral Support Rights:** Neighboring landowner cannot excavate so as to cause a _____ (i.e., subsidence) on an adjacent owner's land.

    o Applicable Standards:

        ▪ Did the neighbor's buildings (structures) contribute to the subsidence? If so, the standard to apply to the one excavating is _____ .

- What if the neighbor's buildings did not contribute to subsidence? The standard to apply is _____.

- **Subjacent Support:** Think mineral rights. The surface landowners has the right not to have their land subside from the activities of the owners of underground rights.

Study hard and good luck on the exam and thanks for your time!

[END OF HANDOUT]

Torts

TORTS
PROFESSOR SHERMAN CLARK
UNIVERSITY OF MICHIGAN LAW SCHOOL

CHAPTER 1:   INTENTIONAL TORTS INVOLVING PHYSICAL INJURY

A. Generally

1. **Three Elements**—in order to prove an intentional tort, the plaintiff must prove:

   o _____

   o _____

   o _____

2. **Intent**

   o The actor acts with the purpose of causing the consequence; OR

   o The actor knows that the consequence is _____ to follow.

   a. **Children and _____ persons**—can be held liable for intentional torts if they act with the requisite intent (i.e., if they act with the purpose of causing the result or know that the consequence is substantially certain to follow.)

   b. **Transferred intent**— the intent to commit one tort suffices for the commission of another; this applies when a person commits:

      ▪ A **different intentional tort** against the **same person** that they intended to harm;

      ▪ The **same intentional tort** against _____; OR

      ▪ A **different intentional tort** against a **different person**.

      Example 1:   *Prof. Clark throws a brick at you, intending to hit you. If the brick hits you, he commits battery. If the brick misses you but puts you in imminent apprehension of being hit, he commits assault.*

      Different tort/same person: The intent to commit battery against you transfers to the tort of assault against you when the brick misses you.

      Same tort/different person: Similarly, if the brick misses you and hits your friend, he commits battery against your friend.

      Different tort/different person: Finally, if Prof. Clark intends to hit you and the brick misses you and your friend but puts your friend in imminent apprehension of being hit, the intent to commit battery against you will transfer to the intentional tort of assault against your friend.

B. Battery

1. Definition

- Defendant causes a _____ or _____ contact with the person of another; and
- Acts with the _____ to cause that contact or the apprehension of that contact.

2. Consent—there is no battery if there is express or implied consent

3. Harmful or Offensive Contact

a. Harmful—causes an _____, pain, or illness

b. Offensive

- A person of ordinary sensibilities would find the contact offensive.

    Example 2: *Spitting on somebody; groping somebody.*

- If the victim is _____, the defendant may still be liable if the defendant is aware but acts nonetheless.

4. Plaintiff's Person—includes anything connected to the plaintiff's person

Example 3: *Pulling a chair out from under someone; knocking a hat off a person's head.*

5. Causation—the act must result in contact of a harmful or offensive nature (need not be _____)

Example 4: *Setting a bucket above a door, such that ice water falls on a person's head when the door is opened.*

6. Intent

- If a contact is not consented to, that suffices to make it _____.
- The doctrine of transferred intent applies to battery.

7. Damages

- No proof of actual harm is required; the plaintiff can recover _____ damages.
- Many states allow _____ damages if the defendant acted:
    - Outrageously; or
    - With _____.
- "_____-plaintiff" rule—a defendant is liable for all harm that flows from a battery, even if it is much worse than the defendant expected it to be.

C. Assault

1. **Definition**—plaintiff's reasonable imminent apprehension of harmful or offensive bodily contact

    > **Editor's Note 1:** The Restatement (Second) of Torts uses the phrase "imminent apprehension" to refer to the apprehension of an imminent harmful or offensive bodily contact.

2. **Bodily Contact**—not required

3. **Plaintiff's Apprehension**

    o   Must be reasonable
    o   The plaintiff must be _____ of the defendant's action.

    > *Example 5:* *If you are sleeping and someone gropes you, that person commits battery even though you are not aware of it. If you are sleeping and someone pretends to hit you, there is no assault because assault requires awareness.*

4. **Imminent**

    o   Must be without significant _____
    o   Threats of future harm or hypothetical harm are not sufficient.

5. **Mere Words**

    o   Generally, "mere words do not constitute an assault."
    o   However, words coupled with the circumstances can, in some cases, be sufficient.

6. **Intent**—present in one of two ways

    o   The defendant must intend to cause either:

    ▪   An apprehension of imminent harmful or offensive contact; or
    ▪   The contact itself.

    o   Transferred intent applies to assault—the defendant may intend to cause the contact itself.

7. **Damages**

    o   No proof of _____ damages is required; the plaintiff can recover nominal damages.
    o   In appropriate cases, _____ damages may be available.
    o   The plaintiff can also recover damages from physical harm flowing from the assault.

CHAPTER 2:   INTENTIONAL TORTS: IIED, FALSE IMPRISONMENT, AND DEFENSES

A. Intentional Infliction of Emotional Distress (IIED)

1. **Definition**—extreme or _____ conduct intentionally causing severe emotional distress

2. **Intent**

   o The defendant must intend to cause severe emotional distress or at least act with _____ as to the risk of causing severe emotional distress.

   o Transferred intent **does not** apply.

3. **Extreme or Outrageous Conduct**—courts are more likely to find conduct or language to be extreme or outrageous if:

   o The defendant is in a position of _____ or _____ over the plaintiff; or

   o The plaintiff is a member of a group that has a _____ _____.

4. **Acts Directed Toward Third Parties (i.e., someone other than the plaintiff)**—a defendant who directs his conduct at a third-party victim can also be liable to:

   o **Victim's** _____ **member**—who is present at the time of the conduct

   > *Example 6:   A mother may be able to recover under the tort of IIED from a defendant who acted outrageously toward the mother's young child, knowingly distressing the mother, who was present.*

   > **Editor's Note 2:** A present immediate family member may be able to recover regardless of whether there has been bodily injury

   o **Bystander**—who is present at the time of the conduct and who suffers distress that results in _____.

5. **Causation**—the defendant's actions were at least a _____ in bringing about the plaintiff's harm

6. **Damages**—severe emotional distress beyond what a reasonable person should endure

   o Often, the extreme and outrageous character of the defendant's conduct is evidence of the plaintiff's distress.

   o **Hypersensitivity**—if the plaintiff experiences an unreasonable level of emotional distress, then the defendant is only liable if aware of the plaintiff's hypersensitivity.

   o Physical injury is not required (except in the case of a bystander, discussed above).

B. **False Imprisonment**

1. **Definition**—three elements

   o Defendant intends to _____ or
     _____ another within fixed boundaries;
   o The actions directly or indirectly result in confinement; and
   o Plaintiff is _____ of the confinement or harmed by it.

   > ***Example 7:*** *Locking a person in a closet.*

2. **Confined Within Bounded Area**

   o The area can be large
   o The area need not be _____

3. **Methods of Confinement**

   o Use of _____, physical force, threats, invalid use of legal authority,
     duress, or refusing to provide a safe means of escape
   o **Shopkeeper's privilege**—a shopkeeper can, for a reasonable time and in a reasonable
     manner, _____ a suspected shoplifter.
   o A court may find false imprisonment when the defendant has refused to perform a
     _____ to help a person escape.

   > ***Example 8:*** *A store clerk refuses to unlock a dressing room in which someone*
   > *is locked.*

4. **Time of Confinement**—immaterial

5. **Intent**

   o Defendant must act:

     ▪ With the purpose of confining the plaintiff; or
     ▪ Knowing that the plaintiff's confinement is substantially certain to result.

   o **Confinement due to defendant's negligence**—defendant will not be liable under the
     intentional tort of false imprisonment (but could be liable under negligence).
   o Transferred intent applies to false imprisonment.

   > ***Example 9:*** *A person throws a log at you, intending to hit you. The log traps*
   > *you in a corner, preventing your escape. The person has committed false*
   > *imprisonment.*

6. **Damages**—actual damages are not required; plaintiff can recover _____
   damages.

C. **Defenses to Intentional Torts Involving Personal Injury**

1. **Consent**

   a. **Express consent**—must be willing and knowing.

   - Consent by **mistake**—a _____ defense unless the defendant caused the mistake or knew of it and took advantage of it
   - Consent by **fraud**—_____ if it goes to an _____ matter

     Example 10: If you engage in physical contact with someone, thinking them to be richer than they really are, that fraud will not invalidate consent because the fraud does not go to an essential matter. However, if you are in a hospital and someone sneaks in and puts on a doctor's coat and the person touches you and you think the person is a doctor, then the fraud goes to an essential matter and consent will not be valid.

   b. **Implied consent**

   - **Emergencies**—it is fair to assume that someone in need of rescuing would allow a rescuer to touch him absent explicit consent.
   - **Injuries arising from athletic contests**

     Editor's Note 3: May be liable if the conduct is "reckless," which in this context means conduct outside the normal scope of the sport.

   - **Mutual consent to combat**

   c. **Capacity**—youth, intoxication, incompetency, etc. (i.e., lack of capacity) may **undermine** the validity of consent

2. **Self-Defense**

   a. **Use of reasonable force**—a person may use reasonable **proportionate** (i.e., not excessive) force to defend against an offensive contact or bodily harm.

   b. **Duty to retreat**

   - Traditionally, most courts required retreat before one could use deadly force.
   - Recently, many jurisdictions state that you need not retreat before using reasonable, proportionate force.

     Editor's Note 4: These are so-called "stand your ground" laws.

   c. **Initial aggressor**—NOT permitted to claim self-defense unless the other party has responded to nondeadly force with deadly force

   d. **Injuries to bystanders**—the actor is not liable for injuries to bystanders as long as the actor was behaving reasonably (not negligent) and the injury was _____.

3. **Defense of Others**—allows you to use reasonable force in defense of others.

4. **Defense of Property**

   a. **Reasonable force**—may be used if the person reasonably believes it is necessary to prevent tortious harm to the property

   b. **Deadly force**

   - Cannot be used

   - A person may never use **deadly mechanical devices** to defend property (e.g., a spring gun).

     Exam Tip 1: Remember that the defense of self-defense may still apply if the person reasonably fears for their own bodily safety.

   c. **Recapture of chattels**

   - Reasonable force may be used to reclaim _____ property that has been wrongfully taken.

   - If the original taking was lawful then only peaceful means may be used.

   d. **Force to regain possession of land**

   - **Common law**—reasonable force permitted
   - **Modern rule**—use of force is no longer permitted; only legal process

5. **Parental Discipline**—parents may use reasonable force as necessary to discipline their children.

6. **Privilege of Arrest**

   a. **Private citizen**

   - Permitted to use reasonable force to make an arrest in the case of a _____ IF:

     • The felony has actually been committed; AND
     • The arresting party has _____ to suspect that the person being arrested has committed the felony.

   - It IS a defense to make a reasonable mistake as to identity of the felon, but it IS NOT a defense to make a mistake as to whether the felony was actually committed.

   b. **Police**

   - Must reasonably believe a felony has been committed and that the person arrested committed it.

   - An officer who makes a mistake as to whether a felony has been committed is _____.

     c. **Misdemeanor**

- An arrest by a police officer only if the misdemeanor was committed in the officer's presence.
- an arrest by a private person may only be made if there is a "_____ of the _____."

CHAPTER 3:   HARMS TO PERSONAL PROPERTY AND LAND

A. Trespass to Chattels

1. **Definition**—an intentional interference with the plaintiff's right to possession of personal property either by:

   o _____ the plaintiff of the chattel;
   o _____ or _____ with the plaintiff's chattel; or
   o Damaging the chattel.

2. **Intent**

   o Only the intent to do the interfering act is necessary.
   o Defendant need not have intended to interfere with another's possession of tangible property.
   o Mistake about the legality of the action is not a defense.

Damages—the plaintiff may recover actual damages, damages resulting from the loss of use, or the cost of repair.

> **Editor's Note 5:** Use or intermeddling—the plaintiff can only recover actual damages (including diminution in value or the cost of repair).

B. Conversion

1. **Definition**—the defendant intentionally commits an act depriving the plaintiff of possession of his or her chattel or interfering with the plaintiff's chattel in a manner so serious as to deprive the plaintiff entirely of the use of the chattel.

2. **Intent**

   o Defendant must only intend to commit the act that interferes.
   o Mistake of law or fact _____ a defense.

3. **Damages**—the plaintiff can recover the chattel's full value at the time of conversion.

4. **Trespass to Chattels vs. Conversion**

   o Courts consider the following factors:

   - The _____ and extent of the interference;

- Defendant's intent to assert a right inconsistent with the rightful possessor;
- Defendant's _____;
- Expense or inconvenience to the plaintiff; and
- Extent of the harm.

o The more extreme the interference, the more likely the court will find conversion.

C. Trespass to Land

1. **Definition**—the defendant intentionally causes a physical invasion of someone's land.

2. **Intent**

   o Defendant need only have the intent to enter the land or cause the physical invasion.
   o NOT the intent to commit a wrongful trespass
   o Mistake of fact is not a defense.

3. **Physical Invasion**— trespass to land includes causing objects to invade the land

4. **Trespass vs. Nuisance**

   o **Nuisance**—may or may not involve a physical invasion or intrusion
   o **Trespass**—**always** involves an actual physical invasion or intrusion upon the land

5. **Rightful Plaintiff**—anyone in possession can bring an action, not just the owner

6. **Damages**—no proof of _____ damages is required.

7. **Necessity as a Defense to Trespass**

   a. **In general**—available to a person who enters onto the land of another or interferes with their personal property to prevent an injury or to prevent another severe harm.

   b. **Private necessity** (partial or qualified privilege)

   - The defendant must pay for actual damages that he has caused.
   - The defendant is not liable for nominal damages.
   - The landowner may not use force to exclude the person.

   c. **Public necessity**

   - Private property is intruded upon or destroyed when necessary to protect a large number of people from public calamities.

     Example 11: *Damaging a swimming pool to protect the public from a fire.*

   - NOT liable for damages to the property

D. **Nuisance**

1. **Private Nuisance**

    a. **Definition**—an activity that **substantially** and unreasonably interferes with another's

    _____ and _____ of land

    Example 12: *Loud noises or foul odors.*

    b. **Interference**

      ▪ Courts are vague regarding what constitutes an unreasonable interference.

        • Must be annoying to the ordinary reasonable person.

          o Someone hypersensitive may not have a cause of action for nuisance.

          o Someone who is not ACTUALLY bothered may still have a cause of action for nuisance if it would bother an ordinary reasonable person.

      ▪ Courts will also balance the interference with the utility of the nuisance.

      ▪ Need not be a physical invasion.

    c. **Not a nuisance**

      ▪ Historically, courts have refused to find the blocking of sunlight or the obstruction of _____ to be a nuisance.

      ▪ **Exception**: The "spite fence"

        • If a person puts up a fence with no _____ except to block their neighbor's view or sunlight, then courts will sometimes find that to be a nuisance.

    d. **Defenses to private nuisance**

      ▪ Compliance with state or local administrative _____.

        • Evidence as to whether the activity is reasonable

        • Not a complete defense

      ▪ **"Coming to the nuisance"**

        • If you move somewhere knowing about a conduct, courts are hesitant to allow you to complain that that conduct unreasonably interferes with your use and enjoyment of the land.

        • NOT a complete defense—one factor considered by the court

2. **Public Nuisance**

    1) An unreasonable interference with a *right common* to the

    _____

Example 13: *Pollution, blocking of a public highway, or interfering with the public's use of public space.*

2) **Special harm**—A private individual generally cannot recover unless the individual has been harmed in a special or _____ way, different from the public.

> **Editor's Note 6:** Best understood as a concept, rather than a tort. If something is interfering with the right of the public as a whole, presumptively the public agencies should deal with it.

CHAPTER 4:   REVIEW OF CHAPTERS 1–3: INTENTIONAL TORTS

1. **One way in which a defendant can be said to have the intent necessary for an intentional tort is if she acted with the purpose of bringing about the consequence. What is the other way in which a defendant can be said to have acted intentionally?**

   If he or she acted knowing that the consequence was _____ to occur.

2. **Does this mean that in order to be liable for an intentional tort the defendant must have intended or anticipated the extent or exact nature of the harm?** _____

3. **What is the doctrine of transferred intent?**

   When a person intends to commit an intentional tort against one person, but instead commits:

   1) The intended tort against a _____ person;

   2) A different intentional tort against that person; or

   3) A different intentional tort against a different person

4. **To what intentional torts does the doctrine of transferred intent apply?**

   Battery, _____, false imprisonment, trespass to land, and trespass to chattels; but does not apply to the tort of _____ infliction of emotional distress

5. **What are the elements of the tort of battery?**

   1) Defendant causes a harmful or offensive contact with the person of another; and

   2) Acts with the intent to cause such contact or the apprehension of such contact.

6. **What is the tort of assault, and how is it different from battery?**

   Assault is the plaintiff's reasonable imminent apprehension that one is about to be the victim of a battery (i.e., harmful or offensive contact).

   If battery is hitting someone, then assault is making someone think they are

   _____.

7. **What constitutes the tort of intentional infliction of emotional distress (IIED)?**

   A defendant is liable for intentionally or _____ causing severe emotional distress with extreme or outrageous conduct.

8. **Does the doctrine of transferred intent apply to IIED?** _____

9. **What are the elements of the tort of false imprisonment?**

   When a person acts:

   1) Intending to confine or restrain another within fixed boundaries;

   2) Those actions directly or indirectly result in such confinement; and

   3) The other is either _____ of the confinement or is harmed by it.

10. **Consent is a defense to intentional torts. Does that consent need to be explicit?**

    _____. Consent can be implied, as by participating in a contact sport.

11. **What are the requirements for the defense of self-defense?**

    A person may use reasonable force to defend against an offensive contact or bodily harm. The force used in self-defense must be _____ to the anticipated harm.

12. **May one use force to defend another person? Is defense of others a defense?**

    _____. One is justified in using reasonable force in defense of others to the same extent that one would be entitled to use self-defense. The force must be proportionate to the anticipated harm.

13. May force ever be used to protect property?

_____, with limits. A person may use reasonable force to defend her property if she reasonably believes it is necessary to prevent tortious harm to her property. _____ force may not be used merely in defense of property.

If someone uses deadly force in defending their _____, it is only valid if in the process of defending their home they reasonably believe themselves, their families, or others to be in danger.

14. What is the tort traditionally known as trespass to chattels?

Intentional interference with the plaintiff's right to chattels (i.e., tangible personal property) by either:

1) Dispossessing the plaintiff of the chattel; or

2) Using or intermeddling with the plaintiff's chattel.

15. What is the tort of conversion?

A defendant is liable for conversion if he intentionally commits an act depriving the plaintiff of _____ of her chattel or interfering with the plaintiff's chattel in a manner so serious as to deprive the plaintiff of the use of the chattel. The plaintiff's damages are the chattel's _____.

16. What is the tort of trespass to land?

When defendant intentionally causes a _____ of land.

17. If the defendant thinks the land is his, has he still committed trespass to land?

_____. The defendant need only have the intent to enter the land (or to cause a physical invasion), not the intent to commit a wrongful trespass. In other words, mistake of fact is not a defense.

18. What is the defense of private necessity?

A defendant who acts to prevent a threatened injury or harm has the privilege to enter onto the property of another and to use that property in that way. The property owner cannot use self-help to exclude the defendant as a _____.

19. **What does it mean to say that private necessity is an incomplete privilege?**

The property owner is entitled to recover _____ damages even though the defendant is not a trespasser.

20. **What is the defense of public necessity?**

A person enters onto the land in order to protect a large number of people from _____, such as the spreading of a fire. He is not liable for any damage to the property.

21. **What is the tort of private nuisance?**

A private nuisance is a thing or activity that substantially and unreasonably interferes with another individual's _____ _____ of his land.

22. **What is a public nuisance?**

A public nuisance is an unreasonable interference with a right common to the public as a whole. A public agency is empowered by statute or regulation to take action to abate the public nuisance.

CHAPTER 5:   NEGLIGENCE: DUTY AND STANDARD OF CARE

A. **In General**

1. **Elements**

   o _____
   o _____
   o _____ (actual and proximate)
   o _____

B. **Duty**

1. **Introduction**

   o Courts may use the term "duty" to cover three concepts:

      ▪ Whether a person has a LEGAL obligation to act a certain way (as opposed to a social or moral one);
      ▪ How careful a person should be when they do act (discussed under "Standard of Care," *infra*); OR
      ▪ The scope of liability (to whom should a person be liable—*Palsgraf* case)

2. **Substantive Rule—Duty as the Standard of Care**

   o   To behave as a reasonable person of ordinary prudence under the circumstances

   o   No duty to act affirmatively

3. **Foreseeability of Harm**—the foreseeability of the harm to others is a factor in determining the scope of duty.

   o   A reasonably prudent person would not engage in activities with an unreasonable risk of harm.

4. **Scope of Duty—Foreseeability of Plaintiff**

   o   While Judge Cardozo used duty to discuss who one is liable to and how much they are liable for in the *Palsgraf* case, today, we generally save that for the proximate cause analysis.

     ▪   Duty of care owed to plaintiff only if plaintiff is a member of the class of persons who might be foreseeably harmed by the conduct.

5. **Rescuers**—a person who comes to the aid of another is a

   _____.

6. **Crime Victims**—considered foreseeable plaintiffs in certain circumstances

   > *Example 14:*   *A driver who leaves a passenger in a high-crime area may be liable in tort if that passenger becomes a victim of a crime.*

7. **Affirmative Duty to Act**

   In general, there is no affirmative duty to help others. The following are exceptions to that rule:

   a.   **Assumption of duty**—a person who voluntarily aids or rescues another is liable for any injury caused by the failure to act with reasonable care in the performance of that aid or rescue.

   > *Example 15:*   *If you pick up a passenger who was cold and then make them leave your vehicle, you may be liable if the passenger freezes.*

   b.   **Placing another in** _____

   > *Example 16:*   *If you see someone drowning in a pool, you do not have a duty to rescue them. However, if you are the one who knocked them in the water, then you have a duty.*

   c.   **By authority**—a person with the ability and actual authority to control another has a duty to exercise reasonable control.

   > *Example 17:*   *A parent's control over a child.*

   d.   **By relationship**

     ▪   The defendant has a special relationship with the plaintiff.

Example 18: Common carrier-passenger; innkeeper-guest.

- Duty to aid or assist those persons and prevent reasonably foreseeable injuries.

CHAPTER 6: NEGLIGENCE: STANDARD OF CARE (CONT'D.)

A. Standard of Care

1. **Reasonably Prudent Person under the Circumstances**—an _____ standard

   a. **Mental and emotional characteristics**—defendant is presumed to have average mental abilities and knowledge

   b. **Physical characteristics**—particular physical characteristics are taken into account

      Example 19: Blindness or deafness.

   c. **Intoxication**—intoxicated people are held to the same standard as sober people unless the intoxication was _____.

   d. **Children**

      - **Ask:** What would a reasonably prudent child of that _____ do?

        - More subjective

      - Children engaged in high-risk adult activities (e.g., driving a car)—the child will be held to an adult standard of care.

2. **Custom**—relevant evidence, but not dispositive evidence

3. **Professionals**

   o Expected to exhibit the same skill and knowledge as another practitioner in the

   _____

   Editor's Note 7: Specialists may be held to a higher standard.

4. **Physicians**

   o **Traditional rule**—physician in the "same or similar" locality
   o **Modern trend**—_____ standard
   o Patients must give informed _____:
      - Must explain risks of medical procedures
      - Doctors are not required to inform of risks that are commonly _____, if a patient is unconscious, if a patient waives/refuses the information, if a patient is incompetent, or if the patient would be harmed by disclosure (e.g., it would cause a heart attack)

5. **Negligence Per Se**—when a law or statute establishes a particular standard of care, the court will apply that standard of care.

   a. **Elements**

      - A criminal law or regulatory statute imposes a particular duty for the protection or benefit of others;
      - Defendant _____ the statute;
      - Plaintiff must be in the **class of people intended to be protected** by the statute;
      - The accident must be the _____ that the statute was intended to protect against;
      - The harm was caused by a **violation of that statute**.

        > **Exam Tip 2:** At the heart of a negligence per se analysis is: is this the type of harm that the statute was intended to prevent.
        >
        > **Exam Tip 3:** Compliance with a statute does not necessarily mean that the defendant was NOT negligent.

   b. **Defenses**

      - Defendant must show that complying with the statute would be even more dangerous than violating the statute.
      - Compliance was impossible or an emergency justified violation of the statute.

   c. **Violation by plaintiff**—counts as comparative or contributory negligence

CHAPTER 7: NEGLIGENCE: STANDARD OF CARE (CONT'D.)

> **Exam Tip 4:** As a general rule, apply the "reasonableness" standard to various types of defendants, then consider what courts have determined to be reasonable for particular circumstances, rather than thinking of these as different rules.

A. **Standards of Care for Specific Situations**

   1. **Common Carriers and Innkeepers**

      o **Traditional rule:** highest duty of care consistent with the practical operation of the business

        - Could be held liable for slight negligence

      o **Many courts today**—liable only for ordinary negligence (not a higher standard)

   2. **Automobile Drivers**

      o **Guests and friends in a car**—drivers were traditionally only liable for, grossly negligent, wanton, or willful misconduct (i.e., "guest statutes").

      o Many jurisdictions have abandoned guest statutes and apply a **general duty of reasonable care** standard to the driver of a car.

3. **Bailors and Bailees**

   o **Bailment**—a bailee temporarily takes _____ of another's (the bailor's) property.

      Example 20: *Driver leaves a car with a valet.*

   o **Common-law:** Complicated rules regarding the standard of care in a bailment; for example:

      ▪ Bailor must warn gratuitous bailee of known

      _____

      ▪ If the bailor receives the sole benefit, the bailee has a lesser duty

      ▪ If the bailee receives a benefit, he has a higher duty of care; even slight negligence can result in liability

4. **Emergency Situations**—the standard of care is that of a reasonable person under the same circumstances.

B. **Possessors of Land**—relates to negligence in the **maintenance** of property (e.g. artificial or natural conditions on the land), not conduct performed on the owner's property

   1. **Two Approaches**

      o One-half of all jurisdictions continue to follow the traditional rules—standard of care owed to people who come onto the land depends on whether the person is an invitee (highest standard of care), a licensee (intermediate standard of care), or a trespasser (lowest standard of care).

      o Other one-half of jurisdictions—status is still relevant, but only as it relates to due care.

   2. **Trespassers**

      On the land without consent or _____

      a. **Traditional Approach**

         ▪ Duty: Possessor is obligated to refrain from _____,

         _____, intentional, or reckless misconduct

         ▪ Use of a _____ or trap will result in liability

         ▪ **Undiscovered trespassers**—no duty owed

         ▪ **Discovered** or **anticipated** trespassers:

            • Must warn or protect them from hidden dangers

         ▪ **"Attractive nuisance"** doctrine—a possessor of land may be liable to injuries to

         _____ trespassing on the land if:

            • An artificial condition exists in a place where the owner

            _____ or has reason to know children are likely to trespass;

- The land possessor knows or has reason to know the artificial condition poses an unreasonable risk of _____ or

_____;
- The children, because of their age, **do not discover** or **cannot appreciate** the danger;
- The utility to the land possessor of maintaining the condition is slight compared to the risk of injury; and
- The land possessor fails to exercise reasonable care.

- **"Flagrant trespassers"**—in some jurisdictions, burglars, etc. are owed an even lesser duty of care

3. Invitees

○ Someone who comes onto the land for your purpose, a mutual or joint purpose.

Example 21: *A customer in your business.*

○ Land possessor owes a duty of _____.

○ **Non-delegable duty:** Cannot avoid the duty by assigning care of your property to an independent contractor

4. Licensees

○ Enters the land with express or implied permission

Example 22: *Allowing neighborhood children to walk across your property on their way to school.*

○ **Traditional rule:** Land possessor has a duty to either make the property reasonably safe or warn licensees of **concealed dangers**

- No duty to _____ for dangers
- Must exercise reasonable care in conducting activities on the land

5. Landlords and Tenants

○ Landlord must maintain safe common areas, must warn of _____ especially for premises that are leased for public use, or and must repair hazardous conditions.

> **Exam Tip 5:** As occupier of land, the tenant continues to be liable for injuries arising from conditions within the tenant's control.

6. Off-Premises Victims

○ Land possessor is generally not liable for injuries resulting from natural conditions.

- Exception: Trees in urban areas

- o **Artificial conditions**—must prevent _____ risk of harm to persons not on the premises.
- o Must exercise reasonable care in conducting activities on the land.

C. Breach of Duty

1. **Traditional Approach**—focuses on a common-sense approach of what the reasonably prudent person would do under the circumstances

2. **Cost-Benefit Analysis**—courts specify what _____ should have been taken, and weigh that against the likelihood of _____

> **Exam Tip 6:** Don't get hung up on the difference here; it's really just two ways of getting to the same result.

CHAPTER 8: NEGLIGENCE: RES IPSA LOQUITUR

A. Res Ipsa Loquitur

1. **General Principle**—in some cases, circumstantial evidence of negligence is sufficient evidence of negligence

> **Example 23:** *A barrel rolls out of a building and crushes a passerby. A jury could reasonably conclude that some type of negligence was the most likely cause of that injury.*

2. **Traditional Elements**

- o The accident was of a kind that ordinarily does not _____ in the absence of negligence;
- o It was caused by an agent or instrumentality within the _____ of the defendant; and
- o It was not due to any action on the part of the _____.

3. **Modern Trends**

a. **Medical malpractice**— in cases in which some doctor, nurse, or other personnel acted negligently to harm a patient, a small number of jurisdictions shift the burden by holding ALL defendants jointly and severally liable unless they can exonerate themselves.

b. **Products liability**—many courts ignore the exclusivity requirement when it is clear that the defect originated upstream of the package's wrapping or sealing.

c. **Comparative-fault jurisdictions**—many comparative-fault jurisdictions (discussed in Chapter 13, *infra*) loosely apply the third element (i.e., that the harm was not caused by any action by the plaintiff).

4. **Third Restatement**—applies the elements generously:

   o The accident is a type of accident that _____ as a result of negligence of a class of actors; and

   o The defendant is a member of that class.

5. **Procedural Effect**

   o Does not result in a _____ for the plaintiff.

   o The court allows the case to go to the jury.

   > **Exam Tip 7:** Res ipsa loquitor reminds the trier of fact that circumstantial evidence can be sufficient.

CHAPTER 9:   NEGLIGENCE: CAUSATION

A. **Causation**—has two components:

   • Cause in fact ("but-for cause")

   • _____ cause

1. **Cause in Fact**

   a. **"But-for" test**—the plaintiff must show that the injury would not have occurred "but for" the defendant's negligence.

      > *Example 24: A car's brakes are negligently repaired. The car is struck by a meteorite, injuring the driver. The person who repaired the brakes is not liable because his negligence is not the but-for cause of the driver's injuries.*

   b. **Multiple/indeterminate tortfeasors**—the "but-for" test can be problematic in the following circumstances:

      ▪ **Multiple tortfeasors**—it cannot be said that any one of the defendant's tortious conduct necessarily was required to produce the harm;

         > *Example 25: Several youths throw a piano off a roof, damaging a car. The plaintiff will have difficulty showing that the conduct of any defendant was necessary to cause the plaintiff's harm.*

      ▪ **Multiple possible _____**—the plaintiff cannot prove which defendant caused the harm; or

      ▪ **Medical misdiagnosis**—increased the probability of the plaintiff's death or injury, but the plaintiff probably would have died or been injured even with a proper diagnosis.

      1) **"Substantial factor"**

         • Used as a "catch-all" when there are conceptual problems with

            _____

- Asks whether the negligence was a "substantial factor" in causing the harm

2) Concurrent tortfeasors contributing to an individual injury

- When the tortious acts of two or more defendants are each a factual cause of one harm, then joint and several liability applies.

Example 26: *A person negligently hangs laundry on a stop sign. A driver negligently speeds through the intersection controlled by the stop sign. The driver injures a pedestrian. The person and the driver are jointly and severally liable for the pedestrian's injuries.*

3) Alternative causation

- Plaintiff's harm was caused by only one of a few defendants (usually two) and each was negligent and it cannot be determined which one caused the harm.
- Courts will **shift the burden of proof to the defendants**—will impose _____ liability on both unless they can show which one of them caused the harm.

4) Concert of action—if two or more tortfeasors were acting together collectively and that causes the plaintiff's harm, all defendants will be jointly and severally liable.

c. Loss of chance of recovery

- Traditionally, a patient with less than a 50% chance of survival would not ever be able to recover for negligence, because they may not be able to prove that they would have survived but for the defendant's actions.

Example 27: *A patient has a 20% chance of survival. The doctor negligently treats that patient by misdiagnosing the patient's condition. Ordinarily, the patient would lose if the normal causation rules applied.*

- If a physician negligently reduces the plaintiff's chance of survival, then that plaintiff can recover.
- In cases in which the plaintiff was likely to die anyway, courts in many jurisdictions alter the rules of causation, allow recovery for the lost chance of survival, but discount damages awarded to the plaintiff.

Example 28: *If the plaintiff's total damages are $1,000,000, and his chances of survival were 40% without the negligent misdiagnosis and 25% after the misdiagnosis, then the plaintiff will recover $150,000: ($1,000,000 × (40% − 25%)).*

B. **Proximate Cause (Legal Cause)**

1. **Foreseeability of Harm**

    Example 29: *If a driver speeds down a street and causes a pedestrian to jump out of the way and sprain an ankle, then the driver is liable. If the sound of the driver's car reminds a passerby of a car the passerby used to own, and the sound makes the passerby want to go for a drive, and the passerby is later in a car accident while driving, the driver is not liable.*

2. **Intervening Acts**

    o If intervening acts are foreseeable, the defendant will still be liable.

      ▪ Intervening acts may be negligent or even criminal and still not break the chain of causation.

      Example 30: *A person negligently leaves several loaded guns at a school playground. A student picks up a loaded gun and shoots another student. That is an intervening criminal act, but the person is still liable. It is not a superseding cause that relieves the person of liability because it is*

      _____.

    o Scope of liability: a person is liable for the _____ that made her conduct negligent.

      Exam Tip 8: When asking whether a particular consequence of negligence is too remote, ask "is this what made the conduct negligent to begin with?"

3. **Extent of Damages**

    o The defendant is liable for the full extent of the plaintiff's injuries, even if the extent is unusual or unforeseeable.

      Exam Tip 9: TYPE of damages must be foreseeable, not EXTENT.

CHAPTER 10:   REVIEW OF CHAPTERS 5–9: NEGLIGENCE

1. **What are the traditional elements of negligence?**

    1) Duty

    2) _____

    3) Causation

    4) Harm

2. **In general, tort law does not impose affirmative duties; when do courts say there is an affirmative duty to help others?**

    1) A person voluntarily aids or rescues another

    2) A person places another in danger, even non-negligently

    3) To perform contractual obligations with due care

    4) One with actual ability and _____ to control another

    5) Defendants with a _____ relationship to plaintiffs (e.g., common carrier-passenger; innkeeper-guest)

3. **What is the basic background standard of care imposed by tort law?**

    A reasonably _____ person under the circumstances

4. **Is this an objective reasonableness standard or a subjective good-faith standard?**

    An _____ standard

5. **What variation of this standard of care is applied to children?**

    The standard of care imposed upon a child is that of a reasonable child of similar age.

    However, a child engaged in an _____ is held to the same standard as an adult.

6. **What factors are taken into account in the cost-benefit approach?**

    1) The likelihood of the harm

    2) The severity of the harm

    3) The _____ that could have been taken

7. **How is custom relevant in determining the standard of care?**

    Evidence of custom in a community or industry is relevant evidence to establish the proper standard of care, but it is not _____.

8. **What variation of the standard of care is applied to doctors?**

    A professional person (e.g., doctor, lawyer, or electrician) is expected to exhibit the same skill, knowledge, and care as another practitioner in the _____.

9. **What does "informed consent" mean in the context of tort law?**

    Physicians are under a specific obligation to explain the _____ of a medical procedure to a patient in advance of a patient's decision to consent to treatment. Failure to do so constitutes a breach of the physician's duty.

10. **What is the doctrine of negligence per se?**

    1) When a statute imposes upon a person a specific standard of care;

    2) Defendant is liable if the person injured is in the _____ of persons protected by the statute;

    3) The harm is the type of harm that statute is intended to _____; and

    4) The violation of that statute was a proximate cause of the harm.

11. **What standard of care has been imposed on common carriers and innkeepers?**

    Traditionally, common carriers and innkeepers were held to the highest duty of care consistent with the practical _____ of the business.

    A majority of courts continue to hold common carriers to this higher standard. However, most courts today hold that an innkeeper (hotel operator) is liable only for ordinary negligence.

12. **What are "guest statutes" in the context of the negligence standard of care?**

    These statutes limited the liability of drivers to passengers in their cars. They held drivers liable only if they had been guilty of gross negligence or wanton or willful misconduct.

13. **In assessing the liability of possessors of land, courts traditionally focused on the status of the person injured on the land, what where the traditional categories?**

    1) _____

    2) _____

    3) _____

14. **What duties were owed to plaintiffs in each category?**

   1) **Trespasser:** _____, except to not engage in willful, wanton, or reckless disregard for their safety

   2) **Licensee:** Duty to warn of hidden dangers

   3) **Invitee:** Duty of _____

15. **What is the attractive nuisance doctrine?**

   A land possessor may be liable for injuries to children trespassing on the land if:

   1) An artificial condition exists in a place where the land possessor knows or has reason to know that children are likely to trespass;

   2) The land possessor knows or has reason to know that the condition poses an unreasonable risk of death or serious bodily injury to children;

   3) The children, because of their youth, do not discover or cannot appreciate the danger presented by the condition;

   4) The utility to the land possessor of maintaining the condition and the burden of eliminating the danger are slight compared to the risk of harm presented to children; and

   5) The land possessor fails to exercise reasonable care to protect children from the harm.

16. **What is the doctrine of res ipsa loquitur?**

   Circumstantial evidence can be sufficient to show negligence. Under the traditional standard for res ipsa loquitur, the plaintiff must prove that:

   1) The accident was of a kind that ordinarily does not occur in the absence of negligence;

   2) It was caused by an agent or instrumentality within the exclusive _____ of the defendant;

   3) It was not due to any action on the part of the plaintiff.

17. **What extension of res ipsa loquitur do some courts apply in some medical malpractice cases?**

   If several people take care of a patient and one may have been negligent, but the plaintiff cannot say which one, then the courts will shift the burden to those defendants, holding them jointly and severally liable unless they can present evidence of which persons were negligent.

18. **Causation can be thought of as having two components. What are they?**

    1) Cause in fact

    2) _____ (or "scope of liability")

19. **What do we mean by "cause in fact"?**

If the plaintiff's injury would not have occurred but for the defendant's negligence, then the defendant's conduct is a factual cause of the harm.

20. **What is "proximate cause"?**

The plaintiff must show that the causal connection was not too _____ or attenuated.

21. **How do courts following the Third Restatement wisely approach proximate cause?**

They ask whether the harm is the kind of risk that made the defendant's conduct

_____.

CHAPTER 11:   NEGLIGENCE: DAMAGES AND SPECIAL RULES OF LIABILITY

A. Damages

1. Actual (Compensatory) Damages

- Purpose is to make the plaintiff whole again
- Sometimes a plaintiff who suffers a _____ injury can also recover for _____ damages (i.e., "parasitic damages")
- **Economic-loss rule**—a plaintiff who suffers only economic loss without any related personal injury or property damage cannot recover in negligence.

  > **Example 31:** *Someone negligently damages a road. A business owner loses business due to the damage to the road, but cannot recover for that economic loss because the business owner has not suffered any personal injury or property damage.*

  - If a plaintiff has proven non-economic injury, then the plaintiff can recover non-economic and economic damages.

2. Mitigation of Damages

- Plaintiff must take steps to mitigate damages
- Not really a "duty"; instead a limitation on recovery

3. **Personal Injury: Categories of Damages**

   o _____, both past and future

   o Pain and suffering

   o Lost income and reduced _____

4. **Property Damage**

   a. **General rule**—the plaintiff may recover the difference between the

      _____ of the property before and after the injury

   b. **Cost of repair or replacement value** are often allowed as an alternative measure of damages

5. **Collateral-Source Rule**

   a. **Traditional rule**

      ▪ Benefits or payments to the plaintiff from outside sources, such as

        _____, are not credited against the liability of any tortfeasor.

      ▪ Evidence of such payments is not admissible at trial.

   b. **Modern trend**

      ▪ Most states have eliminated or substantially modified the rule to avoid double recovery.

      ▪ Payments made to the plaintiff by the defendant's insurer are credited against the defendant's liability.

6. **Punitive Damages**

   o If the defendant acted _____,

      _____, recklessly, or with

      _____, or if an inherently malicious tort is involved, punitive damages may be available.

B. **Special Rules of Liability**

   1. **Negligent Infliction of Emotional Distress (NIED)**

      In general, plaintiffs cannot recover for NIED. Exceptions include:

      a. **Zone of danger**—a plaintiff can recover for NIED if:

         ▪ The plaintiff was within the "zone of danger" of the threatened physical impact; and

         ▪ The threat of physical impact caused emotional distress.

         Exam Tip 10: Think of this as analogous to assault.

      b. **Bystander recovery**—a bystander can recover for NIED if the bystander:

         ▪ Is _____ to the person injured by the defendant;

- Was present at the scene of the injury; and
- _____ the injury.

Exam Tip 11: Lines may seem arbitrary, but draw these lines on the bar exam.

   c. **Special relationship**

- Mishandling of a _____
- Negligent medical information (e.g., a negligent misdiagnosis)

   d. **Physical manifestations**—some jurisdictions still require some physical manifestation of distress, such as nausea, insomnia, miscarriage

2. **Wrongful Death and Survival Actions**

   a. **Wrongful death**

- A decedent's spouse or representative brings suit to recover losses **suffered by the spouse or representative** as a result of the decedent's death
- Damages include loss of support and loss of companionship and society.

   b. **Survival actions**

- Brought by a representative of the decedent's estate **on behalf of the decedent** for claims the decedent would have had at the time of the decedent's death
- Claims include damages resulting from personal injury or property damage

3. **Recovery for Loss Arising from Injury to Family Members**—loss of consortium or companionship

4. **"Wrongful Life" and "Wrongful Birth" Claims**

   a. **Wrongful life**—not permitted in most states

   b. **Wrongful birth**—many states do permit recovery

CHAPTER 12:   NEGLIGENCE: VICARIOUS LIABILITY AND SPECIAL RULES OF LIABILITY

A. **Vicarious Liability**—when one person is held liable for another person's negligence

   1. **Respondeat Superior**

     o The employer is held vicariously liable for the negligence of an employee, if it occurred within the _____

     o **Distinction:** Employer's own negligence v. employer's liability for an employee's conduct

- **Direct negligence**—the employer is liable for the employer's own negligence
- **Vicarious liability**—the employer is strictly liable for the employee's actions

       Example 32: A pizza company hires bad drivers or provides them with alcohol before their shift. Vicarious liability is not applicable; the employer's own actions are negligent. Vicarious liability would apply when, for example, the pizza company is as careful as possible in the hiring, training, and supervising of their employees, yet one employee decides, on his own, contrary to instructions, and without the employer's knowledge, to consume alcohol while delivering pizzas and he negligently gets into an accident.

a. **Intentional torts**—employers are generally not liable for the intentional torts of employees, except when the employee's conduct is within the scope of employment, e.g., force is _____ in the employee's work

> ***Example 33:*** *A bar bouncer beats up a customer thinking he is serving the employer's interests.*

b. **Frolic and detour**

- **Detour** (minor deviation from the scope of employment)—the employer is liable
- **Frolic** (major deviation from the scope of employment)—the employer is not liable

2. **Torts Committed by Independent Contractors**

o An employer is generally not liable for torts committed by independent contractors.

> ***Example 34:*** *You hire someone paint your house while you are on vacation. The painter is negligent in the process and injures someone. You are not liable because the painter is an independent contractor.*

o How to distinguish an independent contractor from an employee—if the employer retains a right of _____ over the way that employee does the work, courts will treat that person as an employee

o An employer MAY be vicariously liable for the torts of independent contractors in the following situations:

- Inherently _____ activities;
- _____ duties;
- Duty of an operator of premises to keep the premises safe for the public; and
- Duty to comply with safety statutes.

3. **Business Partners**—can be liable for the torts of other business partners committed within the scope of the business's purpose.

4. **Automobile Owners**

a. **Negligent entrustment**—an owner can be **directly liable** for negligently entrusting a vehicle (or any other dangerous object) to someone who is not in the position to care for it.

b. **Family-purpose doctrine**—the owner of an automobile may be vicariously liable for the tortious acts of **any family member** driving the car with permission.

    c. **Owner liability statutes**—the owner of an automobile may be vicariously liable for the tortious acts of **anyone** driving the car with permission.

5. **Parents and Children**

    a. **General rule**—parents generally are not vicariously liable for their minor children's torts.

    b. **Negligence of parents**—parents can be liable for their own negligence with respect to their children's conduct.

6. **"Dram Shop" Liability**

    o Holds bars, bartenders, and even _____ liable for injuries caused when people drink too much alcohol and injure third parties.

    o Recognized by many states in statutes or by case law.

    o A form of direct liability; not vicarious liability.

> **Exam Tip 12:** These laws hold the bar or social host liable IN ADDITION to the drunk driver, not INSTEAD OF the drunk driver.

7. **Indemnification**

    o The party held vicariously liable may seek indemnification from the party who was directly responsible.

B. **Immunities**

1. **Federal and State Governments**

    o Traditionally, state and federal governments were immune from tort liability.

    o Immunity has been waived by statute.

    a. **Federal Tort Claims Act**

        ▪ The federal government expressly _____ immunity and allows itself to be sued for certain kinds of torts.

        ▪ There are exceptions (i.e., situations in which the federal government **maintains** immunity)

> **Editor's Note 8:** These exceptions include certain enumerated torts, discretionary functions, and traditional governmental activities.

    b. **State governments and municipalities**

        ▪ Most states have waived immunity to some extent

        ▪ Municipalities are generally governed by the state tort claims statute

        ▪ **Governmental v. proprietary functions**

            • **Governmental functions** (e.g., police, court system)—immunity applies

            • **Proprietary functions** (functions often performed by a private company, e.g., utilities, parking lots)—immunity has been waived

c. **Government officials**

- _____ **functions**—immunity applies
- _____ **functions**—no immunity
- **Westfall Act**—precludes any personal liability on the part of a federal employee under state tort law

2. **Intra-Family Immunities**—largely eviscerated; a family member can be sued for negligently injuring another family member

   o **Core parenting activities**—immunity still applies

3. **Charitable Immunity**—eliminated in most states, though some states still limit recovery

CHAPTER 13: NEGLIGENCE: SHARING LIABILITY AND DEFENSES

A. **Sharing Liability Among Multiple Defendants**

1. **Joint and Several Liability**

   o Each of two or more defendants who is found liable for a single and indivisible harm to the plaintiff is subject to liability to the plaintiff for **the entire harm.**

   o Plaintiff can recover from any negligent party **all** of his damages.

   o **Applications:**

   - Two or more tortfeasors;
   - Tortfeasors acting in _____;
   - Alternative liability;
   - Res ipsa loquitur is used against multiple defendants;
   - Both employer and _____ are liable.

   o In some jurisdictions, a defendant is not jointly and severally liable unless he is at least 10% at fault.

   o **Contribution**—allows a defendant who pays more than his share of the total liability to recover from the other liable defendants.

   - May be pro rata, or may be liable only for proportionate share

2. **Indemnification**—a complete _____ from one party to a party who was forced to pay the damages.

   > ***Example 35:*** *An employer employs an employee who behaves negligently in the scope of employment. The employer may be held liable for the full amount of damages due to vicarious liability but may seek indemnification from the employee because the employer was not at fault.*

> *Example 36:* *A retailer who is held strictly liable for selling a defective product may seek indemnification from an upstream manufacturer who was responsible for the defect.*

B. Defenses to Negligence

1. Contributory Negligence

- If the plaintiff was negligent in some way, that negligence completely _____ the plaintiff's recovery.

- **"Last clear chance" doctrine**—allows a plaintiff to mitigate the consequences of her own contributory negligence by showing that the defendant had the last clear chance to avoid injuring the plaintiff but failed to do so.

    > *Example 37:* *A defendant driving down the street should not feel free to run over a pedestrian who is negligently crossing the street on the theory that the pedestrian's contributory negligence will relieve the defendant of liability. If the defendant had the last clear chance to avoid the harm, he should have done so.*

2. Comparative Fault—a plaintiff's negligence does not completely bar recovery but instead limits the plaintiff's ability to recover; adopted in most jurisdictions.

a. Pure comparative negligence—the plaintiff's recovery is diminished by whatever percentage of fault the jury attributes to the plaintiff's own negligence.

> *Example 38:* *If the jury finds the plaintiff is 10% at fault, the plaintiff's recovery is diminished by 10% and the plaintiff can only recover 90% of her damages. If the jury finds the plaintiff is 90% at fault, the plaintiff can only recover 10% of her damages.*

b. Modified comparative negligence

- If the plaintiff is **MORE at fault** than the defendant: plaintiff's recovery is

    _____

- **Some jurisdictions:** If the plaintiff and defendant are **EQUALLY at fault**: plaintiff's recovery is barred

c. Relationship to other defenses

- Most courts have decided that the last clear chance doctrine is no longer necessary or _____.

- Comparative fault will reduce the plaintiff's recovery even if the defendant's conduct is willful, wanton, or reckless, but it will not reduce the plaintiff's recovery for _____ torts.

> **Editor's Note 9:** The illustrations to which Prof. Clark refers may be found in the Multistate Torts outline, Section IV.K.1.c.5).

     d. **Multiple defendants**—the plaintiff's degree of negligence is compared to the negligence of all of the defendants combined.

3. **Imputed Contributory Negligence**

    o One party's negligence is imputed to the plaintiff to prevent or limit the plaintiff's recovery due to the party's fault.

    o Does NOT apply:

        ▪ A child plaintiff whose parent's negligence was a contributing cause of her harm, in a suit against a third party

        ▪ A married plaintiff whose spouse was contributorily negligent in causing the harm, in a suit against a third party

4. **Assumption of the Risk**

    o Applies when a party _____ embraces a risk for some purpose of his own

    o Analogous to the defense of _____ in intentional torts

    a. **Exculpatory clauses in contracts**

        ▪ In general, parties can contract to disclaim liability on negligence and courts will enforce those disclaimers.

        ▪ Courts will hesitate to enforce exculpatory provisions if:

            • They disclaim liability for reckless or _____ misconduct;

            • There is a gross disparity of _____ between the two parties;

            • The party seeking to enforce the provision offers services of great importance to the public (e.g., medical services);

            • The provision is subject to contract defenses (e.g., fraud or duress);

            • The enforcement would be against public _____.

    b. **Participants and spectators in athletic events**—courts often hold that a participant or spectator cannot recover because the party knew of the risks and chose to accept those risks.

> **Exam Tip 13:** Though they seem related, keep the defenses of contributory negligence and assumption of the risk separate. Contributory negligence is a partial defense; assumption of the risk is a complete defense.

CHAPTER 14:   REVIEW OF CHAPTERS 11–13: NEGLIGENCE (CONT'D.)

1. **What does it mean to say that a plaintiff must prove "actual harm" in a negligence case?**

    Unlike actions for intentional torts, _____ damages are not recoverable in negligence actions. The plaintiff must prove actual harm, i.e., personal injury or property damage.

2. **What is the "economic loss" rule in negligence cases?**

    A plaintiff who suffers **only** economic loss without any related personal injury or property damage cannot recover such loss through a negligence action.

3. **What do courts mean when they talk about a "duty to mitigate" damages?**

    The plaintiff must take reasonable steps to _____ the harm caused by the defendant's negligence. Although sometimes phrased as a "duty to mitigate," this "duty" is a limitation on damages.

4. **What are the main types of compensatory damages available in personal injury cases?**

    The typical categories of damages recoverable in a personal injury action include:

    1) Medical and rehabilitative expenses;

    2) Past and future pain and suffering (e.g., emotional distress); and

    3) Lost _____ and any reduction in future earnings capacity.

    Under the "eggshell-plaintiff" rule the defendant is liable for the full extent of the damages proximately caused by the negligence, even if the extent is unusual or unforeseeable.

5. **What sorts of damages are available in a negligence case involving property damage?**

    The general rule is that the plaintiff may recover the difference between the _____ of the property before and after the damage. In the case of harm to personal property, most courts also allow the cost of repairs as an alternative measure of damages, provided that the cost of repairs does not exceed the value of the property. With household items, courts often hold that replacement value is the measure of damages.

6. **What is the "collateral-source" rule?**

   Under the traditional rule, a defendant would be liable for damages even if the plaintiff had received compensation for that harm from some other collateral source (such as medical insurance).

   Many states have statutes that either eliminate the collateral-source rule entirely or modify it substantially.

7. **Under what circumstances might a plaintiff get punitive damages?**

   The plaintiff may be entitled to punitive damages if he can establish by _____ evidence that the defendant acted willfully and wantonly, recklessly, or with malice.

   Punitive damages are also available for _____ torts.

8. **What special limits apply to Negligent Infliction of Emotional Distress?**

   A plaintiff can recover for negligent infliction of emotional distress from a defendant whose negligence creates a foreseeable risk of foreseeable physical injury to the plaintiff, if the defendant's action causes a threat of physical impact that in turn causes emotional distress. The emotional distress generally must result in some form of bodily harm (e.g., a heart attack). Generally, a plaintiff must show that he was within the "zone of _____."

   Some courts allow recovery for a bystander outside the zone of danger if the plaintiff:

   1) Is closely related to the person injured by the defendant;

   2) Was _____ at the scene of the injury; and

   3) Personally observed the injury.

   In addition, some courts make exceptions to the physical-injury requirement, as in cases of misinforming someone that a family member has died or negligently mishandling a corpse.

9. **What does the term "vicarious liability" mean?**

   One party is held liable for the negligence of another party.

10. **When will an employer be vicariously liable for an employee's negligence?**

    An employer is liable for employee torts within the _____ that includes acts that they do as part of their work or risks that are inherent that inherent in the working relationship.

    This is distinct from primary negligence.

11. **Are employers liable for the torts of independent contractors?**

    No, those who hire independent contractors are generally not vicariously liable for the torts of independent contractors.

12. **How do we tell an independent contractor from an employee?**

    An independent contractor is one who is not subject to the right of control by the employer. If the employer has the right to control how someone does the work, then courts will often consider that person an employee for this purpose.

13. **Under what other circumstances might employers be liable for torts of independent contractors?**

    1) Inherently dangerous activities;

    2) _____ duties;

    3) The duty of an operator of premises open to the public to keep premises safe; and

    4) In some jurisdictions, the duty to comply with state safety statutes.

14. **What is "joint and several" liability?**

    The plaintiff can sue either of two (or more) defendants who are found liable for a single and indivisible harm to the plaintiff; both (all) are liable to liability to the plaintiff for the entire harm. The plaintiff has the choice of collecting the entire judgment from one defendant or the entire judgment from the other defendant.

15. **What is the doctrine of "contribution"?**

    When one defendant has been held liable for the whole harm under joint and several liability, he or she can recover a fair portion of that from other defendants.

16. What is "pure several liability?"

Each defendant is only held liable for his or her own share of the damages.

17. What is the doctrine of "indemnification"?

The shifting of the _____ from one joint tortfeasor to another party

18. When is indemnification available?

It is available when one tortfeasor is _____ liable for the other's wrongdoing. In addition, it is available when there is a prior agreement providing for indemnification.

In some jurisdiction, the doctrine of equitable indemnification can be invoked when one party is more blameworthy than the other. This doctrine is not necessary in jurisdictions that adopt comparative-negligence rules.

19. What is contributory negligence?

Traditionally, and still in a few states, any contributory negligence on the part of the plaintiff will is a _____ recovery.

20. What is "comparative negligence" or "comparative fault"?

A plaintiff's negligence will not necessarily be a complete bar to recovery, but under some circumstances will limit recovery.

21. What are the two basic different forms of comparative fault?

1) **Pure comparative fault:** The plaintiff's recovery is diminished to the extent to which he or she contributed to the harm.

2) **Modified comparative fault:** The plaintiff can only recovery if the injury was mostly the defendant's fault. A plaintiff cannot recover if she was more at fault than the defendant. In some jurisdictions, a plaintiff cannot recover if he or she was equally at fault with the defendant.

22. What is "assumption of the risk"?

The plaintiff knowingly and _____ accepted the risk, and thus cannot recover. It is a complete bar to recovery.

23. Under what circumstances do courts hesitate to enforce exculpatory clauses?

1) Disclaiming liability for reckless or wanton misconduct or gross negligence;

2) Where there is a _____ of bargaining power between the parties;

3) Defendant offers services of great importance to the public which are a necessity for some members of the public; or

4) If the exculpatory clause is subject to typical _____ defenses such as fraud or duress.

Generally, common carrier, innkeepers, and employers cannot disclaim liability for negligence.

24. What is the connection between the assumption of risk and consent defenses?

Assumption of risk applies to _____ cases and consent applies to cases of _____ torts.

CHAPTER 15:   STRICT LIABILITY

- Under strict liability, a defendant will be liable no matter how _____ they were.
- Three general categories:
  - Abnormally dangerous activities;
  - _____;
  - Defective products.

A. Abnormally Dangerous Activities

1. **Basic Rule**—a defendant engaged in an abnormally dangerous activity will be held strictly liable—without any proof of negligence—for personal injuries and property damage caused by the activity, regardless of precautions taken to prevent the harm.

2. **Definition of "Abnormally Dangerous"**—factors in determining whether an activity is an abnormally dangerous activity:
   - Whether it creates a foreseeable and highly _____ risk of harm even when the actor takes due care;

- o   The severity of the harm resulting from the activity;
- o   The appropriateness of the _____ for the activity;
- o   Whether it has great value to the community.

3. **Scope of Liability or Risk**—a defendant is only liable for the harm that _____ from the risk that made the activity abnormally dangerous.

> ***Example 39:*** *If your truck is full of explosives and blows up, then you are strictly liable. If your truck is full of explosives and you run over a pedestrian, then you are only liable if you were negligent, because that is not the risk that made explosives abnormally dangerous.*

> **Exam Tip 14:** This is analogous to proximate cause in a negligence context.

B. **Animals**

1. **Wild Animals**—animals that, as a _____ or _____, are not customarily kept in the service of mankind.

   a. **Dangerous propensity**—owners are strictly liable for the harm arising from the animal's dangerous propensities.

   b. **Liability to trespassers**

   - ▪   Owners are strictly liable for injuries caused to _____ or _____.

   - ▪   Owners are not strictly liable for injuries caused to _____. (**exception in some jurisdictions:** injuries caused by a _____)

2. **Domestic Animals**

   a. **Known to be dangerous**—owners are strictly liable if the owner _____ or has reason to know of the animal's dangerous propensities.

   b. **"Dog-bite" statutes**—many states hold dog owners strictly liable for injuries caused by dogs.

   > **Editor's Note 10:** These statutes vary widely from state to state.

3. **Trespassing Animals**—the owner of any animal is strictly liable for any reasonably foreseeable damage caused by his animal while trespassing on another's land. **Exceptions:**

   - ▪   **Household pets**, unless the owner knows or has reason to know that the pet is _____ on another's property in a harmful way

   - ▪   **Animals on public roads**—a _____ standard applies.

C. **Defenses to Strict Liability**

1. **Contributory Negligence**—the plaintiff's contributory negligence **does not** bar recovery.

2. **Comparative Negligence**—the plaintiff's comparative fault **will _____ the plaintiff's recovery.**

o **General rule**—the plaintiff's carelessness might reduce the plaintiff's recovery if it is clear that the defendant will bear some share of the liability.

3. **Assumption of the Risk**—the plaintiff's assumption of the risk is a _____ to recovery.

CHAPTER 16: PRODUCTS LIABILITY

A product may be defective due to its _____, design, or lack of a warning.

> **Example 40:** A motorcycle may be defective in different ways:
> **Manufacture:** the motorcycle has plastic bolts where there are supposed to be metal bolts; the motorcycle was defectively manufactured;
> **Design:** the motorcycle was built as designed, but is unstable with a passenger or heavy rider; the motorcycle's design is defective;
> **Failure to warn:** the manufacturer should have warned riders that the motorcycle cannot accommodate passengers.

A. **Negligence**—the plaintiff must prove duty, breach, causation, and damages.

B. **Strict Products Liability**

1. **Elements of a Claim**—the plaintiff must show:

   o The product was _____ (in manufacture, design, or failure to warn);

   o The defect existed when the product left the defendant's _____; and

   o The defect caused the plaintiff's injury when the product was used in a _____ way.

2. **Defective Product**

   a. **Manufacturing defect**

      ▪ The product deviated from its intended _____.

      ▪ The product does not conform to the manufacturer's own _____.

   b. **Design defect**—two tests:

      ▪ **Consumer expectation test**—the product is defective in design if it is less safe than the _____ would expect.

      ▪ **Risk-utility test**—the product is defective in design if the risks outweigh its benefits; must show that there is a reasonable _____ design.

   c. **Failure to warn**—of a foreseeable risk that is not _____ to an ordinary user

      1) **Prescription drugs** ("learned intermediary" rule)

- Manufacturers of prescription drugs must warn the _____.
- **Exception:** drugs marketed directly to consumers

   Example 41: *Birth control pills*

  d. **Inference of defect**—courts may allow proof of a defect by _____ evidence (similar to res ipsa loquitur), especially when the defect causes the product to be destroyed.

3. **Plaintiffs**

   o   No privity requirement

   o   Anyone foreseeably injured by a defective product, including purchasers, other users, and _____

4. **Defendants**

   o   Anyone who _____ the product when it is defective is potentially strictly liable.

   ▪   Must be in the business of selling

   o   Must be in the chain of _____The seller may seek indemnification from another party (e.g., the manufacturer).

   o   **Casual sellers**—not strictly liable, but may be liable for negligence

   Example 42: *Selling something to a friend or neighbor.*

CHAPTER 17:   PRODUCTS LIABILITY (CONT'D.)

1. **Damages**

   o   Plaintiff can recover for **personal injury** or _____.

   o   **Purely economic loss**—generally not permissible under a strict liability theory; may be brought as a _____ claim

2. **Defenses**

   a. **Comparative fault**—the plaintiff's own negligence will reduce his recovery in a strict-products-liability action.

   b. **Contributory negligence**—courts hesitate to allow the plaintiff's negligence to completely bar the plaintiff's recovery against the defendant for a defective product.

   c. **Assumption of the risk**—if the risk is one that the plaintiff knew about and voluntarily chose, then the plaintiff will not be allowed to recover.

   > **Exam Tip 15:** Even if assumption of the risk is not a fully effective defense, the courts will be hesitant to hold a defendant strictly liable if the only risk that the

plaintiff can point to is one that the plaintiff knew about, expected, and disregarded.

d. **Product misuse, modification, or alteration**

- Generally, the manufacturer (or seller) will be liable as long as the misuse, modification, or alteration was foreseeable.

    Example 43: *A manufacturer makes a car that explodes at speeds of 80 mph. Drivers are not supposed to speed, but it is foreseeable that drivers exceed the speed limit at times. The manufacturer will be liable for the defect.*

- Foreseeable misuses, modifications, and alterations are viewed as examples of

    _____.

e. **Substantial change in the product**—may bar recovery

    Example 44: *Using a ceiling fan as an airplane propeller.*

f. **Compliance with governmental standards**

- Compliance with safety standards is evidence, that the product is not defective, but not _____ evidence.
- **Exception:** federal preemption—if Congress has preempted regulation in a particular area, then tort claims may be preempted.

g. **"State of the art" defense**

- In some jurisdictions, the relevant state of the art at the time of manufacture or warning is some evidence that the product is not defective.
- In other jurisdictions, compliance with the state of the art is a _____ to recovery.

h. **Disclaimers, limitations, and waivers**—generally do not bar strict liability claims for defective products

B. **Warranties**

1. **Implied warranties**

    a. **Two types**

    - **Merchantability**—the product is _____ for the ordinary purposes for which it is sold.
    - **Fitness for a particular purpose**—the seller knows the particular purpose for which the product is being sold and the buyer relies on the seller's skill or judgment.

2. **Express Warranties**—an affirmation of fact or a promise by the seller that is part of the basis of the bargain; these claims are brought under warranty theory, not tort.

3. **Defenses**

   a. **Disclaimers**

      ▪ These are covered in your Contracts materials

   b. **Tort Defenses**

      ▪ Assumption of the risk
      ▪ Comparative fault
      ▪ Contributory negligence
      ▪ Product misuse
      ▪ Failure to provide notice

C. **Review**

   1. **Three ways a product may be defective:**

      ○ Manufacture
      ○ Design
      ○ Warning

   2. **Three types of suits:**

      ○ Negligence
      ○ Strict liability
      ○ Breach of implied warranty

CHAPTER 18: REVIEW OF CHAPTERS 15–17: STRICT LIABILITY

1. **What does it mean to impose strict liability in tort?**

   The plaintiff need not show _____. The plaintiff can recover when a defendant has caused harm, even if the defendant has not been negligent.

2. **What are the three main situations in which strict liability is imposed?**

   1) Abnormally _____ activities;

   2) _____; and

   3) Defective products

3. **What makes an activity abnormally dangerous?**

   The most important factor is that the conduct creates a _____ and highly _____ risk of physical harm even when reasonable care is exercised. In addition, courts focus on whether the activity has great public value and if it is an uncommon activity.

4. **What activities are commonly considered abnormally dangerous activities?**

   Using _____, mining, fumigation, excavating, hazardous waste disposal

5. **What limitation, analogous to proximate cause, applies to abnormally dangerous activities?**

   Strict liability extends only if the harm that came about is the sort of risk that made the activity abnormally dangerous in the first place.

6. **When is the possessor of an animal liable for harm done by that animal?**

   The possessor of a wild animal is strictly liable for harm done by that animal, if the harm arises from a _____ that is characteristic of such wild animals.

   Generally, an owner of a domestic animal is generally liable if he is _____. An owner of a domestic animal may be strictly liable if the owner knows or has reason to know of the domestic animal's dangerous propensities and the harm results from those dangerous propensities.

   Some states have "dog-bite" statutes that hold owners of dogs or other domestic animals designated in the statute strictly liable for damages resulting from personal injuries.

7. **What type of harm are owners of even domestic animals held strictly liable?**

   Foreseeable harm caused by _____ of the domestic animal

8. **Is the plaintiff's negligence a defense to strict liability?**

   In _____ jurisdictions, the plaintiff's contributory negligence is not a defense to strict liability.

   Most comparative negligence jurisdictions and the Third Restatement, provide that liability based on strict liability should be reduced by the comparative fault of the plaintiff.

9. Is the plaintiff's assumption of risk a defense to strict liability?

_____. The plaintiff's actual and knowing assumption of the risk bars his recovery in a strict-liability action.

10. What are the three ways in which a product can be defective?

A product may be defective because of a defect in _____, in design, or it lacks an adequate _____.

11. Is strict liability the only possible theory under which a manufacturer might be potentially liable for injuries caused by defective products?

No, a plaintiff can bring a _____ claim or a _____ claim.

12. Why is it largely unnecessary and irrelevant to recognize a negligence cause of action?

Plaintiffs do not benefit from a negligence action. Plaintiffs have an additional hurdle of having to prove that the person they are suing is negligent.

13. What must a plaintiff show to recover under strict products liability?

1) The product was _____ (in manufacture, design, or failure to warn);

2) The defect existed at the time the product left the defendant's _____; and

3) The defect caused the plaintiff's injuries when used in an intended or reasonably foreseeable way.

14. What is a manufacturing defect?

The product departs from its intended _____.

15. How do courts determine if a product was defective in design?

Courts apply either the _____ test or the _____ test to determine whether a design defect exists.

16. **Does providing a warning necessarily prevent a product from being considered unreasonably dangerous?** _____

17. **What does it mean to say that a project was defective because of inadequate warning?**

    It essentially is a design defect claim. If a warning should have rendered the product safer, the failure to warning renders the product defective.

18. **What special rule applies to warnings in the context of prescription drugs?**

    The "learned intermediary" rule: The manufacturer of a prescription drug does not have a duty to warn the _____, but has a duty to warn the prescribing

    _____.

19. **What are some exceptions to the "learned intermediary" rule?**

    Most importantly:

    1) If the manufacturer is aware that the drug will be dispensed or administered without the personal intervention or evaluation of a healthcare provider, such as when a vaccine is administered through a mass inoculation; and

    2) As a result of a federal statute, in the case of birth control pills.

20. **Is the distributor or retailer strictly liable for a defective product, or just the manufacturer who manufactured it defectively?**

    Both the distributor and retailer may be strictly liable.

21. **Does that mean that anyone who sells a defective product is strictly liable?**

    No, only if they are in the business of _____. A casual seller of a product does not give rise to strict liability.

22. **Is the plaintiff's negligence a defense to strict liability?**

    Comparative fault—the plaintiff's own negligence _____ recovery in a strict products liability action just in a negligence action.

    Contributory negligence—the plaintiff's negligence generally is not a defense under certain circumstances.

23. Is assumption of the risk a defense to strict products liability?

Voluntary and knowing assumption of the risk is a complete bar to recovery in contributory-negligence jurisdictions and in a small number of the comparative-fault jurisdictions.

In comparative fault jurisdictions, some courts say that a plaintiff's assumption of a risk should not be a complete bar to recovery. However, courts can achieve the same result by finding that a product is not defective.

24. Is compliance with governmental standards a defense to strict liability?

A product can comply with government standards and can still be found to be defective. However, some products liability cases will be _____ by the existence of federal regulatory schemes.

25. What is the "state of the art" defense to strict products liability?

In failure-to-warn or design-defect cases, the manufacturer may introduce relevant evidence of the level of scientific and technological knowledge existing and reasonably feasible at the time of the product's distribution.

In most jurisdictions, courts will allow a party to introduce this evidence. However, a number of states provide that the "state of the art" defense is a complete bar to recovery.

26. Can a manufacturer disclaim or can consumers waive strict products liability?

_____. A disclaimer or limitation of remedies or other contractual exculpation (i.e., waiver) by a product seller or other distributor does not generally bar an otherwise valid products liability claim for personal injury.

CHAPTER 19:   DEFAMATION

A. Defamation

- A plaintiff may bring an action for defamation if the defendant:
  - Made a defamatory statement;
  - That is _____ the plaintiff;
  - The statement is _____ to a third party who understands its defamatory nature; and
  - _____ to the plaintiff's reputation.
- The statement must also be _____.
- In most circumstances, there is a fault requirement.

1. **Defamatory Language**

   o Language that diminishes respect, esteem, or _____ towards the plaintiff, or _____ others from associating with the plaintiff.

   o An _____ is not actionable as defamation.

2. **"Of or Concerning" the Plaintiff**

   o A reasonable person must believe the defamatory language referred to this particular plaintiff.

   o **Statements referring to a group**—a member of the group can only bring an action if the group is so small or that the context is otherwise such that the matter can reasonably be understood to refer to that member.

3. **Publication**

   o The statement must be _____ to a third-party.

   o A person who _____ a defamatory statement may be liable for defamation.

   o Federal statute provides that internet service providers are _____ for purposes of defamation.

4. **Constitutional Requirements**—any Constitutional limitations will depend on the type of PLAINTIFF and on the content of the STATEMENT.

   a. **Types of plaintiffs**

   1) **Public official**—a person who has substantial responsibility or _____ over government office, including political _____

   2) **Public figure**—constitutional requirements are the same as for public officials

      • **General purpose public figure**—a person of persuasive power and _____ in society

      • **Limited purpose public figure**—a person who thrusts themselves into a particular _____

   3) **Private individuals**

   b. **Fault/Constitutional limitations**

   1) **Private individual**

      • **Matter of public concern**—the plaintiff must prove the statement is _____ and that the person who made the statement was at least _____ with respect to the falsehood.

      • **Not a matter of public concern**—unclear whether constitutional limitations apply; a state need not require a plaintiff to prove negligence.

2) **Public official/public figure**—the plaintiff must prove that the person who made the statement either _____ it was false or acted with _____ for the falsehood of the statement ("actual malice").

Exam Tip 17: Malice here does not mean motive, just that the defendant either knew that the statement was false or was reckless with regard to the truth.

5. **Libel and Slander**

   o **Libel**—a written, _____, or recorded statement (including TV/radio broadcasts, email, and electronic communications)

   o **Slander**—a statement that is _____

   o **Damages:**

   ▪ **Libel**—the plaintiff may recover _____ damages (recovery without proof of concrete, _____ harm).

   ▪ **Slander**—the plaintiff must prove _____ damages (requires a more concrete showing of economic loss); exceptions include statements communicating **slander per se**:

      • Commission of a serious _____

      • _____ for a trade or profession

      • Having a _____

      • Severe _____

6. **Constitutional Limitations on Damages**

   a. **Public official or public figure**—the plaintiff can only recover _____ damages (no punitive or presumed damages).

   b. **Private individual and matter of public concern**—the plaintiff can only recover _____ damages unless they show _____.

   c. **Private individual but NOT a matter of public concern**—the plaintiff may recover general damages, including presumed damages, without proving actual malice.

CHAPTER 20: DEFENSES TO DEFAMATION AND PRIVACY TORTS

A. **Defenses to Defamation**

1. **Truth**—absolute defense; a truthful statement cannot be actionable as _____.

2. **Consent**—if you consent to the defamation, then you cannot sue.

3. **Privileges**

   a. **Absolute privileges**—the speaker is completely immune from liability for defamation; includes statements made:

   - In the course of _____ proceedings;
   - In the course of _____ proceedings;
   - Between spouses; and
   - In required publications by radio and TV (e.g., statements by a political candidate that a station must carry and may not censor).

   b. **Conditional privilege**—the statement is made in good faith pursuant to some duty or responsibility; includes statements made:

   - In the interest of the defendant (e.g., defending your reputation);
   - In the interest of the recipient of the statement; or
   - Affecting some important public interest.

     Example 45: Your company is about to hire someone. You tell the HR department that you think the potential candidate has embezzled money from another company. If it turns out to be false, you may be protected by the conditional privilege.

B. **Invasion of Privacy**

   1. **Misappropriation of the Right to Publicity**—a property-like cause of action when someone misappropriates another's _____ for commercial advantage without consent and causing injury

   2. **Intrusion Upon Seclusion**—a defendant's intrusion upon the plaintiff's private affairs, in a manner that is objectionable to a reasonable person

      Example 46: Phone tapping; hacking into medical records; Peeping Toms.

   3. **False Light**—when the defendant makes public facts about the plaintiff that place the plaintiff in a false light, which would be highly _____ to a reasonable person

      Example 47: Writing a story about someone named Bradley Pitt and including a picture of actor Brad Pitt.

   4. **Public Disclosure of Private Facts**

      o Defendant gives _____ to a matter concerning the private life of another and the matter publicized is _____ to a reasonable person, and not of _____ concern to the public

      o This tort is difficult to prove because courts broadly define "legitimate public concern".

   5. **Damages**—the plaintiff need not prove special damages.

6. **Defenses**

- **Qualified and absolute privilege**—applicable to "false light" and "public disclosure" claims
- **Consent**—applicable to invasion of privacy torts; mistake as to consent negates the defense

CHAPTER 21:   MISREPRESENTATION AND BUSINESS TORTS

A. **Intentional Misrepresentation**

1. **False Representation**

- Must be about a _____ fact
- Deceptive or misleading statements
- Can arise through concealing a material fact
- Generally, no duty to _____ material facts to other parties; may be an affirmative duty if:
  - There is a _____ relationship;
  - The other party is likely to be misled by statements the defendant made earlier; or
  - The defendant is aware the other party is mistaken about the basic facts of the transaction and custom suggests that disclosure should be made.

2. **Scienter**—the defendant _____the representation is false or acted with _____ for its falsehood.

3. **Intent**—the defendant must intend to _____ the plaintiff to act in _____ on the misrepresentation.

4. **Causation**—the misrepresentation must have caused the plaintiff to act or refrain from acting.

5. **Justifiable Reliance**—reliance is NOT justifiable if the facts are _____ or it is clear that the defendant was stating an opinion.

6. **Damages**

- Plaintiff must prove actual, economic, pecuniary loss.
- _____ damages are NOT available.
- **Most jurisdictions**—recovery is the "benefit of the _____" (contract-like damages).
- **Some jurisdictions**—allow only out-of-pocket losses.

B. **Negligent Misrepresentation**—failure to take due care in providing information

1. **Elements**

- The defendant provided _____ to a plaintiff;
- As a result of the defendant's _____ in preparing the information;

- During the course of a business or profession;
- Causing justifiable reliance; and
- The plaintiff is either:
    - In a _____ relationship with the defendant; or
    - The plaintiff is a third party known by the defendant to be a member of the limited group for whose benefit the information is supplied.

2. **Defenses**—negligence defenses can be raised.

3. **Damages**—the plaintiff can recover reliance (out-of-pocket) and _____ damages if the negligent representation is proven with sufficient certainty.

> **Exam Tip 18:** Don't confuse this tort with the tort of negligence. Generally, the tort of negligence applies when there has been some physical bodily injury or damage to property.

C. **Intentional Interference With Business Relations**

1. **Intentional Interference with Contract**

    a. **Elements**

    - A valid contract existed between the plaintiff and a third party;
    - Defendant knew of the contractual relationship;
    - Defendant **intentionally interfered** with the contract, resulting in a _____; and
    - The breach caused damages to the plaintiff.

    b. **Nature of the contract**

    - Must be a valid contract
    - CANNOT be terminable _____

    c. **Interference with performance other than inducing breach**

    - The defendant may be liable when he prevents a party from fulfilling its contractual obligations or substantially adds to the burden of performance.
    - The defendant's conduct must exceed _____ and free expression.
        - Interference may be "justified" if there is no improper purpose.

2. **Interference With a Prospective Economic Advantage**

    - The defendant intentionally interferes with a prospective business relationship or benefit between the plaintiff and a third party, even in the absence of a contract.
    - The elements are the same as for intentional interference with a contract (but without the contract); the conduct must be _____

3. Misappropriation of Trade Secrets

- Plaintiff owns information that is not _____ (a valid trade secret);
- Plaintiff has taken reasonable precautions to protect it; and
- Defendant has taken the secret by _____.

D. Injurious Falsehoods

1. Trade Libel—need not necessarily damage the business's reputation

- Publication;
- Of a false or _____ statement;
- With malice;
- Relating to the plaintiff's title to his business property, the quality of his business, or the quality of its products; and
- Causing _____ damages as a result of interference or damage to business relationships.

> *Example 48:* You publish an article in the paper stating, "I would like to congratulate my long-time friend and competitor who retired, closed his business, and moved to Florida. I look forward to serving all of his customers." If this statement is false and damages the business, this can be actionable.

2. Slander of Title

- Publication;
- Of a _____ statement;
- Derogatory to the plaintiff's title;
- With _____;
- Causing special damages; and
- Diminishes value in the eyes of third parties.

E. Wrongful Use of the Legal System

1. Malicious Prosecution

- A person intentionally and maliciously institutes or pursues a legal action for an _____, without _____, and the action is dismissed in favor of the person against whom it was brought.

2. Abuse of Process

- The defendant has set in motion a legal procedure in proper form, but has abused it to achieve some _____ motive;

o   Some willful act perpetrated in the use of the process which is not proper in the regular conduct of that proceeding;

o   The conduct caused damages.

> ***Example 49:*** *A local school board of education sued a teacher's union and subpoenaed 87 teachers for a hearing in order to prevent the teachers from walking a picket line during a labor dispute between the union and the board of education.*

CHAPTER 22:   REVIEW OF CHAPTERS 19–21: CONCLUSION

1. **What are the essential elements of a defamation claim?**

    1) A defamatory statement

    2) _____ the plaintiff

    3) Published to a third party

    4) Damages the plaintiff's _____

    5) Statement must be _____

2. **What counts as "defamatory" language?**

    Language that _____ the plaintiff's reputation in the eyes of others or that deters others from associating with the plaintiff

3. **Must the statement be one that has this effect in everyone who hears or reads it?**

    _____, only in the eyes of a substantial number of respectable members of the community

4. **In order to be actionable as defamation, a statement must be false. What is the key difference between the traditional and modern ways of dealing with this element?**

    Traditionally, truth was a _____; but in modern law, falsehood is an element.

5. **Does "publication" mean the statement must be published in a newspaper or such?**

    No. It must be communicated to a third party who understands its defamatory nature.

6. **Can a statement that refers to a group of people be actionable as defamation?**

   If the defamatory language applies to a group, then a member of the group can maintain a defamation action only if the group is so small that the matter can reasonably be understood to refer to that member, unless there is other evidence that the language refers to that particular member.

7. **Can an expression of an opinion be actionable as defamation?**

   Not generally. If the opinion implies knowledge of facts, then it can be actionable as defamation.

8. **What special burden must be carried by a defamation plaintiff who is either a public official or a public figure?**

   The plaintiff must prove _____.

9. **What does "actual malice" mean in this context?**

   Knowledge of the falsehood or reckless disregard for the truth

10. **In general, even private party plaintiffs must prove that the defendant was at least negligent with respect to the truth or falsity of the statement. But under what circumstances is it constitutionally required that private party plaintiffs show fault?**

    If the statement involves a matter of _____ concern

11. **What is the difference between libel and slander?**

    Libel is written or recorded defamation; slander is _____.

12. **What special requirement, related to damages, has traditionally been imposed on plaintiffs alleging slander rather than libel?**

    For libel, subject to the constitutionally imposed limits, the plaintiff need only prove _____ damages.

    For slander, unless the statement falls into the categories of slander per se, the plaintiff must plead and prove _____ damages.

13. **What does it mean to say that a slander plaintiff must prove special damages?**

    Most often, special damages involve a concrete, measurable economic loss to the plaintiff.

14. **What sorts of statements are considered slander per se, such that a plaintiff alleging slander need not prove special damages?**

    1) Committing a serious crime or crime of moral turpitude

    2) Being unfit for one's _____

    3) Having a loathsome disease

    4) Sexual misconduct (modern cases are rare)

15. **Statements made under the some circumstances are shielded by absolute privilege. What are those circumstances?**

    1) In the course of _____ proceedings;

    2) In the course of legislative proceedings;

    3) Between spouses; and

    4) Required publications by radio, television, or newspaper

16. **The concept of "invasion of privacy" has evolved into four separate causes of action. What are they?**

    1) Misappropriation of "publicity rights"

    2) Intrusion upon seclusion

    3) False light

    4) Public disclosure of _____

17. **What is misappropriation of the right to publicity?**

    1) An unauthorized appropriation of the plaintiff's name, likeness, or identity—

    2) For the defendant's advantage;

    3) Lack of consent; and

    4) Resulting in injury.

18. **What is potentially actionable as "intrusion on seclusion" or "unreasonable intrusion upon the plaintiff's private affairs"?**

    The defendant's act of intruding into the plaintiff's private affairs, solitude, or seclusion in a way objectionable to a _____ person

19. **What is the tort of "false light?"**

    The plaintiff must prove that the defendant (i) made public statements facts about the plaintiff that although each technically true, in total (ii) placed the plaintiff in a false light, (iii) which false light would be highly offensive to a reasonable person.

    Most jurisdictions require that the plaintiff prove _____ by the defendant.

20. **What is the tort of public disclosure of private facts?**

    1) The defendant gave _____ to a matter concerning the private life of another; and

    2) The matter publicized is of a kind that:

       a) Would be highly _____ to a reasonable person; and

       b) Is not of legitimate concern to the public.

21. **What are the elements of the tort of intentional misrepresentation?**

    1) Defendant's false representation

    2) Scienter

    3) _____

    4) Causation

    5) Justifiable _____

    6) Damages

22. **What must be proven to recover for intentional interference with contract?**

    The plaintiff must prove that the defendant:

    1) Knew of a contractual relationship between the plaintiff and a third party;

2) Intentionally interfered with the contract, resulting in a _____;
and

3) The breach caused damages to the plaintiff.

23. Can there be liability for interference with performance other than inducing breach?

The defendant may be liable whenever he induces a party from fulfilling its contractual obligations, even if the defendant does not induce the party to breach its contractual obligation. To be considered tortious, a defendant's actions must substantially exceed fair competition and _____.

24. What do courts mean that interference with contract is justified?

If the alleged interference was motivated by health, safety, morals, or ending poor labor conditions, then the interference is justified. Some jurisdictions, rather than framing it in terms of "justification," require that the defendant's motives or means be "improper."

25. What must be proven to recover for the tort of malicious prosecution?

A person is liable for malicious prosecution when:

1) She intentionally and maliciously institutes or pursues;

2) For an _____ purpose;

3) A legal action that is brought without probable cause; and

4) That action is dismissed in favor of the person against whom it was brought.

26. What must be proven to recover for the tort of abuse of process?

Abuse of process is the misuse of the power of the court. The plaintiff must prove:

1) A legal procedure set in motion in proper form;

2) That is "perverted" to accomplish an _____ motive;

3) A willful act perpetrated in the use of process which is not proper in the regular conduct of the proceeding;

4) Causing the plaintiff to sustain damages.

[END OF HANDOUT]